Vanco
Racial ~~Discourse in Canada, 1875~~

Popular wisdom maintains that the colourful Chinese quarters of Canadian, American, and Australian cities owe their existence to the generations of Chinese immigrants who have made their lives there. The restaurants, pagodas, and neon lights are seen as intrinsically connected to the Chinese and their immigrant experience in the West. Kay Anderson argues, however, that "Chinatown" is a Western construction, illustrative of a process of cultural domination that gave European settlers in North America and Australia the power to define and shape the district according to their own images and interests.

Anderson clearly rejects the concept of "race" as a means of distinguishing between groups of human beings. She argues that race is a set of discursive practices that structure struggles over identity and place. Anderson applies this fresh approach toward the concept of race to a critical examination of popular, media, and academic treatments of the Chinatown in Vancouver.

Vancouver's Chinatown offers an exciting interpretation of a locality, the significance of which extends far beyond the boundaries of Chinatown into the contemporary public affairs of any society in the Western world that receives immigrants. The book will be of special interest to social scientists and students looking for an empirical study of racism, place and multiculturalism that is firmly grounded in social theory.

KAY J. ANDERSON is senior lecturer in geography, University College, University of New South Wales.

MCGILL-QUEEN'S STUDIES IN ETHNIC HISTORY
Series Two: John Zucchi, Editor

Vancouver's Chinatown

Racial Discourse in Canada, 1875–1980

KAY J. ANDERSON

McGill-Queen's University Press
Montreal & Kingston · London · Ithaca

© McGill-Queen's University Press 1991
ISBN 0-7735-0844-9 (cloth)
ISBN 0-7735-1329-9 (paper)

Legal deposit fourth quarter 1991
Bibliothèque nationale du Québec

First paperback edition 1995
Reprinted 1999

Printed in Canada on acid-free paper

This book was first published
with the help of a grant from the
Social Science Federation of Canada,
using funds provided by the
Social Sciences and Humanities
Research Council of Canada.

McGill-Queen's University Press is grateful to the
Canada Council for support of its publishing
program.

Canadian Cataloguing in Publication Data

Anderson, Kay, 1958–
    Vancouver's Chinatown
    (McGill-Queen's studies in ethnic history; 10)
    Includes bibliographical references and index.
    ISBN 0-7735-0844-9 (bnd)
    ISBN 0-7735-1329-9 (pbk)

    1. Chinese Canadians – British Columbia – Vancouver
    – History.
    2. Chinatown (Vancouver, B.C.) – History.
    3. Race.
    I. Title. II. Series.

    FC3847.9.C5A63 1991   305.895'1071   C91-090223-2
    F1089.5.V22A63 1991

Typeset in Palatino 10/12 by Caractéra inc.,
Quebec City

Contents

Illustrative Material

TABLES

Acknowledgments

Establishing the design behind the data of our experience is easier with respect to books than it is with life. Looking back on the making of this book, I return as far as 1978, when as a third-year geography student at Adelaide University I began to feel uneasy about the field of research known as "ethnic studies." I recall asking my cultural geography lecturer if, instead of writing an essay on the Greeks in Melbourne, or the Germans in Adelaide, or the Vietnamese in Sydney, I might examine some aspect of "our" culture, perhaps the rural retreat movement. Professor Fay Gale agreed and encouraged me on to bigger things.

I carried that reservation about ethnic studies with me to Vancouver, Canada, where, with the assistance of a Commonwealth Scholarship, I wrote the PHD thesis on which this book is based. Reading and discussing widely, I began to confront the deeper humanistic issues concerning "us" and "them" that I could only sense as an undergraduate. Somewhat rattled by the epistemological direction in which those issues seemed to point, I made my fitful way through the tangle of threads to "Chinatown."

While I cannot thank individually all the people who gave me thoughtful assistance on the thesis and manuscript, I do want to acknowledge colleagues at the University of British Columbia. In particular, I would like to thank staff and students of the Geography Department, including David Ley and Trevor Barnes, for helping to create the intellectually heightening environment out of which the thesis came. Also helpful was Edgar Wickberg of the History Department who allowed me access to material in the Chinese-Canadian project at the Special Collections division of the main library.

Thanks are due to Peter Goheen of McGill-Queen's University Press for his encouragement throughout the manuscript's review, to two helpful referees, and of course to the Social Science Federation of Canada for the grant that enabled this manuscript to be published.

In Canberra, where this thesis has been converted to a book, I owe thanks to my head of department, Roger McLean, for allowing me time in 1988 to begin the task. I am also grateful to Julie Kesby for her proofreading and assistance with referencing and indexing, to Paul Ballard for his cartographic expertise, and to the University of New South Wales for a small grant that enabled me to use editorial advice, especially on footnoting, from Bill Goff. In Toronto, John Parry did a most professional job of copy-editing.

Thanks, finally, to my parents for instilling in me a steely sense of purpose which sustained me through the long and often difficult writing process. The product, I hope, is some contribution toward a future in which the colour line is neutralized in both theory and practice.

Kay Anderson
Canberra

Vancouver's Chinatown

Introduction

Popular wisdom has it that the colourful Chinese quarters of Canadian, American, and Australian cities owe their existence to the generations of Chinese immigrants who have made their lives in the cities of the West. The restaurants, pagodas, neon lights, and recessed balconies – the Oriental streetscapes – seem to exist through a natural connection between the Chinese and their immigrant experience in the West. In this book I take a fresh, more critical look at Chinatown than that which has appeared in previous popular, media, and academic treatments of the district. In contrast to such portrayals, I examine the evolution of Chinatown from a western perspective rather than as an extension of an innate "Chineseness."

The argument is written in such a way as to reach a range of policy advisers and commentators on society, including social scientists, journalists, and professionals working in ethnic relations, immigration, and human rights. Using a Canadian case study, it breaks with the conceptualization of so-called "ethnic" settlements that features in media, policy, and lay circles. For social scientists – many of whom are now familiar with recent conceptual advances in thinking about "race" – the book attempts to demonstrate empirically the workings of the racialization processes about which theorists have written. It brings micro- and macro-scales of analysis, historical and sociological perspectives, and social and spatial dimensions to the constructivist challenge against essentialist views of race.

The study is based on my PHD dissertation ("East Is West") begun in Vancouver in 1983 (see Bibliography). At the time, the majority of Canadian race-relations research had been conducted at the provincial and national scales, and in the case of British Columbia the subject of "Orientals" had been comprehensively examined. No local history had been written, however, of the relationship between Vancouver's Chinese and European communities. There existed a gap in the empirical literature on overseas Chinese communities in Canada. Moreover, as shall be clear from chapter 1, there seemed strong conceptual reasons for examining the local organization of European assumptions about a Chinese race. From the late 1880s, the enclave of Chinese settlement at Vancouver's Pender Street was an important site through which white society's concepts about the Chinese were constituted and reproduced. A study which examined the local (urban and neighbourhood) scale therefore seemed warranted on both empirical and theoretical grounds. The result is a study that is at once sensitive to the contingencies introduced by the Vancouver setting and applicable to other racial categories and racially defined enclaves in other contexts.

The study of localities brings into simultaneous view a range of forces, only some of which are local in origin and scope. In the case of Vancouver's Chinatown, the influences range near and far. Especially decisive, we shall see, were the practices of all three levels of Canadian government, each influenced by a structure of domination that affected a number of "white" settler societies from the late nineteenth century to the present day. The study of Chinatown's construction opens windows onto this global field of European domination and its domestic extension – national, provincial, and local.

In the absence of adequate secondary material at the local level of Vancouver, and given that my conceptual emphasis here departs widely from previous research at the provincial and national scales, this study relies on primary sources collected at all three levels of Canadian government. The most important government sources consulted for different periods over the century-long time-span were as follows: Vancouver city council's Minutes (1886–1950), the city clerk's Incoming Correspondence (1886–1939), and the Chinatown files of the city's Planning Department (1970–80); the *Journals of the Legislature of British Columbia* (1872–1950) and the relevant BC *Sessional Papers* and *Statutes*; and the *Debates* of the Canadian House of Commons (1879–1980) and the relevant Canada *Sessional Papers* and *Statutes*. I also studied Vancouver's daily newspapers and other publications, including the *Chinatown News* (1958–80) and English translations of the *Chinese Times* (1914–37). Some selectivity in recording events has been necessary, but the aim has been to use historical material with a view to presenting a sociological argument rather than providing a conventionally conceived history of the Chinese in Vancouver.

Canada is an interesting setting in which to examine the process of race definition. For one thing, there is something of a gap in sensibility between the popular rhetoric of a "tolerant" past and a harmonious "multicultural" present, and the reality of a cultural his-

[handwritten: Look into early Canadian history/ government]

tory in which race has been an enduring motif. Furthermore, the management strategies adopted by the Canadian state toward out-groups have been relatively veiled by comparison to the Australian colonies before federation and, of course, the United States and South Africa.

This comparison points to a crucial sub-theme alluded to in chapter 1, which considers generally the idea of race. In Canada, the division of the state, as laid out by the British North America Act (now the Constitution Act) of 1867, into three relatively autonomous levels of jurisdiction set considerable judicial limits on the exercise of European cultural domination (or "hegemony") in the late nineteenth and early twentieth centuries. Municipal and provincial strategies were constrained by the country's constitutional framework in ways that did not impede the separately governed Australian colonies of Victoria and Queensland, for example. Ottawa's power of disallow-ance restrained the excesses of an anti-Chinese provincial legislature, just as at other times the state afforded some of Vancouver's Chinese merchants the means to contest successfully encroachments on their life chances.

[handwritten margin notes: race. / checks and balances]

These constitutional arrangements framed roughly a century of discourse – at the local, provincial, and national levels – on "racial" matters. Chapters 2–7 look at the various players and phases of the discourse as they shaped and were shaped by Vancouver's China-town. Chapter 2 examines how, between 1875 and 1903, a racial cat-egory "Chinese" was constituted by the BC legislative assembly in Victoria and by the dominion parliament in Ottawa. The intellectual context for these measures is identified, including a brief history of the race idea in Western thought. Nation-building and province-building in their symbolic dimension will be seen to focus on con-struction of a white European society, though within limits set by Canada's judicial framework; at the local level, territorial boundaries in Vancouver confirmed the broader cultural and political ones dis-tinguishing "Chineseness."

[handwritten margin note: race.]

Chapter 3 looks at the concept of "Chinatown" – the term by which local whites and municipal officials came to know and manage the area around Dupont Street. The chapter investigates the moral and sanitary dimensions of the Chinatown idea, showing how, with the imprimatur of the state, the area was represented through the filter of European imagining. Successive local administrations between the mid-1880s and about 1920 took their justification from and gave fresh effect to the idea of a (vice-ridden) Chinese race and place.

[handwritten: perceptions lead to reality?]

The 1920s saw the most feverish exploitation of the race idea in British Columbia, and chapter 4 explores the implications of this for government practices, some already in place in the 1910s. Certain measures, including the dominion's Chinese Immigration Act of 1923, were extreme forms of sanction for the idea of a Chinese race, while others directed at resident Chinese were constrained by judicial limits. Within such bounds, the three levels of government strengthened the isolation and stigma of Vancouver's Chinatown in the post–First World War era.

The levelling years of the Depression brought Chinatown its first real allies and the earliest signs of change in European attitudes – as well as some equally fanatical anti-Chinese advocates. Chapter 5 describes events that captured Chinatown's enduring stigma and those that distinguished its emerging definition as Vancouver's "Little Corner of the Far East." The social construction of Chinatown has not always or necessarily been a unilaterally imposed process, however, as indicated by strategies of both accommodation and resistance on the part of Chinatown merchants.

By the late 1950s, when "race" was being dismantled by Canadian policy-makers, the area became the target of the post-war ideology of progress; officially, Chinatown became a "slum." In chapter 6, it is argued that the choice of Chinatown for some major public projects bluntly exposed the power relation that had always underpinned the race-definition process. The efforts of some Chinese groups to use the tourist definition of the district as leverage against the plans for urban renewal and a freeway show how they attempted to manipulate European projections of difference. By the late 1960s, these efforts and pressure by liberal reformists, academics, and architects led to withdrawal of the remaining stages of the public projects in Chinatown, which was now heralded as an "ethnic neighbourhood."

Chapter 7 examines the radically new form of neighbourhood targeting that took place in the 1970s. Ottawa announced a policy of "multiculturalism" to recognize Canada's "ethnic groups," and Chinatown became courted by all three levels of government precisely for the perceived "Chineseness" that for so long had separated it. It will be argued that through all the seemingly "enlightened" rhetoric of multiculturalism and local beautification and zoning schemes, the classification "Chinese" (i.e. non-white) continued. And, as long as the racial frame of reference itself persisted, cultural relativism could easily give way – as it did in Vancouver in the late 1970s – to negative and seemingly more enduring forms of racialization.

The transformative potential of European hegemony underlines the point that the process of racialization is situated in history and society, not biology and nature. It does not take a fixed course whose form for all Western settings can be predicted in advance or "read off" from abstract system needs. It is also a contradictory process, with different levels of state sometimes taking quite different postures toward the "Chinese." In short, European hegemony is no monolithic or mechanical totality, the fragments of which add up to some tidy, theorizable whole. On the contrary, it is an uneven process that defies neat modelling and invites comparative analysis. It also prompts resistance, both from those it includes and those it excludes, suggesting the potential for renegotiation of the relations of dominance. Indeed, although this book reveals the resilience of the race concept in one setting, my deeper ambition is to expose the susceptibility of racial beliefs to change and challenge and the potential therein for their ultimate annulment.

CHAPTER ONE

Race, Place, and the Power of Definition

On 9 February 1985, the Toronto *Globe and Mail*, reporting on South Africa, stated that almost 800 people had had their racial classifications changed in 1984 under apartheid policies. South Africa's home affairs minister, F.W. de Klerk, said in Parliament: "518 coloureds became whites, 14 whites became coloureds and 17 Indians became Malay. There were also 89 blacks who became coloured and five coloureds who became black, three blacks who became Indian, one who became an Asian, and a Malay who became a Chinese."

While few countries have traded as transparently in the currency of race as has South Africa, in many countries powerful institutions such as the state ascribe arbitrary racial identities to select groups of people. Classifications of identity – whether of "West Indians" in Britain, "Aborigines" in Australia, "blacks" in the United States, or "Indians" in Fiji – differ from the South African experience in the degree of force with which they have been invoked but bear the same stamp of a dominant community conferring identity. This book argues that the perception of the "Chinese" in Canada as a "different" group is a comparable cultural abstraction that belongs to the beliefs and institutional practices of white European society and that Chinatowns stand to this day in North America and Australia in large part as physical manifestations of that abstraction.

Neighbourhoods of Chinese settlement in Western societies have attracted a considerable amount of scholarship and media attention throughout the twentieth century. These neighbourhoods have inspired a literature whose volume is distinguished by the corresponding lack of attention given to the enclaves of "host" society members. The neighbourhoods of "whites," by comparison, have escaped attention as objects of study – unless, of course, some aspect of their class, or political, or housing status has been under investi-

gation. We read surprisingly little in newspaper features and social
science about the internal dynamics of British-origin communities in
Western societies, their way of life, their ethnic associations and their
adaptation to overseas settings.[1] There is a sense in which to examine
such matters would be to reproduce the familiar, the mundane. We
know (or we think we know) what is "ours" – our thoughts, our
culture, our local worlds. But in the case of Chinatown, its peculiarity
has stood as the point of departure for a tradition of scholarship and
social comment. Its "difference" from "mainstream" society seems to
have been accepted as a key to new knowledge about the lives of
others. In part, because of its assumed departure from some (assumed)
norm, Chinatown has been an object of study in its own right.

There are good reasons why Chinatowns in Western societies
should be examined. Subjected as most Chinese communities have
been to hostile receiving populations, they serve as commentaries on
the attitudes and behaviour of the host societies.[2] They have also
prompted many important research questions in sociology and
anthropology about cultural transfer overseas and about the dynamics of social organization and community stratification in new environments.[3] In geography, Chinatown has been conceptualized as a
launching point in the assimilation of Chinese settlers, as an urban
village pitted against encroaching land uses, and as a Chinese architectural form.[4] Chinatown has been viewed as either a ghettoized,
minority community or as an "ethnic community." David Lai sum-
marizes the prevailing scientific (and popular) conceptualization of
Chinatown: "Chinatown in North America is characterized by a concentration of Chinese people and economic activities in one or more
city blocks which forms a unique component of the urban fabric. It
is basically an idiosyncratic oriental community amidst an occidental
urban environment."[5] In short, there exists an important school of
thought that sees Chinatown as a colony of the East in the West.

It is possible, however, to adopt a different approach to the study
of Chinatown, one that does not rely on a discrete "Chineseness" as
an implicit explanatory principle. People from China have assuredly
lived in close settlements in the towns and cities of the West, but
"Chinatown" is not "Chinatown" *only* because the Chinese – whether
by choice or constraint – have lived in enclaves. Rather "Chinatown"
is in part a European creation. Like the idea of a Chinese race, "Chinatown" has possessed a tradition of imagery that has lodged it
firmly in the popular consciousness of Europeans (and indeed of the
Chinese themselves). Moreover, the premise of a uniquely Chinese
race and place has shaped and justified practices that have inscribed
it further in European society and space. For more than a century,

in cities such as Vancouver in Canada, assumptions about Chinese "difference" have informed the policies of powerful government institutions toward the Chinese enclave and its inhabitants, in ways that demonstrate the considerable material force and effect of beliefs about a Chinese race and place. In an important and neglected sense, then, "Chinatown" belongs as much to the society with the power to define and shape it as it does to its residents.

At first blush, the study of so local a phenomenon as Chinatown might seem overly restrictive as the basis for a book. After all, as Lai stated, Chinatowns constitute little more than a few blocks in most Western cities. But microscopic portraits can be immensely illuminating of the macro-processes that penetrate, and through which are remade, enclaves like Chinatown. Localities are "complex amalgams," in Dear's words,[6] of past, present, and newly forming processes and patterns whose unravelling requires something of a jeweller's-eye view of the world. In the case of Chinatown, its history in Vancouver can be deconstructed to expose the workings of one of the most influential and resilient of cultural hegemonies. Indeed Chinatown's story – far from being parochial and idiosyncratic – illuminates a European way of seeing and acting whose impact on people's life chances and on Western social and spatial structures is pronounced to the present day.

BEFORE THIS ARGUMENT can be elaborated further, it seems useful to indicate the basis for this book's primary claim that "Chinatown" is a historically situated phenomenon that owes little to primordial differences of "race" or ancestral culture. This can be done briefly by recalling information that is commonplace to contemporary population geneticists and a growing number of social scientists but which, for the most part, has not yet penetrated to lay audiences. For this latter group, the discussion provides the preliminary context for an introduction to the theoretical argument of this study which concerns the role of the Canadian government in the social construction of Vancouver's "Chinatown" and the category "Chinese" from 1880 to 1980. It is a narrative that might be equally relevant to the making of other racial categories in Vancouver, to "Chinese" and "Chinatown" in other settings, and to other racialized people in other settings.

RACE AS A BIOLOGICAL NOTION

Unfortunately, the concept of race, though for many decades being seen as problematic by population geneticists, continues to be used and propounded by many lay people, policy-makers, and journalists as a concept with scientific value.)Belief in the natural existence of race is something they share with nineteenth-century British, American, and western European biologists who assumed the world's races were for all intents and purposes immutable and that each had unique biological and cultural characteristics.)Such biologists never fully agreed on the criteria for classifying the world's populations into races or on the number of races that existed. It was clear from their hopelessly large number of typologies that features such as skin colour, facial angle, cranial shape, and hair texture did not co-vary in any systematic or consistent way.[7] But such nagging problems did not prompt them to question the assumptions behind their classification systems, so powerful was their will to establish naturally occurring regularities behind human variation.

By the 1930s, "population genetics" threw into question a century of research into the visible anatomy of racial types and directed scientists toward the deeper, genotypic variation among populations of individuals. This important conceptual shift enabled scientists to uncover the enormous genetic variation among individuals. Also, scientists discovered that local geographic populations did not differ from other populations absolutely but only in the relative frequency of various genes.(This discovery was signalled by the concept of "geographical race," still used in biology today to refer to reproductively isolated populations of varying individuals, who differ from other local, "inbreeding" populations in the proportions of various genes.)

The implications of this discovery have been decisive for scientific thought about race. Physical differences among people obviously exist and are statistically clear among groups. The well-known Negroid ("black"), Caucasoid ("white"), and Mongoloid ("yellow") divisions, identified in almost every race typology since the eighteenth century, do have some statistical validity. Indeed some physical anthropologists confidently continue to use the term "race" on the grounds that clusters of genetically defined populations can be identified. So too do some contemporary population geneticists, who are interested less in terminology (whether the clusters are "races," "subspecies," "varieties," or "populations") than in what the frequency of given characters says about the processes of natural selection and the dynamics of human evolution.

It is important, however, that social scientists and other commentators on society be aware of the subtleties and difficulties of this more recent use of the term "race" for their own disciplinary concerns. Some biologists argue that the difficulties are sufficient to warrant abandoning the term altogether, especially given the seemingly irresistible emotive baggage it has been made to carry.[8]

That human populations differ in the distribution of their genes is, as mentioned, a biological fact. But no agreement exists among contemporary scientists over whether that fact provides an unambiguous basis for classifying human "races." Apart from the superficial characteristics of skin, hair, and bone by which we have been socialized to see what is called racial difference, there are, as Appiah notes, "few genetic characteristics to be found in the population of England that are not found in similar proportions in Zaire or China."[9] Overall genetic profiles vary considerably more within individuals of a given "race" than between individuals of different "races," the result being that genetic variability within the populations of Asia, Europe, and Africa is much greater than the variation between those populations.

Nor is there a known gene whose form is universally present in one "race" and present only in a different form in another "race." In the case of the gene that determines blood type, for example, every population has some particular mixture of the three forms (A, B, and O) of the gene. How large the difference in the frequency of blood groups or other genetic traits needs to be to warrant a difference of "race" is clearly a matter of judgment. As Lewontin et al. point out, the Kikuya of East Africa differ from the Japanese in gene frequencies, but they also differ from their neighbours, the Masai – and although the differences are less in one case than in the other, it is only a matter of degree. "This means," the authors argue, "that the social and historical definitions of race that put the two East African tribes in the same 'race' but put the Japanese in a different 'race,' were biologically arbitrary."[10]

The point by now is clear. "Racial" differences cannot be conceptualized as absolute because genetic variation is continuous. Statistical groupings cannot be mistaken, as Marger notes, "for actual human groupings founded on unmistakable hereditary traits. Racial categories form a continuum of gradual change, not a set of sharply demarcated types ... The popular division of the human population into three major racial groupings is thus imprecise and largely arbitrary."[11] The short-range differences that exist, and by which society and academics have identified a difference of "race," have been formed and maintained not by biological factors but by geographic and other factors obstructing "intermarriage," such as cultural and legal barriers. There are no natural or intrinsic isolating mechanisms between people, and, given humanity's record of continent-hopping, it is doubtful that there ever were "pure" human "races."[12] By all accounts, differences between sets of reproductively isolated people will be minute as compared with the genetic variability among individuals. The problem of origins may always dog the study of human relations, but, as Lewontin et al. argue, the fact of genetic variability leads us to conclude: (Any use of 'racial' categories must take its justification from some other source than biology."[13])

RACE AS A SOCIAL CONSTRUCT

Reflection on the ontological status of race may not seem a valuable exercise for social scientists. (After all, as W.I. Thomas pointed out many decades ago, if a thing is defined by people as real – as race surely has been for decades – it is real in its consequences, and human perceptions and their consequences are what should concern researchers.) Robert Park was one of the first social scientists to pursue this line of thought, arguing that regardless of the biological significance of race, people's prejudice ensured that very pronounced social distance gradients operated between blacks and whites in American cities.[14])

But the ontological status of race is as critical an issue for students of society as it is for those studying human variation. In geography, the tacit acceptance by many researchers of public beliefs about race has affected the types of questions they have asked. In the ecological tradition of research, for example, there has been a long-standing interest in measuring and analyzing urban patterns of what is said to be "residential segregation by race." Many questions have turned on the relative significance of socioeconomic status and race in determining "racially differentiated" cities.[15] Others have been interested in the dynamics of urban housing markets; how they have become "split" along racial lines and how the "dual" market has been reinforced by financial institutions and such gatekeepers as real estate agents.[16] There has also been widespread interest by geographers, particularly in the United States, in the neighbourhood "transition" that is said to occur when blacks "invade" white neighbourhoods.[17] (The process of white invasion of inner-city black neighbourhoods is commonly termed neighbourhood "revitalization" or "gentrification.") Others have investigated white exclusionary strategies involving government agencies, such as zoning and school segregation.[18]

Now, as Thomas suggested, as long as people believe in the existence of distinct races, geographers and other social scientists have an important function in studying the consequences for urban structure. Notwithstanding the critiques of positivism, the form of such patterns should continue to interest geographers. The crucial issue –

as some geographers have already suggested[19] – is how research questions about the geography of race relations are to be framed. Let's take a different case for the purpose of argument.

Despite scientific evidence to the contrary, people might well still believe that the earth is flat. (The existence of flat-earth societies in England and elsewhere suggests there are people who still accept that view.) But social scientists are unlikely to carry out analyses on a flat-earth premise just to satisfy the populace and reinforce what they know to be false. Their interest in the flat-earth subject would lie in what they might call the effects of the "flat-earth myth," not the effects of the flat-earth itself, as if there were such an explanatory constant. In the example of race research, however, social scientists have not always been so careful. A number still tacitly endorse non-scientific classifications by implying that "races" can be actually distinguished by biologically or culturally relevant criteria. For example, survey research on residence, intermarriage, and occupational patterns often uses census classifications of people's identities in order to try to make measurements and claims about the correlates of "racial" differentiation in cities.[20] Yet as Marshall pointed out some years ago, the groups that census collectors specify and about which social scientists (and journalists) write are those perceived by sets of people in given socio-political contexts, not those formed somehow outside of history.[21]

This methodological problem suggests a more fundamental conceptual difficulty with the kind of survey research just described, one that turns on the explanatory power of race itself. While we need to know more about reality as it presents itself to society, it seems pertinent to ask researchers who describe racial differentiation in cities: is it segregation by distinct and discrete groups that exists, or segregation by skin colour? Differently phrased: do "racial mechanisms" (in Farley's words[22]) sort groups in space and employment, or is it the social significance attached to colour distinctions that engenders residential and occupational differentiation? The question is not simply a semantic (or pedantic) one. Whereas the first position (in each question) gives implicit causal power to race difference itself – it is something objective that somehow ipso facto inspires segregation – the second does not invest race with its own explanatory status. In short, it recognizes that "race" itself must be explained.

There are many examples throughout history, in addition to the extreme South African one, that highlight the entirely sociological nature of racial classifications. Few geographers interested in the "racial" transition of neighbourhoods in the United States today would study the movement of Americans who came from Germany into "Anglo" neighbourhoods. Most would agree that both these groups comprise the "white" population. But, as Solomon points out, this has not always been the case. In New England, between the 1850s and 1920s, those people now regarded as members of a "white race" – Anglo-Saxons, Celts, Teutons, and so on – were perceived as separate "races." Each was considered immutable on the basis of behavioural and physical endowments. Over time, however, New Englanders adapted their evaluation of the "races" of Europe.[23] Similarly, in the western Canadian province of Alberta, in the early decades of the twentieth century, Germans and eastern Europeans were considered not "white" but rather "non-white."

Similarly indicative of the contextual nature of racial assignments is the notion of the "Jewish" race. Only after the 1870s, when the ideology of anti-semitism took root in Germany, were Jewish people classified as a distinct (and inferior) race by white Canadians of Anglo origin. Previously, the external definition of Jewish people had corresponded closely to that people's national self-identity based in religious distinctiveness.[24] Likewise, the Canadian category "native Indian" does not pertain to some constant biological referent. In pre-contact times, members of the Cree, Ojibway, and Iroquois communities identified themselves and were categorized by other indigenous groupings as Cree, Ojibway, and Iroquois. Only to Europeans did "they" all look and act alike, and as a consequence the category "Indian" was coined. The same has been said of the white Australian label "Aboriginal."[25]

The capriciousness of racial classifying can also be seen when one shifts from one society to another. Worsley notes that Kashmiri Brahmins, who think of themselves as "white" in contrast to dark-skinned South Indians, are shocked to find themselves classified as "black" or "coloured" in Britain. The same surprise exists on the part of Nigerian aristocrats and Muslim hadjis.[26] It is also likely that an individual classified as "black" in the United States would be classified as "white" in Brazil because the systems of classification and criteria used differ. In New Guinea what passes in our experience for a "white" person is considered "red" by some "tribes."[27] For that matter, Fried asks, who ever saw a white person, not to mention a yellow one?

RACE AND CULTURE

In the quest to challenge views about essential differences between the world's populations, it would be unhelpful to suggest a vision that turns the Other into the Same. Cultural differences between groups of people assuredly exist, and Brotz's claim to the contrary – that "there is no diversity at all," that "Canada's ethnic groups stand for exactly the same thing which is a bourgeois way of life" – seems an overstatement.[28] To deny cultural differences their subjective significance is to make the mistake of Canadian and Australian postwar assimilation policies that assumed migrants could simply be made over in the image of their receiving societies. The issue, again, is how differences are to be conceptualized.

A growing literature in ethnic studies lends support from a different direction to the argument that the racial classifications we just examined are problematic. Fredrick Barth began the critique in anthropology over twenty years ago when he argued: "We can assume no simple one-to-one relationship between ethnic units and cultural similarities and differences."[29] Since then, many social scientists have challenged the tradition of cultural relativism in North American ethnic studies, where cultural differences were viewed as innate properties of naturally occurring ethnic groups. A more recent argument suggests that ethnic groups are social (not ready-made) phenomena, formed relationally through processes of exclusion and inclusion around symbols of actual or perceived common descent such as language, behavioural practices, and religion.[30] For example, for people of English ethnicity in Canada, their internal criteria of group identification have tended to include white skin colour, English language, and Protestant cultural traditions.

In this recent tradition of work in ethnic studies, researchers have turned their attention to the social process by which boundaries between groups are negotiated, not the "cultural stuff" the boundaries were once assumed to seal hermetically. Implicit in this shift is a different view of ancestral culture itself. Whereas culture used to be defined by social scientists as an objective inventory of characteristics, it now tends to be conceptualized as a framework of values and practices that forms a context for people's lives and which they adapt in changing historical and regional circumstances.[31] It is not something constant or atavistic. Most scholars of anthropology would insist that there is no fixed system of "Chineseness," for example, that is imbibed uniformly across generation and context by a Chinese in Hong Kong, a third-generation Chinese-origin person in Malaysia, a Chinese in mainland China, a Chinese-origin immigrant to South Africa, and a fourth-generation Canadian of Chinese origin living in Vancouver. "We should be wary," one scholar recently remarked when describing the fragmentation of Australia's Chinese-origin population, "of trying to generalize on 'Chinese culture' and of establishing a 'Chinese national character.'"[32] Of course, ethnic self-identification may be strong in the absence of binding cultural traditions. But people's affiliations to ethnic groups cannot be assumed or deduced from differences of skin colour, language, religion, and other markers people use to place themselves and each other in descent groups.

An important distinction needs to be made, then, between self definitions of identity and those classifications that are ascribed from without. Whereas the former are predicated on subjective or inclusive processes (described above in the example of English ethnicity in Canada), the latter are based on processes of exclusion (to be demonstrated in the example of "Chinese" in this study).[33] The analytical distinction between self and other definitions of identity may collapse, of course, in instances where people on the receiving end of identity classifications come to internalize and even assert those assignments, a secondary process we will encounter at interesting moments in the history of the "Chinese" in Vancouver.

The complexity of identity formation processes in multi-ethnic settings is such that anthropologists and other social scientists interested in race and ethnicity have increasingly recognized an epistemological dilemma. One anthropologist calls it a "unit problem," by which he means that "the named ethnic entities we accept, often unthinkingly, as basic givens in the literature are often arbitrarily or, even worse, inaccurately imposed."[34] In geography, Jackson states a similar dilemma in his comment (after Padillo) that "it is only from the standpoint of American society that Puerto Ricans form a group, defined as either a racial group, an ethnic group, or a cultural group."[35] How best, then, for researchers to proceed who want to examine, for example, the settlement and employment patterns and experiences of such people in San Francisco? To whom belongs the status "Puerto Rican"? How "Puerto Rican" is a person born of San Juan parents and raised in the mainland United States? And who is to make this judgment? These issues underline the risk that the boundaries that researchers draw around their subjects will be as capricious as the folk values and practices out of which they are historically constructed.

RACE DEFINITION: "CHINESE" AS A WESTERN REPRESENTATION

If race, ethnicity, and ancestral culture are conceptualized as being problematic rather than axiomatic, some research directions are suggested that depart from conventional studies of racially defined minorities such as the "Chinese" in Western societies. An important

body of research has recently begun to forge such a new direction.
Robert Miles was among the first scholars to argue for more critical
academic study when he coined the term "racialization" to refer to
the process by which attributes such as skin colour, language, birthplace, and cultural practices are given social significance as markers
of distinction.[36] This research is drawing attention to the *idea* of race
and the way in which people's assumptions about essential differences articulate with political, economic, and gender relations.[37] It is
an ambitious agenda, capable of generating fresh insight into processes heretofore masked by languages of permanence and timeless-
ness. It is also opening up a dialogue with larger philosophical
debates in the social sciences, so ending the long disciplinary ghet-
toization of "racial and ethnic studies."

Most of the existing arguments for more rigorous study of race
have been programmatic, theoretical statements. Developments in the
field are proceeding quickly, but as yet only a small amount of
research confronts the epistemological implications of the new thinking about race in substantive research.[38] Still less work traces the
historical construction of particular racial categories in such a way as
to expose their changing form and demonstrate their enduring connection to structures of domination. Despite the political significance
of the leap that has been made in people's minds from differences in
physical features to what has been called "race," there is a dearth of
research on the actual structuring of that cognitive operation. As
Banton suggests: "Though much has been said about the evils associated with racial classification, there has been little systematic study
of the process."[39]

This study contributes to the growing corpus of research on what
I call the race-definition process, by examining the making of the
category "Chinese" in one British settler society. For the "Chinese"
in Vancouver, we shall see that the racial category persisted in European thought and practice for over a century, from the late nineteenth century right up to the present. That period is replete with
evidence of the depth and tenacity of beliefs and government practices that have had an apparently "racial" character. Precisely how the
representation "Chinese" has been fashioned and recast in Vancouver
society and space is the subject of this book.

To be sure, nothing inevitable has brought the notions "Chinese"
and "Chinatown" into European cognition and sustained them in
Vancouver culture and territory. As will be clear by now, race is no
once-and-for-all happening that, of its own accord, inspired the "sinophobia" about which so much has been written since Allport's influential work.[40] Yet conventional approaches to the study of the Chinese

in British Columbia and other colonial settings tend to obscure this important point. The social relations in those settings have for years been interpreted in the language of "prejudice," "ethnocentrism," and "stereotyping" – the stock in trade of liberal social science. Ward's account of white attitudes toward "Orientals" in British Columbia between 1870 and 1947 highlights the problem of such idealist approaches. For Ward, the socio-pyschological tensions between people of Chinese and European origin "inhered in the racially plural situation."[41] The Chinese were stigmatized and penalized, he argues, because "white British Columbians yearned for a racially homogeneous society." From this perspective, the Chinese were victims, hapless targets of white "yearning" against non-whites, and Chinatown (if we are to extend the liberal thesis), an ostracized colony of the East in the West.

Although the prejudice concept has informed a long tradition of race-relations research (and journalism), it is difficult to locate its explanatory value. In itself, prejudice is a rather none-too-revealing concept that implies that white fears of Chinese followed somehow unproblematically from the encounter of the two groups. Again, to quote Ward, "psychological tensions derived from white society's desire for racial homogeneity, a drive continually stimulated by the racially plural condition." But unless the argument is advanced that anti-Chinese feeling (and the policies it informed) were natural, inevitable responses, the question is begged: why were (and are) white people prejudiced? The white-racism thesis stops short of this question, fixing (implicitly) in some mythical human nature the historically and culturally shifting process of ascribing, with markers of skin colour and cultural practices, the "difference" of "race" itself.

In short, it is important to take the step beyond studying white attitudes, because it is not prejudice that has explanatory power but rather the ideology of racial difference that informs it. After all, we shall see that, long after the excesses of "prejudice" were curtailed in British Columbia, there emerged new guises to the underlying European racial frame of reference. It is this framework of ideas that *allows* prejudice and discrimination on the part of more powerful groups to be maintained and that points to the need for a more fundamental critique of such concepts as "Chinese" and "Chinatown" than has been possible within the conventional race-relations paradigm. The remainder of this introduction is devoted to outlining the contours of such a fresh perspective. First, I shall examine – through the concept of cultural hegemony – the historical and theoretical links between racial thought and political practice in British settler societies, and second, I wish to underline the epistemological significance of Chinatown in the history of racialization processes relating to Vancouver's Chinese.

RACIAL IDEOLOGY AND THE STATE: LINKING MICRO- AND MACRO-ANALYSIS

Racial classifications have been cultural ascriptions, but their history reveals that they have also assuredly been political phenomena. Race has not been just another social construction. Like many categories of human cognition, racial representations have to do much less with "truth" (a one-to-one correspondence with what is "out there") than with faith and material interests. Indeed systems of racial classification have been linked so indelibly to historically situated power relations that it is impossible to study anything so benign as the simple ideas of a Chinese race and place. As Edward Said has shown in his excellent history of the European idea of the Orient, social reality is constructed not democratically but within a hegemonic framework that is rarely questioned.[42] Not only, therefore, do we need to uncover what "Chinese" has signified in European thought – as symbolic anthropologists might do – but we also need to address how such categories came to be reproduced as dominant ideological and material forms. This study takes up that challenge to examine the presence of government institutions and territorial arrangements in the process by which one racial category became an authoritative concept in a British settler society. That is, it attempts to demonstrate some important links between the micro-cognitive order of racial representation and the macro-structure of European domination.

Demystification of modes of thought in social life and institutional practice is a popular theme in current sociology and anthropology. Schutz anticipated the trend many years ago: "In putting our questions thus we no longer naively accept the social world and its current idealizations as ready-made ... but we undertake to study the process of idealizing."[43] A common subject of critique in recent years has been the ideas and practices of social-service professionals such as doctors, psychiatrists, welfare workers, and the police. The perceptions and language of such people, it is argued, condition the experiences of those categorized as clients, patients, and victims. This style of cultural critique attempts to expose the interests behind dominant beliefs and, after Foucault, to ground discourses (about, for example, deviance and disease) in the concrete institutional practices that have historically surrounded them.[44] The links between power and what passes as knowledge (folk and scientific) in Western societies are perhaps nowhere more transparent, however, than in the example of racial classification.

The relationship between the cultural and political spheres of Western societies has received relatively little theoretical and empirical attention in the recent writings on the state in capitalist countries. The majority of research in the last fifteen years has explored the links between government and economic interests, often explaining the practices of the former in terms of contradictions, needs, and pressures within capitalist production systems.[45] Yet, as Breton argues, the state is "not only involved in the economy's management, the pursuit of growth, and the initiation or support of changes found necessary in that sphere. It is also engaged in managing the symbolic system, the protection of its integrity and its adaptation to new circumstances."[46]

(Structural Marxist writers on race and the state have been particularly concerned to show the co-operation between governments and owners of capital in colonial and post-colonial settings. Many have argued that racial ideology had its genesis in the exploitative economic system of capitalism that required a cheap and dispensable labour force and a racially divided working class. In meeting both these needs the state fulfilled a vital role, one such writer on Alabama and South Africa contends. "Class actors," Greenberg claims, "breathe life into racial categories bringing the elaboration of a state machinery to control and limit the proletarianization of the subordinate population."[47] Another Marxist writer on British Columbia's early race relations invokes the same forces in her explanation of the state's intervention in the "Oriental" question. She argues that racial hostility is ultimately a product of the "contradiction between the demands of higher wages on the part of (white) workers ... and the demands for cheap (Chinese) labour on the part of employers," a class on whose behalf the Canadian state operated by recruiting and helping to subordinate the necessary labour.[48])

By now there are many Marxist social scientists who would be as uncomfortable with such crude structuralist explanations of the state's relationship to the race question as there are non-Marxists. Scholars at the Centre for Contemporary Cultural Studies in Birmingham, for example, have sought to avoid shrill forms of economic reductionism while emphasizing the material circumstances that enable "racial" awareness to flourish in everyday life.[49] Broadside struggles over causal primacy (as between the economic and superstructural spheres) are fading, then, though less because of philosophical convergence than out of recognition that material and ideological pressures have intersected in irreducible ways in the making of systems of colour-based inequality.

Simple claims of economic determination are also avoided in this account of the Chinese in Vancouver. For one reason, if "racial" tension is the tactic of a capitalist class, on whose behalf the state operates by legislating status divisions among workers, the strategy surely requires pre-existing cultural assumptions about races and their ranking on the part of capitalists and white workers. Structural Marxist and "split labour market" theorists have usefully identified the economic sources of conflict between groups distinguished by colour under conditions of unequal labour costs. But to understand why people from China were cheap labour in the first place requires recognition of both the force of ideological conceptions of the Chinese as a category and the effectiveness of official representations of them as alien. To explain the cheapness of Chinese labour alternatively, in terms, for example, of the "uneven development of capitalism which created low subsistence levels in China" – as one split labour market theorist recently argued[50] – is to invoke only a more sophisticated version of the nineteenth-century view held by white employers and workers that overseas Chinese had an inherently "Chinese" standard of living.

Racial consciousness was undoubtedly systematized during the period from the sixteenth century when Western capitalist labour markets developed.[51] Also, governments in many colonial settings co-operated with business interests over the matter of cheap labour in ways that secured fertile conditions for capital accumulation. But as chapter 2 briefly takes up, the modern race idea inherited and derived its strength from a European cognitive package that since pre-capitalist times distinguished West and East, civilized and uncivilized, Christian and heathen, and master and slave.[52] These us/them dualisms hardened around the idiom of colour by the mid-sixteenth century and supplied to Westerners and non-Westerners a world view without which capitalistic expansion might not have been so extensive or influential. In the case of the "Chinese," there also existed from antiquity a European discourse created by poets, travellers, intellectuals, and colonial bureaucracies that tailored the "Oriental" in the image and interests of the West.[53]

Of course, colour-based inequality cannot be explained solely in ideological terms. Just as the practical task of removing such inequality requires more than changes to people's ideas, so a more ambitious study than this one would examine the mutual structuring of economic pressures and cultural conceptions about the Chinese during the course of British Columbia's development as a capitalist colony. Such a study might inquire into the economic circumstances in which different "racial" groupings were inserted into class relations; also how those relations and struggles between fractions helped preserve the distinctions over time. Such issues are important, but they do not form the focus of this study. As mentioned before, few empirical studies have traced, historically, the persistence and changing forms of racial representation itself. Indeed, the effect and endurance of racial consciousness have been such that its contribution to systems of inequality warrants more attention "on its own terms," in Prager's words.[54] Moreover, to emphasize the influence of the conceptual system of race is not to grant it some explanatory power of its own. Systems of knowledge such as race are not constitutive in themselves but rather are constituted in and through human agency, historical circumstances, and territorial arrangements. This viewpoint forms the basis of what can be called a "constructivist" approach – one that situates the race-definition process in history, politics, and space. As we shall see, politicians in nineteenth-century colonial outposts such as British Columbia sponsored and enforced racial concepts which, through territorial arrangements, became locally organized and embedded.

THE CONCEPT OF CULTURAL HEGEMONY

The links between the polity and culture were primary concerns of the social theorist Antonio Gramsci, whose work offers some fertile concepts for understanding the relationship between the state and racial ideology. In Gramsci's words, the race concept can be thought of as a "critical unifying principle" in consolidating and justifying the rise to "hegemony" of a white European "historical bloc" from the sixteenth century.[55] In using the term "hegemonic," Gramsci and others, such as Raymond Williams, insist on relating the "whole lived social process," by which people and institutions conduct their daily rounds, to specific distributions of power and influence.[56]

For Williams, a hegemonic culture is not simply a set of values – be they European or Islamic – but a "realized complex" of ideas, practices, and social relations that reflect the interests of a dominant sector and which have come to permeate society's private and institutional domains. Just 100 years ago, to take an example, the colony of British Columbia was over 50 per cent "Indian."[57] But through initial strategies of force and later, more routine forms of immigration regulation and control over the division of labour, access to power, and status differentiation, British Columbia imperceptibly but surely became the society of European institutional completeness that it is today. The concept of hegemony is suggestive of precisely this willed and authored process by which a European paradigm came to saturate the practical workings of that colonial society. ⌉

⌈In such a transformation, the legislative assembly established by British officials on Vancouver Island in 1849 and the provincial parliament of British Columbia after 1871 assumed ownership of the means of conceptual control over the definition and status of all settlers to the colony. Their power to shape the discourse out of which different immigrants – including those from Britain and China – were perceived suggests that government agents played a most critical role in constructing categories such as "Chinese" and enforcing their meaning. This "power of definition," in Western's words,[58] suggests that the state should be conceptualized as much more than mere government. From the 1880s through to current times in British Columbia, "Chinese" has signified "non-white" in European culture. It has connoted "them" as opposed to "us," "outsiders" rather than "insiders." But it was Canadian politicians and bureaucrats who in their policies and rhetoric made one way of seeing people from China stand as the official representation of such settlers. Recurring governments did not simply react to popular or economic pressures but, as we shall see, actively sponsored and enforced the we/they distinctions within European culture at large. Their moral and legal authority helped to give the race concept its remarkable material force and effect, embedding it in structures that over time reciprocally reproduced it. ⌉

The insights of Gramsci are interesting here. Though faithful to the Marxist point of departure – that capitalism is a system of production based on the exploitation of wage labour – Gramsci was not deterministic in his theorizing. He argued that it was unhelpful to deduce people's ideas from economic forces because, in organizing people's actions and practices, ideologies do themselves assume a dense material basis. "Mental life is more than a pale reflection of some more basic developments in material life," one interpreter of Gramsci has said. "The link between the two realms is not linear causality but circular interaction within an organic whole."[59]

Gramsci took seriously people's subjectivity because he was interested in the process by which a peasant society in the underdeveloped south of Italy became incorporated into the agenda of capitalist development set by northern industrialists in the late nineteenth century. That is, he was concerned with the problem of how dominant "historical blocs" secure legitimacy for their projects and assimilate other groups to them. To the extent that such blocs are successful, they achieve hegemony, Gramsci claimed, though not through indoctrination or coercion, but as more and more people come to interpret their own interests and consciousness of themselves in the "unifying discourse." In accepting the ruling bloc's moral, political, and cultural values, they facilitate the historical "moment" when the philosophy and practice of a society are fused, when a concept of reality is filtered through a society.

In this process of cultural incorporation, Gramsci argued, political office provides the dominant sector with the necessary official means for "nationalizing" and legitimizing its conceptual and instrumental control. The political sphere is therefore organically linked with the cultural realm in Gramsci's theorizing. The state is not a separate "level" from civil society (as the orthodox base–superstructure model would have it), but part of that society, evolving and legitimizing the rules and framework within which social life is structured.

Although many interpreters of Gramsci, and Gramsci himself, see the ideological struggle as one ultimately between Marx's two "fundamental classes," others have found it useful to extend the notion of a ruling historical bloc to other categories that have amassed cultural, intellectual, moral, and economic solidarity. Potentially hegemonic may be historical groups bound by religious or other ideological ties, as well as economic interest. Among them might be usefully included the authoritative structure known as patriarchy,[60] the cultural formation of Unionism in Northern Ireland,[61] and the influential European hegemony that is the focus of this book. In each of these examples, political and economic control has entailed symbolic domination.

As stated above, race has been a most effective unifying concept in the making and extension of European global hegemony. With more or less force in different colonial settings, racial ideology was adopted by white communities, whose members from all classes indulged it (often in contradictory ways) for the definition and privilege it afforded them as insiders. The race paradigm gave white groups the power of definition in cultural and ideological terms, as well as more instrumental power in the hands of politicians, bureaucrats, owners of capital, labour unions, judges, police, and other influential members of the "ruling" sector.

Among the most influential agents were those who acquired monopolistic control over the state apparatus. In British Columbia, as in other British outposts, we shall see that a colonial bureaucracy quickly specified, officially, the characteristics thought to differentiate outsiders from those deemed to be legitimate citizens. In doing so for the "Chinese," it will be argued, the agents of the Canadian state sanctioned a concept behind which lay the most divisive world view of "us" and "them." In the ambition to build a dominant "Anglo" identity and community, the state sought to secure popular legitimacy by defining people of Chinese origin in opposition to all that could be made to stand for "white" Canada. With all the backing of the imperial mission, politicians took as their mandate the making of a European society in all its institutional and private domains.

The story of how the levels of state achieved this, however, is by no means the predictable outcome of some neat, hegemonic totality. As we shall see, there is no simple or straight-line relationship among racial thought, the will to dominate, and political practice. This is not least because of the legal bounds that existed in Canada on the actions of municipal and provincial politicians and bureaucrats. Such judicial constraints are important to our conceptualization of cultural hegemony in that they point to its uneven and, moreover, its contradictory quality. They underline the fact that cultural domination is no a priori package imposed somehow from above or outside of history. It is still possible, however, to locate within the practices of the past the recurring processes of racialization and domination that informed them. The evidence that we shall consider certainly suggests that, within binding constitutional limits, the Canadian state was a most effective "private apparatus" of European hegemony, in Gramsci's words, centrally implicated in the making of Canada's social order.

Scholars of the more critical race studies mentioned above have been quick to expose classical forms of racialization and domination in the United Kingdom and British settler societies. That *negative* representations of racially defined people shaped adverse attitudes and repressive policies in colonial and post-colonial states is by now well known. Less well documented are other modes of representation in the ideological construction of "Otherness." Yet racial ideology is not a homogeneous ideology, even during periods of blunt "sinophobia" such as existed in Canada in the latter nineteenth and early twentieth centuries. And evidence in this book from the more recent past also suggests that European hegemony has been renewed in *multiple* forms. For this reason, it would be limiting to conclude the study of the race-definition process as it related to the Chinese in Vancouver at the end of the Second World War, when most forms of officially sanctioned discrimination were rescinded. It seems important to bring the analysis forward and uncover the more recent faces of racial ideology. We shall see that, in the 1970s, the Canadian state continued to elaborate a conceptual universe that secured the interests and identity of the dominant white sector. In an era of "cultural pluralism," the Canadian state pronounced fresh concepts of nation-hood that subtly carried forward the essentialist world view (and privilege) of the more powerful "historical bloc."

State practices during the period when policies of multiculturalism have been a place in Canada (and other Western nations such as Australia) illuminate the transformative potential of European hegemony. We shall see that negative stereotyping of a Chinese iden-tity and place gave way, in the 1970s, to promotion of the "Chinese" and "Chinatown" on the part of all three levels of government. Every city needs its Chinatown, it seems, and Vancouver has been no excep-tion. Ideological traces from the past have surfaced in "unity through diversity" policies which, in promoting Chinatown, have broken with repressive practices while at the same time signalling the continuity of racial beliefs. There is a benign face to racial ideology, we shall see, that supports Satzewich's claim that "there is no necessary cor-relation between the belief in the existence of different 'races' and negative evaluations of 'race' difference."[62] Despite placing a positive connotation on "Otherness," multicultural rhetoric supports popular beliefs about "differences" between groups of settlers and strengthens the exclusionary concept of a mainstream (Anglo-European) society to which "others" contribute. In turn this keeps alive the myth of a one-character nation with the privilege and responsibility to deflect apparently contaminating influences. The iconic hegemony of white identity is certainly alive today in a contradictory mix of old and new, blunt and subtle guises.

The influence of European hegemony in Western societies can also be seen in instances where those on the receiving end of identity classifications come to live within the paradigm fashioned by their oppressors and define their own identities accordingly.[63] We shall see this process at work in the example of Vancouver's "Chinese," who at strategic moments in their history consented to and even appropri-ated the identity and neighbourhood stereotypes that since the late nineteenth century had structured their subordination. This is par-ticularly evident in recent years, when Canada's policy of multicul-turalism has made "Chineseness" a politically effective counter-ideology. Chinatown's merchants, in particular, have seen their own advantage in neighbourhood upgrading schemes that attempt to refurbish the district in the image of Western constructs of the East.

At other times, the adverse effects of racial classification were bit-terly contested by people of Chinese origin, suggesting another important aspect about the exercise of hegemonic control. White cul-tural domination in Canada has been resilient and commanding, to be sure, but just as judicial constraints constantly set limits on its form and effect, so those subordinated to it were always on hand to resist its more onerous consequences. Vancouver's "Chinese" have been by no means passive in the race-definition process, sometimes openly challenging, sometimes accommodating, and at other times successfully manipulating to their own ends the symbols of Chinese-ness that have represented them to white society.

THE GEOGRAPHICAL ARTICU-LATION OF RACIAL IDEOLOGY: CHINATOWN IN WESTERN IMAGE AND PRACTICE

In recent years, human geographers have lent their expertise to theorizations of class, politics, race, and gender by focusing on the territorial structures through which such social relations are organized and reproduced.[64] Recent writing in cultural geography on the landscape concept has also contributed to this effort: landscapes have become "texts" that can be "read" for the relations they inscribe and naturalize.[65] What we see "out there" in the built and physical landscape is not objectively given, as many social scientists once assumed, but rather is the transformation into material form of past and newly forming beliefs and practices. The built and physical environments are negotiated realities, in other words, contingent outcomes of changing and often competing versions of reality and practice. In that sense, landscapes are linked in circular relation to ideological formations, systems of power, and sets of social relations.

It will be clear from the comments so far that the study of racial classification is not only about cultural conceptions but also about the reciprocal relationship between beliefs and structures. Often in philosophy the cognitive and external worlds are conceived as being distinct, as if what lies in people's heads is separate from, and bears no relation to, "matter" and its concrete manifestations. Yet, as Hall has persuasively argued, perceptions like race are not idle speculations or forms of belief that operate only at the level of ideas.[66] Such perceptions, in codifying the actions of individuals and institutions, have effects that become practically rooted in the external world. The European premise of a Chinese race has certainly been one such myth that has been used to structure institutional practice, as was argued above.

The argument can, and indeed should, be taken further, however. Racial ideology was institutionalized not only in government policies but also through a set of territorial arrangements. Through these arrangements the racial category "Chinese" became inscribed, both on the ground and in people's minds. Anthropologists and sociologists have been surprisingly silent on this dimension of the racialization process. Yet the epistemological implications are important, as I attempt to demonstrate through the course of the narrative that follows. State practices institutionalized the concept of a Chinese race, but it was in space that the concept became materially cemented and naturalized in everyday life. For over a century in Vancouver, the enclave foundation was a critical locus for the renewal and preservation of white Vancouver's conceptions of a Chinese race. The nexus of race and space operated in two senses: physical and cognitive.

In a physical sense, overseas Chinese settlements in Western cities have been moulded in decisive ways by their receiving societies. As many scholars have already demonstrated, and as the Vancouver example will again attest, pioneers from China concentrated themselves in tight settlements. Their residential segregation was not a direct result of government fiat, but the officially sanctioned process of race definition in Vancouver certainly influenced the social organization of that city's territory. Rich and poor Chinese settlers were confined through informal suasion and defensive reaction to a swampy settlement close to the business centre. In time, the small area came to be associated with Chinese settlement, and movement beyond it was socially classified for many decades as "off limits." During the Depression, the area was further marginalized, and by the 1960s the Canadian state made the declining area the focus of major urban renewal and transportation plans. In the 1970s, the state sponsored redevelopment plans of a quite different kind. To be sure, much of the state's management of the "Chinese" has been directed at Chinese settlement, both its site and its distribution.

It is also important to consider the term "Chinatown" and the sense in which that, too, as a title and a concept, belongs to European society. In Vancouver, from the time of the city's incorporation in 1886, the streets of Dupont, Carrall, and Columbia were home to settlers from China. The spatial fact of Chinese settlement does not in itself, however, account for the name by which this area became known. We might reasonably ask, therefore, how it was that the streets of Dupont, Carrall, and Columbia became apprehended as "Chinatown"? Whose term – in one sense, whose place – was this? No corresponding term – "Anglotown" – existed in local parlance, nor were residents of the likes of Vancouver's West End known as "Occidentals." Why, then, was the home of the pioneers from China known as "Chinatown"?

Consistent with the conventional view of Chinatown as an "ethnic neighbourhood," we might anticipate the response that Chinese people – a visible and culturally distinct minority – settled and made

their lives there through some combination of push and pull factors.
As was stated above, one view might be that Chinatown is a foreign
colony that embodies the values and experiences of the East in the
West. The most recent book on Canada's Chinatowns is written
within this paradigm, outlining a "growth model" for Chinatown that
traces its historical evolution through budding, blooming, withering,
and dying or reviving phases.[67]

That people of Chinese origin, like other pioneers to British colonies, brought with them particular traditions that shaped their activities and choices in new settings can hardly be disputed. An
important tradition of scholarship has outlined the significance of
such traditions for North American (and other) overseas Chinese colonies. Lyman, for example, has argued: "Although sinophobic pressure might explain the existence of a segregated [Chinese] residential
quarter, it does not account for the long maintenance of autonomous
political and legal institutions within the isolated community."[68]

Certainly there is plenty of evidence to support the claim that cultural traditions bound people from China to a localized community,
just as ethnic affiliations were probably a strong unifying force in
Vancouver's British-origin neighbourhood of Shaughnessy. My decision not to give primary attention to the residents' sense of place is
not to deny them an active role in building their neighbourhood or
any attachment they may have felt to their ethnic origins. Some merchants from China might have even been eager to distance themselves from non-Chinese, just as China had obviated contact with
Western "barbarians" over the centuries. Others, given a choice,
might have quickly assimilated.

Another equally important but neglected way of looking at "Chinatown," however, is to conceptualize it as an idea, one that relied
on a range of cultural assumptions held by Europeans about the
Chinese as a type.[69] As we shall see, "Chinatown" was not a neutral
term, referring somehow unproblematically to the physical presence
of people from China in Vancouver. Rather, it was an evaluative term,
ascribed by Europeans no matter how the residents of that territory
might have defined themselves. Regardless of how Chinatown's residents defined themselves and each other – whether by class, gender,
ethnicity, region of origin in China, surname, generation, dialect,
place of birth, and so on – the settlements were perceived by Europeans through lenses of their own tinting. Without needing the recognition of the residents, Chinatown's representers constructed in
their own minds a boundary between "their" territory and "our"
territory.

In his important discussion of "imaginative geographies" such as Europe's Orient, Edward Said argues that this distinction "helps the mind to intensify its own sense of itself by dramatizing the distance and difference between what is close and what is far away."[70] This process suggests that "Chinatown," like "Chinese," has been a historically specific idea, a cultural concept rooted in the symbolic system of those with the power to define such areas as Dupont and Carrall streets in Vancouver. From this vantage point, Chinatown says as much about the frames of mind of the West as it does about the ethnic attributes of the East.

Moreover, Chinatown no less reveals the actions of the West and those of governing élites. As suggested earlier, the European concept of Chinatown would not be so important or enduring but for the fact that it has been legitimized by agents who had the authority to make cognitive categories stand as the official definition of a people and a place. In Vancouver, from the late 1880s, "Chinatown" accrued a field of meaning that became the context and justification for recurring rounds of government practice in the ongoing construction of both the place and the racial category "Chinese." The idea of a Chinese race became objectified in space (as stated above), and through that nexus it was given a local referent in the minds of Europeans, became a social fact, and aided its own reproduction.

Within the social geography of the past few decades, there exists a tendency to treat history as past time, as an undifferentiated backdrop to the present, as if the present were almost an autonomous creation. There has been an unwillingness to venture into the layers of history where might be found the formative elements of contemporary social processes. Yet social theory is replete with appeals of the kind, articulated by C. Wright Mills in the 1950s, for a synthesis of the agendas of history and other human sciences.[71] In sociology, Abrams's "problematic of structuring" and Giddens's theory of "structuration" were programmatic responses to precisely that appeal.[72] There are by now many calls in anthropology for empirical analyses that situate people's symbolic systems in their defining historical contexts,[73] and in human geography for research that actually demonstrates the "contemporaneity of time and space in structuring social process."[74]

This study attempts to trace the "movement in formation" of a territory that has in part been constructed from, and all the time informing of, the race-definition process described above.[75] In what follows, the cultural construction of Vancouver's Chinatown will be documented for a century – from the time of neighbourhood harass-

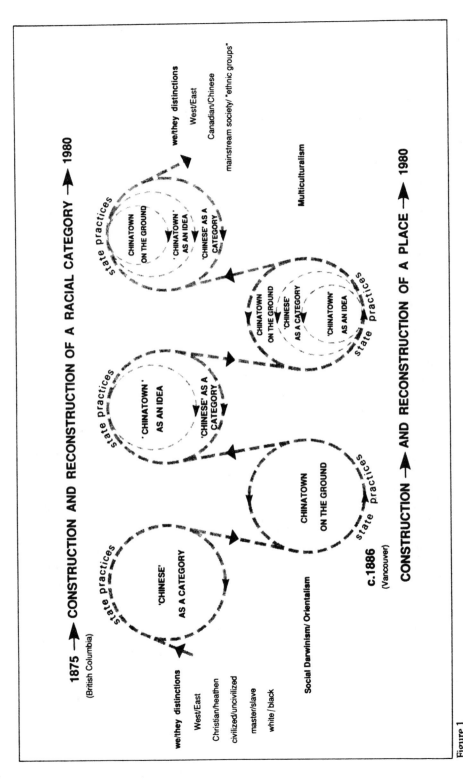

1875 → CONSTRUCTION AND RECONSTRUCTION OF A RACIAL CATEGORY → 1980
(British Columbia)

we/they distinctions

West/East

Canadian/Chinese

mainstream society/ "ethnic groups"

Multiculturalism

state practices

CHINATOWN ON THE GROUND

'CHINATOWN' AS AN IDEA

'CHINESE' AS A CATEGORY

'CHINATOWN' AS AN IDEA

'CHINESE' AS A CATEGORY

CHINATOWN ON THE GROUND

'CHINESE' AS A CATEGORY

'CHINATOWN' AS AN IDEA

state practices

state practices

CHINATOWN ON THE GROUND

c.1886
(Vancouver)

'CHINESE' AS A CATEGORY

state practices

Social Darwinism/ Orientalism

we/they distinctions

West/East

Christian/heathen

civilized/uncivilized

master/slave

white / black

CONSTRUCTION → AND RECONSTRUCTION OF A PLACE → 1980

Figure 1
"East" Is "West": The Historical Geography of a Racial Category

ment in the late nineteenth and early twentieth centuries, through a period of classification as a tourist amenity in the 1930s and a "slum" in the 1950s and 1960s, to the recent era when, under the aegis of Canada's multiculturalism policy, Chinatown has been courted by the Canadian government precisely *for* its perceived "Chineseness." We shall witness the process by which Chinatown became a store of "collective representations," to use Durkheim's expression,[76] where residues of past conceptions of identity and place continually shaped practices that sedimented their image within later formulations and practices (see Figure 1).

Indeed a diachronic approach to the study of Chinatown might be particularly revealing, because what is often taken for granted in conventional approaches to this territory as an implicit explanatory principle – its "Chineseness" – may seem less incisive from an epistemological vantage point that traces over time the construction and transformation of knowledge about the enclave. After many years of research in cultural geography and other disciplines on the "ways of life" of "other" communities, it seems timely to show the sense in which Europeans' constitution of reality has its own exotic and hegemonic quality. What follows, then, is something of an indigenous commentary. It is a historical and cultural critique of the insiders' settled ways of conceptualizing, of the practices that have been framed in terms of those habits of mind, of the power relations on which those habits have been predicated, and of the historical process that has produced the configurations we so often take as naturally given.

CHAPTER TWO

Creating Outsiders, 1875–1903 _ race idea

PIONEERS FROM CHINA

At the time of its creation as a British colony in 1849, Vancouver Island was little more than a fur trade preserve, scattered with settlements of indigenous people and a few trading forts. By 1854, just 450 settlers had made their home in the colony, and no more than 500 acres of land had been developed. By the end of that decade, however, the discovery of placer gold on the Fraser, Thompson, and Columbia rivers attracted thousands of prospectors, miners, and adventurers to the region, and in 1858 the imperial authorities proclaimed a mainland colony of British Columbia to govern the influx of people. The island and mainland colonies merged in 1866, but many of the new residents were no more permanent than the placer camps, and within one year of the merger the total "white" population had fallen below 10,000. The number was, however, sufficient to boost the growth of the main townships of Victoria, New Westminster, and Nanaimo, and the province's early staple industries of mining, agriculture, manufacturing, and fishing.

Immigrants from China were associated with most of British Columbia's pioneering industries. For example, in 1858–9, approximately 2,000 Chinese came from further south on the Pacific coast to the goldfields at the middle course of the Fraser River.[1] The majority ventured north in search of a quick fortune, but a significant number established businesses to serve the growing population in Victoria and the small mining towns of the lower Fraser Valley.

The numbers of Chinese arriving in the province increased considerably after 1859. In that year, an organized recruitment system was established to ship labourers and merchants from Hong Kong to Victoria via San Francisco; also, there were further gold discoveries in the Cariboo and Cassiar regions.[2] Like other immigrants, the overwhelming majority of these workers were men, who ventured alone to the new area in order to earn money for their families in China or to prepare an economic footing so their families could follow. In 1867, there were just 52 women among the 1,995 residents of Chinese origin in mainland British Columbia, an imbalance shared by the white population, in which 443 women were counted in a mainland population of 3,072 in 1866.[3] Population estimates fluctuated widely, however, both seasonally and annually. In 1867, Chinese made up almost 40 per cent of the non-indigenous mainland population, compared with 8 per cent of the number on Vancouver Island; but numbers declined quickly after the boom in gold subsided.[4]

The Chinese found quite a wide variety of employment at this stage of the colony's development. Many took semi-skilled jobs in saw mills on Burrard Inlet and in salmon canneries on the Fraser and Skeena rivers and Puget Sound. Others worked in coal mining at Nanaimo and Wellington, in land clearing, telegraph-line construction, domestic service, laundry operations, vegetable gardening, road construction (such as the Cariboo highway contract of 1863–5), ditch- and dike-building, and on farms. Labourers also worked for Chinese merchants and syndicates in the towns, in enterprises ranging from restaurants for Chinese-origin clientele to export-import houses. Still others were employed by companies in Victoria to transport provisions by mule and wagon to subsidiary businesses in the smaller towns.

Most of the work in canneries and mining, and later in railway construction, was organized on a contract basis. Chinese bosses recruited "gangs" of labourers and then made contracts with industrial managers for the workers' services. In other industries, Chinese sold their labour as part of the normal market for unskilled work at the time. Either way, the labour of immigrants from China was critical to the establishment of British Columbia's economic base at a time when most production work was labour-intensive and white labour was in short supply. Chinese were paid one-half to two-thirds the wage rates of other workers, and they accepted long hours and seasonal work – often in places distant from their homes.[5]

Given the part they played in opening up the BC frontiers, early Chinese settlers won praise from certain quarters of white society. A royal commissioner and judge on the BC Supreme Court, Dr John Hamilton Gray, heard evidence on the "Chinese Question" from a number of entrepreneurs in 1885 and declared in his report: "It may safely be said that there are several industries that would not have succeeded – perhaps it might be said undertaken – if it had not been for the opportunity of obtaining their labour." After describing Chinese as "living machines," Dr Justice Gray went on to say that there was "preponderating testimony as to the sobriety, industry and frugality of the Chinese as manual labourers ... and up to this time their presence in the province has been most useful if not indispensable."[6]

Such praise must have afforded little comfort, however, to the settlers from China themselves. Dr Justice Gray put it this way: "It is fortunate that, in a young and sparsely settled Province, this cheap labour can be obtained, for it enables those whose minds are capable of higher development and whose ambition looks to more enobling industry – to follow pursuits in which they will rise rather than toil and slave in grovelling work, which wears out the body without elevating the mind."[7] Other respected commentators, such as the proprietor of the Wellington Coal Mines, Robert Dunsmuir, held an equally paternalistic view. In 1885, Dunsmuir said that in his mines "the Chinese are put to the work that suits them best – ordinary manual labour."[8] Sixteen years later, the same view was put by Vancouver entrepreneur Henry Bell-Irving, of the Anglo-British Packing Co., who said that "it is the destiny of whitemen to be worked for by the inferior races."[9]

A structure of occupational and social relations among whites and non-whites was organized around precisely such beliefs in the pioneering days of capitalist development in British Columbia. In the canning industry, Chinese were in their place – can-making, soldering, and filling. In the homes of the provincial élite, young Chinese men, in the absence of sufficient young white women, helped with the menial activities of domestic life. Only in those industries where Chinese secured an early monopoly, such as laundering and vegetable gardening, did they escape almost uniform relegation to the lowest occupational tasks. It was, according to Dr Justice Gray, a natural outcome of "the dispensations of Providence by which the highest good can be obtained for mankind."[10]

The alien status of settlers from China was more bluntly apparent in the conduct of white labourers, who saw Chinese workers as a direct threat to their efforts to establish a comfortable existence in the province. The first, albeit sporadic and non-violent, signs of antagonism surfaced in the mining fields of the Cariboo in the 1860s. Many of the "whites" who arrived there from the us west coast brought with them anti-Chinese sentiments and excluded the Chinese from both their digging companies and the most lucrative goldfields. At Nanaimo, the miners threatened violence as early as 1867, when the local coal company announced that it would hire Chinese labour.

In fact, many BC labourers came to view the Chinese, rather than their employers, as their most formidable enemy, and this disposition soon became a channel for the political protest of the province's labour. White workers – ignoring the demonstrated willingness of early Chinese labourers to strike over job and pay discrimination – believed that the "Chinese" were endowed as a category with the capacity to undersell more deserving labour. They also felt strongly that the Chinese could be used by employers (as indeed they were) to break the strikes mounted by white labourers for higher pay and better working conditions. (Dr Justice Gray's report of 1885 reveals that employers themselves were quite open about their willingness to use Chinese for just that purpose.) In evidence to the same commission, a representative of the Knights of Labor from Nanaimo pursued what became a familiar theme when he accused the Chinese of "unfair competition": "The degraded Asiatics ... live generally in wretched hovels, dark, ill-ventilated and unwholesome, and crowded together in such numbers as must utterly preclude all ideas of comfort, morality and even decency".[11]

For white workers of British Columbia then, just as for entrepreneurs, Chinese immigrants were somehow irremediably beyond the body of eligible citizenry from the time they entered the province. According to a complex ideological matrix, the Chinese in this New World society were an undifferentiated category of outsiders, fundamentally and constitutively "different" from those immigrants for whom British Columbia became home automatically. The different classes of European immigrants had different (economic) reasons for embracing the idea of an essential "John Chinaman." There may also have been significant gender variations in the European response to immigrants from China. It is clear, however, that belief in "John's" existence, and his alien status in the new community, transcended sectional interests. In March 1859, the first colonial newspaper, the *Gazette*, captured such overriding sentiments as it editorialized on the theme of Chinese immigration: "They are, with few exceptions, not desirable as permanent settlers in a country peopled by the Caucasian race and governed by civilized enactments. No greater obstacle to the coming of the class of immigrants needed in British Columbia could be devised, than the presence of Chinamen in large numbers."[12]

IT WILL BE NECESSARY TO EXAMINE the role of the different levels of Canadian government in constructing this category of aliens in British Columbia. Before doing so, however, we should consider the intellectual context out of which the categorization "Chinese" arose and acquired its meaning for "white" British Columbians. I speak here of a broader field than the white prejudices which, for Ward, derived from the "psychological tensions ... continually stimulated by the racially plural situation."[13] In particular, I am interested in the cultural filter through which prospective Canadians from China were "seen" in early British Columbia. Only by emphasizing this conceptual screen can one avoid flattening past European subjectivities in the unhelpful psychologism of the prejudice framework.

The context of ideas is also more important (as noted in chapter 1) than has been acknowledged by simple structural Marxist explanations. According to those arguments, the separation and antagonism between whites and Chinese were ultimately an expression of the deeper structural contradiction set up by the capitalists' drive for profit (through the use of cheap labour) and the workers' struggle for higher wages. The conflict between whites and Chinese is thus said to be a secondary reflection of class cleavages. As was argued in chapter 1, however, both these positions are impoverished by their silence on cultural pressures of the kind that ensured that the claims to a new life by Chinese immigrants would be evaluated quite differently – by all classes – from those of other pioneers. It is to one important element of that nineteenth-century European outlook that this chapter now turns.

THE RACE IDEA
IN BRIEF REVIEW

Early immigrants from China arrived in British Columbia at a time when modern race theory was beginning to earn the respect of the scientific community of North America and Britain and to captivate the popular imagination of North America. Ironically, just as the battle over slavery in the United States was being won by the abolitionists, new currents of thought emerged in the United States and Britain that ensured that the "Negro" and his or her colonial counterparts such as the "Chinese" would remain as "living machines." A stream of deterministic thinking began to seduce Western culture and science from the mid-nineteenth century, undermining all the optimistic Enlightenment beliefs in the unity and adaptability of humanity's universal nature.

This deterministic turn was not born into an intellectual vacuum, however; rather it sprang from a cultural tradition long disposed to viewing the world's population in terms of essences, or created types. The idea of the racial type cannot be traced to a single source or era, and it is not the intention here to give a comprehensive account of so complex a topic. It is possible, however, to provide some general historical context for white British Columbia's predisposition toward the "Chinese."

Many centuries before European societies interpreted human variation in biological or racial terms, the rest of the world was measured against a romanticized or idealized version of Europe itself. Just as generations of Chinese long held myths of a civilized ingroup,[14] so Europeans interpreted the world with the use of concepts that dramatized the distinctions between themselves and others. From ancient times through to the Middle Ages, Europeans thought of the world as being composed of three formal parts, namely "Asia," "Africa," and "Europe." Overlapping this threefold division from antiquity was another more nebulous and less areally specific division between "Orientis" and "Occidentis," or "East" and "West." March argues that these regionalizations were in large part social and literary constructs, concepts by which Europeans established a framework for group identification in a universe of known and unknown civilizations. Accordingly, as other scholars have argued, Asia and Africa took their earliest definitions against Europe in such a way as to lend precision to the emerging idea of Europe itself.[15] Their essential characteristics tended to become those things that were non-European. Whereas the Orient, for example, was old, excessive, slavish, despotic, opulent, uniform, and non-Christian, Europe was modern, rational, progressive, free, civilized and, later on, Christian.

In the context of such beliefs, notions of "race" crept slowly and without coherent or consistent meaning into the European vocabulary. Around 300 BC, Aristotle spoke of his own "Hellenic race" as being "high spirited and intelligent. Hence it continues free, and is the best-governed of any nation, and, if it could be formed into one state, would be able to rule the world."[16] Against this race were pitted the "barbarians," or all the rest of the world's people. These included the "Ethiopians," as "blacks" were called by Egyptians, Greeks, Romans, and early Christians, and the "Asiatics," who were said to be "inventive" but "wanting in spirit." At the time, however, it was ethnocentrism more than assumptions about biological difference that formed the basis for judgments of non-Greeks.[17] Montagu has also noted that Hellenism was more "a thing of the spirit rather than of 'race'."[18] There was a colour symbolism associated with Christianity that drew on the sensitivities of the classical era to black-white antinomies,[19] but the earliest racial thought was essentially non-racialist.

The seeds of the modern race doctrine were sown by a stronger interpretation of "difference" that came with the growth in contact of

Christians and non-Christians between the fifteenth and seventeenth centuries. In 1455, Pope Nicholas v approved the subjugation of "infidels" to Christians on the grounds that although mankind was one, the Negroes, American Indians, and other "heathens" would have much to gain from Christian ways of life. Soon after that, the Portuguese trade in slaves, particularly in Africa, began in earnest, drawing from and cementing the old Arabic mythology of blacks as a brutish and satanic type. A similar connection has also been drawn between the non-Christian status of "Negroes" and the institutionalization of slavery in America from 1660. Montagu states that the choice of blacks, and the severity of the system of economic subordination to which they were subjected, were "based virtually entirely on the view that the Negro was a benighted heathen, unable to read or write, and belonging to a class and caste clearly inferior to those of his masters."[20] As Jordan points out in his examination of the colonial images of blacks in the United States, "to be Christian in mid-seventeenth century America was to be civilized rather than barbarous, English rather than African and [by 1680] white rather than black."[21]

By the eighteenth century, European expeditions of various kinds were straddling the globe, and in the wake of these journeys, other populations, such as the "yellow" populations of "the East," joined "Africans" on the list of inferior peoples. For example, Karl von Linné's famous correlation of custom and race in *Systema naturae* (1735) had it that Asians were "severe, haughty and miserly," Europeans "light, active and ingenious," and Africans "lazy, negligent and governed by whim." In 1748, David Hume wrote the essay "Of National Characters," which posited a naturally rooted relationship between complexion, character, and intellectual capacity, and within twenty years, Kant drew on that essay to make one of the earliest syntheses of colour and intelligence in European philosophy. The explanation for these variations was still largely environmental, however, the non-white races being assumed "perfectible." Furthermore, there were signs of almost sarcastic intellectual dissent from the developing mainstream theory. In his 1775 book *On the Natural Variety of Mankind*, Johann Blumenbach wrote that "one variety of mankind does so sensibly pass into the other, that you cannot mark out the limits between them. Very arbitrary indeed in both number and definition have been the varieties of mankind accepted by eminent men."[22]

During the seventeenth and eighteenth centuries, the monogenist view that the races of humanity owed their origin to a single common ancestor had been the basis for an optimistic sense of humanity's ultimate unity. Savages and Negroes, though members of a semi-permanent stock, could eventually become European in the American melting pot. By the mid-nineteenth century, however, with the imperialist requirement for "subject" races growing, polygenists began putting a contrary view. The Alabama physician Josiah Nott, for instance, claimed that human races were separated by immutable mental, moral, and physical differences owing to their distinct origins. Nott went into some polemical detail about skull shapes and sizes to conclude that each "race" represented a separately created species and that all "the dark-skinned races" were inferior to Europeans.[23] The mid-century did indeed mark a dramatic switch, in Stepan's words, "from a sense of man as primarily a social being, governed by social laws and standing apart from nature, to a sense of man as primarily a biological being, embedded in nature and governed by biological laws."[24]

According to Harris, one of the keys to this new pessimism was the early-nineteenth-century discovery of the vast dimension of geological time, which gave a fresh perspective to discussions about the transformation of the races. Further, the fossil record lent credibility to the ancient idea of gradation, where life was believed to be a linear progression from simplicity to complexity. A new-found naturalness was seen in Aristotle's "great chain of being," where it was imagined that nature produced living things in a continuous chain from God through the angels to people and, with decreasing complexity, to vegetables and inanimate objects. Applied to people, the chain offered a ready-made social hierarchy onto which the separately created "racial" types could be grafted with the sanction of nature.

On that platform was also set a mandate of Western scientists: the measurement of man's finite forms of biological organization. The scientific goal of establishing laws behind variation had a fresh object, and in the course of discovery a generation of nineteenth-century specialists recast the beliefs of previous centuries into a radical biological determinism.

Among outstanding examples of this new research were comparative anatomy and phrenology.[25] Comparative anatomy simply accepted the racial type as a sine qua non. This science purported to document the grades of complexity in the nervous systems of the world's human types. Phrenology, described as a science of the mind, measured the shape, weight, and volume of human skulls. It too assumed that the skull was an outward sign of innate biological organization. Moreover, in addition to holding the key to mental ability, the skull was taken as an index of cultural behaviour, including traits such as benevolence and temperance. Needless to say, the "races of men," as Knox called them in a book of that name in 1850, were measured on a scale where the "Saxon race" was the standard for comparison. An editorial in the *Anthropological Review* in 1866 applied the same benchmark: "As the type of the Negro is foetal, that of the Mongol is infantile. And in strict accordance with this we find their government, literature and art are infantile also."[26] (At the time that editorial was published, many Chinese settlers were about to enter British Columbia on the encouragement of new gold discoveries and the establishment of organized migration procedures from Hong Kong.)

One of the most intriguing developments in the history of the race idea is the interpretation that race scientists (and in turn other intellectuals and laypeople) put on the work of Charles Darwin. The complexities of this theme have been explored elsewhere,[27] but some discussion of it is helpful to complete this account of the cultural and intellectual setting in which perceptions of a "Chinese race" in British Columbia developed. Darwin's *Origin of Species by Means of Natural Selection* (1859) and *The Descent of Man* (1871) offered a conceptual framework that had the capacity to discredit the concept of the permanent racial type. Darwin believed that just as the animal world was a continuously changing species, so the human population was part of an evolutionary process of natural change by variation, struggle, and a selection of traits conducive to survival. Accordingly, his work made a strong case for the unity of the species and its capacity for change – sufficient, one might expect, to challenge the science of static types. In *The Descent of Man*, Darwin insisted that evolutionists "will feel no doubt that all the races of man are descended from a single primitive stock." But the work of the first evolutionists produced precisely the opposite result. Not only did it inspire new extremes of cranial measurement in the natural sciences, but *The Descent of Man* fostered a stream of popular and social scientific ideas that wedded the notion of the permanent type to a new ideology called "Social Darwinism." This combination became so seductive that it pervaded the popular consciousness of North America and Britain for decades – until long after it was discredited by the science of genetics, which integrated Darwin's argument into a new theory of heredity.

Despite being novel for its anti-creationism, Darwin's work was in fact compatible with earlier racial discourse, if not the strict polygenist view. For one thing, he fully revived the notion of a "chain of being" by integrating humanity's ancestry with that of the animal world. It was possible for lay and academic interpreters of Darwin to graft on to his views of evolution in nature the prior notions of difference between and "fitness" of races. For Stepan, this application of the competitive struggle in nature to the human races was less a perversion of Darwin than a product of the internal logic of his own evolutionary argument. "That argument," she claims, "was one of continuity – continuity seemed essential if he were to prove that man's mental, moral as well as physical features had arisen naturally by slow evolution from animal forms. But the argument for continuity led almost inevitably to the use of the lower races to fill the gap between man and the animals."[28]

Jones also argues that in asserting his main hypothesis of natural selection as the motor of evolutionary change throughout the species, Darwin passed seemingly unconsciously from the individual to the group or racial type as the unit on which natural selection operated. In so doing, Darwin's "belief in the human equality of origin to which other areas of [his] work testifies, was sacrificed," Jones claims.[29]

As many read it at the time, Darwin's work reinforced the view that history was a progression from barbarism to civilization. Liberals, socialists and conservatives alike saw something in his theory for their views of class, government, and social reform. As for ideas about race, many post-Darwinian scientists and social scientists, including the evolutionary theorist Herbert Spencer, adopted the view that although primitive peoples were intrinsically capable of evolving to civilization, in practice they would require an infinite time to do so – perhaps as long as the geological time scale itself. For all contemporary purposes, the races were immutable. Commissioner Dr Joseph Chapleau certainly felt that way after the 1885 royal commission on the "Chinese question" in British Columbia. "Races change slowly," he said, "but the stationariness of the Chinese race seems phenomenal."[30]

Evidence is abundant that post-Darwinian biologists, while reaffirming the monogenist view of a unitary origin, fostered "none of the egalitarian conclusions that had characterized their eighteenth century predecessors."[31] Vague evolutionary metaphors offered an almost irresistible intellectual and popular idiom for old prejudices. Anthropologists began to argue that even national institutions were peculiarly racial products. For example, it was argued that American democracy was an outgrowth of Teutonic "seeds" that had been brought from northwestern Europe and controlled the nation's cultural evolution.[32]

Some took the argument for the racial basis of institutions as a guarantee that the superior races had nothing to fear from their inferiors, while others warned that it rendered institutions vulnerable to "hybridization" and "contamination" by the influences of unfit immigrants. On similar grounds, race was taken to be the key to the rise and fall of nations, which themselves were species involved in inexorable struggle. Just as struggle was the rule in nature, so conflict among nations was also inevitable. Bannister argues that it was this reading of Darwin by American intellectuals that prompted the violent extremism in the American South during the 1880s and 1890s – an extremism that dismantled the existing paternalistic relations and faith in the strategy of educating blacks.[33]

As long as Darwin and the other early evolutionary theorists could not explain the source of variation in organisms, they and their contemporary interpreters found it difficult to resist the notion of the racial type. As mentioned earlier, Darwin in a sense invited this thinking because he implied that the process of natural selection operated on races as biological units, rather than on populations of individuals. Hence, by the late 1880s, a quasi-polygenist theory of racial stability had become successfully integrated into evolutionary science and, in turn, popular opinion in Britain. Stepan attributes this to faith in the racial type, which, at a time of formidable imperialist expansion, was far deeper than any acknowledgment of the possibility of biological change.

Whatever their origins, the twin ideas – that every human being belonged to an essence or type whose physical expression was an index of innate biological and cultural organization and that the types were ranked by nature in a struggle for survival – were axioms of late-nineteenth-century science and culture. The result "was to give a mental abstraction an independent reality, to make real or reify the idea of racial type when in fact the type was a social construct."[34]

VICTORIA FORMALIZES OUTSIDER STATUS

When the colony of British Columbia joined the Confederation of Canada in 1871 and its legislative assembly became a provincial parliament, the architects of the province's nascent political culture quickly assumed responsibility for defining a society in the image of their own European profile. Table 1 shows that in the majority of elections between 1871 and 1900 those elected to the legislature were predominantly British-born. They were the immigrants who saw it as their imperialist responsibility to build a *British* British Columbia from the loose collection of workers and entrepreneurs that existed under colonial administration. Charles Wilson, elected to the legislature from Cariboo in 1882, made the mandate explicit while arguing

Table 1
Birthplaces of Members of BC Legislature, 1871–1900

Election Year	United Kingdom	Canada	Other	Not Listed
1871	11	9	–	5
1875	21	4	–	–
1878	13	6	1	5
1882	12	7	2	4
1886	21	4	1	1
1890	18	7	3	–
1894	19	13	1	–
1898	18	13	4	3
1900	17	18	2	–

Source: The Canadian Parliamentary Companion and Annual Register, 1862–1987
(Ottawa: Gazette Printing); continues Canadian Parliamentary Guide
(Montreal: Gazette Printing)

for restriction on Chinese immigration: "We must not overlook the fact that we are establishing a British colony," he said. "It is true that we may have less capital, but it would be more beneficial in the end having loyal subjects of the Queen."[35]

The first Royal Commission on Chinese Immigration, of 1885, is replete with evidence that the race idea, as we have seen it developed in Europe and North America from classical times through to the latter half of the century, enjoyed widespread currency in British Columbia. Almost every one of the forty-eight BC witnesses invited to testify on the Chinese presence in the province traded freely in the language of racial types, racial instincts, and racial antipathy.

A former BC agent-general in London, Mr G. Sproat, boldly invoked the idea of a Chinese race when he told the commission: "The Chinese character is of a fixed, persistent type, alien, beyond any control or chance of change, to everything that concerns Western civilization."[36] Echoing the Californian witnesses to the same commission, others dwelt on the impossibility of assimilation between the "two kinds of civilization, the one modern and West and the other ancient and East." A few witnesses argued that it was the pride of the "sons of Han" that kept the races apart. Others claimed that the groups could never mix because of the amoral style of living of the "Chinese," their idolatrous religious practices, their objectionable living quarters, their capacity to undercut white labour with their own "docile" labour, their disregard for truth, their predisposition for crime, their inhumanity, and so on. Such characteristics were part of an essential

Chineseness, it was believed, that rendered the Chinaman alien in blood and spirit and inspired conflict between the "white" and "Mongolian" races. "There seems to be an instinctive feeling of preference for whites, independent of any reasoned opinion respecting their merits or demerits as compared with Chinamen," summarized Commissioner Chapleau in the commission's report. "Race antipathy seems to be at the bottom of this," he concluded, "and though to the philosopher such antipathy may appear narrow, a profounder insight may find in it a natural – perhaps divinely implanted – safeguard against great evils."[37] Sir Matthew Begbie, chief justice of British Columbia, had a similar view of the inevitability of conflict and the station of the two races (or at least, apparently, of the two races' men): "There seems to be an impulsive force which brings into action the ever-present dislike between the IndoCaucasian and this branch of Mongolians ... The Chinaman is in every respect the reverse of a European except that he is a man."[38]

In the hands of British Columbia's early provincial politicians, the race idea was a useful idiom around which to forge a regional consciousness. Race was an influential language with which to cement the collective sense of an in-group, in part because it enabled politicians to concentrate into a "counter-idea" everything that was thought to be in conflict with the building of an ideal community.[39] This argument is supported by evidence to the 1885 royal commission, at which many witnesses singled out politicians as chief among the instigators of an anti-Chinese movement in British Columbia. Chief Justice Begbie, for example, remarked that he could not recollect anything that could be called agitation against the Chinese until Confederation. John Robson, provincial secretary, agreed that the agitation began as a political question in 1872, while Mr B. Pearse, the surveyor-general, said that the movement against Chinese was "begun and carried forward, chiefly by politicians." The manager of the Bank of British Columbia, Mr W. Ward, was more specific: "The agitation has been chiefly political with a view to the labouring class vote. I think it is mainly led by politicians (following the Californian experience) though there is a general feeling that the immigration should now be restricted, if not entirely stopped."[40]

As this testimony shows, and notwithstanding widespread beliefs that fundamental biological differences guaranteed a natural separation of the races, governing élites showed little hesitation in intervening in, and fomenting, British Columbia's race question. From the first session of the legislature in 1872, their actions and rhetoric contributed significantly to the construction of a culture wherein "Chinese" signified non-white, non-Christian – "them" as opposed to "us." We now turn to a review of the practices that the early provincial governments instituted or attempted to institute as part of the social construction of the alien category Chinese. We are dealing with a period when residents from Britain also shared a "charter ideology," as Porter has called it – of themselves as founding people and the others as immigrants.[41] In flat defiance of the fact that British Columbia was almost 75 per cent "Indian" in 1870, British immigrants confidently claimed, and began to rule, the territory as their own.

THERE WAS FAR MORE enthusiasm than subtlety in the way the provincial legislature set about building a morality of "us" and "them" in British Columbia. As we shall see shortly, its strategies encountered legal and constitutional barriers along the way, but it struck one major blow very early. When the colony of British Columbia became a province in 1871, the Chinese enjoyed the right to vote and exercised it fully in at least some districts where they lived. But in the first session of the provincial legislature, an Act to Amend the Qualification and Registration of Voters Act was passed which precluded Chinese (and native Indians), even if they were British subjects, from voting.[42] The implications of this act for Chinese-origin residents were significant well beyond their sudden loss of the franchise. It would later restrict them from certain occupational choices, such as pharmacy, law, and political office. Also, by another law passed in 1883, only registered voters were eligible to serve as jurors in all courts of civil and criminal jurisdiction.[43] *racist practices against Chinese by govern.*

Perhaps more critical, however, were the symbolic implications of such legal targeting. The disenfranchisement act officially sealed the alien or non-settler status of the category "Chinese." It also enabled and justified further social and economic closure. Robert Dunsmuir, one of the largest employers of Chinese labour in the province, actually conceded that the ascription of non-settler status by the state was an independent source of anti-Chinese sentiment, when he advised the commissioners of 1885: "If it were possible for Parliament to bring in a bill speedily to give the Chinaman the franchise, there would be less anti-Chinese agitation." It was obvious to Dunsmuir that from the time Chinese were disenfranchised, politicians could vent any inflammatory opinions regarding their presence in order to gain popular legitimacy.

The first session of the legislative assembly thus quickly asserted the marginal political status of "Chinese." Resolutions to tax them fifty dollars per annum and to prohibit them from employment on provincial and federal works were also presented, but both were defeated.[44] Some members protested that in a free society the labour market should also be free, while others expressed doubt regarding the legal competence of the province to enact such measures.[45] Another act of little practical, but some degree of symbolic significance was passed that prevented Chinese from registering their vital statistics.[46]

During the 1870s, the legislature became increasingly concerned at the prospect of "the province being over-run with a Chinese population, to the injury of the settled population of the country." A motion to devise steps to prevent such injury was carried unanimously under the government of Premier Andrew Elliott in May, 1876.[47] By 1878, with Chinese immigration from the United States and Hong Kong increasing rapidly, the legislature voted to insert a clause in contracts for public works prohibiting the employment of Chinese labour.[48] The province also decided to test its legal power in an attempt to appease anti-Chinese sentiment without alienating the employers of Chinese labour. In August 1878, Premier George Walkem introduced and won approval for the Chinese Tax Act, drafted ostensibly "for the better collection of provincial taxes from Chinese."[49] This statute imposed a quarterly licence in the form of a ten-dollar levy for every Chinese employee over twelve years of age and stipulated that employers of Chinese retain the licences for routine inspection. Just months after the act had been passed, however, a Mr Tai Sing appealed against the seizure of some of his goods in default of his tax payment. Two hundred and fifty Chinese residents of Victoria went on a five-day strike against the measure, and a number of cannery operators protested the bill on the grounds that it threatened to ruin their businesses.[50]

Given the critical nature of the precedent, it must have been of deep concern to the Walkem government when Dr Justice Gray declared in Tai Sing's case that the Chinese Tax Act was ultra vires provincial jurisdiction. Since proclamation of the British North America Act of 1867, authority for establishing the privileges and disabilities of aliens in Canada was vested exclusively with the dominion parliament, Gray pointed out.[51] And, just in case the "spoilt child of Confederation" did not yet know its legal place, the minister of justice in Ottawa decided to confirm the fate of the bill by recommending to the governor-general the following year that the Tax Act be disallowed.[52]

The constitutional limits on the political will of those who would extend European domination to the colony were thus solidly confirmed in this first provincial encounter with Ottawa. The province's lieutenant-governor exhorted members of the legislature to try other means of achieving their goal,[53] but the dictates from above silenced provincial politicians for the time, and the Chinese question, like many provincial issues, became infused with a strong anti-federal invective. British Columbia would certainly come to regret its surrender of power over the matters of immigration and aliens to the dominion parliament when it joined Confederation in 1871. The Walkem government, for one, looked enviously to the separately governed colonies of Australia, which had only a generally sympathetic home government to convince of the virtue of anti-Chinese measures.

In response to the Tax Act decision and concern over Chinese immigration, Walkem in 1879 appointed a select committee to report on the best means "to deal with the Chinese population, and to prevent further immigration of Chinese into the province." The committee's report was to "set forth the baneful effect of the presence of the Chinese in our midst" and form the basis of an appeal to the dominion government to restrict Chinese immigration.[54] This committee's report on the "Chinese question" did precisely as instructed and used language that demonstrated the moral authority the provincial government could afford the idea of a "Chinese race," in the absence of sufficient legal competence to enact desired anti-Chinese measures. "Their [the 6,000 Chinese] moral and social condition is degraded in the extreme," the committee wrote. "A large majority of the men are in a state of semi-bondage, while all the women are prostitutes ... A state of marriage is unknown among them; hence the influence exerted upon society by such wholesale vice cannot be otherwise than highly pernicious, as no attempt is made at concealment." Their "slave labour has a degrading effect," the report continued, "as it causes an inconquerable and not unreasonable prejudice on the part of the free members of a community." It also attributed the "strong and growing antipathy to their presence in the community" to the fact that "they are undesirable settlers ... wholly opposed to any amalgamation of races or to becoming a portion of the permanent population of the country." (The sojourning charge was a dubious one, as Commissioner Chapleau noted in 1885: "It is hard to deal seriously with those who complain they will not stay, for the very same person will grow querulous over the fact that he is here."[55])

THE LATE-NINETEENTH-CENTURY legislatures of British Columbia were unreservedly opposed to the inflow of cheap labour from China, despite their commitment to economic growth and their deference toward private companies in the province.[56] There was division in the house from year to year over whether Chinese labour should be regulated by government intervention, but there was unanimity that further Chinese immigration should be restricted, if not excluded. In that conviction, the legislative body ran uncharacteristically but resolutely against its own frontier-acquisitive mentality. Only one form of labour was to develop the province, it was urged, and in 1883 a unanimously carried resolution under the Smithe government requested the dominion government to inaugurate a "liberal scheme of white immigration to British Columbia."[57] An address on the Chinese question at the same time declared that with a "white population alone, we can hope to build up our country and render it fit for the Anglo-Saxon race."[58]

The Walkem, Beaven, and Smithe governments also went to considerable lengths in the late 1870s and early 1880s to try to avert the threat that had been pending since British Columbia joined Confederation – the employment of Chinese labour on the transnational rail link. Walkem actually visited Ottawa in 1880 to request that Chinese labour be prohibited from railway construction. By 1882, however, when a resolution was passed by Robert Beaven's government "to induce the contractors on the Canadian Pacific Railway to import and employ white labour on their works, instead of Chinese,"[59] contractor Andrew Onderdonk had already secured the co-operation of Chinese labour recruitment companies in San Francisco. Between them, the companies found approximately 15,000 Chinese to build the mountainous section of the transnational connection.[60]

The proportion of the province's population of Chinese origin thus increased to 9 per cent by the mid-1880s, a development that so perturbed the Smithe government that in 1884 it decided to take matters completely into its own hands. While submitting to Prime Minister John A. Macdonald that "the hordes of Chinese ... surge in upon the country and carry with them the elements of disease, pestilence and degradation over the face of the fair land," William Smithe presented to his own legislature an Act to Prevent the Immigration of Chinese, carried in February 1884.[61] According to this bill, entry to the province was denied to "any native of China or its dependencies not born of British parents, or any person born of Chinese parents." Another bill, the Act to Regulate the Chinese Population of British Columbia, insisted that "any person of Chinese race" over fourteen years of age pay an annual tax of ten dollars for a licence to work.[62] The tax was warranted, according to the act's preamble, because "the incoming of Chinese to British Columbia largely exceeds that of any other class of immigrant, and the population so introduced are fast becoming superior in number to our own race; [they] are not disposed to be governed by our laws; are dissimilar in habits and occupation from our people; evade the payment of taxes justly due to the Government; are governed by pestilential habits; are useless in instances of emergency; habitually desecrate grave yards by the removal of bodies therein; and generally ... Chinese are inclined to habits subversive of the comfort and well-being of the community."

Within six weeks, the Act to Prevent the Immigration of Chinese was disallowed by the governor-general-in-council, possibly as much in the interests of completing the railway as ensuring conformity with the British North America Act. The Regulation Act was eventually declared unconstitutional by the BC Supreme Court, but a third act passed in the 1884 session was allowed to stand. According to clause 122 of the Land Act, it was deemed unlawful "for a Commissioner to issue a pre-emption record of any Crown land, or sell any portion thereof, to any Chinese, nor grant authority to any Chinese to record or divert any water from any natural channel of any stream, lake or river of the province."[63] acts against Chinese

Such a measure was hardly enough to halt the animosity that swelled in British Columbia when, with the rail track completed in Vancouver in 1885, thousands of relatively underpaid Chinese labourers were discharged onto the regular labour market. As theorists of the "split labour market" in the province have argued, the market of cheap, racialized labour bred an independent economic grievance that compounded conflict between the European and Chinese-origin population.[64] Ottawa's failure to "abate the evil" therefore grew increasingly provocative, and in 1885 a stronger appeal was made by the Smithe government to the dominion to act on behalf of the province. A resolution drafted for transmission to Ottawa in 1885 said:

The Chinese are alien in sentiment and habits. They do not become settlers in any sense of that word ... The Chinese population chiefly consists of male adults, and thus they come into unfair competition with white labour ... Their presence exerts a baneful influence in restricting the immigration of white labour, especially house-servants, who will not be brought into contact with this race. They have a system of secret societies which encourages crime amongst themselves ... The use of opium has extended throughout the Province to the demoralization of the native races ... This House urgently requests that some restrictive legislation be passed to prevent our Province from becoming completely overrun by Chinese.[65]

And in case Ottawa did not register the sincerity of this plea, the Smithe government re-enacted the disallowed act of 1884 by levying a fifty-dollar tax on all Chinese immigrants to Canada – only to have it overruled again.[66]

Thoroughly hampered in its attempts to control the entry of immigrants from China, the Smithe government turned again to residents. In 1890, the legislature forbade the employment of Chinese in underground work at coal mines. Perhaps more significant, a standard anti-Chinese employment clause was prepared by a select committee in 1886 for inclusion in private bills. However, the relentless member for Victoria, Robert Beaven, found it difficult to muster the necessary support for his clause when decisions over incorporation bills for private companies were presented to the assembly. As mentioned earlier, the legislature was split on the issue of restricting so docile, sober, and industrious a work-force as Chinese were perceived to be, especially at a time when rail networks were opening up the seemingly infinite resources of the province. Some members did not want Chinese at any price; others felt the inherently cheap nature of their alien labour sufficient justification to use it. Both groups, however, shared the view that Chinese labour should be managed in the "public interest" of establishing a European society. Beaven's day of glory did arrive in fact, in 1891, when the house set a precedent by carrying his motion to include a Chinese-exclusion clause in the Act to Incorporate the British Columbia Dyking and Improvement Co.[67]

In 1897, the government of Premier John Turner, facing a year of economic recession and labour unrest, attempted a more decisive stand on Chinese employment with the passage of an ambitious Act to Regulate the Employment of Chinese (and Japanese) Persons on Works Carried on under Franchises granted by Private Acts.[68] The legislature once again ran into constitutional problems, however. The lieutenant-governor reserved assent of the bill, and, when the act was renamed and recarried in 1898 as the Labour Regulation Act, it suffered at the hands of the dominion minister of justice the same fate as other measures involving the rights of aliens.

One significant, unanimously carried anti-Chinese clause that did remain on the statute books in this period (through insertion in contracts rather than as blanket legislation) determined that "if any Provincial aid be granted in the way of contributions of public funds of the province, or a grant of Crown lands in aid of public works undertaken, [it shall] be conditional upon a contract being entered into ... that no Chinese or Japanese be employed upon any such undertaking."[69] In this way the legislature set an example of discriminatory action; it could not enforce such action across the private sector by law, but it could provide it with de facto legitimacy through the spirit of its own employment practices.

In the last years of the century, the legislative assembly intensified its efforts to transmit local definitions of the "Chinese" to legislators and officials in Ottawa, who at the time did not have first-hand experience of "them." Successive governments carried resolutions in 1893, 1894, 1897, and 1899 calling for more stringent restrictions on Chinese immigration than had eventually been introduced by the House of Commons in 1885. That dominion measure (discussed in the next section of this chapter) had proved effective in limiting Chinese immigration to less than 300 for several years until 1892, when over 3,000 Chinese entered Canada. The provincial resolution of 1899 declared that, without more effective measures, "the destructive incursion of Asiatics" would drive "workingmen of British race and blood out of many of the fields of labour" and threatened "to leave very little occupation remaining for the white labourer." In 1900, another provincial government (under Premier Joseph Martin) attempted to cater to its anti-Chinese electorate with yet another Act to Regulate Chinese Immigration. It was promptly disallowed.

In the mean time, provincial régimes of the late 1890s did what they could to curtail the public-health risk which was assumed to accompany increasing numbers of Chinese in the province. With Charles Semlin's government in power in 1899, the assembly unanimously carried a motion "that the attention of the government be directed to the urgency of enforcing the sanitary regulations laid down in the provincial Health Act where ever Chinese congregate," while in 1894 and 1897, motions had been carried asking the dominion for more strict quarantine inspections of incoming Chinese or "Mongolians."[70]

Another request to Ottawa in 1900 revealed the strength of the provincial government's belief in some essential Chineseness, independent of citizenship, birthplace, and adopted country of residence. The assembly unanimously carried a motion "that this House views with alarm the admission of Mongolians to the rights of citizenship, and that the Dominion Government be requested so to change the naturalization laws that it will be impossible for any Mongolian, or person belonging to the native races of Asia, to become British subjects."[71] Within British Columbia, some movement toward this goal had been achieved five years earlier, under the Turner government. The Provincial Elections Act of 1895 denied the franchise to naturalized and Canadian-born subjects of Chinese (and Japanese) origin. "Chinese" had been legally labelled as alien in 1875, and in turn this had been used to justify denying them further access to insider status. Commissioner Gray put it this way in his 1885 report: "By provincial legislation in British Columbia and the general hostility towards them, the Chinese are practically prohibited from becoming attached to the country. They are made so far as provincial legislation can go, perpetual aliens."[72]

IN THIS SECTION WE HAVE seen that, within strict judicial limits, the early provincial governments of British Columbia played a pivotal role in transforming people of Chinese origin into members of an undifferentiated, alien category in BC culture and politics. "Chinese" is a concept that must be studied as part of society rather than nature, and the province's early politicians, in their practices and rhetoric, legitimized the meaning and strengthened the material effects of that categorization. Theirs was no "prejudice," but rather an appeal to origins that helped forge and justify the making of a European order within the parameters of a constitutional system. The words of Surveyor General Pearse to the 1885 royal commission reveal the power relations out of which emerged the classification process we have been examining. "We want here," he said, "a white man's community, with civilized habits and religious aspirations, and not a community of 'Heathen Chinee' who can never assimilate with us, or do ought to elevate us, and who can be of no possible value to a state in any capacity other than that of drawers of water and hewers of wood."[73]

Notwithstanding the power of colonial authorities in England, the dominion parliament had ultimate control over the definition and status of these settlers, and we now examine its part in the making of the authoritative idea of a separate Chinese race.

THE VIEW FROM OTTAWA

Consistent with economic theorizing of the day, many members of Canada's House of Commons appeared uncomfortable with the requests of BC representatives for dominion intervention in the free flow of labour. When Arthur Bunster (Vancouver) moved in 1878 that an anti-Chinese clause be inserted in Canadian Pacific Railway (CPR) contracts, Alexander Mackenzie, leader of the opposition, protested: "It [the motion] is one unprecedented in its character and spirit, and at variance with those tolerant laws which afford asylum to all who come into our country, irrespective of colour, hair or anything else."[74] The following year, Mackenzie informed the restless BC members that "the principle that some classes of the human family were not fit to be residents of this Dominion, would be dangerous and contrary to the Law of Nations ... however unpleasant the neighbourhood of the Chinese might be."[75]

Ideological support for open immigration came easily to a government that had construction of a transnational railway as a primary mandate. Prime Minister John A. Macdonald, more explicit than most, made a blunt statement of the race-development dilemma to BC member Amor de Cosmos in 1882. Just like many BC entrepreneurs and labourers, Macdonald assumed an intrinsic quality to Chinese labour that made it automatically cheaper than other labour and eminently suited to the menial and onerous tasks of an expanding economy, such as railway construction. He told de Cosmos: "I share very much the feeling of the people of the United States and the Australian colonies against a Mongolian or Chinese population in our country as permanent settlers. I believe that it is an alien race in every sense, that would not and could not be expected to assimilate with our Aryan population. [But] ... it is simply a question of alternatives – either you must have this labour or you cannot have the railway."[76] One year later, Macdonald deflected another appeal from British Columbia: "I am sufficient of a physiologist to believe that the two races cannot combine, and that no great middle race can arise from the mixture of the Mongolian and the Aryan. I believe it would tend to the degradation of the people of the Pacific; and that no permanent immigration of the Chinese people into Canada is to be encouraged, but under the present system there is no fear of that ... They are not permanent settlers ... and therefore there is no fear of a permanent degradation of the country by a mongrel race."[77]

The idea of a Chinese race clearly lent itself to all manner of politically convenient twists. It was used to argue against immigration restriction at the same time as it could be used to argue in favour of it. For Canadian and foreign entrepreneurs and the dominion government in the early 1880s, it was precisely the (putatively) inherent nature of Chinese labour – docile, industrious, and alien – that entitled the country to use it and dismiss it; for others, the competition created by the uniquely Chinese living standard was sufficient reason to reject Chinese labour altogether.

Linking these apparently alternative voices was the force of the race idea itself in Canadian culture and the political utility of such a cross-class belief. The class divisions of Canada's emerging industrial base ensured that owners of capital had good reasons for using Chinese labour – reasons that when translated into employment practices entrenched occupational segregation along colour lines and boosted profits to owners. But it was the prevailing racial frame of reference that justified the recruitment and exploitation of labour from China during a labour-intensive stage of Canadian economic development.

This view more adequately explains the co-operation between the dominion and the CPR on the use of Chinese labour than the arguments of Warburton and others. These scholars have seen it in terms of "the class relations, which [as] the essential mechanism of the system of production, required these workers."[78] Aside from its silence on the question of why "these workers" were chosen or why they were cheap, that view overlooks the fact that Ottawa had its own reasons for contracting Chinese in the early 1880s – namely, to promote colonization of Canada's territories, unite a nation, and render it European. As long as the mutually beneficial arrangement with the railway company existed, then, the protests of BC members in Ottawa, against the "worse than worthless element," "the greatest pagans on earth," and the like, were simply deflected.[79]

But the voices of the west were not forgotten entirely. With the end of the railway in sight in 1884, Macdonald set up the Royal Commission into the Chinese Question in British Columbia, "to obtain proof that the principle of restricting Chinese immigration is proper and in the interest of the Province and the Dominion." The commissioners, Dr Justice Gray of the BC Supreme Court, and Dr Joseph Adolphe Chapleau, dominion secretary of state, entered the investigation with relatively open minds. Their commitment to laissez-faire political philosophy seems to have predisposed them against government intervention in the issue. But laissez-faire thinking lent itself easily to Darwinist arguments about the "fit" and "unfit" races, and both commissioners were well versed in evolutionary theory.

Dr Justice Gray argued, for example, that "it is something strange to hear the strong, broad-shouldered superior race, superior physically and mentally, sprung from the highest types of the old and new world, expressing a fear of competition with a small, inferior and comparatively speaking, feminine race."[80] He believed that society, like nature, was a harmonious hierarchical structure, with each element set in its appointed place. Trading heavily in the language of the "great chain of being," he said in the commission's 1885 report: "How derogatory to the French, English and American races in Canada to assert that the presence of a few labouring ignorant Chinese will cause the Canadian people to abandon the religion of their fathers, the morals, education and higher Christian civilization of their institutions, to adopt the idol worship and debasing morals and habits of the heathen ... In moral and social habits, beyond a very limited circle, the influence of the foreigner in a debasing direction will be extremely small, and upon the great masses of the people absolutely imperceptible when the country into which they come is of a higher organization in morals and civilization."[81]

Applying this version of race logic to dominion concerns of the day, the commissioners recommended a cautious policy of "limited restraint" on Chinese immigration. This accommodated laissez-faire views, while accepting the "objection that there is no homogeneity of race between them and ourselves, nor can they comprehend or assimilate themselves to our institutions." To bring about this limited restraint, the commissioners suggested a ten-dollar duty on each entrant from China. Dr Justice Gray argued that such a tax would be "judicious," because "sound policy will regulate the coming of the Chinese, not stop it, any more than a clear-headed farmer would dry up a river because it may sometimes overflow its banks and perchance create temporary derangement in the lands through which it flows, but which when properly restrained, its waters irrigate and enrich." The politics of race could assume poetic heights indeed.

Soon after the commission reported, Chapleau himself introduced in the House of Commons a Bill to Restrict and Regulate Chinese Immigration into the Dominion of Canada. While observing his fellow commissioner's fears about stemming the "flow," it conceded more to BC pressure by raising the tax on Chinese immigrants to fifty dollars. Chapleau was well aware of the significance of this first act of intervention by the Canadian government in the free flow of labour to the country's shores. He sought to defend it, therefore, in a way that struck a chord with mounting public opinion about race. He asked the house: "Is it not a natural and well-founded desire of British subjects, of the white population of the Dominion, who come from either British or other European States and settle in this country, that their country should be inhabited by a vigorous, energetic and white race of people?"[82]

ON 2 JULY 1885, PARLIAMENT approved Chapleau's poll tax, and henceforth the dominion government became more united in its mode of implementing the concept of a Chinese race. The government also became a chief mediator of the composition and idea of "Canada." The new act, for example, divided potential immigrants to Canada into two classes. One comprised people of Chinese origin; the other, all people not of Chinese origin, who were covered by the general Immigration Act. The new law also led to the appointment of officials whose task was to execute the spirit and the letter of a law strictly for "Chinese." A chief controller of Chinese immigration at the ports of Victoria and Vancouver was entrusted to enforce the act, and special records of Chinese entry, exit, occupation, and other statistics began to be compiled. In such ways, the act gave the category "Chinese" an administrative existence and a reality in Canadian official life that did not need to acknowledge the criteria immigrants from China might have used to define themselves and each other. This system of racial classification had major ramifications for those who were defined in its terms, and also for dominion politics in Canada, as the following analysis of the act and its administration and amendment to the turn of the century will demonstrate.

The 1885 Act to Restrict and Regulate Chinese Immigration was cumbersome compared with the simpler, 1882 Exclusion Act of the United States. It demanded fifty dollars from any person of Chinese origin entering Canada and not entitled to exemption.[83] Those exempt from the tax were diplomatic and consular representatives, tourists, merchants, and students. Merchants, it was believed, would contribute capital and trade arrangements to Canada's development, and state officials were reluctant to deter their entry. Such merchants were not on equal terms with white immigrants of commerce, however; their racialization still set them administratively apart.

A further barrier to Chinese entry was the imposition by a section of the act of a maximum ratio of one immigrant for every fifty tons of ship's weight. Another section recognized the right of an immigrant to visit China and return to Canada without paying the tax again on presentation of a certificate of entry. The provision proved exceedingly troublesome to port officials, however, because certificates were routinely sold in China. The act was therefore amended in 1887 to make the registration of all Chinese in Canada compulsory. The amendment did not stop fraudulent practices surrounding return certificates – a fact that encouraged accusations about the untrustworthiness of the "Chinese" character – and by 1892 return certificates were replaced by a system in which returning Chinese were obliged to prove their identity to the satisfaction of the controller.

The 1887 amendment also refined the official definition of "Chinese," which became "a person born of a Chinese father irrespective of the nationality of the mother" and extended exemption from the tax to women of Chinese origin married to "British and Christian subjects." These changes flowed directly from a controversy surrounding the entry of a Mr Moore, "an Englishman of standing," who arrived in Canada to find that he was required to pay a tax for his Chinese wife and their children.[84] According to the revised act of 1887 such women and children were no longer officially "Chinese."

The Moore incident was seized on by those in the house who considered the tax on women from China an ultimate menace to the community. The member for Bothwell, seeing the double standard of the amendment, requested that all women of Chinese origin be relieved of the tax so as to encourage family settlement. However,

John A. Macdonald saw his own opportunity in the suggestion: "The whole point of this measure is to restrict the immigration of the Chinese into British Columbia and into Canada ... If wives are allowed, not a single immigrant would come over without a wife, and the immorality existing to a very great extent along the Pacific coast would be greatly aggravated ... I do not think that it would be to the advantage of Canada or any other country occupied by Aryans for members of the Mongolian race to become permanent inhabitants of the country."[85] Chapleau similarly subscribed to the logic that allowing Chinese wives to come in would promote not morality but greater immorality. As he had noted in the royal commission report of 1885: "If they came with their women they would come to settle and what with immigration and their extraordinary fecundity, would soon overrun the country."[86] Limited family settlement was an important effect of the official recognition of the category "Chinese." Like the head tax itself, it further realized the alien and non-settler status of residents of Chinese origin.

Public debate about the merits of the tax continued from its implementation into the next century. Questions concerning trade and commerce, diplomacy, and even basic justice were recognized as militating against the law. Sir Richard Cartwright, minister for trade and commerce, felt moved to excuse the act in this way: "It appears to me, although it may be said that this practice of taxing Chinamen is opposed to British practice ... to a very considerable extent the instinctive feeling which prevails in British Columbia has its origin in a wholesome feeling of self-preservation."[87]

ON THE EVE OF HIS ELECTION victory in 1896, Liberal leader Wilfrid Laurier's political reading of the issue led him to promise (to a BC audience) that while "Chinese immigration restriction is not an issue in the East, the views of Liberals in the West must prevail."[88] However, his new government remained cautious in its management of the "Oriental question," as the issue came to be called when increasing numbers of Japanese immigrated to Canada in the late 1890s. The Department of Trade and Commerce on a number of occasions warned against increasing the head tax because of its concern to protect trade links between China and Canada.

The dominion authorities were also at pains not to offend Japan, a major trading partner of the British Empire and a nation perceived to hold a conception of progress and civilization more assimilable to the European cultural tradition than that of its more mysterious Oriental neighbour. For example, while appeals against the head tax to the Colonial Office by the Chinese legation in London failed to move the imperial authorities to act in Canada, the colonial secretary, Joseph Chamberlain, was sensitive to measures adopted in parts of Canada against immigrants from Japan. The dominion parliament's opposition to legislation that affected both Japanese and Chinese seemed to provide a slight cushion for the discriminatory posture toward Chinese. In fact, after the provincial Labour Regulation Act of 1898 was disallowed in Ottawa, Laurier himself advised the BC legislature against restraining Chinese and Japanese labour together, in view of the cherished relations between the home country and Japan.[89]

Along with these international considerations, there were more specific influences on policy, such as the steamship service across the Pacific Ocean, which had much to lose from government restrictions on migration from China. Nevertheless the dominion House of Commons grew increasingly receptive to the views of British Columbians. In July 1899, Edward Prior, member for Victoria, told the house: "I believe that the Chinese are a malignant cancer eating in the very vitals of the workingman of Canada but with this difference: that while up to the present time, no cure is known for cancer ... there is a cure for this Chinese cancer, and that is by the Government providing a sufficient poll tax to keep them out ... The aim should be to people Canada with those who have the courage and the wish to build up the British Empire and perpetuate British institutions."[90]

Laurier by then had realized that to ignore such a forceful lobby might impair his electoral prospects in the west. Moreover, the fifty-dollar head tax was losing its effect – in 1897, 2,447 Chinese paid the tax at British Columbia's ports, compared with just 211 in 1886, the year after its introduction – and population growth figures defied the argument that the Chinese were mere sojourners in Canada. For Laurier, the time had come to surrender to the self-solacing thought that prejudice was inevitable, innate, and proper. On the same day that the member for Victoria spoke about the "malignant cancer," Laurier had this to say: "It is a fact for which there must be a strong ethical reason that the Anglo-Saxon race, which has proved itself to be one of the most tolerant of all races ... shows an invincible repugnance to the people of the Mongolian races ... Wherever the Mongolian race presents itself, the English race immediately shows a strong repugnance. That is the fact, and though perhaps it is a sentiment to be deplored, still it exists, and we have to reckon with it. I say at once that it will not do for this Government, or for any Government to ignore it; on the contrary the Government is quite prepared to recognize it and to deal with it accordingly."[91]

The following year, the House of Commons agreed to an amendment to the immigration law of 1885 that increased the entry tax to $100. And in September 1900, three royal commissioners, including two BC residents, were appointed to investigate "Oriental" immigration to Canada and assess whether prohibitive measures were in order.

THE NINETEENTH CENTURY CLOSED with the idea of race well entrenched in North American public opinion and science. Despite the nagging difficulties being encountered by scientists and anthropologists in their attempts to typify the globe's populations, few white people – including intellectuals and governing élites – questioned the belief that the mental, moral, and physical differences between "the races" were profound. Monogenist beliefs in the unity of the globe's people had been solidly overturned, not least in white Canada, by deterministic thinking about racial difference.

The nature and strength of the consensus about race were amply demonstrated in the proceedings of the new royal commission, conducted by Roger Chute, Daniel Munn, and Christopher Foley. During 1901, they received more than 300 submissions from British Columbia, and virtually none expressed opposition to the proposal that immigration from China be prohibited completely. This despite the fact that the province's Chinese population, numbering 16,000 in 1900, was solidly outnumbered by the 129,000 "whites."[92]

While in 1900 Chinese labourers were still regarded favourably by employers in the province for "their sobriety, machine-like regularity, economy and their disposition to remain with one employer,"[93] the majority of large entrepreneurs interviewed by the commissioners claimed that Chinese immigrants of all classes had outgrown their usefulness. Sufficient white labour had been available since the rail link was completed, they suggested, and the major economic activities of the province (except for the canneries) would not suffer from greater restriction of their labour. The changed mood among employers was highlighted in the testimony of Samuel Robins, of the New Vancouver Coal Co. In the 1885 royal commission, Robins had on balance favoured the continued employment of Chinese labour. In 1901, he told the commissioners that Chinese immigration was an evil that "should be stopped before it grows to unmanageable dimensions." White self-employed businessmen had also joined the cry against Chinese immigration, as more Chinese immigrants turned to the urban trades. In its 1902 report, the royal commission described the "under-consumption" of the Chinese and their predisposition to "live under conditions insufferable to a white man." The white working class had for decades charged that this amounted to "unfair competition"; by 1901 royal commissioners agreed that such competition was no less than "deadly ... because it strikes at home life."[94]

Chute, Foley, and Munn also invoked a "numerously signed petition from the residents of British Columbia" to the governor-general-in-council in May 1900. The petition protested: "The province is flooded with an undesirable class of people non-assimilative and most detrimental to the wage-earning classes of the people of the province." It also urged that "it is in the interest of the Empire that the Pacific Province of the Dominion should be occupied by a large and thoroughly British population rather than one in which the number of aliens forms a large proportion."[95] The commissioners concluded that further immigration from China would indeed be injurious and unanimously recommended that the head tax on Chinese immigrants be raised to $500.

Given a report so lacking in equivocation, the Laurier government wasted no time in implementing its recommendations. The 1903 session of parliament amended the immigration act of 1885 to raise the entry tax to a hefty $500, with the dissent of only a few "free traders," as the member for Russell called himself.[96]

Such dominion endorsement of the racial category was not an uncomplicated or automatic response to beliefs about race, as we have seen. But clearly the twin ideas of a Chinese race and of Chinese inferiority had grown in force and political utility, so that by 1903 most members of parliament – the large majority of whom were yet to have local experience with "Chinese" – were prepared to overcome whatever moral, economic, and diplomatic reservations remained about legally imposed discrimination.

The prime minister defended the outcome in 1903, when he said that "the difference between the two races" bred an antagonism that even the state needed to respect. "It seems impossible to reconcile them [the differences]," Laurier said, "and the conclusion of all who have considered the matter seems to be that the amalgamation of the two is neither possible [nor] desirable. There are so many differences of character that it is supposed to be impossible to overcome them. At all events in the province of British Columbia, this feeling is very strong."[97]

Even with immigrants from Japan, Laurier continued, "the ethnical differences are of such a character as to make it very doubtful whether assimilation of the two races could ever take place."[98] The marginality of the "Oriental" in Canada had been divinely ordained, or so Laurier wanted to believe, and his government's responsibility was to respect and facilitate the unfolding of that higher will. Thenceforth, immigration from China to Canada fell to a trickle.

FRANK PARKIN HAS SPECIFIED THE importance of the state in the making of outsiders in Western society: "In all known instances where racial, religious, linguistic, or sex characteristics have been seized upon for closure purposes," he argues, "the group in question has already at some time been defined as legally inferior by the state."[99] Exclusionary possibilities can be "realized" by the rest of society, Parkin claims, only if the state has already created the appropriate legally and politically vulnerable category. We have seen that during the late nineteenth and early twentieth centuries, the government of Canada was instrumental in specifying "Chinese" as such a category, through speeches and practices that appropriated and wielded beliefs about their difference.

Such official intervention in the race issue cannot be adequately explained as the prejudice of successive politicians. Nor is it sufficient to claim that they stepped in because of a structural imperative within the capitalist economy to maintain "the marginal status of a group whose labour was necessary for economic expansion,"[100] although economic solidarity surely consolidated the white sector's hegemony. A more neglected factor influencing state action on the Chinese question was the respect of Ottawa's politicians for the idea of racial difference and the moral commitment it generated in them for nation-building. Dominion legislators also saw political capital in the mandate to propagate a European society in the British colony. The idea of a "Chinese" race was a most convenient concept for political manipulation, as we have seen at both provincial and dominion levels, used (not necessarily consciously) to win electoral support and inspire a collective sense of identification among a "white" in-group. And, once separate statutory provisions strictly for "Chinese" were erected in 1885, Ottawa became committed to a course of discrimination that required its own justification and refinement. By the close of the nineteenth century, the morality of separation between "them" and "us" had all the force of national official status and, as we shall see, at the local level all the confirmation of territorial boundaries.

THE GEOGRAPHY OF RACE IN VANCOUVER

During the 1860s white, Chinese, and native Indian pioneers lived relatively cordially in and around the small town of Granville on

Burrard Inlet. Something of a pecking order of occupational tasks was in place which "sorted" the living and working relationships between camps of pioneers. Chinese settlers from California and Victoria, for example, were employed in unskilled capacities at the Hastings, Moodyville, and Stamps saw mills. A minority also established stores to supply the mill hands, hand-loggers, and their employers with amenities, including laundry service. By 1884, there were five merchants, sixty sawmill hands, ten store employees, thirty washermen and cooks, five children, three married women, and one single woman – a total of 114 settlers of Chinese origin – on Burrard Inlet.[101] Well known among the stores was the Wah Chong laundry on Water Street, the Gin Tei Hing wash-house and general store (which supported a family of six), and the Dupont Street grocery of Goon Ling Dang (who had arrived in Victoria early enough to vote in the dominion and provincial elections). Some of the Chinese settlers in Granville lived in wooden shacks around the shore of False Creek near Hastings Street, some lived to the west in the vicinity of Dupont (later Pender) and Carrall streets, and others were sparsely scattered throughout the Old Granville Townsite and environs.

Ottawa's decision in 1884 to extend the western terminus of the CPR from Port Moody to Coal Harbour on the inlet transformed Granville from a small, rough village of transients into the prosperous new town of Vancouver. It also brought many discharged Chinese railway labourers, only a minority of whom opened businesses to serve the rapidly growing numbers of eastern Canadians, British, and Americans settling in British Columbia. With the growth and turbulence wrought by completion of the railway, the once peaceful and paternalistic group relations around Burrard Inlet grew increasingly competitive.

The staking of a new town and citizenry was – like the defining of a new province – a territorial process, and by 1886, with anti-Chinese measures in place at both senior levels of government, Vancouver's "white" pioneers were as accepting as other British Columbians of officially sanctioned definitions of "us" and "them." Many saw the primary challenge facing the new town to be the prevention of permanent Chinese settlement. The reported sale to Chinese of two lots in the business section of town in April 1886 certainly sparked indignation throughout the white community. It was, for the *Vancouver World*, no less than "a violent wrench to the public sentiment," a danger, the *Herald* warned, to property values in the emerging commercial section.[102] When a "small horde of unemployed Chinamen" tried to locate a new business in the section, the *Vancouver News* said: "Let their efforts, however little we know them, be promptly discouraged ... The thin edge of the wedge, in this case, had better be obstructed."[103]

In the mean time, white residents did what they could to discourage Chinese settlement. At the first municipal election, of May 1886, the cultural and political bounds of the new community were quickly asserted when sixty men of Chinese origin were chased from the polls back to the Hastings Mill, from which they had been brought by manager and mayoral candidate Mr R.H. Alexander.[104] It had been inscribed in the statute to incorporate the city of Vancouver that no "Chinese" or "Indian" was entitled to the municipal franchise – and this closure was vigilantly enforced with clubs and fists at the first opportunity.

Driving the Chinese back as far as the Hastings Mill was not far enough for many Vancouver citizens. They saw a better opportunity in the great fire of 13 June 1886, which levelled the new city and with it the residences and businesses of Chinese. In the week after the fire, three street meetings, held with the support of the new Scottish-born mayor, Alderman M.A. MacLean, and fellow Scots-born Alderman L.A. Hamilton, passed resolutions aimed at preventing Chinese from re-establishing themselves. But by July, the *News* lamented: "They seem to have recovered from the fire scare which drove them out," and a "number are coming into the city taking up their locations principally on the outskirts."[105] From the outskirts, which included a 160–acre tract that "a colony of Mongolians" had leased for cultivation on the road to New Westminster, Chinese supplied private residences, hotels, and boarding-houses which depended almost entirely on them for their vegetable products. Hamilton found the threat so serious as to take the matter to council in November of that year, when he pressed for the city to "take some action in trying as far as possible to prevent Chinese from locating within the City limits."[106]

Local assemblies of the Knights of Labor, also mounted a campaign to "avert the evil effects which are sure to follow wherever those miserly rice eaters locate."[107] In November 1886, they passed a resolution declaring that "the employment of Chinese not only lowers the dignity of labour but is exceedingly injurious and detrimental to the best interests of the working classes," and for this reason, they resolved "to do [their] utmost ... to lessen the grievance by an active and persistent action against all persons who continue to employ Chinese."[108] True to their word, the Knights organized a boycott of all Vancouver businessmen who employed, sold food to, or in any way patronized Chinese residents; they painted a black cross in front of any store that broke with white solidarity. Hotel-keepers agreed to discharge Chinese help. The city also respected the initiative by refusing to hire Chinese and by prohibiting the employment of "any person of Chinese race" on municipal contracts or city-assisted projects – an exclusion the Vancouver Trades and Labour Council scrupulously monitored.

The fear that Chinese labourers would undercut white workers was not without foundation. As stated earlier, BC employers exploited the race concept to their own advantage and paid Chinese workers a wage in proportion to their perceived worth. Thus in late 1886, when John McDougall recruited "batches of Mongolians" from Victoria for his 350-acre clearing contract in Vancouver's West End (see Map 1, page 69), he quickly came under attack from the local white labouring class. At $1.25 to $1.50 per day, Chinese labour would halve his costs, the contractor explained. It was a defence that few accepted, and McDougall's action bristled workers and also community-minded citizens, businessmen, and officials who were trying hard "to stop the growing evil while yet it is in its infancy."[109]

In early January 1887, a citizens' meeting at City Hall appointed a committee, which included Mayor MacLean and Alderman Joseph Humphries, to establish a fund for defraying the expense of returning Chinese "to the place from whence they came." A second committee, also including the mayor, was chosen "to wait upon all employers of Chinese labour for the purpose of inducing them to replace it with white help." Within two days, the committee had convinced twenty or so West End workers to decamp and sail away to Victoria, to the "hearty cheers" of "fully 600 citizens."[110] Others were escorted to the road to New Westminster, while substitute Chinese workers from Victoria quickly sensed the reception they would get in Vancouver and sailed on to Port Moody.

The intimidation strategy was quickly strengthened and diversified. A joint-stock company was formed to buy out Chinese-owned laundries in the Old Granville Townsite; a vegetable ranch at False Creek was said to have been vacated, and it was rumoured that some of the more eager citizens raided Alderman Hamilton's house and packed off his two houseboys on the steamer to Victoria.[111]

One Chinese "boss," Lew Shew, refused to be harassed in this fashion, and in late January he retained a lawyer to bring action against Mayor MacLean, Alderman Humphries, and others on the new citizens' committees, for molestation he allegedly suffered in an attempt to expel him from the city limits. Although the defendants were exonerated, Lew Shew and "McDougall Chinee," as the clearance contractor became dubbed, won an injunction from the BC Supreme Court discouraging similar acts of expulsion in the future.[112] Armed with this injunction, and determined to complete his contract to clear the Brighouse Estate, McDougall brought back the necessary labour in February 1887, only to find that an anti-Chinese league had been formed with the specific intention of preventing Chinese from relocating within the city limits. Popular support for anti-Chinese activities had grown extensively in the weeks since the citizens' committees were formed. During four well-attended January meetings at City Hall, various means of soliciting pledges from the community had been devised to prevent Chinese securing another foothold. When it was rumoured that Chinese were en route from Victoria, some 300 people had sped to the wharf.[113] Citizens had also continued to paint crosses on establishments that were said to deal with Chinese.]

It was into this atmosphere of anxiety and growing antagonism that the Brighouse Estate workers returned, with the defiant "McDougall Chinee" no doubt preparing for strong reaction, but not quite for what transpired on 24 February 1887. On that evening, the frustration of residents came to a head at a crammed public meeting at City Hall. Unimpeded by local police, approximately 300 angry men surged from the meeting to the camps of sleeping workers at Coal Harbour, with their own solution to the Chinese presence in mind. Shanties were pulled down, bedding, clothing, and provisions thrown into a fire, and some twenty-five workers, it was said by the press, "kicked and knocked about." Around midnight a smaller mob completed the deed at Carrall Street, where the homes of some ninety Chinese residents were burnt or damaged.

The following day, Chinese living in the vicinity of Carrall Street were notified to leave the city. They agreed to do so peaceably on condition that one person could be left in charge of each store. With those terms met, the settlers were carried off to New Westminster. Three rioters (a logger, a milkman, and a clerk) were arrested, given bail by Magistrate J. Blake (a member of the original citizens' committee), and later discharged for what was said to be lack of evidence. The riot marked the first act of concerted physical violence against the Chinese in Canada. In Victoria, the events of 24 February drew official disapproval, despite the obvious sympathy of the legislature and the province's difficulty in translating its own political will into legal action. Even anti-Chinese champion John Robson said that while Vancouver's civic authorities possessed ample powers, they had "strangely and persistently refrained from exercising them in upholding the law."[114]

Attorney-General Davie immediately drafted urgent legislation. A Bill to Preserve the Peace in Vancouver passed through all three readings in the house in one day, effectively suspending the city's charter and annulling its judicial powers.[115] Much to the resentment of Vancouver's mayor and council, some forty special constables were also sent from Victoria to take charge of what the attorney-general described as a decline into "mob rule."

Ironically, then, the protection of a reluctant provincial government allowed the immigrants from China to return to Vancouver and re-establish residence. Most returned to the vicinity of Carrall and Dupont streets on district lot 196, the land some had been expelled from. Many of the Brighouse labourers also gravitated there after they finally completed the clearing contract in 1888. By 1889, according to Henderson's *British Columbia Directory* published in Victoria in that year, the settlers of Chinese origin had become concentrated in the vicinity of Dupont and Carrall streets. While nine of fourteen Chinese laundries were scattered through the Old Granville Townsite and district lot 196, the twenty-nine Chinese companies and merchant premises were confined almost entirely to Dupont and Carrall streets. Of the merchants, five were grocers, three owned general stores, one was a shoemaker, one was a labour contractor, one owned a store, and the trades of the others were not specified. A Chinese school was located at 115 Hastings Street. No mention was made in the directory of the sundry shacks of labourers, but many were located on the tidal flat on block 14 with good access to industrial and commercial wharfs, industrial shops, the gas works, and the Royal City Planing Mill, built in 1886. By 1892, this spatial pattern was consolidated, as was the relative concentration of Chinese in Vancouver (see Map 1).

The area of concentrated settlement was a depressed, swampy district, covered at high tide by the waters of False Creek, which flowed closest to Burrard Inlet between Carrall and Columbia streets. At Hastings and Carrall streets, a rocky outcrop further enclosed and protected the area, the adverse physical character of which parallelled its residents' marginal cultural, legal, and economic status. The spatial referent of the category "Chinese" was not a legislated one, however; settlers from China did not locate in a concentrated pattern through formal civic suasion or restrictive covenant. When the city attempted to rid Stanley Park of some Chinese squatters by such direct means in the years 1888–90, Attorney-General Davie was quick to query its jurisdictional competence. (City council in turn advised the board of health to indict the squatters as a public nuisance to facilitate their removal.)[116]

WHAT IS CLEAR, HOWEVER, from events in early Vancouver, is that the council was eager to lend whatever moral authority it could to the

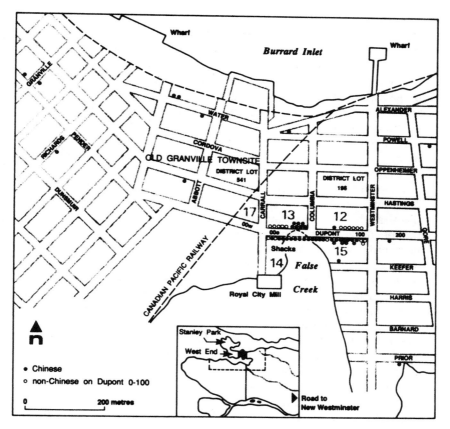

Map 1
Distribution of Chinese in Vancouver, 1892
Source: Based on *Williams' Illustrated Official British Columbia Directory*, 1892

anti-Chinese vendetta. There is little doubt that the force with which the racial category was being wielded in Vancouver, with the support (or in the case of the riot, the blind eye) of City Hall, convinced many Chinese of the wisdom of locating together, especially after 1887. This was acknowledged by at least some participants in both the 1885 and 1901 royal commissions. Mr Justice Henry Crease of the BC Supreme Court said in 1885 that "their tendency to congregate ... in British Columbia is directly owing to the fact that as foreigners, held in dangerous disesteem by an active section of whites, they naturally cling together for protection and support."[117] At the 1901 commission, the solicitor for the Chinese Board of Trade said that "the Chinese live in aggregation, but this is more a matter of necessity than choice."

Won Alexander Cumyow of Vancouver also claimed that the chief reason for the congregation of Chinese in one part of the city was companionship. "The Chinese know that the white people have had no friendly feeling towards them for a number of years," he said.[118]

Of course, some immigrants from China may well have preferred to distance themselves from Europeans. Sharing a district with fellow countrymen would probably have been an attractive option in the circumstances for some. But it seems unlikely that the majority of merchants, at least, chose to live beneath their often substantial means in a waterlogged district. And even if they elected to live near the captive market of labourers they had at their disposal, this decision too must be situated within the culture of race and the host of secondary effects such a context had from the time the Chinese were disenfranchised. Important among the effects was the creation of a pool of single and poorly paid men who were dependent on Chinese merchants for their employment, their lodgings, and sometimes their head-tax payment.

We have seen that the emergence of this enclave in Vancouver resulted from a complex set of factors. While the protection afforded by the state partly enabled formation of the district, state action also constrained Chinese people to live together. In Vancouver, no less than in other parts of British Columbia, there were limits on how far and by what means the idea of a Chinese race could be implemented. The upshot of the provincial intervention in civic affairs in 1887 – and ultimately the dominion control over provincial initiatives – was that the city of Vancouver was forced to accept the Chinese presence. Canada's senior politicians respected not only the quest for a European society but also the reputedly "Anglo-Saxon" virtues of justice, fair play, and law and order. In a sense, therefore, the boundaries of the district of settlers from China signified the limits to the popular implementation of the race idea. Within the meagre confines of a few sodden streets, Chinese people would be afforded the minimal right to a livelihood and property. (This principle was affirmed again in 1907, when the dominion government, on the advice of imperial authorities, stepped in to compensate Vancouver's Chinese residents for property damage suffered in another, more serious riot.[119])

The complexities surrounding the origins of the Chinese enclave in Vancouver, and indeed of the Chinese experience in early British Columbia, suggest that European hegemony cannot be conceptualized as a structure implanted somehow from above or outside the contingencies of particular settings. What we have seen are details of the historical process by which cultural domination was negotiated in Canada and Vancouver, its contradictory expression at different levels of state, and the judicial limits within which it was elaborated.

Within such limits, civic authorities would come to ensure that if a Chinese claim to Vancouver did exist, it would assuredly be a contested one. Certainly the tenor of civic attitudes did not change as a result of Victoria's reprimand of 1887. That intervention affected the city's means, but not the end, of securing a "white" cultural and institutional fabric for Vancouver. When anti-Chinese agitation peaked again in the late 1890s, the municipality symbolically led the movement with public meetings at City Hall.[120] The anti-Chinese league of 1896 boasted many politicians among its members, including the mayor, five aldermen, some ex-aldermen, and a number of members of parliament. In 1897, Mayor J. Templeton presided over the league's meetings, including one convened to lobby Ottawa for an increase in the head tax. Alderman Nicolai Schou circulated a petition calling for a prohibitive Chinese head tax – enrolling some 3,000 signatures in Vancouver. Through such efforts, the city became the focus of the anti-Chinese movement both in British Columbia and in Canada as a whole, and many politicians from Victoria, Nanaimo, and New Westminster attended the league's meetings. Meanwhile, Vancouver's major daily newspaper had this to say about a contingent of English settlers in 1902: "They are our own kith and kin ... entertaining for British laws and customs and for the British flag the same respect which we ourselves hold."[121]

CONCLUSION

This chapter has examined the roles of the different levels of Canadian government in shaping the definition and status of immigrants from China in British Columbia in the late nineteenth century. For governing élites, no less than other members of Canadian society, "John Chinaman" stood as the image of all men and women from China. This typification can be traced to the modern idea of race which collapsed class and gender divisions among Chinese and assimilated an ancient and medieval baggage of distinctions between "West" and "East," civilized and barbarian, master and slave, Christian and heathen, white and non-white into a doctrine of discrete and immutable types. By the mid-nineteenth century, with British power straddling the globe, the oppositions had congealed into an ideological structure of formidable rigidity. Darwinism was adapted to lend scientific status to the views that there existed such things as races; that there were lower and higher races, progressive and non-progressive races ("John" being a prime example of the latter); and that a natural antipathy engendered conflict between the races. This influential ideology of "difference" informed the outlook of white British Columbians from the 1870s, when settlers from China began arriving there. Thirty years later, despite the fact that people of Chinese origin constituted less than half of one per cent of Canada's population, it was entrenched in the ethos and institutions of the province, and a whole epistemology of separation had been built between "Chinese" and "whites."

The state played a crucial role in sponsoring and enforcing this arbitrary distinction of race as a line of division around which both rhetoric and practice were directed. After the province joined a confederated Canada, the social cleavage was etched firmly as politicians began to stake out a *British* British Columbia. One of the means by which they marked the limits of, and boosted collective legitimacy for, their staked claim was by imposing disabilities on the out-group labelled "Chinese." They did so not out of irrational prejudice, nor as blind agents of capital, but as active propagators of a legally bound cultural hegemony. Greater caution was exercised in Ottawa, but eventually dominion politicians were content to forfeit an open immigration policy in the interests of control over Chinese entry. At the local level, Vancouver's city council gave moral force to racial categorization through its support for strategies, including violence, to rid the city of Chinese. Its leadership was an important factor in setting the context for a settlement that, as we shall see further in the following chapter, gave concrete form to the concept of a "Chinese race."

The Canadian state's institutional authority carried a stamp of legitimacy that collective opinion of the time lacked. Through a combination of "proactive" and reactive measures, the levels of government rendered the idea of a Chinese race a social fact of considerable material consequence, both for those so defined and for white society. By the close of the nineteenth century, "John's" perceived threat to this British settler society had achieved a magnitude that prompted the intervention of all three levels of government, the momentum of which was to resound through the decades to come.

CHAPTER THREE

Constructing Race through Place – community. and Practice, 1886–1920

In 1902, dominion royal commissioners Roger Chute, Christopher Foley, and Daniel Munn summed up their findings concerning Chinese labourers in British Columbia with these words:

They come from southern China ... with customs, habits and modes of life fixed and unalterable, resulting from an ancient and effete civilization. They form, on their arrival, a community within a community, separate and apart, a foreign substance within but not of our body politic, with no love for our laws or institutions; a people that cannot assimilate and become an integral part of our race and nation. With their habits of overcrowding, and an utter disregard for all sanitary laws, they are a continual menace to health. From a moral and social point of view, living as they do without home life, schools or churches, and so nearly approaching a servile class, their effect upon the rest of the community is bad ... Upon this point there was entire unanimity.[1]

It would be easy to interpret the commissioners' words as further evidence, if more were needed, of the weight of racial discrimination in British Columbia at the turn of the century. Like many other official utterances of the period, their words strengthen the claim that Chinese settlers were subjected to many forms of victimization at the hands of the European community. Chapter 2 attempted to take the analysis of the "Chinese" in early British Columbia beyond the level of white attitudes, however, to examine the ideology behind sentiments such as the commissioners'. In particular, the chapter addressed the official means by which the paradigm of race was sanctioned and "John Chinaman" defined and disempowered in the province.

As was pointed out in chapter 1, the study of racial concepts should not be restricted to the behaviour of historical actors. It is important to show how such concepts become linked reciprocally to the material world. Government agents mediated this relation, as we have seen, and at the local level the exercise of cultural domination served in part to inscribe in Vancouver's territory the premise of a Chinese race. Henceforth, the settlement at Dupont Street became a critical nexus through which racial ideology was structured and realized. China-town has existed on the ground, as we have observed, and it has also been a European concept, as this chapter will argue, one made up of images which screened the enclave as "a foreign substance, within but not of our body politic." The "ideal" and the "material" have been mutually confirming axes, then, in this story of the historical inter-connections among race, place, government, and power in one West-ern setting. But let us first look further at the Chinese enclave discussed in the last chapter.

community.

THE SETTLEMENT AT DUPONT STREET

During the first decade of the twentieth century, a neighbourhood of predominantly "Chinese" residents developed in inner Vancouver. It was bounded by Carrall Street on the west (until 1904), Hastings Street to the north, Columbia and Westminster streets on the east, and False Creek on the south. Only a small minority lived in other areas of the city (see Maps 2 and 3). In 1901, the district housed an estimated 2,053 men, twenty-seven women, and twenty-six children.[2] The year before, the city's health inspector counted 1,500 inmates in 105 boarding-houses in the Dupont Street area, making for a density of approximately fourteen per house.[3] Sixteen of the women were wives of merchants and eight of labourers, while the single women performed household chores for merchant families, were home seam-stresses for Chinese tailors, or were prostitutes. A tiny minority of women worked for wage labour in the 1900s and 1910s.[4] The com-munity rarely supported its total number of residents at any one time, however. Much labouring work, especially in the Lower Mainland canneries, was seasonal.

The most permanent settlers in 1901 were the 143 merchants, whose commercial enterprises served and were supported by the local Chinese community and, in the case of silk and shoe retailers and tailors, by some non-Chinese. The merchants included fifteen greengrocers, three rice millers, eight manufacturing clothiers, eight importers and exporters, two silk merchants, two custom tailors, and various numbers of butchers and poultry dealers, general retailers, labour contractors, lodging-house owners and managers, pawnbrokers, intelligence officers, opium manufacturers, and barbers.[5] Often, owners amassed the necessary capital for their ventures through various forms of partnership. In particular, rotating credit associations, organized along lines of clan or locality affiliation, offered mutual credit to members.[6] By 1911, the number of Chinese businesses in Vancouver had trebled from 71 to 236.[7]

Wage labour was sold both inside and outside the Chinese community. In 1901, those working outside the community included over 260 Chinese "houseboys," a good many cooks and cleaners in hotels, itinerant vegetable pedlars, brickyard and market-garden workers, approximately 550 cannery workers, and 172 who worked in the city's lumber mills. (By 1908, the number employed in Vancouver's saw, shingle, and planing mills had increased to 1,500, or just over a quarter of the Chinese-origin population in the city for that year.[8]) Others worked for Chinese "bosses" who depended on the labour of their countrymen. In 1901, for example, 100 worked for tailoring firms producing overalls, suits, coats, and silk products, while almost 200 were employed in the Chinese laundry trade. That line of business was popular among Chinese because it required only a small outlay of capital and depended heavily on manual labour, and Chinese had established an early comparative advantage in the trade. Other labourers found work in the Chinese community in construction, restaurants, and miscellaneous jobs such as rag collection for mattress and furniture dealers.

Class distinctions within the Chinese community were pronounced, and perhaps even more rigid than in the European community, given the relative poverty of Chinese workers. On the basis of unusually detailed data collected by the dominion deputy minister of labour, William Lyon Mackenzie King, in 1907, one author has constructed a pyramid of economic power in Vancouver's Chinese community.[9] At its apex, the pyramid featured the four firms of Sam Kee, Gim Lee Yuen, Lee Yuen, and Hip Tuck Luck, which each earned between $150,000 and $180,000 annually, or six times the average income of two-thirds of Chinese businesses in Vancouver. Their main interests included importing and exporting, real estate investment, opium manufacture, labour contracting, and steamship commissions. At the second highest tier, Yee placed five merchants who earned between $66,000 and $85,000 per year for importing and supplying wholesale provisions to canneries. A diverse group of sixteen businesses, earning between $31,000 and $55,000 annually, comprised the third level, while thirty-six firms with incomes ranging from $1,000 to $30,000 made up the base. Between them, these mer-

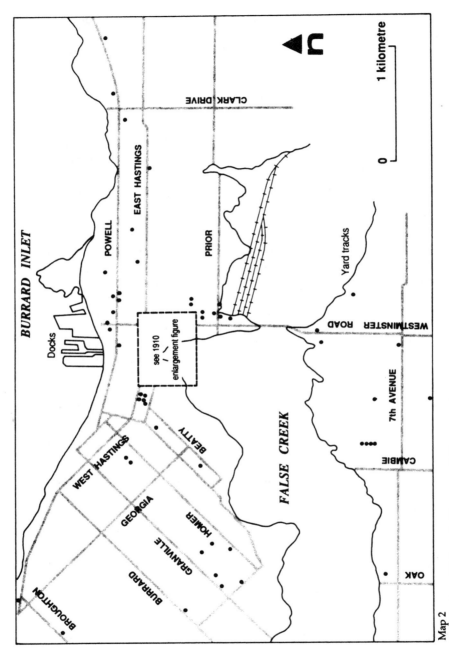

Map 2
Distribution of Chinese in Vancouver, 1910
Source: Based on *Henderson's Directory, British Columbia,* 1910

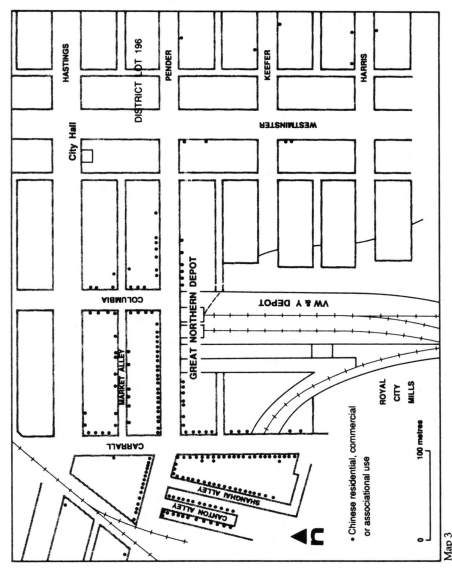

Map 3
Chinatown Area, 1910 (Detail of Map 2)
Source: Based on *Henderson's Directory*, 1910

Text within the figure:

HASTINGS

DISTRICT LOT 196

City Hall

PENDER

KEEFER

HARRIS

WESTMINSTER

COLUMBIA

MARKET ALLEY

GREAT NORTHERN DEPOT

VW & Y DEPOT

CARRALL

SHANGHAI ALLEY

CANTON ALLEY

ROYAL CITY MILLS

N

• Chinese residential, commercial or associational use

0   100 metres

chants built a sub-economy that was "self sufficient to the degree
that it provided its inhabitants with a full range of services including
restaurants, lodgings, employment contractors, barbers and clothing."[10]

As in many overseas Chinese communities, interlocking loci of
power linked members of the merchant élite of Vancouver's Chinese
population to each other. In 1889, members of the Lee Yuen and Sam
Kee companies established a branch of the Chinese Benevolent Association (CBA), in part to support destitute railway workers, although
the association was not formally incorporated until 1906.[11] In 1896,
the separate Chinese chambers of commerce amalgamated as the
Chinese Board of Trade at 5 Dupont Street, growing to forty-seven
member firms by 1901. The board's leaders included Yip Sang and
Lum Duck-shew from the Gim Lee Yuen Co.[12] Three years later, Won
Alexander Cumyow, a BC-born labour contractor and court interpreter, founded the influential Empire Reform Association on Columbia Avenue; a women's counterpart, composed mainly of merchants'
wives, was formed in 1903. By 1910, 90 per cent of Chinese women
in Vancouver belonged to the association, while in the same year
another community-based organization, the Chinese Women's Missionary Band of Vancouver, had forty members.[13]

The merchants also established the property base for a "Chinese"
district in Vancouver. For them, the area became a field of investment
as much as a social community of families and homes.[14] The first
legal claim to the area was made in 1892 with the purchase of lot 25,
block 13, district lot 196. The acquisition was made through a non-
Chinese mortgaging institution, as became customary in subsequent
purchases. By 1901, in the area called "Chinatown" by the royal commission, the total assessed value of real property was $260,255, of
which $67,255 worth was in Chinese hands. Seven years later, Chi-
nese ownership of land, stores, houses, and stock in the district was
estimated at $2 million.[15] Of this, Gim Lee Yuen owned nine lots,
forming three distinct sites in the area; the company of Wing Sang,
sixteen lots, including the eleven lots of Canton Alley; Lee Yuen, two
lots; and Sam Kee, various others. The firms also invested in properties outside Chinatown,[16] but in the first decade of the century
theirs were the purchases that accounted to a large extent for the
physical expansion of the "Chinese" district. Businesses and lodgings
spread along Carrall Street, north toward Hastings Street, south
toward False Creek, and west along Pender Street.[17] Claim was later
made to the 100- and 200- blocks on East Pender Street (formerly
Dupont Street), and by 1914, Chinese in Vancouver had purchased
twenty-one of the twenty-four separate pieces of property in the forty-

three lots of the unit block and the 100- block on East Pender Street and the unit block at West Pender and Carrall streets.[18]

The community of Chinese pioneers in Vancouver was economically differentiated into a small élite of well-to-do merchants and their wives, a significant minority of small businessmen, and a large number of workers. Family life was the preserve of a minuscule proportion of the merchant sector who could afford the onerous head tax and whose often elegant living conditions set them widely apart from the less privileged "bachelors." (In 1910, a reporter from the *Province* newspaper visited one "beautifully neat" house and wrote glowingly of stained-glass doors that opened onto a sheltered balcony, carved wood cabinets, tasteful furnishings with a "combination of Oriental and European ideas," and a large print of Confucius.[19])

Outside these few merchants, the constraints on family settlement imposed by Ottawa's head tax system and other disabilities were very real. Won Alexander Cumyow told the royal commissioners of 1901 about the loneliness of many Chinese men in Vancouver. "A large proportion of them would bring their families here," he said, "were it not for the unfriendly reception ... which creates an unsettled feeling." A Nanaimo market gardener told the same commission: "I have been here 12 years. My wife and two children are in China ... I would like to bring my wife and children here ... The people in this country talk so much against the Chinese I don't care to bring them here."[20] The impact of such factors is illustrated by the fact that in 1907 just ninety-eight "Chinese" children were enrolled at Vancouver's schools.[21]

For the impoverished, then, a rather circumscribed life was spent within the confines of the Dupont Street district. China's statesman, Liang Ch'i-ch'ao, described their plight as very "distressed and cramped" during a visit to Vancouver in 1903. "Their situation is pitiable beyond description," he said.[22] The Chinese Theatre off Carrall Street and the Chinese Opera House built in the late 1890s probably relieved the cheerless circumstances for some, gambling provided a forum for socializing (and large profits to operators), and the Chinese missions no doubt helped comfort their small number of converts. There were also Chinese New Year's festivities that united the community in celebration once a year, at least for those who did not return to China for the event (as many did), and Chinese-language newspapers, the first of which, the daily *Chinese Times*, was established by the Ying Wang Bo Publishing Co. in 1894. Notwithstanding the social focus assisted by these activities, the material reality of many workers' lives was long working hours, a small room with a bunk, a table, and a stove, and a harsh routine relieved by

Community.

gatherings with countrymen in the lodging-house common room. Such was the marginal territory from which Vancouver's Chinese population launched their contested claim to Canadian life in the twentieth century.

"CHINATOWN" AS A EUROPEAN CONCEPT

The home to the Chinese pioneers of Vancouver was a place of considerable resonance in the minds of other settlers in the city. It drew no neutral response from them; rather it was known and evaluated, from the early days of white settlement, as "Chinatown." This, in turn, prompts an important question: whose term, indeed in one sense, whose place, was this? As noted in chapter 1, no corresponding unit of knowledge called "Anglotown" existed in local parlance, nor were the concentrations of southern Europeans in Strathcona explicitly defined as discrete places. In the case of Chinese, however, "Chinatown" was accepted vocabulary. The *Daily Colonist* in Victoria, for example, reported in 1860 that 264 Chinese arrived from Hong Kong and "finally camped on Cumberland Street near Chinatown."[23] Scholars have used the same terminology. The most recent history of Canada's Chinatowns, for example, writes that the "cluster of Chinese labourers and stores in one location constitute[s] the nucleus of a budding Chinatown."[24]

Of course, the mere word "Chinatown" is not in itself important. The simple existence of a label is not controversial per se; the issues raised here are neither semantic or pedantic. What is significant is the meaning the term acquired and the functions it performed. In 1885, Commissioner Chapleau described to the House of Commons his view of Chinatown: "The Chinese custom of living in quarters of their own – in China towns," he said, "is attended with evils, such as the depreciation of property, and, owing to their habits of lodging crowded quarters and accumulating filth, is offensive if not likely to breed disease."[25] After his visit to California in 1884, Chapleau used these words in his report to the Royal Commission on Chinese Immigration: "Had Dante been able to visit Chinatown, San Francisco, he would have added yet darker strokes of horror to his inferno."

Well before any substantial settlement of Chinese was identified as such in Vancouver, then, a "place" for them already had a distinct reality in the consciousness of Europeans. Californian gold-diggers were probably the most direct source, along with written interpretations of the Chinese presence in the New World. Many Californian witnesses at the 1885 royal commission, for example, referred to "Chi-

natown" in their testimony and told British Columbians what to
expect. "The aggregation of Chinese in any city or town in my opinion, is a sort of moral blight," said Arthur Briggs, president of the
Immigration Association of California. "You can form a better idea
of their habits by going into Chinatown than any one can give you
by talking." The evidence of such witnesses was so consistent, Chapleau concluded, because "the Chinaman seems to be the same everywhere."[26]

Certainly the Dupont Street area in Vancouver was thought by
white residents to be the product of qualities intrinsic to those "saffron coloured sons of the East," in the words of the *Vancouver News*
of 3 June 1886. Citizens seemed to believe that the Chinese district
was a natural outcome of the "herd instinct" of the "clannish Chinese" with their "habit of huddling in limited quarters of their own,
directly opposed to our conceptions of civilized progress, morality
and hygiene."[27] As a separate (and inferior) race who "scorn our civilization, who scorn our morals, who scorn our Christianity and who
live amongst themselves," the Chinese gravitated to a settlement
where they could express their unique mode of living, it was claimed.

It was just as Commissioner Chapleau had anticipated in 1885. He
had observed that, unlike the more familiar situation where "those
who inhabit Whitechapel are the dregs of a population, thousands
of whom live surrounded by the most refined civilization ... Chinese
immigrants will herd together in a quarter of their own,"[28] and in a
"most unenviable neighbourhood" at that, he told the House of Commons the same year.[29] There was a style of living that all classes of
Chinese possessed, certain uniquely "Chinese" habits that accounted
for the concentration, the commissioner remarked. Furthermore, their
mode of life and sanitary standards were such that – in a twist of
Darwinist logic – they might eventually subvert or contaminate the
superior white race if not carefully monitored. "The air is polluted
by disgusting offal with which they are surrounded," Chapleau
warned after his Californian investigation, "and vile accumulations
are apt to spread fever and sickness in the neighbourhood which in
the end may affect extensive districts."[30] In short, Chinese settlement
was an "ulcer," the commissioner told the House of Commons in
1885, "lodged like a piece of wood in the tissues of the human body,
which unless treated must cause disease in the places around it and
ultimately to the whole body."[31]

THE DIAGNOSIS ALREADY having been made, how did respective officials of the city of Vancouver confront Dupont Street? How did they

manage "Chinatown" and invest it, through their practices and rhetoric, with the authority of some natural truth? The answer to those
questions may be divided into two parts; the first concerns the European image of Chinatown as an unsanitary sink, and the second
deals with the perception of Chinatown as a morally aberrant community. These interpretations stemmed from an intellectual climate
and a set of interests that combined under the régime of European
hegemony we are tracing for Vancouver. The components of the Chinatown idea were certainly powerful calls to action for local administrators who wanted to advance their political legitimacy and justify
white ascendancy over the alien Chinese. In so doing, they lent their
support to the concepts of a Chinese race and place and to the process by which Chinese were marginalized in Vancouver's society and
space.

"CELESTIAL CESSPOOL": SANITARY DIMENSIONS

Shortly before the anti-Chinese riot of 1887, a reporter for the *Vancouver News* observed that at False Creek "an evil is only just beginning to take shape," one that risked becoming "so well defined that
it will be next to impossible to expunge" if the city delayed taking
action against it.[32] A month later, a reporter for the same paper wrote:
"The China Town where the Celestials congregate is an eyesore to
civilization." If the city could be "aroused to the necessity of checking
the abuse of sanitary laws which is invariably a concomitant of the
Chinese [it] will help materially in preventing the Mongolian settlement from becoming permanent."[33] Four months later, a row of "hate-
ful haunts" on Carrall Street was singled out for the attention of
council. There, warned the *News*, "in the nucleus of the pest-produc-
ing Chinese quarter ... strict surveillance by the City will be necessary to prevent the spread of this curse."

TRUE TO CHAPLEAU'S IMAGE OF the "ulcer," it was the ordinary Chinese
wash-houses scattered over the city that became the first targets of
civic concern in Vancouver. Their dispersal began to attract people's
attention in the first decade after the city's incorporation, when residential sorting was beginning. In 1889, ten of the fourteen Chinese-
owned laundries in Vancouver were located outside "Chinatown" to
serve the city-wide market they had cornered.[34] For a "race" so dirty,
there was certainly plenty of work to be had in the business of clean-

liness! Yet despite the extensive service they offered, the medical health officer of 1900 found the Chinese wash-house "an unmixed evil, an unmitigated nuisance," and, from the late nineteenth century on, council sought ways to restrict Chinese-operated laundries to "locations least offensive to the public."[35]

Early attempts to achieve this goal met similar legal problems to those discussed in the previous chapter. In an important precedent, Mock Fee successfully appealed to the Supreme Court against the city's refusal to renew his pawnbroker's licence in 1888. In upholding the appeal, the court ruled that neither the provincial legislature nor a municipality could "deprive generally, particular nationalities or individuals of the capacity to take out municipal trade licences."[36]

Thus denied the strategy of licence restriction, the city devised indirect measures to confront the encroaching wash-houses. The most effective was Alderman W. McGuigan's by-law of 1893, which specified spatial boundaries beyond which laundries could not be erected, "that is to say beyond Dupont Street and 120 feet on Columbia Avenue and Carrall Street, southerly from Hastings."[37] Numerous residents in areas beyond the limits made sure that the city enforced the by-law in precisely the way its architects had intended. For example, twenty-eight ratepayers from the West End complained to council in 1900 that the laundry at 1107 Hornby Street will "give this part of the city a set-back that it will not get over. If this nuisance cannot be put down we would be as well living in China-town on Dupont Street and this would hardly be a nice place to bring up a family of small children."[38] Council duly instructed the relevant authorities to stop the erection of the wash-house. McGuigan's by-law remained in place for fifteen years, until 1908, when Alderman Stewart applied to open a steam laundry outside the by-law's boundaries.

Checks on location were not the only form of civic targeting of the Chinese wash-house. In March 1900, Health and Plumbing Inspector Marrion insisted on compulsory smallpox vaccination for Chinese laundrymen.[39] In December of the same year, the Vancouver Trades and Labour Council secured a victory over Chinese launderers when a new Sunday observance by-law required laundries to close on Sundays.[40] Another by-law passed the same month prevented clothes being exposed to the open air for drying, a clause which operated in favour of the newer, non-Chinese steam laundries (including those of Alderman Stewart).[41] By 1904, in an attempt to "drive Chinamen out of the trade," to use the words of the counsel for several Chinese laundrymen, council increased the annual licence fee for laundry operations from $10 to $50.[42]

CIVIC AUTHORITIES DID NOT confine their scrutiny of the "Chinese" to the laundry question. During the 1890s an equally vigorous campaign was launched, this time in the name of sanitary reform, on the wooden shacks of the Dupont Street settlement. In 1890, fear of cholera gripped Vancouver's residents, and the local press demanded that council take action against the people of Dupont Street, given that "in Chinese style ... they will not fall into line for the purpose of maintaining cleanliness. Imagine cholera or any other deadly disease once getting into their midst," a news report stated.[43] The discovery of two alleged Chinese lepers in 1891 inflamed this fear and fuelled proscriptions against the entire neighbourhood. "I defy any writer to pen-picture that awful place," one citizen wrote in a letter to the editor in 1893. "The degraded humanity from the Orient, more beastly than human, live in places that a hog would die in stench of."[44]

The legislative arm of European sentiment was quick to act on such claims. Chinatown was for the city the embodiment of an inferior mode of existence that represented a mandate for action. One of the city's most significant acts came in the mid-1890s, when council formally designated "Chinatown" an official entity in the medical health officer's rounds and health committee reports. Along with water, sewerage, scavenging, infectious disease, slaughter houses, and pig ranches, Chinatown was listed as a separate category and assigned a special officer to supervise it under the by-laws.[45] One such officer reported in 1895: "In my inspections of Chinatown this year, I have not observed any improvement in the cleanliness of the dwellings and surroundings. The former are becoming increasingly dilapidated and filthy and the latter, together with the shores of False Creek, are more and more saturated with manurial refuse and garbage ... All the cabins on the foreshore should be condemned and destroyed. In no other way is it possible to abate the nuisance arising from the constant deposition of filth and refuse by the occupants. At present they cannot be other than a standing menace to public health."[46]

Chinatown elicited a similar response from Medical Health Officer Thomas the following year: "All the buildings on the south side of Dupont Street between Carrall and Columbia are standing over a huge cesspool," he stated (without mention of the fact that Dupont Street had not been connected with public sewers). Furthermore, "there is abundant evidence of the continued deposition of refuse and filth of all kinds with the result that the atmosphere of the neighbourhood is saturated with evil odours."[47] The city's health records of the period are strewn with similar graphic accounts from officials charged with inspecting the vicinity.

In response to these descriptions and to an examination of the south side of Dupont Street by city health officials in 1896, four rows of wooden shacks and cottages in blocks 13 and 14 of district lot 196 were destroyed in the latter part of the decade.[48] In 1897, Thomas recommended the destruction of more shacks on Dupont Street because of their alleged health risk, while two years later, the *World* reported: "Another lot of Chinese shacks, on Carrall Street this time, will be destroyed ... and soon there will be that much less to crowd Chinatown."[49] Mayor Garden ventured to Dupont Street that year, and soon after his visit Marrion served notices to some owners on blocks 13 and 14 under the newly enacted Boarding House Bylaw. Like others before it, the by-law had been passed, without being so framed, "in order to secure better regulation and supervision in the case of Chinese dwelling places."[50]

Health Inspector Robert Marrion adopted a firm stance toward Chinatown from the time of his appointment in 1893. "The Chinese method of living is totally different to that of white people," he claimed in 1901. "The Japs try to obey the laws, but the Chinese are always on the lookout to evade them."[51] He believed that the Chinese required "constant vigilance," and he set about providing just that. In 1902, for example, Chinese merchants were forced to expand their operations to the southern side of Hastings Street, so particular was Marrion about density and sanitation by-laws in Chinatown.[52] "The whole appearance of things is enough to shock the sensibilities of a European and there is no doubt that the inspector's action will be supported," said one journalist.[53] Of course, in the minds of Marrion and the reporter, the "whole appearance of things" had little to do with the constraints on Chinese family settlement, job and pay discrimination, or the physical condition of the tidal flats. Rather, such "things" could be explained, as Marrion told the commissioners in 1901, by "the difficulty to get Chinese people to adopt sanitary methods ... Even when every convenience is provided, Chinese are generally dirtier than whites." While "the whole of Chinatown is governed by bylaws the same as any other part of the city," he said, "it takes more to enforce sanitary regulations there than in a similar area in any other part of the city."[54]

Though blunt, Marrion's statements were entirely conformist for his day; he spoke not out of some irrational prejudice or unfortunate flaw in the human psyche, but rather in the accepted vocabulary for describing the district that housed these pioneers to Vancouver. Identity and place were inextricably conflated in European consciousness, and the process of racial classification was corroborated with every official expedition.

Given this nearly universal scheme by which Chinatown was comprehended, it was remarkable for a non-Chinese to argue in a letter to the editor in 1896: "It would be extremely difficult, if not impossible, even in the worst Chinese quarter, to parallel the state of affairs revealed amongst some white men in our city not so long ago in some of the cabins behind the Imperial Opera-House."[55] Even this correspondent, however, found it natural to use conditions in Chinatown as a referent against which to measure the evils of which he complained.

Other evidence reveals that the bias of the municipal authorities' attention to sanitary matters in Dupont Street stemmed from their respect for, and manipulation of, the race idea. Medical Health Officer I. Maclean was convinced that since China was an "infected" country, "Chinese immigration is the most dangerous element against which we have to contend."[56] Yet no actual evidence that disease originated in Chinatown was ever provided in the health inspectors' reports, in health committee minutes, or in the vigilant local press. The solicitor for the Chinese Board of Trade, Mr A. Taylor, reminded the commissioners in 1901, with the help of city statistics on infectious disease: "No instance is given of the origin of any contagious disease in the Chinatown of either city (Vancouver or Victoria)."[57] A greater proportion of Chinese than non-Chinese died of tuberculosis – in 1900, 50 per cent of the city's tuberculosis victims were Chinese[58] – but, as the Chinese Benevolent Association of Victoria maintained some years later, most cases were contracted in distant mines, and Chinese did not have easy access to special hospitals for sufferers from the disease.

At the same time, a number of Chinese merchants made known their willingness to establish an amenable environment for business and residence. At odds with the typification projected on the area (see Figure 2), the merchants appealed to City Hall for neighbourhood improvement, some of which they undertook themselves. In 1896, for example, a group of Chinese residents lodged a complaint with council about the "bad condition" of Dupont Street and its sidewalks;[59] in 1898, a request was made for a plank crossing over Dupont Street;[60] in 1899, twenty-four firms, including those of Lee Yuen, Sam Kee, and Hip Tuck Lung, requested that Dupont Street be sprinkled twice a day in the summer and that back lanes be repaired;[61] and in 1905, a group of businessmen asked the board of works to pave Shanghai Alley and another petitioned council for improvements to Pender and Hastings streets.[62]

Far from lesser beings steeped in a racially determined standard of living, as most whites viewed the Chinese, or hapless victims of some eternal white prejudice, as the liberal race-relations paradigm

Figure 2
"The Unanswerable Argument"
Source: Saturday Sunset, 10 August 1907

suggests, the entrepreneurial élite of Chinatown often disputed the city's arbitrary actions and used its understanding of civic politics to try to elevate the physical condition and social status of the neighbourhood. Just as earlier discussions about the courts and Ottawa's power of disallowance have shown that European hegemony, though influential, was not unbounded, so the following incidents indicate that white cultural domination in Vancouver did not go uncontested by those it sought to subordinate.

The Lim Dat Co. was so dissatisfied with the city's refuse collection in the area that, in 1906, it applied for a licence to conduct its own street-cleaning operation.[63] Other Chinese merchants were prepared to challenge what they felt were unwarranted municipal encroachments on their neighbourhood. The firm of Jun Kee took the city to the BC Supreme Court in 1897 to claim for damages wrought by a fire lit by the then city engineer. The engineer had been ordered by council to destroy a row of cabins in the vicinity of the firm's property.[64] A Lee Chung appealed to the city in 1890 for compensation for his eleven hogs, destroyed by the health inspector on the alleged grounds they had "hog cholera." The city paid Lee Chung $50.[65] In 1899, the lawyer for Sam Yuen applied for an injunction restraining council from burning a building of his that had been condemned by Marrion.[66] "The Chinese appear to be made for litigation," lamented Marrion in 1901, and in the same year he was granted an order from the health committee of council to visit "the Chinese quarters" at night, so to strengthen his hand in cases of litigation about crowding violations.[67]

THE EUROPEAN INTERPRETATION cast on the area was carried forward in government rhetoric and practices into the new century. In the same month as the savage riot of 1907 in "Celestialland," Inspector Marrion could describe the area in no more original terms than its "fowls, refuse, filth, dead dogs and offal."[68] The point here is not so much that image-makers like Marrion were "wrong," as if the concepts of "Chinese" and "Chinatown" were ghastly errors existing in opposition to some definitive truth. The point rather stems from Foucault, who has argued that what becomes defined as real or "true" is a selective process that is linked in circular relation to the systems of power that produce and sustain it.[69] Such was Marrion's faith in the idea of a foreign and inferior Chinese race that he saw it as his contribution to the making of a European society (and his means of professional mobility) to monitor Chinatown in select ways. His perceptions of Chinatown shaped his actions which themselves vindicated the myths and social relations on which they were predicated.

Certainly the city was not prepared to compromise its idea of some essentially "Chinese" Chinatown in the face of challenges to its authority from the courts. Such obstructions served only to inspire new strategies, so assured were city officials of the integrity of their mission. By 1910, for example, a circle of local officials that included Mayor L.D. Taylor, Chief of Police Chamberlain, Building Inspector S.N. Jarrett, Medical Health Officer Dr F. Underhill, and City Solicitor

MacDonald sought to achieve "full control of conditions in China-town."[70]

The success of Chinese in fighting by-laws, especially with injunc-tions that prevented condemned buildings from being torn down, prompted Vancouver officials to seek wider powers of by-law enforce-ment at the 1910 session of the provincial legislature. Such powers were expected to "avert the legal difficulties which beset the path of the civic authorities in their efforts at the reform of the Chinese quar-ter." Jarrett and Chamberlain were particularly irritated by a require-ment that they produce a search warrant before entering any suspect premises. Chamberlain also protested that police raids on Chinatown were being stymied as "wily Chinese" added "secret partitions and trapdoors" to their buildings. Fortunately for the residents, the leg-islature was not inclined to grant the extended powers demanded. There was no recourse for residents the following year, however, when the city served notice on "two to three dozen buildings ... occupied by a large number of Chinamen" to make way for the track-age required by the Great Northern Railway Co. at the unit block East Pender Street and southward on Carrall Street.[71] This was an early sign of the city's readiness to encourage non-residential func-tions in the Chinatown area.

PERHAPS AS A RESPONSE BY Chinese merchants to this industrial en-croachment, or perhaps on the city's initiative, an attempt was made in 1911 to move Chinatown to a separate location to the east of the existing district. Unfortunately only scant details of this project are available. Apparently three firms, including the real estate syn-dicate Chung Hing Co. and the Chow T. Tonge Co., bought lots worth $167,000 in the East End, where Albert Street was to be "solely reserved" for the Chinese.[72] Council made one or two other prepar-atory decisions, and some sections of the press anticipated that the scheme would provide an opportunity to clear out the tenants of the worst buildings and "force them to move to more respectable quar-ters."[73] However, the city failed to pay the price demanded by the Chinese residents for their original properties, and the project was disbanded.[74]

There were other districts in Vancouver, of actual or perceived low sanitary status, that rivalled the East Pender Street area. In 1914, Inspector Hynes visited a district in the East End that was home to some Italian residents and found conditions as "abominable" as on East Pender. "The condition in the Italian district was filthy ... There is overcrowding in almost every house to an alarming extent. The stench in houses ... was sickening in the extreme."[75] But only the Pender Street settlement was publicly known and defined as a social and spatial unit according to putatively immutable "racial" qualities. Even the much disliked settlement of pioneers from Japan on Powell Street appears to have escaped the crude neighbourhood characterization that gave Chinatown its name in the early decades of the century. There was a widely held view that, although the Japanese were also a foreign "race," their homeland was a potential world power that boasted "qualities" more assimilable to the European cultural tradition than China. (Such a generous view gave way to extreme forms of discrimination against Canadians of Japanese origin by the Second World War.[76])

THE DISTILLED CONCEPT THAT WAS Vancouver's Chinatown was, for the city, a pressing mandate, and well into the twentieth century its actions reinforced the vision and reality of a neighbourhood apart. Almost immediately after the 1914 murder of the wife of well-known West End Railway administrator Charles Millard by Jack Kong, her "China-boy," council led the clamour to have all Chinese removed from the schools. Based solely on the fact that the "boy" had been educated in the school system, council stated its "grave apprehension" at

the prevailing practice of the School Board in permitting children and young men of Oriental race to attend our public schools and to associate with our children of tender years on terms of equality. In the opinion of this Council, such association of the two races must result in a condition detrimental to the future welfare of our children who have nothing to gain, either mentally or morally, by daily association with Orientals. By being indiscriminately thrown into contact with Orientals many years their senior, our children are wantonly exposed to Oriental vices at an age when revolting incidents may be indelibly stamped upon their minds. Furthermore the health of our children is endangered by such close association with Oriental children, many of whom hail from habitations where reasonable sanitation and cleanliness are not only despised but utterly disregarded. In some cases, these Orientals come into our public school classrooms with their apparel polluted with the fumes of noxious drugs and germs of loathsome diseases on their persons.[77]

The possibility of school segregation had been raised some four years earlier in the legislature, with the member for Nanaimo asserting that "forced association" was "degrading and dangerous."[78] However, council's request to Richard McBride's government for

segregation following the Millard murder foundered on legal obstacles, as the city solicitor had warned.[79] The Chinese consul, Lin Shih-
Yuan, publicly denounced council's attempt as a vindictive response
to a single alleged crime and reminded council, as reported by the
Sun, that "next to 'native-born Canadians', the percentage of criminals among Chinese in British Columbia was the lowest."[80]

school segregation

The lack of legal authority to enforce school segregation did not
deter the city from wielding power where it could. The year after the
segregation issue came to a head, the local press described Chinatown as no less than "besieged" in "the battle for morality and health"
being waged by council. The *Sun* saw the opposing forces in a way
that left no doubt about its editorial stance: "Lined up on this side is
the civic authority led by the medical health officer, the building
inspector and the chairman of the Health Committee supported by
the City aldermen. This great civic force has as its ally the law in the
form of health bylaws, building regulations, police officers and pen-
alties, etc. Arrayed against this seemingly formidable army is the
wily Oriental of Chinatown with his fondness for defying the civic
powers in the matter of health ... Civic regulations are dust to the
Chinaman of Chinatown to be stamped underfoot ... For 25 years
the same forces have been at war."[81]

The residents had one valuable ally in Ambassador Lim, the guard-
ian of his countrymen's welfare in Canada. In 1915, Lim had taken
to publishing warnings of health inspections in the *Chinese Times* and
advised owners to apply chloride of lime treatments to ensure that
places were incontestably clean.[82] District Inspector Kinneston had
closed more than forty sleeping apartments in Chinatown in 1914,[83]
and further notices had been served on buildings visited by members
of the health committee in April and October 1915, with instructions
that owners comply with the building by-law regarding interior partitions. Meanwhile, the city engineer was given orders to "demolish
the old shacks bordering on False Creek adjacent to Main Street,"
whose occupants were "loathe to leave."[84] Kinneston was certainly
conscientious, and in 1917 Medical Health Officer Underhill
remarked: "Practically all of this section of the city is occupied by
foreigners who would live in filthy condition but for the daily supervision of the district inspector."[85]

IT IS CLEAR FROM THIS RECORD of local government activities in the
East Pender Street district from the mid-1880s through the 1910s that
the "Chinatown" concept was being inherited by successive administrations whose members traded in the discourse and outlook of

their predecessors. Recurring municipal practices legitimized Europeans' way of seeing people of Chinese origin and their settlement on Pender Street. Chinatown was not only an idea, however. As we saw in chapter 2, it had a concrete referent in the form of a segregated community whose physical presence propped up the selective vision of identity and place we have been examining. State practices not only supported this vision but further inscribed the spatial marginality of the Chinese in Vancouver. Furthermore, the circumstances of Chinese immigration to Canada probably encouraged objectively poor living conditions in many sectors of the community. In that sense, the material reality of Pender Street justified and fulfilled the prophecy of Chapleau's "China town."

It was the mutually reinforcing concepts of race and place, however, and their scope and influence in BC culture, that gave the district its coherence as a discrete place in the consciousness of those with the power to define it. In the eyes of successive civic officials, "Chinatown" signified no less than the encounter between "West" and "East," to be administered and controlled in select ways. Their operative assumption was that Chinatown embodied the vast asymmetry between two civilizations and two races. In that sense, Chinatown was more than a cultural construct of European imagining; it was a political projection through which a divisive system of racial classification was being structured and reproduced.

VICE-TOWN:
MORAL DIMENSIONS

Much as the "West" has defined the "Orient" (as Said has expertly shown in his book *Orientalism*), Vancouver's Chinatown was for its representers a collection of essences that seemed to set the Chinese fundamentally apart. It was a set of absences (non-white, non-Christian, uncivilized, and amoral) that revealed the biases of European cognition and served the social distinctions between insider and outsider that were being made in Vancouver society and space.

Matters of hygiene were only part of the vision and vocabulary out of which a racially defined territory was constructed. Equally significant and perhaps more effective, it will be seen, were moral associations. Because the Chinese were seen as inveterate gamblers, Chinatown was lawless; as the home of opium addicts, the area was a pestilential den; as the home of evil and inscrutable men, it was a morally retrograde prostitution base where white women were lured as slaves. "Is there harm in the Chinaman?" Reverend Dr Fraser asked a meeting of the Asiatic Exclusion League in 1907. "In this city," he

Figure 3
"Vancouver Must Keep This Team"
Source: Saturday Sunset, 1 February 1908

said, "that could be answered with one word, 'Chinatown', with its wickedness unmentionable."[86]

Two city hardliners, Police Magistrate Alexander and Chief of Police Chamberlain, in their everyday business supported a specialized vision of Chinatown that is captured eloquently by a cartoon (see Figure 3) from the *Saturday Sunset* in 1908. As the home of the "racial Other,"[87] Chinatown seems to have signified many of the impulses that Europeans feared and attempted to repress in themselves: gambling, drug addiction, prostitution, slavery in women, licentiousness, and crime. That is, only those aspects of Chinese living in Vancouver that fitted the racial categorization were being filtered (as they were by European communities throughout North America and Australia[88]). Little allusion was made in white Vancouver circles to the distinctions that residents of Chinatown, like all communities, defined among themselves. Such distinctions did not form part of the historically available information about such settlers, and if they were encountered, they tended not to alter the more comforting conflations of homogeneous racial identity and place. Chinatown was a blunt characterization indeed, and as this section sets out to demonstrate, it was one streamlined by the local state and its "moral reform squad," appointed in 1913 to take special charge of the district.

Before this relationship between Chinatown and City Hall is discussed, it seems important to press one question further: why did municipal officials reach the conclusions they did when describing and managing issues of public morality in Chinatown? How was it that Chamberlain and Alexander were concerned with the few elements depicted in the cartoon and not others? The relevance of this question has been obscured by the conventional white-prejudice framework for the study of race relations. As was suggested in chapter 1, that paradigm has tended to explain away such systems of imagery, and racial categories themselves, in some taken-for-granted white predisposition toward non-whites. The familiar chronicle of forms of prejudice, discrimination, and other imperialist sins has obscured the active process by which definitions of identity and place are constructed and reproduced in certain contexts and particular ways, around the idiom of "race."

Or again, economic competition was a major rallying point for anti-Chinese sentiment in British Columbia, as it was in other areas of Chinese settlement.[89] It might be argued that the officials' views originated in a system of economic production that required a racially segmented labour force. But economic competition, too, has been less a primary cause of such sentiment than an outcome of the collective conceptions about the cheap and docile "Chinese" held, and used, by Europeans during a historical conjuncture when capitalist development was being consolidated. Ideological formulations about race have made a powerful and distinct contribution to structures of capitalist inequality and must be examined, as was pointed out in chapter 1, on their own terms.

A different approach would attempt to expose the shared representations that the likes of Chamberlain and Alexander drew on to make sense of the East Pender Street district in Vancouver. The most critical component of the symbolic system they inherited – the race idea – has already been analysed and illustrated in some detail in

chapter 2. But to understand the civic management of the Chinese
presence in Vancouver, we also need to examine the vocabulary and
images through which the West saw China in the late eighteenth and
the nineteenth centuries. Those features – and their predecessors,
dating back another five centuries – antedated local figures like
Chamberlain and Alexander and prepared them (and their succes-
sors) to encounter Pender Street "intelligently" rather than "blindly."[90]
The topic has enormous scope but may be addressed briefly for the
purposes of this work.

THE DESIRE OF WESTERN EUROPEANS to measure China against an
idealized vision of themselves dates as far back as the thirteenth
century, when travellers, imbued with the Greek dualisms of
"Europe" and "Asia," "East" and "West," and "Orientis" and "Occidentis" set out to uncover the unknown. March notes the importance
of the classical regionalization of the world in these travellers' minds:
"Long before there was more than one or two sentences worth of
knowledge (even fabulous) about China itself, the genus into which
new information would be fitted was ready prepared in the European
mind."[91] "Asia" was perceived as the oldest, richest, and most populous of civilizations, and China, as the farthest outpost to the East,
was ipso facto the most "Oriental" of all. Medieval travellers were
certainly enchanted by that country's "ritcheness and plentiffull-
nesse," and Marco Polo, for one, wrote glowing accounts of the splendour and size of its cities and palaces, the abundance of silks, rugs,
and porcelains, and the opulence of its god-like ruler.

The romantic view lingered in European consciousness for more
than three centuries. Seventeenth-century Jesuit missionaries saw
China through spectacles tinted by the enthusiasm of earlier writers
and confirmed the positive image in their writings on the Confucian
state. Along with its scholarly bureaucracy, it was, for the Catholic
priests, a benevolent agency for the timeless perpetuation of sage
ideals.[92]

By the late seventeenth and certainly by the eighteenth century,
Europe's emerging image of itself as imperial, industrial, enlightened,
and progressive provided the benchmark for different perceptions of
China. A new construction on China's antiquity was beginning to be
put forward, one that emphasized its changelessness, homogeneity,
and uniformity – "the despotism of Custom," as John Stuart Mill
wrote in his mid-nineteenth-century essay *On Liberty*. With British
military power in ascendancy, the European image of China began
to darken. Not that the romantic view of a "grand and imposing

civilization," as Lord Macartney described it on his diplomatic mission in the late 1790s,[93] was lost for ever. We shall see in later chapters that it was recalled from time to time throughout the history of Europeans' perception of the Chinese in Vancouver and remains a source of neighbourhood imagery to this day. But as a prevailing image, it was submerged during the late eighteenth century. The Chinese became "a people of eternal standstill."

Nineteenth-century philosophers such as Hegel and Spencer lent intellectual authority to this view. They envisioned unilinear courses to progress and conceptualized civilization as a scale that left China (inventor of printing) somewhere around the bronze age. In so conceiving China (and more generally "Asia") as a negative construct – that is, non-European – Europe was giving force to its own idea of itself.[94] Europe became what the Orient was not, and vice-versa, and by mid-century, with the support of biological determinism in science, the constructs of "East" and "West" were confirmed in rigid opposition.

Miller traces this decline in China's status from the time of its first trade with the United States in 1785. It was around that time that frustrated traders, diplomats, and missionaries relayed home reports of China's resistance to their commercial and evangelical entreaties. From the records of fifty traders to China between 1785 and 1840, Miller identified the following themes: China's technological and scientific backwardness; its military ineptitude, from which many traders deduced national cowardice; the venality of the Chinese character, as revealed by the devotion of Chinese to gambling and their "diabolical cunning"; and, above all, their peculiarity, for which one had only to look to their theatre (their "detestible discord" as one trader put it), their insistence on writing up instead of down the page, their use of chopsticks, their slant eyes, their propensity for eating shark's fin, and so on.[95]

The memoirs of diplomats and accounts by commentators on European diplomatic missions – from Lord Macartney in 1792 to the embassy sent by US President Andrew Jackson in 1832 – were more influential than the traders in shaping American public opinion. Whatever their accuracy, they were regularly used in the first half of the nineteenth century by American editors, writers, and academics, especially geographers. Most memoirs were contemptuous of the backwardness and vice that China's despotism was thought to inspire. Military impotence, depravity, addiction to pernicious drugs, and infanticide were all taken as signs of a civilization in decline, a civilization that opposed to its detriment the improvements Western embassies would introduce.[96]

As opinion-maker, it was the Protestant missionary, however, armed with his own press, who commanded the widest audience in North America. Unlike his Jesuit counterpart, who had seen in Confucianism valuable preparation for Christian teachings, the Protestant missionary was a scathing critic. For him, there could be no more damning evidence against Confucianism than the rampant idolatry, infanticide, slavery in women, polygamy, opium obsession, noonday orgies, treachery, and endemic gambling – all pagan rites that frustrated his best efforts. So puny was their record of conversions, in fact, that some missionaries concluded that the wily Chinese were conscious agents of Satan who purposely dishonoured God with acts of licentiousness.

IN FEBRUARY 1912, A FEATURE on Vancouver's Chinatown in the *World* began: "Conditions prevailing in the cities of China are familiar topics of the returned missionary, who will dwell at length upon the awful condition of the slums, the armies of the unwashed, and the prevalence of vice in the shape of opium smoking and gambling, in the empire across the seas. Would you believe that the same condition of affairs is in existence in the city of Vancouver in our Chinatown, which constitutes a considerable quarter on Pender Street between Canton and Shanghai alleys?"[97] Yet how else, we might ask, could Pender Street be known?

The plight of the fallen woman disappearing into the clutches of procurers in segregated "Oriental" vice districts was, from the turn of the century, a pressing concern for moral reform groups in North America. Not surprisingly, therefore, the anxiety was heightened in Vancouver by the location of its "restricted area" (where prostitution was tolerated by the police) right next to the predominantly male Chinese quarter from the time the city was incorporated. The worst fears of all were realized in 1906, when prostitutes moved en masse to the very heart of Chinatown on Shanghai Alley, following a request by city council for their eviction from their former location. No police protection like that offered the residents of Mount Pleasant – the area that had been expected to receive the dislodged prostitutes – was extended to Chinatown, and for some time it became the new "restricted area" for prostitution in Vancouver. Later, in the face of much local protest about the unhappy combination of prostitutes and "Chinamen" in the one location, the restricted area was moved to Shore Street and from there to Alexander Street, in the East End.[98]

Of the various niches where prostitution enjoyed a blind eye in Vancouver, it was only in Chinatown, as the cartoon (see Figure 4)

Figure 4
"The Foreign Mission Field in Vancouver"
Source: Saturday Sunset, 10 October 1908

demonstrates, that an especially evil construction was cast upon the practice. "The helpless are shackled," wrote a reporter for the *World* in 1892, by these "past-masters in the art of duplicity and in cheating the devil."[99] An indignant citizen wrote in the *Saturday Sunset* on 10 October 1908: "A regular traffic in women is conducted by the Chinese in Vancouver. The Chinese are the most persistent criminals against the person of any woman of any class in this country ... Now all this goes on in a Christian community." Most often, protests in petitions to council concerning prostitution dwelt on the risk to property values.[100] In Chinatown, however, the voice of the nineteenth-century Protestant missionary to China reverberated. One resident reported that she was "shocked to discover the streets of Shanghai and Canton (in Vancouver's Chinatown) filled by Houses of Ill-Repute and a lot of brazen women plying their trade." Another: "It is a disgrace to our city to have that evil in that location."[101]

The Vancouver press occasionally took to lampooning Chinese residents with references to "John's" peculiarity. His "racial oddities,"

such as his "quixotic" New Year's festivities, were a source of some
wry amusement.[102] So too was his diet. "The only one of the lower
animals Vancouver's Chinese do not eat," wrote the *Province* on 23
July 1910, "is the cat." However, the dominant image of the time had
it that the Chinese were a filthy and depraved people.

Stamped with the weight of a racial typification, Chinatown was
intelligible only in terms of a few criteria. A contributing factor to
this selectivity was the assimilation into one generic identity of the
experiences of both men and women from China.[103] While it is true
that men well outnumbered women in Vancouver's Chinese community (until the 1960s), the racialization of people from China
absorbed mostly male images to its service. The compounding of
sexism and racism was no more clear than in the assumption that
"John" was a lascivious trader in white women.

Class distinctions also paled before the more influential racial characterization of the neighbourhood. For example, council simply
ignored a 1906 petition from the Chinese Board of Trade which, in
protesting the unimpeded movement of prostitutes into Shanghai
Alley and Canton Street, reflected concerns of the Chinese élite that
were not far removed from the most traditional of white Christian
mission ministers in Chinatown. "We the undersigned (30) merchants and others," it said, "beg leave to call your attention to the fact
that several of the women of ill-repute who are being ordered off
Dupont Street are moving into Shanghai Alley and Canton Streets.
This we consider most undesirable. It is our desire to have our children grow up learning what is best in Western civilization and not
to have them forced into daily contact with its worst phases."[104]

A number of Vancouver's Chinese business leaders undertook a
campaign against another perceived vice out of which the non-Chinese concept of Chinatown was constructed. Indeed, the vice label
was resisted as vigorously by local merchants as were charges about
Chinatown's filth. In 1908, the merchants' anti-opium league sent a
petition to Ottawa, asking the dominion government to "decisively
exercise its authority and powers to prohibit the importation, manufacture and sale of opium into Canada so that the social, physical
and moral condition of both Chinese and Europeans may be vastly
improved."[105]

But try as the merchants did to counter the idea of a generic Chinatown, the drug that Britain had in fact introduced into China in
the 1840s was now a powerful metaphor for neighbourhood definition, as the cartoon (see Figure 5) conveys. In 1899, a newspaper
reporter, who had accompanied Marrion on one of his tours of Chinatown's bachelor shacks, remarked in the 28 April edition of the *World*

Figure 5
"The Opium Fiend at Home in Vancouver's Chinatown"
Source: Vancouver World, 10 February 1912

that "the luxury of smoking opium is beyond comprehension in such
tight boxes." Newspaper reports during the following decade continued to invoke Chinatown's "bargain rate heaven," as opium's power
as a symbol of Chinese afflictions continued to grow. By 1912, when
the first tourists began visiting Chinatown, the *Vancouver World* felt
moved to draw together much of the local sentiment in a profile of
what it called the City's "plague spot." This article spoke of inhabitants not only stupefied by opium, but also engrossed in gambling,
surrounded by stagnant air, worshipping strange idols, feasting on
dead birds, with "two white women reposing on couches." It was a
"most repellant sight," wrote the reporter, who advised that the most
"loathsome spectacle" was to be had in the small hours of the morning, when the majority were at home "passed out."[106]
    Like the construction placed on white participation in Chinatown's
bawdy houses, the large use of opium by non-Chinese in Vancouver,

revealed by Mackenzie King in his 1908 investigation, only confirmed the view that Chinatown was a menace to civilized life.[107] White drug use did not prejudice but rather validated the more comforting racial and spatial category, as one resident's allegation in 1907 highlighted. In Chinatown's "underworld," he wrote, "Chinamen keep opium dens where our young men are led into contracting this habit which marks them for utter ruination and pushes them deeper into the mire of immorality."[108]

In the study of criminology, it is well accepted that for petty crimes such as gambling, where the victim is a willing participant, "the appearance of the act as a crime known to police will depend on the initiative of the law enforcement agencies; policies of enforcement in these areas are notoriously variable."[109] In Vancouver, the "heathen Chinee" was known for inveterate gambling. Successive officers of the city police certainly accepted the label, and they pursued Chinatown's gambling vigorously for five decades, from the 1890s until the late 1940s, when the extent of the harassment became embarrassingly transparent even to the city. Until then, however, it was rare to find a year that the *Chinese Times* and the rest of the local press did not report at least one raid on Chinatown's gambling quarters. Won Alexander Cumyow, whose testimony to the 1901 royal commission we have met before, laid the blame for this state of affairs squarely on discriminatory police enforcement practices. After telling the commissioners that there was proportionately a large amount of gambling among the Chinese, Cumyow went on: "Some do gamble for large amounts, but more commonly, the play is for amusement only and for small sums to pass the time as this is done in the common room of the boarding house. If a police raid is made and any are caught playing, all are arrested for gambling and looking on. If the same course were pursued in relation to white men, gamblers would be caught in barrooms and of course all who were at the bar would be arrested as onlookers."[110]

Just as raids on opium dens vindicated white people's assumptions about the moral laxity of the Chinese, civic scrutiny of gambling in Chinatown sprang from and confirmed popular assumptions about a generically addicted "Chinaman." And one vice bred another, as Alderman McIntosh charged in 1915. Chinese gambling and opium required constant vigilance, he said, because they were associated not only with white women slavery, but also with tuberculosis.[111]

Yet gambling in Vancouver was not confined to this one area. A letter to the editor of the *Province* on 30 January 1900, appealing for greater control of gambling in the city, said: "Everyone knows that gambling goes on promiscuously all over Vancouver, in clubs, in hotels, in saloons, in rooms connected with saloons and in private

Trouble in Chinatown

By W. R. Gordon

There's trouble down in Chinatown and the Chinks are spitting blue;
The cops have yanked old Tai Kee's bank and all his layout, too.
The fan-tan game and the py-gow frame and the chuck-luck mat all went
In one fell swoop when Sergeant Troop and his "bulls" collected rent.

The games were going with a handsome showing and a noisy, smoky hum,
While thoughts of raids and police parades were far from the yellow scum.
The air was thick as burnt clay brick; the smoke you could cut in chunks,
But the monks were gay in their saffron way as they bet their hard-earned plunks.

A swell young Chink in a jacket pink lounged by the outer door.
His eyes were closed and you'd swear he dozed, but he saw a whole lot more
Than you or I, if we passed by, would take in at a look,
For he was scout for the whole layout and the street was his lesson book.

A cop walked by and the Chink's slant eye read trouble as he passed,
And before another could follow the other that outer door slammed fast.
He pulled a string, and, funny thing, two more banged down the hall,
While in the room the noisy hum had changed to a heathenish bawl.

But the cops were wise; they had used their eyes to size up Tai Kee's joint.
They went at the wall in the dark back hall with an axe and a crowbar point.
In a minute or two they laid plain to view the murky gambling den;
They swarmed inside and the way they tied those Chinks was worth a ten.

Five at a time in a jabbering line, they knotted them queue to queue,
While the "muck-a-hai's" and "mo-bing-kai-tai's" turned the place an indigo blue.
There were forty odd, too heavy a load for the "Black Maria" van,
So some had to walk for many a block, pig-tailed like a human fan.

Now that is why the big ki-yi is heard in Chinatown.
The row they'll raise will be heard all ways round the streets that they hold down;
But it's all in the game, it's ever the same; they're raided from day to day.
When work is slack the cops fall back on the Chinks for a grandstand play.

Figure 6
"Trouble in Chinatown"
Source: British Columbia Magazine, September 1911

houses. Not a night passes, not a day passes, that it is not indulged in." In Chinatown, however, a neighbourhood image was built around both its practice and police attempts to suppress it, as bluntly conveyed by the poem (see Figure 6) published in *B.C. Magazine* in 1911. The local press relished in the struggles of the "Chinatown plain-clothes squad," trapped behind "ingenious Oriental systems of spring doors" and "getaway rat tunnels."[112] Mysterious Chinatown, a place white residents did not need to experience to "know," certainly offered the capacity to entertain, and the press was quick to exploit it. Deputy Chief of Police McLennan, for example, was dubbed "the terrible axe man" and bore the media distinction of "never being trapped by a door."[113]

At the end of 1915, the *Sun* declared, nostalgically and somewhat prematurely, that "Chinatown is a dead issue." Civic efforts to "tame" it were being contested successfully by its residents in the courts, an editorial lamented. Chinese residents had resorted increasingly to litigation over police harassment (as they had during Health Inspector Marrion's crusade against buildings), when their protests to city council proved futile. This complaint from the Chinese Board of Trade in 1905 was one such appeal that fell on council's deaf ears: "The members of our board are law abiding citizens. Many of them have been residents of this country for a number of years and are large holders of real estate, payers of taxes and other civic assessments. The members ... have been constantly annoyed by what we believe to be an unjustifiable intrusion of certain members of the Vancouver Police Force ... in the habit of going into our stores and rooms where our families live, showing no warrant whatsoever, nor do they claim any business with us ... We are subjected to indignities and discriminating treatment to which no other class would submit and to which *your* laws, we are advised, we are not required to submit."[114]

If the *Sun* thought the use of the courts was making Chinatown a dead issue, an incident surrounding litigation only a few months earlier suggests that the civic authorities thought otherwise. In February 1914, the merchant Chow Foo Kay sued a Detective McLaughlin for wrongfully searching his store and person for evidence of gambling paraphernalia and opium. In the same month, a police sergeant illegally arrested a white businessman. The sergeant had his rank reduced to first constable. Detective McLaughlin, meanwhile, was fined a mere fifty dollars – and Mayor Baxter proceeded to refund it out of the public purse.[115]

Just as part of the merchant sector worked hard to suppress the other vices that stigmatized Chinatown, a small group seemed to be as interested in the reform of gambling activities as Police Chief Chamberlain himself. In 1917, for example, a group of merchants petitioned council for even stricter regulation of gambling on Pender Street than already existed.[116] Despite the prevailing view that the community was united by a habit ingrained in the celestial nature, there was significant conflict over gambling among certain merchants, recruits to the Christian missions,[117] vice resort operators, and their regular customers. Some of the latter even became police informants, and almost all showed themselves quite capable of dispensing with the "habit" in the late 1930s, when neighbourhood organizations urged them to give generously to the war effort of the homeland against Japan.[118]

CONCLUSION

"Chinatown" was a concept that belonged to Vancouver's white European community which, like its contemporaries throughout North America, perceived the district of Chinese settlement according to an influential culture of race. For Europeans, Chinatown embodied all those features that seemed to set the Chinese apart. Possible convergences of class, gender, immigrant status, and so on between whites and Chinese were obscured by the overriding beliefs in the natural occurrence of the two races and the superior race and culture of Europeans. Thus, out of the infinity of things that could have been said about the settlers on Vancouver's Pender Street, it was their apparently standard appearance, heathenism, clannishness, propensity to sleep twelve to a room, opium and gambling addiction, eating habits, strange language, odd graveyard practices, and so on that became ingredients of their image. In other words, Chinatown was almost everything white society was not.

This is not to suggest that Chinatown was a fiction; nor does it deny gambling, opium addiction, and unsanitary conditions in the district where Chinese settled in Vancouver. Moreover, there were probably divided opinions among Europeans about the extent of vice and unsanitary behaviour in Chinatown, and such variation in European's responses as existed along class, gender, and other lines should be the subject of further research. The point is that "Chinatown" was a shared characterization constructed by and for Europeans who – out of conformity toward, and support for, a régime that bestowed on them identity, status, power, and economic advancement – sought to confirm the "otherness" of the Chinese. That they directed that purpose in large part through the medium of Chinatown attests to the importance of such enclaves in the making of systems of racial classification. That sectors within the Chinatown community also resisted the purpose is testimony to the potential for renegotiation of the forms of dominance we have been describing.

In so defining and targeting Chinatown, the European authorities of early Vancouver ensured that the racial category "Chinese" would be carried forward in the society and space of their city. "Chinatown"

was their unit of knowledge, and its "Chineseness" belonged to them. Both notions continued to be reinvented at the symbolic and material levels in the years to come, and while various governments were mapping the career of the Chinese they would at the same time be defining the insider community whose boundaries and privilege it was their ambition to protect.

CHAPTER FOUR

Marginalizing Chinatown, 1920–1935

A geographer has written that landscape impressions, though subjective in origin, "acquire an objective content in so far as they have
a history: a history of authorship, diffusion and impact."[1] In late-
nineteenth- and early-twentieth-century Vancouver, Chinatown was
one such concept to shape practices that further objectified the idea
and its concrete referent at Pender Street. As we have seen, Chinatown was for white residents of Vancouver the embodiment of a
unique Chineseness that set it inevitably apart from the mainstream
of respectable settlers. Chinatown was "their" domain, "their" home
away from home, "their" doing, "their" evil. And all the while, such
a claim to truth was being made more legitimate by policy-makers
and more "real" in a physical sense as its consequences became
locally embedded.

So, in the late 1910s, when some ambitious Chinese merchants
attempted to breach the moral order of place and race in Vancouver
by moving to the suburbs, the disturbance was for Europeans particularly visible and jarring. According to the ethos of separation
between "us" and "them" that had been inscribed in Vancouver's
landscape since the late 1880s, the merchant Chinese were "out of
place." They were a "polluting" influence that needed to be expelled,
much like other categories of aliens (examined in the field of "mainstream–outsider" relations) that have been the target of exclusionary
tactics on the part of suburban communities.[2] The jolt to Vancouver's
white suburbs reverberated throughout the province, as restless Chinese took the opportunity of the First World War, when white troops
were away, to "infiltrate" property and occupations that for decades
had been the unspoken preserves of white British Columbians. It
was a "Yellow Peril" of the gravest order.

This book is tracing the process by which the concept of a Chinese race fed into political practices that reproduced the racial concept and its underlying social relations. Strategies that marginalized the out-group, both symbolically and spatially, were among the more effective of such practices. This chapter develops that theme and, in particular, examines the variety of means by which the three levels of the Canadian state responded to the threat of Chinese mobility during the post–First World War period. In their direct application, these official strategies attempted to seal the limits of Chinese entitlement in Vancouver at the boundaries of Pender Street. Not all the measures met with legal success, but taken together the national, provincial, and neighbourhood practices further institutionalized the racialization of British Columbia's "Chinese" and its enclave foundation at Pender Street. By the time the Depression arrived, Chinatown had become for European society a metaphor for racial contamination and for Vancouver's Chinese a maximum entitlement.

THE IDEA OF "RACE HYGIENE"

From the 1890s through the 1910s, the race idea had been given fresh sanction from a branch of science that built on former race typologies. The science of heredity, or "eugenics," had achieved considerable influence and respect in the United States and to a lesser extent in Britain, and in both countries it lent authority to the morphological races of Western biology and physical anthropology. Essentially, eugenics was a science and a practical program of racial improvement through selective breeding of the human species. In science, Stepan claims, it "provided yet one more channel for the transmission of the racialist tradition."[3] In society, it was institutionalized throughout the world by the 1920s, when Germany, Russia, Japan, and the United States all boasted active eugenic or "race hygiene" societies.

The term "eugenics" was coined by Charles Darwin's cousin, Francis Galton, a geographer and biologist. As Galton interpreted The Descent of Man, scientific support was finally available for "social hereditarianism," a theory in vogue from the mid-nineteenth century.[4] That theory held that many forms of human behaviour, including criminality, idiocy, ability, degeneracy, alcoholism, and insanity were inherited; just as man's physical peculiarities were passed on, so did like behaviour beget like behaviour in a most deterministic fashion. Obviously there was comfort to be had in Darwin's theory of the natural selection of inherited, adaptive physical characteristics in nature, and commentators on society, including Galton, saw no impediment to applying the spirit of Darwin to man's behavioural, mental, and moral condition.

Faith in the priority of heredity over environment was not completely new; biologists had long believed that innate differences in ability and behaviour separated the races. But eugenics purported to give behavioural differences more scientific credibility by linking them explicitly to Darwinian concepts of fitness and heredity. For the first time in scientific thought, ability and intelligence became discrete and measurable qualities inherited differentially by individuals and races. The goal of the science was to explore the hereditary nature of traits and to measure their variability in individuals and groups, a goal well suited to increasingly popular statistical methods of inquiry and verification.

In practice, much dispute about the mechanisms of genetic transmission diluted the force of the theory as a science, especially in Britain. But methodological disputes did not alter adherents' belief in the power of nature over nurture, and the language of the "fit" and the "unfit" retained its popular appeal. Galton believed that mankind could even improve the human stock by promoting the breeding of "fit" (races and individuals) and discouraging the reproduction of the "unfit." Indeed technical disputes did not alter the conviction that the science's virtue was its capacity for practical application.

During the 1900s and 1910s, eugenists and others attempted to promote programs that would hasten for society what nature could only slowly achieve. In Britain, their first (and last) legislative success occurred in 1913 with passage of the Mental Deficiency Bill, which called for the segregation of mentally ill people in order to prevent them from breeding. British eugenists also saw possibilities for controlling the biological fitness of the working class, but in time the movement came to alienate the political left.

In the United States, eugenics became deeply wedded to the race question, which by the first decade of the twentieth century embraced the emancipated "Negro" and the "masses" of Europe.[5] The latter had been arriving since the 1890s, and their perceived threat to the quality of "true" Americans generated a vigorous campaign for immigration restriction and, to a lesser extent, sterilization laws. Eugenists presented their cause as a patriotic one. Fine Nordic traits had created American institutions, it was held, and the traits of lowly races threatened to undermine them. The challenge was a sort of negative eugenics – to prevent the national organism from being compromised by those who would pass on their deficiency. On that point, analogies to nineteenth-century agricultural breeding theory were particularly helpful. The mixing of distant "strains" would induce "reversions" or wild types of "hybrids," it was argued. And, of course, there was no need to specify carefully the close from the distant strains because a whole history of race science had already done that, at least in the case of the yellow and black races.

As for the non-yellow and non-black people, Stepan notes that eugenists in both Britain and the United States tended to refer to a range of different categories as "races," without much regard for consistency.[6] Along with the old (seemingly unambiguous) races, "Russians," "Slavs," "Mediterraneans," "Irish," and "Jews" were also "races" in the pages of the *Eugenics Review,* and their collective entry to the United States was seen as an "influx" that threatened to overwhelm the native-born "stock." By 1924, when the most pressing needs of the new industrial economy had been served, an immigration restriction campaign by American whites, fuelled in large part by eugenist prophecies, brought about a legislative solution. Ten years later, the concept of race hygiene found perhaps its most supreme expression in Nazi Germany.

RACE AND PROVINCIAL LEGISLATION

When Ottawa acceded in 1903 to British Columbia's demands for a prohibitive head tax on Chinese immigrants, the provincial legislature's appetite for anti-Chinese legislation was satisfied, at least for a time. In the years that immediately followed, the attention of the provincial house turned to the "Japanese problem" and the difficulties of effecting legal measures against a population with whose country of origin the imperial government had valuable treaty relations. By the 1910s, the house had exhausted all possible avenues in that direction, and the Chinese and Japanese populations (as different from each other as both were from Europeans) were increasingly defined as the "Asiatic" or "Oriental problem." The legislature next turned to the issue of race, and the place of aliens in white British Columbia, in 1919. The reappearance of the race issue at that time was at least partly a product of the First World War, which stirred "racial" self-consciousness in British Columbia, as it did throughout the Western world, in a climate of narrow nationalisms and imperialistic competition.

The milieu was ripe for such crude Darwinist treatises as Lothrop Stoddard's immensely popular and lurid *The Rising Tide of Color,* published in New York in 1920 (and recommended to the Canadian House of Commons by the member for Burrard in 1922).[7] The book's premise was that the war had destroyed "white race-unity," leaving that race fractured and vulnerable to the vast hordes of the Far East. "There is no immediate danger of the world being swamped by black blood," the American political scientist and eugenist wrote, "but there is a very imminent danger that the white stocks may be swamped by Asiatic blood." It was not that the "yellow race" was necessarily inferior, Stoddard argued. On the contrary, "the Asiatics have by their own efforts built up admirable cultures rooted in remote antiquity," and it was for that reason that "white men cannot, under peril of their very race-existence, allow wholesale Asiatic immigration into white race areas."[8] The awakening of Asia foreshadowed coloured domination, "mongrelization," and the destruction of white civilization. The vocabulary of race, it appears, had moved to the defensive.

The war also precipitated a period of socioeconomic dislocation in British Columbia. The brief economic prosperity of wartime collapsed from 1919 to 1922, when closure of the munitions industry and the return of veterans brought unemployment, general discontent, labour unrest, union formation, new heights of working-class consciousness, and agitation for political rights among women. A general strike in Winnipeg in May 1919 raised the spectre of the "red scare" and exacerbated general panic and pessimism in what seemed a most unstable world.

Many social scientists have observed that during times of economic recession social groups whose own organizing and defensive capacities have been diminished are subjected to further estrangement from society at large.[9] Post-war British Columbia was no exception. Moreover, the racial paradigm with which the province's inhabitants had grown up became more explicit as the ideological discourse of "nation" became harnessed to it. In the minds of whites, "race" and "nation" became interchangeable idioms around which socio-political units were built and conquered.[10] More bluntly affirmed than perhaps ever before was the exclusiveness of the insider community of whites and the boundaries of the nation that was seen to be their rightful hold on identity and power. No amount of war-bond purchases by Chinese to support Canada's war effort, for example, could convert their status to that of "allies." (The Chinese people of Vancouver contributed over $100,000 to the war effort through bond purchases.[11])

In this climate of nationalism immediately after the armistice, a new and strenuous round of lobbying began in Victoria for immigration exclusion of Chinese and all such alien others. In March 1919, the legislature unanimously carried the following motion: "That in the opinion of this House the Federal authorities should forthwith cable the Hon Sir R.L. Borden, Premier of Canada, to urge the Peace

Conference, as a matter of safeguarding and keeping undisturbed international relations, the prohibition of the immigration into Canada of those races which will not readily assimilate with the Caucasian race."[12] The war had given the white community new incentive to seize what was "theirs" and much greater certainty that what was "theirs" was under siege.

Perhaps the greatest irritant for white British Columbians was the wartime "Oriental" penetration of agricultural lands and jobs and increasing ownership of valuable property. Even before the war, a *Colonist* news report stated: "The boards of trade throughout the Okanagan Valley are extensively taking up the problem by giving white landowners the preference over Chinese."[13] After the war, this infiltration became so serious to members of the BC Board of Trade that in February 1920 they lobbied the provincial government for a commission that would "inquire into and devise means of providing a remedy to the serious menace of an Oriental influx into several of the richer agricultural sections of British Columbia, and particularly to make it impossible for Orientals and undesirable aliens to own, lease and otherwise control land in Canada."[14] Other representations were made during 1919 and 1920 by the Farmers' Institute, the United Farmers of British Columbia, the British Columbia Fruit Growers' Association, and the British Columbia Stockbreeders' Association, and by 1921 Mr E.D. Barrows, minister of agriculture, had commissioned the study.[15]

The report on "Oriental" ownership did not provide comparative figures for other nationalities, it being simply assumed that any degree of "Oriental" ownership was an infringement.[16] The study found that in 1921 Chinese owned nearly 5,000 acres of farm land and held 10,030 acres on lease. Most of the land was given over to mixed farming, while orchards and dairying occupied a small portion. Ninety per cent of the province's supply of "truck produce" was cultivated and distributed by Chinese, as was 55 per cent of its potato crop. The presence of Japanese in agriculture was thought to be still more threatening because they owned more property than they leased.

The grievance of landowners was echoed by several retail merchants' associations in the urban areas, where job and pay discrimination against Chinese had encouraged a growing number to open small business operations. In Victoria, local retailers informed the legislature in 1922: "The worst feature about it is that this Oriental invasion is spreading out into various lines of business. At first the Chinese who came here were content to work in the home or to be simply laundrymen, but now they are in the green grocery business and many other lines; they are in possession of vast tracts of land on this Island and the Mainland."[17]

It was an old grievance – that "Orientals" created unfair economic competition. Because of their distinctive standard of living, Chinese could farm the land more cheaply, offer more competitive prices, and reap greater profits (or so the logic went). As one observer wrote in 1921: "The Chinese are successful [in truck gardening] owing to their tremendous energy and to their frugal habits of life ... Where the average wage of the white labourer is $5 a day, the Chinaman will work for $3 to $4.50 a day."[18] What was new was the size and influence of the lobby that vented the grievance. Whatever partiality some white entrepreneurs once showed Chinese labour was diminishing, as retailers too manipulated the race idea to suit their immediate economic interests.

In this context, newly mobile "John" was violating the rules of a racialized occupational hierarchy that put him strictly in a position of service for whites, not profit-making from whites. "He" was also breaching the boundaries of a racialized residential arrangement. The Vancouver Board of Trade felt moved to vent the concern in its submission to the Special Oriental Immigration Committee in July 1921: "During late years the matter has become serious in that the Oriental is no longer content to seclude himself in the Chinese or Japanese quarters of the towns in the Province, but is either occupying land in advantageous localities or is branching out in the retail or wholesale trades in the best districts in the cities ... There is a natural repugnance inherent in the soul of our people to fraternize with the Oriental with the ultimate result that they secure control of the surrounding land ... We strongly feel that we should retain British Columbia for our own people. We realize that the owners of land must eventually control the destinies of any country and we must urge that every precaution should be taken to preserve us and our children this great heritage of ours."[19]

At the same time, the minister of lands, Thomas Dufferin ("Duff") Pattullo, found the penetration of the "Oriental strain" beyond its quarters so menacing as to be "detrimental to the progress of the Anglo-Saxon civilization of the Pacific Coast."[20] A year later, in November 1922, he eschewed the idea of extending "ill-will" to Orientals but restated that there was a great biological difference between whites and Oriental races: "We must trade together, but I think it is sufficient to suggest that we should occupy our own spheres."[21]

One of the ways by which the provincial attorney-general, Alex Manson, attempted to placate unemployed veterans and other BC residents in the early 1920s was to campaign among primary and manufacturing industrialists against the employment of "Asiatics." "The man who is not patriotic enough to employ white men in his industry is not a good citizen and I am not hesitating to tell him so," Manson said.[22] In 1922, almost 6,000 Chinese (and 3,000 Japanese) were employed in the province's industries, the majority in the various branches of the lumber industry and in railway construction. By mid-1922, the *Colonist* happily reported: "Through his [Manson's] activities, the railway companies and other large employing concerns have been induced to ... issue instructions that hereafter, whites must be employed instead of Orientals on track and other rail work."[23] Some shingle-mill operators also responded to Manson's call and gave their first consideration to a minimum wage that would, among other things, remove the advantage of Chinese in the labour market. (In 1926, a minimum wage policy was introduced in the lumber industry bringing hardship to many Chinese.[24])

The minister of finance, John Hart, endorsed Manson's campaign for the self-preservation of the province: "We want British Columbia to be a white province," he said in June 1922.[25] For both ministers, the issue of Oriental penetration was simple but serious, as Manson told the legislature in November 1922: "I have no real objection to the Oriental, but the real objection to him and the one that is permanent and incurable is that there is an ethnological difference which cannot be overcome. The two races cannot mix and I believe our first duty is to our own people ... It is a matter of our own domestic affairs that we should endeavour to protect the white race from the necessity of intermingling with Oriental blood, and I think we have every warrant for fighting to prevent a situation that will inevitably result in race deterioration."[26]

The provincial government under Premier John Oliver was solidly behind Manson's campaign, and in 1921 it decided to re-enact an old (1902) order-in-council which excluded Chinese and Japanese from employment on government contracts. The imperial privy council subsequently ruled that the order as applied to Japanese was beyond the power of the province, but for Chinese it was held that "Canada's treaty with China permits the Dominion and inferentially its Provinces, to exclude Chinese from employment on government undertakings, or in connection with Government leases or licences."[27]

Despite that partial success, Oliver's government knew that if Chinese occupational and residential mobility were to be ultimately contained, it would be necessary for Ottawa to co-operate. Thus there followed a period of lively political activity at the provincial and dominion levels, with manifestations of the fear of "racial contamination" at the forefront. No other period in BC history brought forward as concerted a front against Chinese immigration to Canada. All politicians seemed to feel that they needed an "Oriental exclusion" platform to guarantee electoral success, and such electioneering added more fuel to the already inflamed race debate. The dominion election of 1921, for example, raised a furore in British Columbia, with respective candidates accusing their opposition of encouraging the "Yellow Race." In the December 1921 *Province* advertisement (see Figure 7), Conservative Prime Minister Arthur Meighen is depicted by the Liberals extending a welcome to an "Oriental."

This round of province-wide agitation has been comprehensively examined elsewhere, and it is sufficient to note here that protests against further "Oriental" immigration to Canada hailed from a multitude of organizations and interests of all class backgrounds and political affiliations.[28] Chinese and Japanese, both thought to be a threat to white domination by virtue of the vast hordes waiting in China and the high Japanese birth rate in British Columbia, became useful targets of military metaphors in the press. For example, the *Colonist*, in its editorial of 12 November 1922 (about the possibility of returning the $500 tax to Chinese on condition they leave Canada), said: "These are times when the rights of nations have been asserted on the battlefield, when the policy of self determination has been vindicated as a cardinal principle." Concern about the possibility of "race suicide," "extinction," "invasion," and an "Asian takeover" pervaded the province despite the fact that in 1921 Chinese constituted just 4.5 per cent of its population, nearly 75 per cent of its population was of British origin, and that from 1911 to 1941 it had the highest proportion of British-born residents of any province of Canada.[29]

Exclusionary sentiments were injected into legislative debate late in 1922 when Victoria began its most strenuous drive for dominion action. For the Oliver government, manipulation of the race idea was an effective, perhaps even necessary, source of political legitimacy, so pervasive was the culture of race in the province. But the political prominence given the issue was not simply expedient. In mid-November 1922, the minister of mines, William Sloan, saw the matter as transcending "political football"; for him it was not so much a "social or a labour question; [but] more vitally a question of racial domination and, eventually, of our national existence."[30] In the provincial parliament, the minister underlined the moral mandate of politicians, and in 1922 his resolution that the assembly "place itself on record as being in favour of complete prohibition of Asiatic immigration" was unanimously carried by the house.[31] The Liberal member for Vancouver, Ian Mackenzie, shared Sloan's concern and in the

Liberal
Candidates

are pledged to a

Brigadier General
VICTOR ODLUM
"A Clean Hard Fighter"
Liberal Candidate
VANCOUVER SOUTH

White British Columbia

COPY OF TELEGRAM
CANADIAN PACIFIC RAILWAY COMPANY'S TELEGRAPHS
TELEGRAM

Who is to dominate British Columbia---the White or the Yellow man? Shall it be through the negligence of the Meighen Government as represented by the Hon. H. H. Stevens, that the development of this wonderful Province of ours is to come under the domination of the Yellow Race? Speaking at the Opera House on the evening of September 19, eleven years ago, Mr. Stevens promised—

"that one of my first acts, if elected, would be to try to improve the conditions of fishing on the Pacific Coast." The report of that meeting also states that Mr. Stevens "regretted to see the B.C. fisheries so largely in the hands of the Asiatics." And, still at another meeting at the Horse Show Building on Monday night of September 18, in the same year, the report reads: "Mr. Stevens, waving his hands about, told them" what mighty things he would do, if he were sent to Ottawa. About eleven years have passed. What has Mr. Stevens done? Absolutely nothing! What are the results? 7466 Japanese and 20,342 Chinese have been admitted in the last ten years. One birth in every nine in British Columbia this year is that of an Oriental child. Over one hundred logging and shingle camps are now entirely Japanese. Out of 3961 salmon licenses the Japanese hold 2004. The Japanese control 10,167,004 acres of British Columbia's choicest orchard lands. The Chinese control 16,751.73 of the choicest truck farm lands. These are the bare facts.

MAYOR GALE
"And a Bigger Vancouver"
Liberal Candidate
VANCOUVER CENTRE

What is the Remedy?

Each Liberal Candidate has pledged himself to make a White British Columbia. Sitting on the Government side----as they undoubtedly will under the new Government---- they can achieve this purpose. They will make British Columbia a White man's country. They will develop our boundless resources, our mines, our forests, our fisheries, and our fertile valleys for the profit of the White man. Each Liberal Candidate believes that every "job" in British Columbia should be occupied by the White Man. It is indeed a sorry state of affairs when a returned citizen, who has won the highest reward at the disposal of his country—Michael O'Rourke, V.C—publicly states that "the Meighen Government and the Oriental have forced him into the bread line." If you would remedy these conditions you will mark your ballot on December 6 FOR THE LIBERAL CANDIDATE!

M. A. Macdonald,
K.C.
"Canada's Able Young Statesman"
Liberal Candidate
BURRARD

Figure 7
"Liberal Candidates Are Pledged to a White British Columbia"
Source: Province, 3 December 1921

same session introduced an ambitious motion which, after several recitals, came to the point as follows: "And whereas it is essential, if the Caucasian race of the Province of British Columbia is to be permitted to work out, unfettered, the high ideals of Anglo-Saxon civilization both in the development of the country's natural resources

and in the application of those ideals to proper standards of living;
Therefore be it resolved that the Dominion of Canada be petitioned
to grant its assent and accord its active assistance to the obtaining of
amendments to the BNA Act, giving the province of British Columbia,
at present most affected, and the other provinces of Canada, the
power to make laws prohibiting Asiatics from acquiring proprietary
interest in any form whatsoever."[32]

The motion was unanimously carried, and with it the Oliver government confirmed that the "Chinese quarter" had become for white
British Columbians a maximum entitlement beyond which Oriental
strains threatened to taint, and Oriental competition disturb, a natural Darwinist order.

CIVIC STRATEGIES

Jobs were scarce in Vancouver after the real estate boom collapsed in
1913, and local feeling turned strongly against the long-despised
competition from Chinese workers (see, for example, the advertisement in Figure 8). City council responded quickly with a campaign
against Chinese employment, a tactic that led to a bout of mutual
animosity between the Chinese and white communities. The official
campaign came at a time when unemployment among Chinese was
already so severe that the Chinese Benevolent Association in Vancouver had sent a circular to China advising countrymen not to emi-
grate. (Local Chinese entrepreneurs, who profited from the glut of
labour, opposed the forwarding of the circular.)[33]

The city's vendetta began in 1914 when "antipathy to Orientals, to
Chinese in particular," as a result of Mrs Millard's murder prompted
council to give preference to lumber mills employing white labour.
Council voted to use the white-only Anglo-American Lumber Co. for
future municipal contracts and purchases. "It might not be absolutely
legal," said Alderman Hamilton, "but it could be the unwritten law
of Council."[34] At the same time, council reaffirmed that Chinese
labour could not be used on city works.[35]

Next, in 1916, the board of licence commissioners resolved to
exclude Chinese workers from all liquor-licensed premises – despite
strong opposition from both white employers and Chinese spokesmen. The managers of the Vancouver Hotel and the Hotel Metropole,
for instance, protested that "only Chinese provide the right class of
domestics and cooks."[36] Chinese Consul Lin Shih-Yuan contested the
exclusion both before and after the board acted. When the consul
heard of the impending resolution, he appealed to the board to "consider further, that the class of workmen you would deprive of their

A Message to the People of Vancouver

Will you help to provide employment for 500 WHITE girls, women and men? You can do it without the least inconvenience. You can help keep ONE MILLION DOLLARS in Vancouver this year, which will otherwise leave the Province permanently

For several months' past the WHITE LAUNDRIES OF VANCOUVER have been considering the best method of approaching the people of this city regarding THE IMPORTANCE OF PATRONIZING LAUNDRIES OWNED AND OPERATED BY WHITE PEOPLE AND EMPLOYING WHITE MEN AND WOMEN. There are, in this city, many hundreds of WHITE women and WHITE men who could be regularly employed by the WHITE laundries if the people would send their laundry work ONLY to the WHITE LAUNDRIES.

It is not our point to attack the CHINESE. Our appeal is to WHITE men and women of Vancouver in the best interests of WHITE men and women. If every family now patronizing CHINESE laundries will, in future, send their work to WHITE laundries, more than FIVE HUNDRED WHITE MEN AND WOMEN would FIND WORK AT ONCE. Also, more than ONE MILLION DOLLARS PER ANNUM would remain right here in Vancouver to support WHITE families, many of whom have given their fathers and brothers to the great cause which is so dear to loyal Canadians.

We are going to do our part, beginning Monday, by reducing our prices on laundry work

Figure 8
"Message to the People of Vancouver"
Source: World, 1 May 1915

means of livelihood ... have paid the sum of Five Hundred Dollars to enter this country at the stipulation and acquiesence of your Government."[37] In a searing letter to the licence board in June 1916, after it had agreed to the exclusion, he threatened to take the matter to a British court and denounced the board's "continuous class legislation which hampers my countrymen in every field of employment."[38]

Among the worst casualties of the sensitivity surrounding employment in the late 1910s were the itinerant Chinese pedlars of Vancouver. The story of the city and the pedlars illustrates the vigour with which "white" Vancouver applied the race thinking of the day but also sees the continuation of forms of resistance within the Chinese community that were to play an important longer-term role in the history of Chinatown.

Vegetable peddling had always provided a secure, if modest, livelihood for Chinese in Vancouver. There existed a ready market available in Chinese domestics and restaurant cooks, and supplies were assured because the cultivation of fresh produce was one occupational venture that had been open to Chinese from Vancouver's early days. Civic harassment of pedlars began early, however; in 1894 council passed a by-law preventing the sale of produce outside normal store hours. The hours available for legal peddling were further regulated in a 1908 amendment to the Market Bylaw, a move that the BC Supreme Court upheld in an appeal by a Chinese pedlar.[39]

These early restrictions were slight, however, compared with what the Chinese pedlars faced in the atmosphere of the 1910s. "In hundreds of families that should be the white man's best customers," wrote the *Sun* in August 1913, "the Chinese cook wields his malevolent influence ... For the Chinese cook buys Chinese grown vegetables." In the same year, Alderman McMaster proposed that pedlars be licensed, in an effort "to put the white man on a more equal basis in the growing of vegetables."[40] In 1915, a major new obstacle to the trade was erected. Council originally proposed to control the location and hours for peddling in the city, but in February 1915 the Private Bills Committee of the provincial legislature declined to accept council's request for the necessary enabling power.[41] It did appear, however, that the city had the power to charge a fee for the licensing of pedlars, and in May of the same year, to the delight of the Vancouver Retail Merchants' Association, a hefty fifty-dollar annual tax was set by council.[42]

By August 1918, one of the earliest labour organizations in Chinatown was established in the form of a 300–400-member Vegetable Sellers Association.[43] Its first target was the council's proposed Trades Licence Law, which aimed to exclude "Orientals" and others classified as unfair competition against so-called legitimate dealers. The new consul for China, Koliang Yih, joined the vegetable sellers in the fight. In a letter to council in December 1918, he wrote: "The discrimination against the Chinese and the unrighteousness of such a course, Gentlemen, has moved me to appeal to your spirit of fair play in this trying time of readjustment."[44] Not only was the appeal in vain, but council decided upon a still more aggressive course in the new year. While retail stores were required to pay a ten-dollar licence fee per year, the levy for peddling was raised to $100.[45] The consul

was outraged and sent this strongly worded response to the mayor
and council in April 1919:

This Bylaw is purposely established to destroy and prohibit the business
carried on by peddlers, and to discriminate indirectly against the Chinese
only and directly against them in favour of retail merchants and shops. May
I ask you, if you can impose $100 on these peddlers, who can make only a
gross profit of $350 a year, how many Hundreds or Thousands of dollars will
you impose on a lawyer or a doctor or even yourselves, who can make ten
or one hundred times more profit than those peddlers? The City is supposed
to look after the interest and welfare of the public. Now the City is to use a
kind of means to help retail merchants to hold up to the public to suffer
high cost of living and inconvenience. The $100 licence fee is prohibitive,
therefore it is unlawful, impracticable, unobservable and unreasonable.[46]

Ambassador Yeung also stepped in to protest council's action, and
in June 1919 the finance committee saw fit to return the fee to fifty
dollars. The itinerant vendors were no longer prepared to accept any
discriminatory fee, however, and in November, when the BC Supreme
Court upheld its validity, they decided to back their protest with
strike action. To rally support, the pedlars distributed circulars to
households in Vancouver defending their position, warning of higher
prices, and appealing for support. The door-to-door vendors, an
indispensable institution to Vancouver householders who were keen
to avoid cumbersome trips to the city market, won the support of
over 5,000 women in a 1920 petition to council.[47]
    The Vancouver Retail Merchants' Association and the Vancouver
Chamber of Commerce, however, were powerful adversaries whose
interests council was keen to protect. Both of these organizations
supported the fifty-dollar tax on peddling and called on council to
retain it – which it decided to do, despite the tireless efforts of an
attorney for the pedlars. Within three years, there were just 152 Chinese pedlars in business in Vancouver, less than half the number the
consul for China reported were in operation in 1918.[48]
    In harassing the Chinese pedlar, council (and the Retail Merchants'
Association) unwittingly invited what to them was a much graver
menace. In conjunction with other factors, civic persecution of peddling during the 1910s encouraged the rise of Chinese-owned and
-operated grocery stores in locations outside Pender Street. Chinese
pedlars had built up a busy trade throughout the city with their
competitive prices. Given this assured suburban market and the
guarantee of reliable suppliers, they began to establish small businesses, with attached residences, at locations more convenient to their

Table 2

Licences Issued to Chinese in Vancouver, 1920, 1922, 1924, 1926

Class of Licence	Chinese				Other Nationalities				Distribution outside Chinatown			
	1920	1922	1924	1926	1920	1922	1924	1926	1920	1922	1924	1926
Apartment Houses	–	4	4	2	–	368	481	547	–	3	4	–
Auto (Gas and Rpr)	1	1	1	–	117	276	289	231	–	–	–	–
Auto (Taxi)	8	8	9	7	282	211	309	258	–	–	–	–
Auto Livery	–	–	–	–	60	16	59	62	–	–	–	–
Auto Painter	–	–	–	2	–	–	21	–	–	–	–	–
Baker	1	1	2	2	180	182	199	206	–	–	–	–
Barber	17	20	17	20	12	15	26	32	–	–	–	–
Bath Prl and Mssg	–	–	–	–	12	12	13	11	1	–	–	–
Bath, plain	2	4	5	5	8	23	48	–	–	–	–	–
Beauty Parlour	–	–	–	–	75	55	53	–	–	–	–	–
Billiards	3	1	2	2	59	73	53	60	–	–	–	3
Boot and Shoe Dealer	2	2	4	4	136	152	142	144	–	–	1	3
Boot and Shoe Rpr	8	10	8	7	243	136	229	280	3	3	2	4
Broker	4	2	1	2	116	124	121	126	1	–	–	–
Butcher	6	8	8	5	386	301	375	326	–	–	–	–
Candy, etc.	37	33	29	22	144	127	112	111	1	3	4	3
Cleaner and Dryer	5	12	12	10	68	174	195	210	2	5	6	–
Contractor	1	2	1	1	–	39	–	49	–	–	–	–
Delicatessen	–	1	–	1	28	29	34	43	–	–	–	–
Dressmaker	–	–	–	–	85	115	91	87	–	–	–	–
Drygoods	4	8	15	13	96	95	66	–	3	3	4	2
Electrician	–	–	–	–	615	471	512	503	–	–	–	–
Express and Dray	30	27	21	13	22	19	15	5	–	–	–	–
Fish Dealer	6	5	3	3	–	–	–	36	–	–	–	–
Florist	–	–	–	–	–	–	–	–	–	–	–	–
Flour and Feed	6	4	–	–	11	13	8	–	5	3	–	–
Fuel Dealer	1	1	1	–	46	53	50	56	–	–	–	–

Table 2
(continued)

Class of Licence	Chinese				Other Nationalities				Distribution outside Chinatown			
	1920	1922	1924	1926	1920	1922	1924	1926	1920	1922	1924	1926
Furniture Dealer	–	–	–	1	43	–	–	29	–	–	–	–
Gents Clothier	11	4	6	5	87	54	71	71	1	–	–	–
Green Grocer	31	46	70	74	9	6	7	11	25	40	66	71
Grocer	88	73	68	67	411	377	377	426	30	25	28	35
Hardware	2	1	4	2	46	42	39	40	–	–	–	–
Insurance Agt	–	–	–	1	–	–	54	54	–	–	1	1
Jeweller	13	18	14	9	89	59	60	66	–	–	–	1
Laundry	43	39	40	40	15	16	14	12	38	36	36	37
Laundry Offices	–	–	–	17	–	–	–	13	–	–	–	13
Lodging House	17	16	15	17	328	329	330	387	7	7	6	8
Milk Vendor	–	–	–	–	–	–	36	38	1	–	–	–
Miscellaneous	1	11	14	4	688	374	325	224	–	–	–	–
Music Dealer	–	–	–	–	16	27	28	32	–	6	9	–
Photo and Art Dealer	4	6	5	3	47	50	51	41	2	2	2	2
Plumber	–	–	–	–	77	–	–	–	–	–	–	–
Poulterer	9	11	11	9	16	9	7	8	–	–	2	–
Printer and Publisher	3	3	4	5	63	74	71	74	–	–	2	3
Real Estate Dealer	1	–	–	–	244	187	175	179	–	–	–	–
Restaurant	50	61	69	54	253	236	246	257	15	25	24	20
Second-Hand Dlr	12	12	9	5	172	133	152	150	2	–	1	–
Sheet Metal	1	1	–	–	28	44	–	–	–	–	–	–
Sign Writer	–	–	–	–	–	29	–	23	–	–	–	–
Stationery and Books	2	3	3	4	52	51	50	46	–	–	–	–
Tailor	28	27	24	26	Not Specified		50		Not Specified			
Tobacco	110	106	105	102	855	777	759	823	20	25	27	34
Wholesale Dealer	16	22	13	21	560	847	914	772	9	11	6	14

Source: CVA, Van. City, In Correspondence, Vol. 126, L File 1929

clients. By 1920, thirty of the eighty-eight Chinese grocers and as many as twenty-five of the thirty-one Chinese greengrocers were located outside Chinatown. Six years later, seventy-one of the seventy-four Chinese greengrocers had set up shop outside the district. As Table 2 indicates rather dramatically, Chinese in Vancouver virtually began the separate line of stores called "greengrocers" in the early 1920s, partly in response to the colour-based division of labour that denied them open employment choice. Prior to then, produce was sold by pedlars, in groceries or at the city market. Only nine greengrocer shops were owned by "other nationalities" in Vancouver in 1920. Of the other trades in which Chinese held licences in 1920, only laundries, and to a lesser extent restaurants, were disproportionately located outside Chinatown.

DESPITE THIS MOVEMENT BY greengrocers, Chinese settlement in Vancouver was still highly concentrated in 1920. Three years earlier, the annual report of the civic health committee noted that the Chinese population in the city appeared to be increasing rapidly, occupying a district bounded by Campbell Avenue on the east and the CPR tracks (near Carrall Street) on the west. The map of settlement for 1920 confirms this new spill of Chinese into Strathcona and also indicates that a minority had moved since 1910 to other districts of the city, such as Fairview, Mount Pleasant, and Grandview (see Maps 4 and 5). Most of these non-Chinatown residents lived on laundry or grocery premises, according to the address and occupation information in the directory – a notable new concentration of which was located near the Granville Street bridge on the west side of the city. The small concentration near Commercial Drive and Hastings Street lay on Woodland Drive and Albert Street, in the vicinity of the district that was to have been reserved for Chinese in the aborted move of Chinatown during 1911–12.

Evidence is spotty, but it is clear that informal practices on the part of white real estate agents and landlords limited the residential choices of Chinese in Vancouver in the first part of this century. Such evidence includes newspaper advertisements for lots that Chinese were not eligible to buy; statements by community spokesmen in later years about the lack of residential choice of Chinese before the late 1950s (see chapter 6); references to steering practices by real estate agents; and other evidence such as the operation of restrictive covenants in various districts of the city, as we shall see later.

Also revealing are the protests about Chinese spatial and occupational mobility from a number of ratepayer groups and the Vancouver

Retail Merchants' Association in the late 1910s and early 1920s. In 1914, the Grandview and Ward Three ratepayers' associations, for example, passed resolutions calling for the prevention of property ownership by Chinese in Vancouver and throughout British Columbia during the war.[49] By 1919, the Grandview Chamber of Commerce had joined them, and in February of that year the *Highland Echo*, the chamber's official organ, reported under the heading "To Fight the Yellow Peril": "Grandview merchants, besides many prominent men in the district were out in full force last Monday ... The first speaker was Alderman Jos. Hoskins who promised his every endeavour to stamp out the evil. However the landlord, he said, was the only man who could effectively keep the Oriental out of the district by refusing to sell or rent to him. Before closing Ald. Hoskins made a motion that efforts be made to bring about a bylaw, whereby no licences would be given to any Oriental, who had not been an ally of Britain, to do business in the city. The motion was unanimously carried."[50]

Alarmed by the spirit of such gatherings, all the Chinese merchants at Grandview and Fairview petitioned the consul for China, complaining that "on account of the recent agitation their business has suffered to a marked degree."[51] But in the same month, the Grandview and the Central ratepayers' associations protested to council about the inroads Chinese had begun to make and the deleterious effects these were assumed to have for property values and hygiene in their areas.[52] The merchants of Upper Granville, Davie, and Robson streets, indignant and somewhat alarmed at this new form of competition from "John," joined in with a petition for measures that would restrict Chinese settlement to one area of the city.[53]

Until this time council had not found it necessary to take formal action with regard to Chinese residence in the city. As the city clerk had informed his Calgary counterpart back in 1910: "The City of Vancouver has not had to take any action with reference to the matter of segregating the Chinese for residential purposes ... They are mostly confined to one district of the city."[54] But by the end of the decade, when the Chinese population of the city had reached approximately 6,000 (about 3.5 per cent of the city's population),[55] council was moved to take action on behalf of the white commercial and residential lobbies which had made their views so clear.

For Aldermen Elkins and Hoskins, the threat of Chinese infiltration into the residential districts was so grave that it warranted a strongly worded appeal to Ottawa for Chinese immigration exclusion. Otherwise it would be necessary to "take up arms to drive them into the sea," Hoskins told the *Province* in early February 1919. On 10 February, council resolved to appoint a committee of aldermen "to

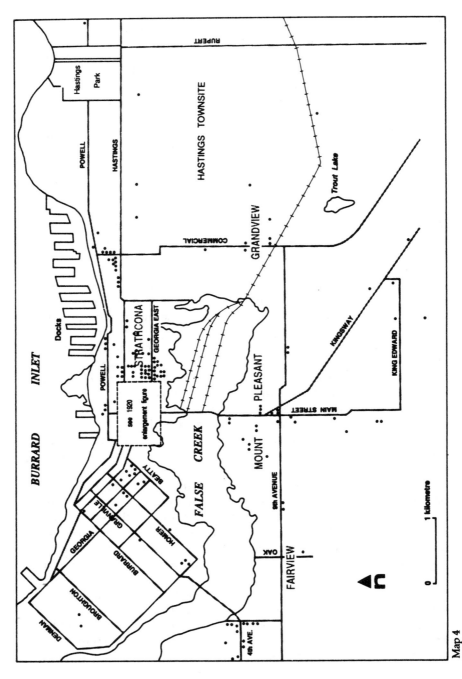

Map 4
Distribution of Chinese in Vancouver, 1920
Source: Based on *Henderson's Directory*, 1920

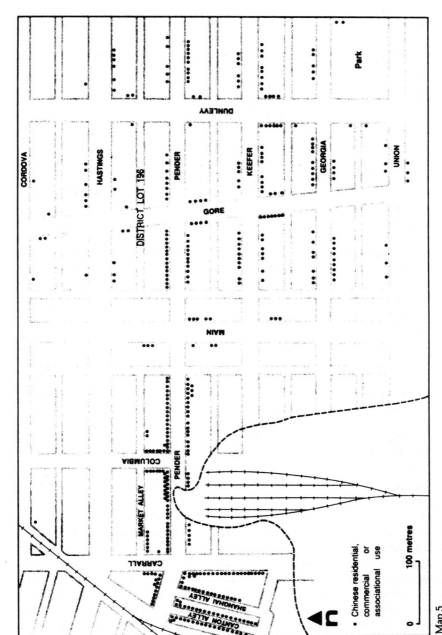

Map 5
Chinatown Area, 1920 (Detail of Map 4)
Source: Based on *Henderson's Directory*, 1920

(Map labels:)
CORDOVA
HASTINGS
DISTRICT LOT 196
PENDER
GORE
MAIN
COLUMBIA
MARKET ALLEY
PENDER
CARRALL
SHANGHAI ALLEY
CANTON ALLEY
DUNLEVY
KEEFER
GEORGIA
UNION
Park

- Chinese residential, commercial or associational use

N

0   100 metres

enquire fully into the question of the immigration of Asiatics into the Province and their employment subsequent to arrival." A month later, it unanimously carried Elkins's motion, giving moral force once more to the agitation of the day:

Whereas the number of Chinese of all classes immigrating to the Province of British Columbia is too large and at the present time there are too many Chinese residing in this Province ... And whereas ... a large number of Chinese are operating farms and stores throughout this City and Province in unrestricted competition with our own citizens, and such conditions being prejudicial to the best interest of this City and Province; And whereas the great majority of these immigrants to Canada remain in the Province of British Columbia on account of the climatic conditions and it is undesirable that they should assimilate with our citizens on account of racial prejudice; And whereas it is undesirable to increase the difficulties of providing sufficient employment for our soldiers now returning from overseas ... And whereas we believe the system of collecting $500 head tax is wrong in principle and tends to create a condition of slavery in our midst with its attendant evil; Be it therefore resolved –: 1. That this Council memorialize the Dominion Government asking that the necessary regulations be immediately enacted to prevent further Chinese immigration into Canada.[56]

If immigration exclusion offered part of an ultimate solution, a more immediate task in the eyes of council was to seal the limits of the Chinese claim to Vancouver at Pender Street, and it quickly began investigating ways of achieving a form of spatial segregation of the Chinese and European populations. In line with that strategy, Mayor R. Gale simply ignored a February 1919 request from Consul Koliang Yih that he "warn the editors of the *Highland Echo* to stop further agitation against the Orientals and to assure us that the owners of property will not use their efforts to force Chinese tenants to vacate, or to unreasonably advance the rent to a prohibitive price."[57] Gale's allegiance on the question lay with the Retail Merchants' Association, as he assured its members two years later as the Liberal dominion candidate for Vancouver Centre.[58]

In a letter read to council in March 1919, the Chinese consul again sought to influence the debate, writing: "The proposition to segregate the Oriental residents is certainly ill-advised, thoughtless and unwarranted in the first place."[59] On the same day, council carried a motion by Alderman Hoskins which showed that the consul had even less effect on this issue than he had on the pedlars' licences: "Whereas the City Council has been approached by deputations representing retail business and residential districts of Vancouver requesting relief from encroachment of Asiatics into business and residence sections; And whereas the said spread of Asiatics is daily growing to be a graver aggravation; Be it therefore resolved that the City Solicitor be instructed to advise the Council whether or not some system of segregating cannot be legally adopted to confine Asiatic retail business into some well defined given area of the city."[60]

AFTER AN EXTENSIVE INQUIRY by legal advisers to council and by the Retail Merchants' Association of Canada, City Solicitor J.B. Williams finally had to inform council in 1923 that it did not have the power to restrict "Orientals" to any particular section of the city. "The only effective solution from a practical standpoint, would appear to be for enabling legislation of both a Federal and Provincial character to be secured, delegating powers to municipalities to deal with the matter."[61] American municipal authorities had enjoyed similar powers until the US Supreme Court ruled them unconstitutional in 1917,[62] but Canadian municipalities, with senior levels of government perhaps wary of the American precedent, did not get their legislation.

In Vancouver, the strength of purpose of municipal authorities and those they represented ensured that their exclusionary aims were realized in fact, if not in statute. Some strictly residential areas simply overcame the constitutional limitation on their powers by establishing "gentlemen's agreements," or unwritten rules, by which segregation was assured through adherence to the common goal of denying property rights to "out-groups." The authorities are known to have turned a blind eye to such collusion, and gentlemen's agreements in such districts as Point Grey, the University Endowment Lands, Capilano Highlands, Shaughnessy, the British Properties, sections in the Hastings Townsite, and Mount Pleasant survived until the late 1940s, and in some instances beyond this.[63] Only in the mid-1950s did the courts demolish the legal validity of these restrictive covenants. In other mixed residential and commercial districts of the city, such as Grandview, there was little – bar the informal pressure that had the indulgence of officials of council – to prevent Chinese from operating greengroceries on premises that usually doubled as houses.

MEANWHILE, THE FULL MISCELLANY of legal and political discrimination had continued unabated. The cultural belief that "whites" were an in-group – a community needing firm boundaries and strong safeguards against loss of its standards – was justification to marginalize the Chinese in whatever ways were open to the governing élites.

Consul for China Yih reminded Mayor Gale after a meeting at City
Hall in 1919 that Chinese in Vancouver and Victoria alone were paying approximately $300,000 municipal taxes annually, as well as a
considerable amount in provincial taxes. Yet, while all naturalized
British subjects over twenty-one years of age were entitled to the
provincial and civic vote, Chinese were denied it. Yih protested that
this was a "most unjustifiable condition [of] taxation without representation."[64]

The professions of pharmacy, dentistry, and law were also closed
to non-voters, and in Vancouver occupational closure against people
of Chinese origin extended de facto to other jobs in banking, in the
department stores, and in nursing at the Vancouver General Hospital,
an institution where in the 1920s sick Chinese were treated only in
the basement.[65] Chinese in Vancouver's schools also became targets
in 1921, when the Vancouver School Board decided to pursue the
possibility of school segregation, despite the assurances of all but
four of the city's thirty-four school principals that Chinese students
were not a hindrance to the achievements of white students.[66]

The lines of social and political closure also continued to be drawn
around the sacred preserve of Canadian nationality, depending of
course on the discretion of respective judges. Naturalization was so
jealously guarded by some judges that they would go to absurd
lengths to justify denying it to "Chinese." In 1922, for example, Judge
Grant of Vancouver refused the application of one Yew Gan Hoy on
the grounds that, having taken the trouble "to investigate the kind
of farmers they make, I am told from an agricultural point of view
they are ruining the Lower Mainland ... My duty is not to approve
any person whom I do not believe would keep this country as good
as it is." Unfortunately for his honour's otherwise impeccable logic,
Yew was a Chinatown tailor![67]

Within the same strict judicial bounds that we observed in earlier
chapters, white Vancouver had come to demonstrate the excesses of
a solidly rooted cultural hegemony, fuelled by eugenist prophecies
about the dilution of the white race. One rather spectacular expression of this determination was the Asiatic Exclusion League, formed
with Vancouver as its base in 1921. In that year, according to the chief
controller of Chinese immigration for the port of Vancouver, every
household in the city was canvassed to support the league, with
considerable success.[68] The following year, the league's secretary,
Charles Macauley, reported membership of 40,000 throughout the
province.[69] Its hysterical publication called *Danger: The Anti-Asiatic
Weekly* sought, in the words of Macauley, "to educate the people of
this country to the terrible effect of allowing Orientals a foothold in

Canada."[70] In its lurid tone and language, it was rivalled by Hilda Glynn-Ward's fiction *The Writing on the Wall*, which the mainstream *Vancouver Sun* saw fit to publish in 1921. "The leopard cannot change his spots any more than a white man can be Orientalized or an Oriental be brought to live by the customs and laws of the European," Glynn-Ward wrote. In a story that envisaged a future in which the mayor of Vancouver and most of the aldermen were Chinese, the author conveyed her deeper message: "Between the Orient and the Occident, there lies more than a mere ocean, there is a great divide, intangible and insurmountable.") — all restrictions against Chinese.

"SNOW-PARTIES"
IN CHINATOWN

Behind the walls of Glynn-Ward's "great divide," Vancouver's Chinatown continued to be defined and monitored through the early 1920s according to its perceived "Chineseness." Administrations at City Hall took a leadership role in neighbourhood definition, policing the divide in ways similar to the régimes examined in the last chapter. Legal limits had constrained the most direct means of enforcing the divide, as was shown, but in the management of the ghetto itself council continued stridently to impose its will. The *British Columbia Monthly* gave council a clear mandate in 1921: "For years its [Chinatown's] unsavoury reputation has been a sidewalk topic. Different authorities on the shady side of the city have condemned it in no uncertain terms as not only the breeding place of such diseases as flourish in the dens of the Oriental, but also as a crime centre in Vancouver. Opium, gambling – to each Chinatown is a home ... The manner of life of its inhabitants is indescribable. And this district has, of late years, spread amazingly. Residential localities which, until lately, were occupied by people who were white, are now entirely Chinese. Business blocks, which a few years ago were occupied by Canadian firms are now filled with the goods of the Oriental. It may be said that this is part of the price of war but, if so, it is surely nonetheless deplorable."[71]

Ever mindful of the legitimacy to be earned from Chinatown vendettas, the city responded to such views with characteristic dedication. Administrations drew on prior definitions of the "Chinese" and "Chinatown" to justify close scrutiny of the Pender Street district. Sanitary reform certainly proceeded apace, and the familiar remedies were brought to bear. In 1919, for example, Chinatown was denounced by the health committee of council as a propagating ground for disease, and an inspection team was set up to monitor the hygiene of the area.[72] Within ten months, the owners of more than twenty lodgings were threatened with orders to condemn their properties, including the Chinese Hospital at 106 East Pender Street.[73] In March 1921, the entire city council inspected Chinatown, and some weeks later three officials ordered 278 of the 280 owners it had visited to upgrade and paint their homes, failing which they would be pulled down. Not surprisingly, the *Chinese Times* complained of discrimination.[74] Another effort to control density violations in Chinatown came in 1922, when council established a minimum of 400 square inches of breathing space per person per room.[75] Gambling and opium raids and arrests also took their usual busy course, and in the first few months of 1921 nearly 1,000 gamblers were arrested and fined.[76] By another civic dictum of 1922, noodle and confectionery stores and restaurants using what were thought to be inferior eggs imported from China had to indicate this in their windows.[77]

In the early 1920s, the image-makers of "Chinatown" found new ammunition to compound the old. Former vice associations became incorporated into a new perception of the district that carried forward the earlier public nuisance definition. In particular, the image of Chinatown as an opium den was assimilated into a fresh image of the area as a narcotics base and a perception of "Chinese" as dangerous drug distributors. On 22 March 1920, for example, a *Sun* editorial asserted: "It has been proved beyond all peradventure that the traffic in habit-forming drugs centres in Chinatown ... If the only way to save our children is to abolish Chinatown, then Chinatown must and will go, and go quickly."

Consul-General Yip appealed to the provincial government and twice to Mayor W. Owen for an end to such unsubstantiated claims in the press. The mayor, however, argued that Chinese were frequent drug users, and the *Sun* continued its charges.[78] He did nothing, for example, to silence an April 1921 editorial that described Chinatown as a "cancer corroding the vitals of this community ... overstraining the power of civic endurance" and attacked Chinese merchants for forcing on the public the belief "that no degradation is too vile to be inflicted upon the white people so long as it brings easy money in Chinatown."[79] A *World* editorial took greater licence in 1922 when it described the district as the "corrupter of white girls who are taken round in curtained taxis to Chinese labour camps and lodging houses so that they might earn the money to purchase more of the foul stuff."[80]

Consul-General Yip and the Chinese Benevolent Association (CBA) of Vancouver had by now become concerned at the degree to which this media sensationalism was being matched by official anti-Chinese sentiment, particularly in the House of Commons. In 1921 they formed a Self Improvement Committee to try to elevate the public image of Chinatown.[81] The old campaigner Won Alexander Cumyow, by this time president of the CBA, had already taken a stand against press characterizations of drugs in Chinatown in this 1920 letter to the editor of the *Sun*:

It is indeed too obvious to state that habit-forming drugs do not of their own accord drop from the heavens into Chinatown and it is needless for us to state that all means of ingress and egress by which this illegal drug traffic can be carried on is neither directly or indirectly controlled by the Chinese ... That Chinese vendors have been engaged in the traffic we do not deny, and we greatly deprecate this condition of affairs, but at the same time we deem it pertinent to call to mind the suggestion of Police Commissioner Buckworth that Chinese vendors are merely conveniently used and that the traffic is controlled by persons other than Chinese ... In conclusion we wish to assure the general public that we are only too glad to render any assistance in eradicating this nefarious trade and that the Chinese people are not afraid to attempt to prevent this illegal drug traffic is more than proven by the fact that not so very long ago China went to war with Great Britain in an endeavour to stamp out that evil.[82]

As Chinatown's Self Improvement Committee fought to contain anti-Chinese feeling in Vancouver itself, its fears that such sentiments were being carried into the dominion arena were proving well founded, with British Columbian representatives acting as prime movers in Ottawa. The irrepressibly anti-Chinese member of parliament for Vancouver Centre, Henry Herbert Stevens, played a leading role in this transmission of ideas and sentiments. The former secretary of the Vancouver Moral Reform Association made a series of emphatic speeches on the question in the House of Commons in the early 1920s.[83] In a speech in May 1920 aimed at convincing the house that Chinese "are incapable of assimilation," Stevens declared that the basis for the "pernicious drug habit" on the Pacific Coast was Asiatic: "We have seen in Vancouver almost innumerable cases of clean, decent, respectable, young women from some of the best homes dragged down by the dope traffic and very, very largely through the medium of the opium dens in the Chinese quarter."[84]

Two years later, a more detailed tale of Chinatown's "snow parties" was related to parliament by Leon Ladner of Vancouver South as part of his appeal to Prime Minister King (a hardliner on the Chinese drug question since his 1908 opium investigation) for exclusion of Chinese immigration. Ladner spent a considerable amount of his speech describing how the traffic in cocaine and morphine, organized "almost entirely by Chinese," was orchestrated: "Chinamen of great wealth, engaged in this odious practice, give parties at which white women, whom they employ, act as hostesses. Young girls are invited from about the city ... Interspersed among these young people are two or three addicts who are trained and whose business it is to inveigle other people into the use of narcotics."[85]

Other BC members also used this new ingredient of the Chinatown concept to great effect in that session of parliament. The member for Yale, John MacKelvie, interpreted the "drug evil," as he called it, to the rest of the house by appealing to the notion of "Chinatown" itself. He said: "If any member wishes to acquaint himself with how degraded human nature may under certain circumstances become, all he has to do is to visit certain Oriental quarters in British Columbia cities, where he will find a condition of filth and vice, vice which must be unmentionable before audiences such as this, which ought to convince him that the fewer of this class of people that any country has within its bounds, the better it will be for its people and for its civilization to progress upon really proper lines."[86]

Spurred to action, dominion authorities decided in 1922 to strengthen their control over Chinese drug abuses by amending the Opium and Narcotic Drug Act to provide for deportation of aliens found guilty of any drug offence.[87] In such ways, the Chinatown idea informed recurring rounds of legislative activity at all levels of government in the ongoing construction of the category of outsiders "Chinese." We turn now to the decisive measures adopted by the dominion government in the period following the First World War.

OTTAWA: THE HEAD TAX AND EXCLUSION

The racial classification "Chinese" had been institutionalized in dominion policy since the Act to Restrict and Regulate Chinese Immigration was passed in 1885 and the head-tax system introduced. The category was not a neutral one, as we have seen. According to the epistemological framework through which people of Chinese origin in Canada were "seen" and out of which the guardians of European cultural domination acted, "Chinese" signified non-white, non-Christian, and non-Canadian. This classification overrode, among other possible criteria of self-definition, those of nationality, birthplace, gender, and adopted country of residence. In short, "Chinese" signified an essence that was eternal and foreign. And once the category was a legal and administrative entity, it provided the medium and justification for successively tighter restrictions on people of Chinese origin. The category aided its own reproduction, in other words, and the status of outsider became self-fulfilling.

As noted in chapter 2, the legislation of 1885 was cumbersome from the outset. It granted exempt status to certain classes of Chinese – merchants, students, scientists, tourists, and diplomats – and the rest were charged a $100 head tax in 1901 and a $500 levy from 1903. *head tax.* In subsequent years, administrators of the act in various departments – Trade and Commerce initially, Interior after 1911, and Immigration and Colonization from 1919 – were preoccupied with refining the qualification for exempt status and the procedure for determining the status of persons claiming exemption. Their problem lay with the enforcement machinery of the act which was ill-fitted to manage abuses of exempt status. This difficulty had been invited by the framers of the legislation, who – as the chief controller for Chinese immigration, Mr W.D. Scott, told a barrister for a Chinese student in 1913 – set out "to place obstacles in the way of the Chinese desirous of entering the country, but at the same time to avoid provisions which would tend to diminish trade between the Dominion and the Chinese Empire."[88]

As an example of the administrative difficulties created by the act, prior to 1908 a distinction was made between students having student status prior to their landing in Canada and those declaring their intention to enter Canadian schools. Those in the first class were exempt from the tax, and those in the second were required to pay it on the understanding that they would be eligible for a refund upon producing, within eighteen months, a certificate showing regular school attendance for at least one year.

By 1908, suspicion was being cast on the entry of "students" to British Columbia. In that year, the number of Chinese entering Canada had risen to 2,234 (of whom 752 were exempt), nearly ten times the number who had entered the year before.[89] A BC member claimed in the House of Commons that Chinese labourers were entering the country, getting an education from the province for a year, and then joining the regular labour market. "I don't see why we should leave a loop-hole for these people to escape from the head-tax," the member stated.[90] Soon afterward, the act was amended to require the tax from all students on entry, with the provision that it would be refunded to students who complied with new conditions, on leaving Canada.[91] From that time, a student had to be registered at a university with "satisfactory proof" of his student status in both Canada and China.

A similar management problem arose with regard to the admission of Chinese merchants. Here again, the operational definition and

student racism

procedure for assessing this status devolved to officials in Ottawa and the ports of entry, who confronted the problem of fraudulent entries of non-merchants posing as merchants. In the face of an increase of tax-exempt entries beginning in 1908, a royal commission was appointed in 1911 to inquire into Chinese immigration at the port of Vancouver.[92] The customs interpreter at the port and some government officials were found implicated in scandals surrounding the processing of spurious merchants. These findings led to closer scrutiny of incoming migrants, and the number of exempt entrants fell to 498 in 1911–12, nearly half the number for 1910–11.[93]

The entry to Canada of non-exempt Chinese migrants had also been proscribed, despite requests for a more relaxed policy from employers such as railway entrepreneurs. Successive dominion governments increasingly restricted the entry of Chinese labour, not merely through tightening the operational definition of exempt categories but more directly through extending the application of various orders-in-council to Chinese immigrants. On the eve of the First World War, officials in the Department of Interior recommended that the provisions of an order-in-council, passed in 1913 to exclude labourers and artisans from landing in British Columbia, be extended to Chinese immigrants even if they could pay the $500 head tax.[94] The extension had an immediate impact; the number of Chinese paying the entry tax decreased from 5,274 in 1913–14 to 1,155 in 1914–15 and 20 (students) in 1915–16.[95] The extended regulations remained in force under various orders-in-council for the following seven years, despite continuing pressure from Canada's larger employers of labour.[96] These mostly extra-parliamentary controls were used to circumscribe the avenues for Chinese immigration throughout the 1910s. Meanwhile, concerted immigration recruitment programs were commenced by the Department of Immigration and Colonization in the British Isles, Scandinavia, Holland, Belgium, France, and Switzerland.[97]

ATTEMPTS BY CHINESE TO CIRCUMVENT the outsider status built in to the immigration act of 1885 were normally sufficient to prompt amendments to the law, but external political pressure, channelled through members of the House of Commons, ensured that administrators would look to the strictest interpretation of the exempt-status provisions in the act.

As mentioned earlier, Henry Stevens, Conservative member for Vancouver Centre, was perhaps the most outspoken BC critic of the Chinese in the 1910s and early 1920s. Stevens began his crusade to exorcise Orientals (and "Hindus") as soon as he was elected in 1911. He regularly made florid speeches on the subject to his constituency (Oriental immigration was for instance "an unmitigated curse, and foul from the bottom up"[98]), and built a prominent political profile around the "Yellow Peril" slogan. Inside the house, what distinguished Stevens from previous BC members was the unapologetic language he introduced to debate in an institution that had generally attempted to steer a diplomatic path around crude vocabulary. In March 1914, while charging southern China with hookworm infestation, Stevens said in one of his more controlled speeches: "Orientals have a distinct life, distinct in ideals, in habits, in conditions, in morals and every other way. I care not what value you may place upon it, it is distinct from ours, and that life and these ideals are what guide them in their decisions ... I hold that civilization finds its best exemplification in the civilization which we see in the British Empire and in the other countries of northern Europe. I hold that it is the sacred trust of the Anglo-Saxon and kindred peoples to hold that civilization and to cherish it ... We cannot hope to preserve our national type if we allow Asiatics to enter Canada in any large number."[99]

Stevens paved the way for other blunt invocations of the race idea. On the same day as Stevens identified the nation's "sacred trust," Frank Oliver (Edmonton) spoke out in favour of extending the order-in-council of 1913 to Chinese with words that appealed to Glynn-Ward's "great divide": "I will admit that the labour feature of the question is important, but I maintain it is a less important part of it. As the civilization of the West differs radically from the civilization of the East, it will be agreed that if western or European civilization is to prevail on this continent, it must be without the influence of Asiatic civilization ... The two civilizations are radically different and cannot exist together and maintain their own characteristics."[100]

Three years later, Oliver appealed to the moral equation of race and nation to try to convince the house to reject an amendment to the act that would return Chinese students to regular exempt status. He said: "For my own part, I desire in this House to promote the idea of a white Canada and the exclusion so far as it is reasonably possible, of those races, who, by a policy of peaceful penetration permitted to be carried on, would change the condition of this Canada of ours from being a white Canada to being a Canada of some other character."[101] The amendment on student exempt status passed the house, despite the efforts of Oliver and many other members. It had been prompted by criticism from the Chinese government concerning the lack of diplomacy involved in Canada's treatment of Chinese university students, when compared with that of the American government.

True to the fears of the amendment's critics, the old menace of fraudulent entries soon reappeared. In 1918, over 4,000 Chinese were admitted with "student" status, many of whom were shown on investigation to be labourers. Within months, Scott had advised port officials to refuse head taxes from all Chinese immigrants except merchants' sons less than sixteen years old, whose fathers had deposited an affidavit with the department guaranteeing that the child would attend school and nothing more.[102] The agents of all steamship lines were also given instructions to limit transportation to returning and exempt Chinese. These measures to tighten Chinese immigration had the desired effect of reducing, to approximately 500, the total number of entries in 1919–20.

In 1921, however, another influx broke the calm for the officials. To enter Canada, merchants required a certificate of entry issued by a recognized official of the Chinese government or a British consul in China. Suspicions about the methods by which the certificates were obtained lingered well after the 1911 royal commission exposed some corruption, and as soon as the 1921 rise in merchant entries was detected legislation was introduced to close what was seen as a loophole. In an important amendment to the 1885 legislation made in April 1921, all Chinese applying for admission to Canada, regardless of whether they were bearers of certificates (i.e. exempt), had to substantiate their status to the satisfaction of the controller of Chinese immigration, subject to the approval of the minister of immigration, whose decision was final.[103]

Soon afterward, the first Chinese merchant possessing a certificate but unable to substantiate his merchant status arrived at Vancouver. He applied for and won a writ of habeas corpus, which effectively allowed him exempt admission – and set a significant legal precedent. Such troublesome litigation finally led Mr A.L. Jolliffe, controller of Chinese immigration, to complain to Immigration Superintendent Mr W.D. Scott, in February 1922: "In so far as the Chinese Immigration Act [sic] is concerned, this statute does not now serve the purpose for which it was created ... The department's officials are experiencing considerable difficulty in carrying out the policy now in existence, due in my opinion to the fact that existing legislation does not meet the situation ... The present enforcement of the regulations is being systematically opposed by Chinese now in Canada as shown by the number of habeas corpus applications."[104]

THE HEAD-TAX SYSTEM OF CONTROL seems to have contained the seeds of its own ultimate impracticability. By 1922, when, as we shall see, the clamour in the house for exclusion was at its most feverish, the only option left open to a Liberal government needing to demonstrate again its solidarity with "white" Canada was to repeal the 1885 immigration act and draw up a new law. By this time, eastern and central Canadian members were aligned with the BC contingent against the Chinese, many of whom had "infiltrated" over the Rocky Mountains during the First World War. By 1921, the proportion of Canada's Chinese living in British Columbia had fallen to 59 per cent (from 86 per cent in 1901).[105] Returned soldiers' associations, trade unions, and other organizations from across Canada petitioned Ottawa for an end to Asiatic immigration.[106] Still, it was the experienced BC members in both political parties who provided the tone and vocabulary for debate.

In May 1922, the member for New Westminster, William McQuarrie, introduced a resolution to exclude "Oriental aliens" from Canada.[107] The resolution received much sympathy during the course of an entire day of debate. McQuarrie defended his resolution with words that indicated the extent to which the race idea and eugenist concepts were entrenched in the culture and lexicon of post-war British Columbia: "They (Orientals) cannot be assimilated. They will always exist as a foreign element in our midst. The real test of assimilation is intermarriage. The divergence of characteristics of the two races is so marked that intermarriage does not tend to perpetuate the good qualities of either race. The races are fundamentally different. Their morals are different, and language, heredity, religion and ideals will militate against and prevent even sociological assimilation."[108] McQuarrie's other reasons for presenting the motion were the inevitability of racial conflict in British Columbia, the lower standard of living of Orientals, their economic competition in certain lines, their responsibility for the drug traffic, and their unsuitability for naturalization.

The well-organized BC members reiterated these claims using the powerful conceptual opposition of "ours" and "theirs." Alfred Stork of Skeena argued: "It is good policy to settle this Oriental problem while the white population is still in possession of British Columbia." It was all the more pressing, he argued, because the contest was unequal. "The white man is handicapped by the responsibilities of civilization; the Oriental is prepared to struggle for his solitary existence." The member for Burrard, John Clark, also used words that invoked less the hidden workings of some latent white prejudice or the imperatives of a capitalist system of production and more the cultural and political force of the race idea itself. "In my opinion," he said, "the basic factor is the future of the white race as a racial type. That is the basic factor in the future of the Dominion, and if our race is to be mixed with that of an Oriental country, we cannot have that racial type." Charles Dickie of Nanaimo agreed: "We cannot conceive of a commingling of the blood of our Canadians with that of the Ethiopians; we cannot conceive of a commingling of our blood with that of Asiatics." In addition to mentioning the drug issue, Leon Ladner also appealed to basic matters of "blood." "I submit," said Ladner, "that in order to have national harmony, the people must hold in common such great fundamentals of nationhood as, national ideals and aims, the Christian religion, race tradition – the colour and habits of the race, and perhaps, most important of all from the standpoint of immigration, the practice of intermarriage."[109]

But it was Stevens who, as the final BC speaker, attempted to interpret the issue for the rest of the house, with his concluding question: "Shall Canada remain white, or shall Canada become multi-coloured? Shall British institutions, traditions, ethics, and social standards prevail; or shall they, by blind neglect and purposeless procrastination, submit to a peaceful conquest by the forerunners of the hordes of Asia? Shall Canadianism, which we are always proud to picture as the perfection of British democracy, prevail; or shall it recede before the races that, as I have already said, are incongruous and incompatible with our mode of life?"[110]

Presented with the patriotic conviction of their Pacific coast counterparts, members less directly experienced with the Chinese readily conformed. The member for Yukon, who was "happy to say" that there were "no Chinamen" in his constituency, was none the less well versed in myths about essential racial characters. "Canada wants settlers," George Black stated, "but she wants only settlers who will become Canadians. We want only races which will intermingle and which can intermarry with our people and become not only with us, but of us." Edward McMurray of Winnipeg North admitted the Chinaman's "pronounced integrity" but continued: "We must look at this question from the point of view of its national importance ... The nations that succeed are those that have been built up slowly of one homogeneous people."[111]

Prime Minister King preferred to argue in analogies. He thought it particularly instructive to go to the "law governing the precious metals," which had it that when "two kinds of metals are in circulation as coinage, if one [is] of finer quality than the other, the baser metal tend[s] to drive the finer metal out of circulation."[112] The prime minister therefore fully supported McQuarrie's resolution, at least as it affected Chinese immigration. After all, China was "a second rate power, not a first class power," said King, and whereas the government's hands were tied with regard to Japanese immigration, for Chinese immigration there was, as McQuarrie had observed, an open field. That being said, the prime minister insisted that the wording of the resolution be changed from "exclusion" to "effective restriction" in the interests of diplomacy. At the time, King was planning to visit Beijing to try to secure a bilateral arrangement with the Chinese government. The amended resolution calling for "effective restriction" was carried by the house, without the support of diehard prohibitionists such as Stevens.[113]

On his visit to China in February 1923, King successfully negotiated a gentlemen's agreement by which the Chinese government would control migration to Canada.[114] Despite that success, and despite the most concerted lobbying efforts from Chinese organizations across Canada,[115] the minister of immigration soon afterward brought down a bill massively restricting Chinese immigration. It was in effect an exclusion act, but, consistent with Canada's history of veiled strategies on alien entry, it was not framed as such. It eliminated the troublesome head-tax system and substituted a system whereby entry was granted only to specified classes, subject to the discretion of the minister of immigration, who was granted the final authority for admission.[116] Under the new law, entry could be granted to merchants, university students for the period of their degree program, Canadian-borns returning from several years of education in China, and representatives of the Chinese government.

However, the law was designed to prevent these categories from meeting the operational qualifications, which were left to discretion rather than statute. For example, even if merchants did, as required, possess a minimum of $2,500 invested in a business at least three years old in China dealing exclusively in goods produced in China, they could bring their families to Canada only for short terms. The act also required all people of Chinese origin in Canada to register – an experience that proved to be both humiliating and difficult.[117] Finally, through the placing of a Canadian official in Hong Kong, rather than at the port of entry, troublesome litigation could be avoided and discretion exercised effectively to cover, as King put it, "what we want to have understood as coming within the provisions of the law."[118]

But for the lone and, for his time, remarkable attack by James S. Woodsworth, member for Winnipeg Centre (and soon to become founder of the Co-operative Commonwealth Federation), parliament solidly supported the bill. Woodsworth said: "It seems to me that we must definitely and consciously attempt to overcome the prejudices which we have against men of other races and other than our own. All students of ethnology recognize that, after all, there are many more things in common between the different races than things which separate us and the apparent divergences are not so great as sometimes we imagine."[119]

The House of Commons ignored Woodsworth's plea and passed an act that was to exclude all but a handful of people of Chinese origin from entering Canada for the next twenty-five years.

THE EXCLUSION LEGISLATION REPRESENTED the most extreme of the post-war attempts by different levels of Canadian government to enforce the cultural distinction of race. It was a bold confirmation of the relative entitlements of a socially constructed order of insider and outsider, the contours of which were decisively drawn in Vancouver society and space. As we have seen, "Chinatown" was for its representers an incubator of vice and disease that threatened to corrode the pure "stock" of a race and nation. If eugenists were correct, as many Canadians believed them to be in the 1920s, race deterioration, even suicide, would follow where the "unfit" encroached. Legislators took this as their call to action. As guardians and enforcers of European domination in a British outpost, they attempted to contain the disease-carriers by restraining their mobility and opportunities. The member for Yale put it bluntly during the day-long debate of 1922: "We say cut right down to the root of the evil, cut right home to the very marrow of this disease and apply the only effective remedy that will meet the situation – absolute and complete exclusion."[120]

The decision to restrict Chinese entry to Canada cannot be conceptualized simply as a reactive one, in which politicians blindly acted out the role of representing white interests. Insofar as politicians attempted to legitimize their control over the social order, they actively wielded and dramatized their calling, in part to secure votes, but also to build a national unit in the image of a European society. In that sense, the state-society relationship was reciprocal in the making of a culturally based hegemony. Although at the civic level it had not been possible to administer a direct remedy to Chinese mobility, we have seen that at the dominion level the power to engrave further the boundaries of a socially constructed order was decisively exercised. If leakage from the ghetto could not be directly plugged, the flow into Chinatown could at least be stemmed at the source. Henceforth 1 July, celebrated in Canada as Dominion Day, was to be observed for another reason. It marked the day in 1923 on which the Immigration Act came into force, and it became known to the Chinese as their own Humiliation Day.)

THE PENDER STREET
SOUP KITCHEN

Long on ageing bachelors, short on women of child-bearing age, and denied the direct means of demographic replenishment, Vancouver's Chinatown began to stagnate in the years after exclusion. A *Province* editorial some years later anticipated the most final of solutions as the effects of the 1923 act were beginning to be felt: "The number of Chinese in British Columbia declined by 25 percent from 27,139 in 1931 (of which 2,239 were women) to 21,740 in 1936."[121] In Vancouver itself, the Chinese community lost 6,000, or half of its number, during the 1930s.[122] Residents given no prospect of being joined in Canada by their families returned to China; others died, and some migrated to the eastern provinces, especially Ontario.

While white Vancouver society embraced the optimism of the 1920s, the cultural and political marginalization of the Pender Street community was brought home in a number of ways. In 1924, the city treasurer presented a case to council for moving Chinatown on the grounds that its site could be put to valuable industrial use.[123] In the same year, Attorney-General Manson launched a year-long investigation into the murder of Janet Smith, a Shaughnessy "nurse girl" who was allegedly killed by the home's "China-boy." The "China-boy" was eventually acquitted, but in the mean time the provincial legislature and, in particular, the press played wickedly on the notoriety of Chinatown.[124] Manson also lobbied Ottawa for repatriation of Orientals on the familiar grounds that "Oriental and European blood" could not be "mixed with advantage."[125]

In the mid-1920s, a spate of robbings and physical attacks took place in Vancouver's Chinatown, and when police consistently turned a blind eye the Chinese Benevolent Association (CBA) was forced to ask city council to afford greater protection to life and property in Chinatown.[126] The city also refused to sell a piece of its own land to a Chinese buyer in 1927,[127] while in 1928 Mayor W.H. Malkin was elected on a platform that included curtailment of the spread of Chinese in Vancouver. Their encroachment "constituted a menace and should be stopped by confining all Oriental stores to fixed Oriental districts," Malkin stated.[128] Three years later, the Tolmie provincial government reclassified married Chinese men as single workers and taxed them accordingly.[129] In the same year, a dominion order-in-council limited the issue of naturalization certificates to those Chinese who could produce evidence that they had renounced their Chinese citizenship. By 1941, just 5 per cent of the Chinese population who were not born in Canada were naturalized Canadians.[130]

WHITE VANCOUVER'S IMAGE AND assessment of Chinatown came to have some of its more onerous effects for "Chinese" during the Depression. Chinatown's organizations had traditionally supported the indigent, sick, and needy within their own welfare structures, but the Depression exerted enormous pressure on these internal networks and exposed the vulnerability of the Chinese community at large, and Chinese labour in particular.

The dependence of Chinese on economically vulnerable service industries, the closure of most shingle mills near Vancouver in 1929, and the general displacement of unskilled manpower because of mechanization exerted a formidable strain on Chinese employment in Vancouver. The CBA was so concerned by the pressure that unemployment placed on Chinatown's resources that it petitioned city council on 30 November 1931:

Whereas 40 per cent of the Chinese community are at present unemployed; And whereas for the last two years the Chinese Benevolent Association and other Chinese associations have carried on relief work amongst Chinese nationals without any assistance whatsoever from the Dominion or Provincial Governments or the City Council; And whereas the funds appropriated by the Chinese Benevolent Association are now utterly exhausted; And whereas there are at present in the City of Vancouver approximately 260 Chinese nationals who are absolutely destitute; And whereas there are at present only approximately 75 Chinese nationals on City Relief ... Now therefore we the Chinese Benevolent Association do humbly request and recommend that cognizance of these facts be taken by the City Council and that instructions be given to the Relief Department of the City of Vancouver to provide such relief as may be necessary to alleviate the suffering of the members of the Chinese community who require assistance by way of food and lodging to keep body and soul together and to prevent death by starvation which is the only alternative unless immediate action is taken.[131]

In response to this, and a complaint from white workers that Chinese on relief could use their meal tickets and live where they chose (at least theoretically), while non-Chinese were sent to relief camps, the civic relief officer contracted the Oriental Missions (run by the Church of England) to feed Chinese men on relief.[132] Thus in mid-1932 a separate scheme for Chinese relief was established.

By the following year fifty Chinese felt moved to march to City Hall to protest against the poor relief treatment and to demand welfare assistance. In the confusion over who was responsible for Chinese relief, the mayor deflected the grievance. At about the same time, a restaurant association was set up to fight the exclusion of Chinese restaurants from the right to redeem meal coupons.[133] By January 1935, the appeal of Chinatown had grown more desperate. A petition was submitted to Mayor McGeer and Premier Pattullo regarding "the inhuman and menacing conditions that exist among Chinese people in Vancouver, who are subject to the deplorable conditions existing in the soup kitchen at 143 Pender Street East, operated by the Board of Oriental Missions."[134] No less than 520 Chinatown residents signed this petition. The men particularly resented the provision of "two meagre meals per day which do not cost more than 3 cents a meal, while the Board receives from the Government 8 cents a meal. In addition, the Chinese unemployed have not received an issue of clothing or shoes since January 1934."

The petition closed with a plea for closure of the soup kitchen and for unemployed Chinese to be granted relief through the same system as the rest of Vancouver's unemployed. But as late in the Depression as June 1936, the provincial relief administrator still found the idea of equal relief payments to Chinese unfitting. He advised the civic relief officer that "a lower scale should be applied to Oriental cases ... We can never expect Orientals who have a much lower standard ... to become self-supporting as long as they are getting more on relief than they ever earned in good times."[135] Some Chinese did eventually receive cash payments; others, especially elderly men and the sick, were repatriated to China during 1934–6 under a provincial offer.[136] Still others failed to register for relief, perhaps because of language difficulties, ignorance of welfare regulations, or simply fear, in what for many was probably a first encounter with non-Chinese officials since their arrival.

There should be no doubt about the degree to which the process of racialization materially affected the lives of the people of Vancouver's Chinatown, above all in the Depression. The Canadian state, particularly the local government, quite simply abdicated responsibility for an unprotected bloc of workers. Through the Pender Street soup kitchen, the ultimate expression of the vulnerability of alien status was played out from 1931 to 1935, when at least 175 Chinese customers of the soup kitchen died of starvation.[137] If they died for a cause, it was certainly not their own. The cause was their marginalization by the state, whose practices confirmed not just the cultural boundaries of the Chinese racial category but the limits to the very survival of a neighbourhood apart.

CHAPTER FIVE

New Allies,
New Perceptions,
1935–1949

Vancouver's Chinatown found its first real allies during the Depression, although white people's concern for the neighbourhood was not prompted by their sudden rejection of beliefs about race. Rather, the abdication of responsibility for the Chinese during the Depression was, in the eyes of some nascent political reform groups, an obstacle to the much broader ideological struggle against a stratified society. Some incidents during the 1930s illustrate how this new political dimension to "the Chinese question" came to be recognized. The Provincial Workers' Council and the Scandinavian Workers' Club told Premier Duff Pattullo and Mayor Gerry McGeer in 1935 that the Chinese were "the only foreign race in Canada that is discriminated against in such a brutal and inhuman manner." Protests against the Pender Street soup kitchen were also made to the senior levels of government by the Canadian Co-operative Federation, the Canadian Labour Defence League, the North Fraser Workers' Protective Association, the Provincial Workers' Council on Unemployment, and the Women's Labour League.[1]

But if the Depression encouraged some sympathy for Chinatown, it also produced a new generation of equally ideologically inspired critics who, as we shall see, carried on with much the same sort of arbitrary "category legislation" examined in earlier chapters.[2] Armed with the still influential Darwinist logic, they desperately continued the challenge of trying to limit the residential and occupational entitlements of Vancouver's Chinese. The tension between these developments, the one reaching back to an "intolerant" past and the other extending to a more "tolerant" future, is the empirical concern of this chapter.

The study of race relations has typically been concerned with situations of negative ascription, conflict, and oppression on the part of more powerful groups. Rex's views can be taken as representative when he states that one of the "necessary elements" of a "race relations situation" is "abnormally harsh exploitation, coercion and competition."[3] Such a narrow conceptualization of a race-relations situation has tended to rely on an equally limiting definition of racism as the invidious belief in the superiority of one race over another. For decades, such definitions have foreclosed the types of questions asked in the field. The liberal tradition of race-relations research on the Chinese in Western societies has certainly amply documented "elements" that meet Rex's definition. It has chronicled the forms of exploitation and discrimination that belonged to eras less tolerant than most Western societies enjoy at present. The assumption behind such work is that changes in white attitudes have held the key to "better" race relations. This possibly accounts for the fact that many conventional histories of the Chinese in Western societies end their accounts at the Second World War, when the harshest forms of discrimination were outlawed. What has gone unnoticed, however, is that beliefs in the existence of "races" have themselves endured beneath changes in white attitudes.

(The more recent body of critical "race" research has also focused almost exclusively on negative evaluations of phenotypical and cultural differences. Husband, for example, suggests that people's beliefs in "race" have usually been accompanied by the racist belief that races are ranked on a hierarchy which has whites at the apex.[4] Husband is of course correct, and we have seen that in British Columbia "John Chinaman" was, for the most part, placed well beneath white settlers on the pecking order of perceived worth. But as was stated in chapter 1 of this book, the process of racialization need not always be accompanied by classically racist thought and action. To claim so is to obscure the multiplicity of forms that racialization is capable of assuming.)

In addition to its empirical aims, therefore, this chapter attempts to trace the persistence of the concepts of a Chinese race and place as they informed established, and emerging, white attitudes and practices during the 1930s. It will be seen that a more positive definition of "Chinatown" arose during that decade that drew on Western romantic conceptions of "Orientals" and their ancient and opulent civilization (referred to briefly in chapter 3). To be sure, this more amiable perception held the promise of better life chances for Chinatown's residents than they had experienced since arriving in British Columbia. But it also signalled the endurance of the process of racial categorization that is the subject of this study. White Vancouver's beliefs in the existence of a separate "Chinese race" were invigorated from a more benign perspective in the mid-1930s and structured, as they had been in the past, through the physical and symbolic medium of the Pender Street enclave.

The exotic image of Chinatown did not begin entirely afresh, however, simply displacing what went before, as if history were a string of beads. Just as the past is always sedimented within the present, so the romantic idea of Chinatown relied on prior conceptions of it as an aberration from white society. It grew out of the earlier vice discourse in a continuous process, and, as will be seen in this and the following chapters, the old and new conceptions converged in a more or less uneasy alliance – chameleon-like in European image and practice – for the balance of Chinatown's career. The residents, too, displayed varied responses. In some interesting developments, we shall see that the merchant élite was as committed to supplying the exotic concept of Chinatown that many Europeans sought to discover as it was at challenging the enduring, unflattering images of its neighbourhood.

In what follows, therefore, I seek to convey a sense of the transformational quality of European domination over Vancouver's Chinatown. White hegemony did not statically exist as a form of dominance; it was continually adapted to pressures from white society and was all the while capable of being modified and even harnessed to the interests of those it ultimately marginalized.

UPDATE ON CHINATOWN

In our concern for the European idea of "Chinatown," we must not overlook the fact that a Chinese community was eking out its own life in Vancouver, quite independent of the beliefs of white society. As will be clear by now, this study does not contribute to the body of scholarship about that settlement as a lived community from the vantage point of the residents. For the purposes of this argument, however, the Chinatown concept had a continuous physical referent at Vancouver's Pender Street, and what follows is an update of the brief description given in chapter 3 for the earlier decades.

In 1931, Vancouver possessed a Chinese-origin population of 13,011, the largest such community in Canada.[5] As mentioned in the last chapter, however, the demographic future of Chinatown looked bleak in the late 1920s. The exclusion legislation terminated growth, and Chinese residents' birth rate of six per 1,000 in Canada in 1931 (compared with the national birth rate of 23.2 per 1,000 in that year) did not augur well for the natural growth of Chinese communities anywhere in Canada.[6] Also, between 1931 and 1938, nearly 5,000

Chinese emigrated from Canada to China.[7] By 1941, a Vancouver news report headlined "City Chinese Face Racial Extinction" anticipated the ultimate solution when it stated that the Chinese birth rate had sunk to half the death rate.[8] One important demographic implication of these developments was that, despite the low birth rate, the local-born population of Chinese origin gradually grew in numerical significance in Chinese communities during the 1930s and 1940s.

Dispersal of Chinese business and residential activities increased somewhat after 1920, as the map of Chinese school attendance in Vancouver for 1937 indirectly indicates (compare Maps 4 and 6). The concentration in Strathcona was still pronounced, but during the 1930s there had also been further movement into Fairview, Grandview, Hastings East, and Mount Pleasant. It is possible that the demographic constraints on Chinese community growth, together with the economic stringency of the 1930s, compelled merchants to seek more expanded markets. By 1939, Chinese held licences for 133 of the 156 greengrocers in Vancouver and twenty-six of the forty laundries.[9] Both of these trades were disproportionately located outside of Chinatown, as was noted in chapter 4.

The spatial boundaries of "Chinatown" itself were specified by Quene Yip, a district merchant who wrote a short pamphlet on the neighbourhood for Vancouver's Jubilee celebrations in 1936. "Chinatown," he stated, "is situated on Pender Street, stretching from Carrall Street to Gore Avenue, including the whole of Canton and Shanghai Alleys, part of Carrall Street, part of Columbia and part of Main Street. Also a small colony is located at Keefer and Georgia streets which for the most part caters to wholesale produce."[10]

Within these boundaries, Yip identified six schools that operated after public-school hours, twelve "large societies," four churches, the premises of the *Chinese Times* newspaper, six hotels, one theatre, two cabaret halls, nine cafés, six butcher shops, nine "chop-suey houses," two "genuine chop-suey houses," eighteen tailor stores, twelve barber shops, twenty-four merchandise stores, two jewellery stores, one antique store, a Chinese-language branch of the Bank of Montreal, agencies of the Canadian Pacific, Blue Funnel, and Admiral lines, a doctor's office, and St Joseph's Hospital on Campbell Avenue. He might also have included a number of lodging-houses and various other small businesses – for example, laundries, shoemakers, booksellers, gambling houses, and pawnshops. These outlets and the map of Chinatown land use for 1943 (see Map 7) suggest that after the First World War, the territorial base of the Chinese community in Vancouver continued to be supported by institutional and business activity and, very probably, by the desire of immigrants from the

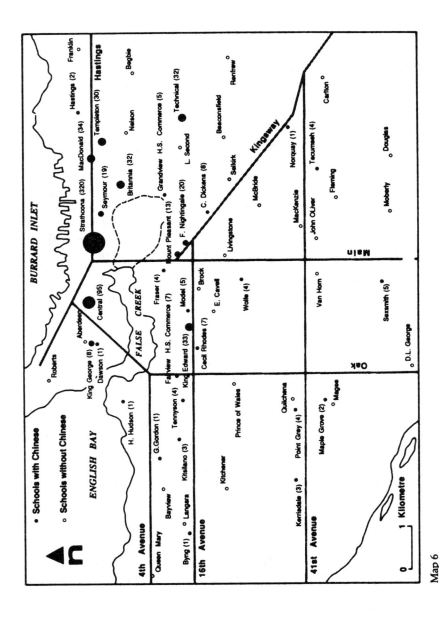

Map 6
Distribution of Chinese in Vancouver Schools, 1937
Source: Data in Halford Wilson Papers, Vol. 1/17, Provincial Archives of British Columbia, Catalogue No. E/D W69

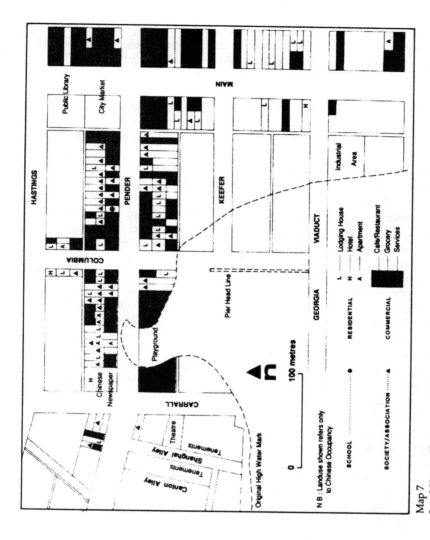

Map 7
Land Use in Chinatown, 1943
Source: University of British Columbia, Special Collections Map File, Acc. No. 2698

same country to participate in common activities. The Chinatown sub-economy kept many labourers in jobs, and there was also work in suburban market gardens, in the wholesaling and distribution of produce, in various unskilled capacities around the city, and increasingly in service industries such as restaurants.

These Chinese employment niches were evident province-wide in data collected for the 1931 Census of Canada.[11] There were 8,203 Chinese in unskilled work (other than agriculture, mining, and logging), 5,182 in the "personnel" sector (over half of whom were cooks, and a significant minority, waiters and restaurant keepers), 4,193 in agriculture (two-thirds were farm labourers), 1,841 in commercial sectors (half were owners/managers of retail stores while the rest were salesmen and pedlars), 997 domestic servants, 749 in the laundry trade (about 600 were workers and 106 were owners/managers), and 653 in the logging business (four were owners/managers). The categories in which Chinese were noticeably under-represented were the professions (where just 78 were employed as teachers, musicians, clergymen, health professionals, journalists, photographers, and "others"); few also worked in building and construction, in fishing, and in the finance/insurance category. In total, 22,999 Chinese men and just 161 women were employed in British Columbia in 1931.

The two most significant trends to note from these figures are, first, the rise in Chinese numbers employed in the service industry and in particular restaurant work since the turn of the century, and, second, the movement of unskilled labourers to agriculture, which followed the introduction in 1926 of minimum wage legislation in the lumber, canning, and mining industries. (In 1925, over 3,800 Chinese had been employed in the province's lumber industry.[12]) Finally, professional work outside the Chinatown sub-economy remained virtually non-existent, while public service was prohibited by law.

The associational life of Vancouver's Chinatown flourished after 1923 as the Chinese community looked inward for support and protection. The impetus for organizational change came largely from shifts in China's national politics and also from the strain of the Depression and various forms of external harassment. Both Kuomintang and freemasons' organizations consolidated their support (and mutual antagonisms) after the Kuomintang's rise to power in China in 1928; new district and clan associations were formed; others amalgamated, some developed cross-Canada links, and others such as wholesalers' organizations and the Mainland Growers' Cooperative Association were established in response to outside economic discrimination. As in other North American Chinatowns, the Depression brought forth labour organizations such as the Chinese Workers'

Protective Association to fight for jobs and economic security.[13] Other organizations devoted themselves to local welfare and fund-raising for projects in China, a cause that consumed the community after the outbreak of war between China and Japan in 1937. Women played a particularly significant role in orchestrating various fund-raising drives. In conjunction with the exclusion legislation, the homeland's involvement in a war created conditions for some degree of unity within a community that was more accustomed to internal discord, conflict, and stratification.

LABOUR, THE CCF, AND
A SPIRIT OF SOLIDARITY

The drastic curtailment of production and the upward spiralling of unemployment in the vulnerable resource-based economy of British Columbia from 1929 to 1933 sparked new heights of union solidarity and politicization among white workers. Out of the ferment, socialism was reborn, and in August 1932 the Socialist Party of British Columbia voted to affiliate itself with a new national socialist organization, the Co-operative Commonwealth Federation. Under the CCF's wing came various reformers and proponents of a new social order such as teachers, social workers, doctors, women's leagues, church associations, and some farmers. By 1933, the CCF had mounted an energetic BC election campaign, and when a rejuvenated Liberal party defeated the Conservative Tolmie government that year, the CCF became the official opposition.[14]

Prior to the Depression, organized labour throughout Canada had viewed Chinese workers in a spirit of competition and conflict. The Trades and Labour Congress of Canada (established in 1883) had never initiated a campaign among Chinese workers to encourage them to seek higher wages. For the most part, it had adopted expedient, short-run actions aimed at white workers' solidarity at the expense of a non-white enemy, rather than actions geared to long-run class solidarity. At the time, organized labour was, in the words of Ireland, "fighting to define its role and to secure its place in the total Canadian social structure."[15] Something of a change of heart might have occurred in 1919, when the British Columbia Labour Union opened an office in Chinatown to recruit supporters for the general strike, but it proved to be a short-lived gesture.[16]

Amid the levelling experience of the Depression, such expediency gave way to recognition by the Trades and Labour Congress that the source of conflict between "Orientals" and "white" labour was caused by the competitive position into which Orientals had been forced and that legalized discrimination ultimately militated against the interests of all workers. Some important political action by branches of organized labour followed from that realization. In 1929, for example, the Vancouver Trades and Labour Council registered its non-participation in the newly formed White Canada Association because it "would not support any movement which would relieve the pressure on one class of the community at the expense of the other classes."[17] Two years later, the same organization protested the exclusion of Chinese from registration on unemployment rolls.[18] Some labour organizations even began to recruit Chinese, Japanese, and native Indian workers, a form of co-operation made easier in the case of Chinese workers by the demise of the labour contract system. One member of the CCF encouraged this alliance in a campaign speech in October 1935: "The Oriental is a better man than some of the superior whites in the matter of class consciousness."[19] Beliefs in the fixity, reality, and to some extent hierarchy of human types remained, but the tenor of attitudes was clearly undergoing a transformation.

IT WAS THE ENFRANCHISEMENT ISSUE that forced into relief the polarization between the agents of change and the defenders of the Darwinist order. Important among the players attempting to crack the anti-Chinese stigma were James S. Woodsworth (whose caution to the House of Commons in 1923 was noted in chapter 4), Vancouver East member Angus MacInnis, and, outside parliament, Professor Henry Angus, head of the Department of Economics at the University of British Columbia.

Angus was particularly interested in the status of local-born Canadians of Chinese origin and spoke out eloquently against their treatment as aliens. As early as 1931, he pointed out that the disabilities of fellow "underprivileged Canadians" were a reflection on Canadian democratic principles and that inequality was not a function of the attributes of the minority communities themselves but a consequence of prejudiced thought and discriminatory action within the receiving society.[20] It was an important breakthrough, and one consistent with views that were beginning to be articulated by a school of race relations in North American universities.[21] For Angus, the problem could be solved only by a policy of accelerated assimilation, beginning with an amendment to the BC Provincial Elections Act and repeal of the 1923 exclusion legislation. He labelled the latter "a contribution to international ill-will" and set about a strenuous lobbying campaign for reform of the former.[22] (In the 1930s, the Elections Act still provided that any person of "Chinese, Japanese and East Indian" race could not have the provincial franchise. It also excluded them from election to the legislature, nomination for municipal office, nomination at an election of school trustees, jury service, possessing licences for hand-logging, admission to the professions of law and pharmacy, and the dominion franchise.)

In the House of Commons, agitation for the enfranchisement of Canadian-born Chinese began in 1934. In debate about a plan to disenfranchise "subversives," such as the immigrants called "Doukhobours," Woodsworth expressed his opposition by arguing that the house should in fact enfranchise those already denied the right. Known for his fearlessness in espousing unpopular causes, Woodsworth stated: "If these people are qualified, there is no reason why a colour line should be drawn on the right of voting."[23]

The right to vote was one of the key issues of the dominion election campaign in 1935, although in British Columbia the CCF candidates had to steer a careful course. There, opposing campaigns made much of the fact that the CCF stood for "Oriental" enfranchisement. They attempted to counter the "socialist" position with more explicit appeals to the race idea than had perhaps been necessary in previous elections. The advertisement (see Figure 9) illustrates the Liberals' strategy, while Mr P. Winch, secretary of the newly formed Anti-Oriental Penetration League of British Columbia, called for Angus's dismissal by the minister of education. Winch described the enfranchisement question in terms that suggested that the race issue had devolved around the ideological interests of the political left and right: "What he (Angus) advocates is the foundation wedge of Communism, the brotherhood of man. Obviously democratic ideals among a homogeneous population of Nordic blood is one thing, but it is quite another for the white man to share his blood with, or entrust his ideals to brown, yellow or red men. This is suicide pure and simple and the first victim of this amazing folly will be the white man himself."[24]

With the election over, CCF members became more daring in their pledge to grant political rights "without regard for race." MacInnis, for example, put forward a motion in February 1936 to secure voting rights for Chinese and Japanese born in Canada. It was solidly defeated in the House of Commons, but in an important moment in the history of human rights in Canada a special house committee was formed to examine the issue.[25]

With the franchise issue being openly confronted in political circles, other new allies of the Chinese felt moved to express their sympathies. A letter to the editor of the *Province* in December 1929 was perhaps ahead of its time when it argued that "as a chain is no

50,000 ORIENTALS IN B.C.

For Vancouver Centre

Hon. Ian Mackenzie

For Vancouver Burrard

G. G. McGeer, K.C.

For Vancouver East

J. Lorne (Jack) MacDougall

C.C.F. Party Stands PLEDGED to Give THEM the Vote

The LIBERAL Party Is OPPOSED to Giving These Orientals the Vote

WHERE WILL YOU STAND ON ELECTION DAY?

A Vote for ANY C.C.F. CANDIDATE is a VOTE TO GIVE the CHINAMAN and JAPANESE the same Voting Right that you have! A Vote for a Liberal Candidate is a VOTE AGAINST ORIENTAL Enfranchisement

Canada's Next Government Will Be Liberal!

Under the new Liberal regime Canada will follow Britain's lead forward to prosperity ---even as Australia and South Africa already have done. It is important that the Vancouver and the Lower Mainland have a solid Liberal representation at Ottawa in harmony with the new Mackenzie King Government which will be in power after October 14th.

Vote For Vancouver!

When you go to the polls on Monday, Oct. 14, remember a vote for your Liberal Candidate is a vote for Greater Vancouver.

Calendar of Liberal Meetings First Three Days of This Week

Vancouver Centre	Vancouver Burrard	Vancouver East	Vancouver South

Remember, polls open at 8 a.m.; polls close at 6 p.m.

For Vancouver South

Alex M. Manson, K.C.

For Vancouver North

A. E. Munn

For New Westminster

Thomas Reid

INSURE VANCOUVER'S FUTURE BY VOTING LIBERAL ON OCTOBER 14

Figure 9
"50,000 Orientals in B.C."
Source: Province, 7 October 1935

stronger than its weakest link, so no nation is greater than its suppressed minority," but it was a promise of things to come.[26] In March 1932, the Vancouver General Hospital decided to allow Chinese membership in its alumni on the grounds that Chinese had a right to "equality of treatment," as the provincial health officer put it.[27] By the mid-1930s, a small number of letters to the editor began to express support for the CCF position, beginning with the grudging rationale that "if we have to live with them, better to live with good than bad citizens."[28] Come 1934, the *Province* was willing to publish a feature article that insisted on treating "as equal citizens in the fullest sense, all men and women born in Canada, to close no occupation to them, to withhold no political right from them and to make them feel that Canada is their native country deserving their undivided loyalty."[29]

Two years later, the British Columbia Conference of the United Church of Canada went on record as favouring the enfranchisement of all residents born in Canada, just as the "Aryan myth" began to make itself heard in the letters pages of the local press.[30] The opinions of Angus and of the CCF were by no means universally accepted, but their very expression signalled a shift in mood in the European community, one from which emerged an expanded interpretation of the racial category Chinese and its geographic referent at Pender Street.

"EAST MEETS WEST": CHINATOWN AS CIVIC SPECTACLE, 1936

Vancouver's "Little Orient," as *British Columbia Magazine* called Chinatown in 1911, had always been a mysterious place in the minds of local white society. For the most part the mystery had been informed and fed by unflattering stereotypes about the inscrutable heathens and their disease-ridden homes. The area's early stigma had been relieved only by a fond curiosity about "John's" peculiar diet and his festivity at the Chinese New Year, as was noted in chapter 3. Occasionally, it was also seen to hold an epic quality, "undomesticated and natural," to use the words of a news report in 1914. Continuing, the report speculated that "when City Hall eradicates the evils of Chinatown, with it will pass the last vestige of romance in the Oriental quarter which so long has been a place of mystery and adventure to the visitors to the Pacific Coast and Vancouver."[31] At the time, however, the burden of negative attitudes militated against a broadly shared or developed conception of Chinatown as a tourist attraction.

In the context of the new mood that developed in parts of white Vancouver society in the mid-1930s, a more innocuous vision of "Little China" began to be articulated. Age-old fantasies about China's ancient and venerated civilization began to be invoked and absorbed into the historically established imagery and discourse about Chinatown. City council played a major role in focusing public attention on the area's "quaint peculiarity," as did some members of the Chinese community itself. In addition, the local press lent its stamp of authority and helped promote the neighbourhood's tourist image. In a *Province* feature on 21 May 1936, "our little city-within-a-city" was a place where "Yellow Gods rule and the Occident fades into the background." It continued: "Even in western garb Vancouver's Chinese carry the look of the East. And the East lurks in windows crowded with strange merchandise. In the queer shops of the Orient, there are ... herbs and bark and healing root, the properties of which were known when the Dragon Kingdom was young ... while up and down the street is a steady soft shuffle." At a time when Chinatown's façade was in fact becoming more "Westernized" and "modernized," Europe's once romantic concept of the Celestial Empire filtered back into Western consciousness.[32]

The *Province*'s colourful feature of May 1936 coincided with a notable reversal of the way the city had traditionally acknowledged the presence of Chinatown within the community. That same month, council approved an application by the Chinese Benevolent Association to erect Chinese buildings adjoining the southeast corner of Pender and Carrall streets during the city's Golden Jubilee celebrations.[33] Equally significant was the decision of the district's merchant élite to encourage images about Chinatown's exotic quality by offering $40,000 toward the "Chinese Village" project. A guide to Chinatown written for the occasion by Quene Yip demonstrated strategic awareness by merchants of the rewards to be had from "re-orienting" Chinatown in conformity with European images. It guaranteed "100 per cent Celestial atmosphere" to readers during the Jubilee festivities. "The Chinese village," Yip wrote, "will be most artistically and becomingly decorated with Chinese lanterns and hundreds of Oriental splendours ... directly imported from the Celestial Empire."[34] Council was captivated by the appeal to opulent Old Cathay, and Chinatown merchants, eager to find ways of alleviating the rigours of the Depression, set about implementing the route to profit and status that had already proved effective for their counterparts in San Francisco and New York City.[35]

The local press also revelled in the idea of an artistic contribution to the Golden Jubilee from "our Chinese colony." In anticipation of the event, it told readers to expect an ornate eighty-foot bamboo arch tower at Pender and Carrall streets and a nine-tier Chinese pagoda in all its Oriental grandeur.[36] On exhibition would also be items of Chinese material culture that had left such an impression on Westerners in the eighteenth century that a "cult of chinoiserie," as Dawson put it in the *Chinese Chameleon*, flourished in Europe at the time. Jubilee visitors would witness similar "specimens of Chinese artistry," such as antiques, art pieces, porcelains, and tapestries. A Mandarin house complete with carved and jewelled furnishings and a "Buddhist temple never before exhibited to the Occidental eye" would also be featured. A week before the celebrations, the *Sun* anticipated that the village would "reveal to Occidental eyes many of the wonders and mysteries of the Orient."[37]

The Chinese village was officially opened by Mayor Gerry McGeer on 17 July 1936. A *Province* reporter was there to record the "gay parade" over to Granville Street that was "symbolic of customs and traditions that were old when the oldest firs on the coast were seedlings."[38] Thousands watched the procession, the paper reported, including "the weird Chinese ceremony [in which] the spirit of the ancient warrior was invoked to aid the carnival." Another story reported that "the mingled crowd of Orientals and Occidentals" was "treated to an exhibition of Chinese acrobatics and strength."[39] This "quaint gesture of the Orient" was followed by "Occidental formality," when Mayor McGeer spoke of "the destiny of young Vancouver as it entered into commerce and commune with the vast millions of the Orient" and expressed his pride at the work the local Chinese had done on the Chinese Village. The moment was captured in a photograph of the mayor on the arm of "Chinese Queen" Grace Kwan, which appeared on the front page of the *Province*. "Here in the Chinese village," wrote one reporter, "East and West are meeting each other."[40]

So popular was the village that the city's Jubilee Management Board decided to extend the display for two weeks after the other celebrations were closed. The board also registered its appreciation later in the year: "The contribution of our Oriental friends, notably the Chinese, was a matter of great satisfaction. The care that was taken in securing and exhibiting precious specimens of art and culture from China should receive our heartfelt thanks. The committee of Chinese residents who raised the funds and supervised the venture did so without trouble or worry to us and displayed a fine cooperative spirit."[41] The *Sun* also declared that the efforts to which the local Chinese had gone to "glorify the birthday of a city that speaks an alien tongue, thinks alien thoughts and worships alien gods" could only make Vancouver's people "proud of the energy, initiative and citizenship of our fellow Canadians of Chinese birth or extraction."[42]

By the mid-1930s, then, and with the acknowledgment and participation of certain Chinese themselves, Chinatown was becoming a European commodity. A news report in 1936 put it bluntly:

Vancouver is chiefly indebted to the sponsors of this interesting Chinese village in the fact that it calls attention to the Chinese community as a permanent tourist attraction. It is something the city apparently has never realized. Other cities – New York, San Francisco and even London have utilized their Chinese colonies very freely as a point of interest for visitors. Vancouver has never taken advantage from a tourist standpoint of the interest that attaches itself to the life and manners of our Oriental citizens. Even without the pagodas and palaces and bazaar of the Chinese village, Chinatown has a rare fascination for eastern visitors. Perhaps the present exhibit will remind us that our Chinatown is worth exploiting as a tourist attraction year in and year out.[43]

WITHIN TWO YEARS OF THE Jubilee celebration, the district was officially opened up to tourism.[44] Gray Line negotiated financing arrangements for a coach tour. A guide was also appointed, and for a short while during 1938 a Christy McDevitt – with the consent of Chinese leaders – hired jobless Chinese to run yelling through the streets holding rubber daggers covered with ketchup to convey to his sightseers the infamous Chinatown Tong Wars.[45] By 1940, the area had become so tailored for European consumption that a news report could boast: "No other city in Canada possesses a Chinatown which has retained the glamour, fascination and customs of the parent country to the same extent as this Little Corner of the Far East located in Vancouver. It is China itself, age old, mysterious, inscrutable."[46]

SPARING WHITE WOMEN,
1936–37

The European tendency to interpret Chinatown's peculiarity in ways that affirmed white society's own cultural sense of itself took new forms through the 1930s, of the kind just described. It also assumed old expressions more akin to racialization processes described in earlier chapters. Taken together, the diverse forms of racialization suggest that the making of Vancouver's "Chinatown" concept was not a tidy, linear process in which one image was born, to be replaced by a second, which was in turn transformed by a third. Rather, it became a store of competing conceptions in which residues of old associations with vice informed and became embedded within the later tourist definition. In this way, unflattering visions of "Chinatown" and the "Chinese" endured, undislodged, in the city's race discourse.

In 1929, the White Canada Association was formed in Vancouver to "prevent further Oriental penetration in British Columbia, and [to] reduce the present menace to our national life."[47] At its founding meeting on 27 November 1929, no less than twenty-seven organizations favoured its formation, including the British Columbia School

Trustees Association, the Central Ratepayers' Association, the Native Sons of British Columbia, the Retail Merchants' Association, the Union of British Columbia Municipalities, the Vancouver Board of Trade, and Vancouver's city council. The provincial minister of agriculture, Mr W. Atkinson, also participated in the first meeting.[48]

The attitudinal climate that yielded such organizations also produced individuals such as Alderman Halford Wilson and other anti-Chinese civic officials who saw the first rumblings of sympathy for the Chinese as part of a politically threatening critique from the left wing. As such, it was a call for conservatives to enforce more actively the geographical props of the old Darwinist order. This mandate applied most directly and obviously to the encroaching Chinese, but in the 1930s it also had an inverse application to some "whites."

As a category, whites too had their properly appointed place in European consciousness. In 1919, the Women and Girls Protection Act had been passed by the BC legislature outlawing white women's employment on Oriental restaurant premises. At the time of its passage, the act had raised a spate of protests from Chinese diplomats in Victoria, Vancouver, and Ottawa, and in 1923 it was amended to dispense with the stigma of "exclusion nominatum" and to vest discretionary authority on the issue in the hands of the chief of municipal police.[49] It was left to the chief's judgment to decide in which places it was unsuitable for women to be employed. The legal path was thereby cleared for any such officer to wield old conceptions of the "lascivious Oriental" (see Figure 4) and to appeal to lurking fears and fantasies about the wickedness of "inter-racial" sexual union (a carry-over perhaps of the complex sexual tensions that had been projected onto relationships between white women and the "libidinous Negro" in the United States[50]).

The statute was enforced only sporadically in the years following its enactment. In 1931, however, Mary Shaw, a waitress in Vancouver's Chinatown, was murdered, allegedly by her admirer, Lee Dick, who was said to have shot himself to complete the deed. The jury urged council to enforce whatever legislation might exist to prevent such occurrences in the future.[51] Vancouver contractor and insurance agent Halford Wilson was only too eager to take up this mandate when he entered civic politics in 1934. On behalf of the West Point Grey branch of the Canadian Legion, the United Scottish Association, and other organizations, Wilson pressed the matter before council and Mayor McGeer's recent appointment, Chief Constable W.W. Foster, quickly winning their support.[52]

FOR THE PURPOSE OF ATTRACTING non-Chinese customers and maintaining a supply of cheap employees, Chinese restaurateurs, like others in Vancouver in the 1930s, saw the advantage of employing young white women. But in Chinatown, Chief Constable Foster saw a more sinister motive afoot. In 1935, he invoked the Act for the Protection of Women and Girls by advising three restaurants in Chinatown to release their white employees. In Foster's words: "The restaurants affected by the ban are situated entirely in the Chinatown district and are patronized exclusively by Chinese with the possible exception of a few low type whites."[53] According to the chief, action was to be taken on "moral grounds," the police not being concerned with questions affecting minimum wages or hours of work.

What particularly concerned the retired colonel were the deeds he claimed were being committed against young and inexperienced waitresses who were "induced ... to prostitute themselves with Chinese." Foster believed that contact would be set up inside restaurant booths and that after working hours women would go to Chinese quarters, "where immorality took place." New staff members were very quickly influenced to become "loose." It was also established, said Foster, "that the majority of Vancouver's known prostitutes had formerly been employed in Chinatown restaurants, thus indicating they had started on their careers of vice through their early association with those cafes." The old vice characterization of Chinatown was clearly serviceable for those who wished to justify and reinforce the alien status of the Chinese.

By the end of November 1936, eight Pender Street restaurants employing a total of twenty-nine women and girls had been given the notices required by the act to dismiss their white help.[54] But when put to a legal test, the act proved ineffective in securing convictions. Foster did not see this as an impediment to his mission, however, and decided to enlist the services of Licence Inspector H.A. Urquhart, another official known for his moral discipline. A new round of warnings to the restaurants followed, this time carrying the threat of licence cancellations. City by-laws were also amended to oblige Vancouver's restaurant owners to eliminate closed-curtain booths, narrow passageways, and screens that obstructed the view of civic officials.

Early in the new year, 1937, Foster and Urquhart decided that licence renewal applications for the Chinatown cafés under notice would be withheld until the owners promised to dismiss white women and forgo employing them in the future.[55] This ultimatum produced a number of protests to city council, on the grounds that it was unfair and discriminatory against Chinese.[56] Such biased conduct was slowly becoming frowned on by society at large, and Alderman Wilson suggested a compromise policy of what Foster called "attrition."[57] This would allow restaurateurs to retain their current white help on the understanding that they would not take on further white women when positions were vacated. On this supposed new understanding, the 1937 licences were granted.[58]

In February 1937, however, the Chinese Benevolent Association (CBA) informed officials at a meeting in its Chinatown headquarters that no such arrangement had been made. As it understood the agreement, extra white help could not be hired, but white women could be employed to replace any that left.[59] A lawyer was hired to act on behalf of the Chinese, and a meeting was convened between the concerned parties early in April.[60] One month later, the Chinese presented an ultimatum of their own to the new mayor, Alderman George Miller. They agreed to upgrade their restaurants in any way the city felt necessary for sanitary purposes and to discharge any waitress whom the police could prove was guilty of improper conduct, on condition that they "not be singled out for any special treatment over and above what treatment is handed out to other reputable restaurant proprietors."[61]

The arm of the law was diligent to its intent, however, and when Foster and his so-called morality officers discovered some turnover of white staff in the Chinatown cafés, the chief constable, with the support of the mayor, set about devising a new strategy.[62] This time, Prosecutor Oscar Orr came to the assistance of Foster with the advice "that we should use the remedy that we have got, namely, the power to cancel licences ... Proceedings for the cancellation of licences need not be conducted with the same strictness of proof as a criminal prosecution and I do not say this with the idea that we should punish persons without proof but merely that a great many things are perfectly obvious to a Licence Inspector ... which would be difficult to paint in Court. Suppose, for instance, the Licence Inspector makes a personal visit to one of these places and finds loose conduct, such as, a white waitress sitting down with a Chinese. No outward crime is being committed but the chances are that procuring may be well under way."[63]

On 14 September 1937, Licence Inspector Urquhart, acting under the authority of council, cancelled (as an example to the others) the licence of the Hong Kong Cafe at 126 East Pender Street, owned by none other than the president of the CBA, Charlie Ting. Also cancelled were the licences of the Gee Kong Cafe of Harry Lee at 168 East Pender and Toy Wing's B.C. Royal Cafe at 61 East Pender.[64] Mayor Miller took the opportunity to announce to the press that he was "out to clean up Chinatown."[65] The owners immediately applied for injunctions restraining the city from interfering with their businesses. In the mean time they continued their operations in defiance of the city but were quickly issued summonses for operating without a licence. Some days later, Mr Justice Fisher of the BC Supreme Court, convinced of the city's power to act in the matter, dismissed the application from the Chinese on the grounds that proceedings brought by Urquhart concerning their defiance of licence cancellations were still pending in the police court.[66]

The city's disciplinary action provoked many merchants and prominent Chinatown figures to speak out on the restaurant issue in particular and neighbourhood targeting in general. Foon Sien, secretary of the CBA, complained: "In every licence case concerning white men the City gives a warning. In every case of a Chinaman, the City cancels first and talks later."[67] Lum Fung Ting, one of Vancouver's wealthiest Chinese, said he saw no reason why the city should make "these spasmodic attempts" to clean up Chinatown. "And anyway, if the girls are allowed to work in Oriental cafes uptown, why should they not be allowed to do likewise in Chinatown?" he asked.[68] But perhaps the most revealing protests came from the waitresses themselves, who took strong exception to the practice of race and gender stereotyping. One woman attacked the "self-appointed directors of the morals" for the women in Chinatown. "We must live and heaven knows if a girl is inclined to go wrong, she can do it just as readily on Granville Street as she can down here," she said.[69] Another waitress, Kay Martin, said that she would "much prefer working for a Chinese employer than for some other nationalities."[70] The women felt so strongly about their right to choose their own place of employment that a delegation of sixteen waitresses from the three restaurants marched to City Hall on 24 September 1937 to protest the ban on their employment in Chinatown (see Figure 10). The mayor refused them a hearing.

Three days later, the Chinatown proprietors, faced with such implacable opposition, finally accepted the city's terms for reinstatement of their licences, and council agreed to abandon its police court prosecutions.[71] Other café owners reluctantly agreed to observe the civic ruling, although their solicitor informed Prosecutor Orr that it was doubtful that the city's legal power to regulate businesses extended to prohibition on such grounds.[72] The CBA decided not to pursue its legal proceedings against the ruling, perhaps because there was no assurance of winning and a good chance of completely alienating a demonstrably unsympathetic civic administration. In a last-ditch effort some two weeks later, a group of thirty waitresses,

Figure 10
"Dismissed Girls Parade to City Hall"
Source: Sun, 25 September 1937

armed with a lawyer, demanded reinstatement in their old jobs at a
meeting of the Civic Services Committee, but again they left City
Hall unassisted.[73] On the same day, one member of council, Alderman Alfred Hurry, contended that the city, in concentrating on Chinatown, was overlooking vice in other areas. He too was ignored.[74]
The following year, the CBA's president attempted to test the colour
line by employing white women once again – and promptly had his
licence cancelled.[75] Foster threw one crumb to the opponents of his
crusade when, in March 1939, he allowed white women to be re-
employed in Chinese-owned restaurants that served only "English
meals to English customers."[76]

THE FIGHT OVER THE EMPLOYMENT of white women took place precisely as white society was being encouraged to visit Vancouver's
latest attraction on Pender Street. Chinatown's tourist definition, set

out as it was by the European community, clearly extended only as far as that society's curiosity in terms of Chinese "life and manners." Certainly the actions of City Hall officials point up a tension behind the overtures to the city's "Oriental friends" during the Jubilee episode just one year earlier. Their actions affected only a few restaurants and waitresses, but they demonstrated the endurance of adverse images of the Chinese and the state's power to recycle them. The city's leadership on the matter was alluded to in the *Sun* in an August 1938 editorial: "No matter how harmless the practice may be in itself, this City and this Province is determined that Orientals shall not employ white women in their business establishments. This prejudice may be well founded, or it may be absurd. This is not the question. What matters is that the law ... supports the prejudice and condemns the practice."[77]

A circle of determined officials had lent fresh authority to the Chinatown concept in a way that assimilated the increasingly stale beliefs of an earlier age into an emerging, more complex formulation. The sinister and the exotic in "Chinatown" had been distinguished in two successive years. As chapter 6 will show, the city would continue to juggle the images in ways consistent with its own interests and agendas. For the time, mayors McGeer and Miller had, in different ways, paid tribute to the racial category "Chinese" through the medium and imagery attached to a locality. In their actions, they carried forward the European racial frame of reference which, in providing a rallying point for the self-definition of a category of insiders, ensured that Chinatown, whether viewed positively as an exotic village or negatively as a vice town, told for ever of some deeper "Chineseness" – some pre-existing, unalterable, and ultimately foreign essence.

WILSON'S VENDETTA

The agreement between Chinatown café proprietors and City Hall marked the end of just one of many episodes in the harassment of Chinese restaurateurs, cooks, and restaurant help during the 1930s. In March 1935, for example, Chinese cooks in Western restaurants were obliged to undergo a physical examination for infectious disease.[78] During the second half of the decade, the Vancouver Restaurant Owners' Association attempted to secure from the city more strict enforcement of civic health by-laws in Chinese restaurants (which were growing in popularity and number) and in restaurants where Chinese were employed.[79] Obligingly, the Metropolitan Health Board, while it could not openly target Chinese restaurants, did so indirectly by devising more refined by-law standards for Vancouver's restaurants. The CBA was quick to recognize this thinly veiled strategy and protested to members of council's health committee in February 1936.[80] But its grievances were deflected, and in May 1937 the board decided to examine "Oriental establishments for traces of communicable disease." Legal action by the CBA thwarted the city's attempt to include in this process medical examinations specifically of Chinese restaurant employees,[81] but in 1939 the Restaurant Bylaw was again amended, granting power to the city's food inspector to compel any person preparing or serving food to submit to a medical examination.[82]

Right in the thick of such incidents was Alderman Halford Wilson, whose role in the white waitresses affair has already been noted. For Wilson, the moral and sanitary cleansing of Vancouver's Chinese restaurants was just a practice run. The penetration of Vancouver's produce and retailing industry by Chinese who usually lived on their shop premises became one of Wilson's main political missions. A typical expression of his style was a protracted battle over one row of Chinese-owned and -operated premises on 19th Street, between Main and Quebec streets. In May 1935, a special committee of council was established to investigate that particular wholesale vegetable-distributing centre in response to repeated complaints from nearby residents.[83] The committee concluded that the city should "take every step within its power to have this business removed" and set Wilson, the city solicitor, and the building inspector on a search for legal means to do so. At the end of June, Wilson successfully moved in council that the medical health officer be instructed "to placard as unfit for human habitation" the premises at 19th and Main.[84] Two years later, the city's properties, licences, and claims committee carried a Wilson motion that no licence be issued to "Orientals" without first being approved by the committee.[85] This had the advantage of allowing the city health department to inspect the proposed premises of applicants, but the results were not always as Wilson might have expected. One such inspection of a Chinese establishment in Dunbar in May 1938 found "that the premises of the applicants are in good condition; also that there are no living quarters in the said premises."[86]

In March 1939, concern about Chinese residential mobility led council's social service committee to set up a special group to investigate living quarters at the rear of stores. A letter to Wilson the following year from a Mount Pleasant resident concerning the movement of Chinese into the district of Cambie and 24th Street reveals the alderman's hand in trying to fight their encroachment. "On March 6, 1940 you wrote me advising that you would make every effort to prevent Orientals using their stores as places of residence ... "[87] The same resident in another letter wrote: "The district has been zoned for stores but we do not intend accepting the position of stores being used as places of residence as well as business, especially by Orientals. We look to the Aldermen to protect our interests and we know that especially from you, Mr Wilson, we are assured of every effort in this direction."[88]

Meanwhile, amendments were made to the Building Bylaw which granted broad discretionary power to building inspectors and medical health officers regarding enforcement of such things as partitioning of stores from living quarters, ventilation, and placement of conveniences. The efforts of Chinese to escape their stigmatized homes in the Pender Street area were thus discouraged at every turn. The surest way to fight residential encroachment, however, was to deny Chinese the economic means for mobility. Mock Fee had known the power of such a strategy back in 1888, when, as was noted in chapter 3, he successfully contested the right of the state to deny him a business licence. But Wilson was not one to let legal obstacles deter him from a display of anti-Oriental action before his constituency. Besides, he believed in his cause. "It is imperative," he wrote to a member of the Royal Society of St George in March 1938, "that those possessed of British ideals and imbued with British tradition must stand together in an effort to combat any movement that would, in time, dominate and suppress British influence in our Province."

In 1938, Wilson attempted to fix a quota on "Oriental" business licensing, reasoning that "Orientals are creeping into the retail trade, taking possession of it and enforcing lower standards of living."[89] Wilson wanted to limit Chinese and Japanese to 5 per cent of the total number of licences issued by the city. When counsel advised that the city had no such power in its charter, Wilson moved "that the City proceed to advertise and apply for a proposed amendment to the Charter to limit to a stipulated quota, the granting of licences to persons of Asiatic extraction."[90] The motion was passed with the support of the entire council except CCF member Alderman Helena Gutteridge, who later claimed that such discrimination "could extend to other nationalities in the same way as in Europe."[91] When the proposal went to the Private Bills Committee of the provincial legislature, chairman Harry Perry also denounced it as smacking of "Hitlerism," and the amendment to Vancouver's charter was rejected.[92]

The loss did not deter Wilson, who responded by suggesting to council the appointment of a special committee on legislation. In

1939, that group won council's support for a second bid to Victoria with Wilson's quota plan, but again Perry's committee declined support.[93] The determined alderman tried another strategy, sponsoring a 1940 council request for a trades licence board that would grant powers to council to control licences "in the public interest of the city."[94] Perry's committee again stood firm. Meanwhile, Wilson had suffered another setback with an unsuccessful attempt to enter the provincial parliament from East Vancouver in the 1939 election. During the campaign he had declared: "A vote for the Liberal candidate means a standard of living of fish and rice; a vote for Wilson means one of beef and bread."[95] Whether the voters of East Vancouver opted for fish and rice is not clear, but Wilson's political career remained at City Hall. He bounced back again in municipal politics in 1942, when council carried his motion to relay support to the dominion government for a measure that would remove residents of Japanese origin from the Pacific coast. Buoyed by this success, Wilson proposed another round of negotiations on his licence quota in Victoria, but by then he had lost the support even of his fellow aldermen.[96]

THOUGH FAILING TO WIN ELECTION to the BC legislature, Wilson did have allies there in the late 1930s, including one Clive Planta. After Wilson, Planta likened the expansion beyond Chinatown of Chinese-owned and -operated produce outlets to a disease that threatened to engulf the whole of Vancouver. A *Province* editorial, supporting Planta's position in 1937, commented: "Twenty years ago lowly John Chinaman leased a parcel of land from its white owner and mostly by hand, produced what he could peddle through the streets of town. Today that picture is quite outmoded. Big Chinese corporations own large farms ... and their produce is sent to market in trucks owned by Orientals, driven by Oriental chauffeurs, delivered to Oriental warehouses, sold finally to Oriental retail stores – where the salesgirl is very apt to be a brilliant young Chinese graduate of UBC."[97]

As Planta protested before the legislature, "a financial web runs through the Chinese operations."[98] What with their singular living standards and their filthy and amoral habits, Planta charged, the Chinese would take over whole industries. Whereas in 1922 there was only one Chinese wholesale vegetable dealer in Vancouver, by 1936 there were twenty-one. In the West End, Kitsilano, Point Grey, and Fairview districts of Vancouver, there were sixty-nine Chinese retail stores handling produce, Planta warned.[99] But what for Planta was the financial web of "too many cousins" was, in the eyes of one Chinese, merely the unity and co-operation needed to surmount a history of occupational marginalization and discriminatory practices such as the provincial Produce Marketing Act of 1927.[100] According to that law, produce had to be marketed through a centralized marketing control board which fixed prices in order to eliminate Chinese competition.

THE EUROPEAN CATEGORY "CHINESE" collapsed whatever distinctions people of Chinese origin made among themselves, to the service of one distinction – that of differentiating "them" from "whites" and white domains. Critical among these domains were "the better residential districts," to use Wilson's words in 1941, when he and his main ally on council, Alderman Harry de Graves, took up the cause of defending white (and especially élite) living areas from Oriental encroachment.[101] The quest of Wilson (whom the *Chinese Times* knew by this time as "the bad member of Council"[102]) involved confining Orientals "to their own recognized localities," as the *Province* reported in February 1941.

During the early 1940s, a number of area associations in Vancouver joined the cry against Chinese residential mobility. The South Granville Chamber of Commerce protested to council the movement of Chinese into the Fairview district, while the English Bay Improvement Association and the Kitsilano Chamber of Commerce made similar complaints.[103] The following year (1941), residents from Little Mountain complained about the intrusion of Chinese.[104] A Vancouver judge had summed up the situation well in 1938: "The status of the Oriental family in the white community is low. White tenants voice resentment when an Oriental settles down in the neighbourhood; houses rented to Orientals can seldom be rented later to white families."[105]

The protest that finally rallied council to action was a February 1941 delegation, bearing a petition with more than eighty signatures, from the residents of Southlands, an exclusive corner of Point Grey. Their grievance was the purchase by a Chinese and his non-Chinese wife of a property for which they had bid the highest amount. Residents in the Highbury Street area insisted that council lower their tax assessments to correspond to an anticipated 20-per-cent fall in property values and that it devise more general measures to "prevent the intrusion of the Oriental into desirable residential districts."[106] Wilson needed little more encouragement. "They simply don't comply with our standards," he said. "Real estate values are falling. Where one Oriental buys property another follows ... The time has come to do what has been done in other Pacific Coast and eastern cities."[107]

With Wilson leading the way, council acted immediately on the petition, appointing a special committee to draft a by-law that would prevent "Orientals" from being either tenants or owners in areas other than "their own localities." Wilson allayed one fear of his constituency by telling the press that the by-law would not affect the movement of Oriental servants. Next, discounting previous rulings from its own lawyers that the city could not implement the plan, Wilson defended his initiative on the grounds that "Orientals" were already discriminated against by the municipal government and that any further discrimination must therefore be acceptable. This extraordinary logic provoked Chinese Consul-General Chunhow H. Pao to join the debate, describing council's proposal as "prejudicial, discriminatory, a gross miscarriage of justice and a reflection on the national dignity of China."[108]

Whether or not the attempt to confine Chinese to Chinatown was any of these things, it was certainly illegal. Once again, the constitutional division of powers in Canada – the requirement that each level of government confine itself to its allotted sphere of competence – exerted a check on political will. Some days after council pondered the measure, Wilson conceded that he had misunderstood what he had thought was a legal precedent for council action in a restrictive Toronto by-law. Meanwhile, though, Alderman H.L. Corey advised the Point Grey delegation what could be done within the law – namely, to include anti-Oriental clauses in the titles of new subdivisions.[109] This strategy, as noted in the previous chapter, was at work in a number of areas of the city until 1956, when a new Real Estate Act abolished the clauses' legal status.[110]

ALDERMAN HALFORD WILSON'S single-minded and outspoken crusade against the threat of the "heathen Chinee" is important for two reasons. First, it is clear from council's support for most of his initiatives that there was still, in the early 1940s, a degree of political legitimacy in anti-Chinese vendettas. Aldermen less vociferous than he remained willing to encourage or at least indulge his crusade. As Mayor J.W. Cornett said in 1941: "If anything can be done to segregate them and put the Orientals in the same districts, we are all for it."[111] In that sense, Wilson was less on the fringe of BC society than his bold enunciations and practices might suggest. His, perhaps more than that of any others who went before him in Vancouver, was the cause to consign the Chinese to their lowly place, and in that pursuit he was backed by a supportive council and constituency.

Second, Wilson failed, however, to take sufficient account not only of the power of the courts to limit his ambition and the capacity of the Chinese to resist him but also of the growth of liberalism in Canada. This development required him to modify his language and conduct in a way that conformed to the rhetoric of an increasingly liberal society. Wilson, therefore, like his fundamentalist counterparts elsewhere in the world in the 1930s, brought bluntly hostile manipulations of the race idea into disrepute by dint of sheer volume and repetition. Virtually no one questioned the distinctiveness of races, but many had begun to doubt the once axiomatic belief that they were ordered on a hierarchy of superiority. What we have witnessed was the last full-throated roar of classical racism before decades of cultural hegemony gave way to a more subtle, if no less proscriptive, agenda by which the Chinese would continue to be singled out.

DISMANTLING THE RACIAL HIERARCHY IN THE 1940S

Unlike the First World War, where nations struggled over territory, the Second World War was a battle of competing ideologies, of the liberal democratic order and of communism against fascism. The Depression had challenged the confidence of the West in unfettered laissez-faire capitalism, and the Soviet example had shown an alternative to the free market. The Second World War became a pivotal clash, therefore, which, in its duration and atrocities, alerted the West to its vulnerability and to the possibility of subjugation by powerful adversaries – one of which was "Asiatic."

At home, the Second World War tested people's consciences, including those of many scientists who saw Nazi crimes as a ghastly perversion of science for political ends. The confidence of scientists in racial typologies waned considerably, and eugenics fell, if it had not already, into scientific disrepute. In British Columbia, the gap between the rhetoric of the West's international struggle for "liberation," "democracy," and "freedom" and public practices at home was not lost on white residents. As noted earlier, the chairman of the provincial private bills committee saw Vancouver's 1938 and 1940 requests for greater licensing powers as requests to persecute Orientals. "Substitute the Jews for Chinamen," he remarked in 1940, "and you are copying Hitler."[112] Editorialists also chastized home-front violations of democratic rights, especially against Chinese, who were fighting a long war against their old foe, Japan. "Justice is not a racial prerogative," said one editorialist in 1943. "Rabid racialism is an evil which leads to the Master Race idea and the lengths to which anti-Semitism has been taken," another stated the following year. And in a 1945 editorial advocating Oriental enfranchisement, the *Province* said: "Canada must not sabotage the efforts on the field of battle by practising racial intolerance at home while they fight for tolerance abroad."[113]

Despite the pressure of international events in the 1940s, some legislated props of white supremacy proved resistant to change. The most important was the denial of the franchise to people of Chinese and Japanese origin, including local-born residents and naturalized Canadians. Wartime brought this issue into very sharp focus, as one Chinatown resident was able to demonstrate in 1940. In that year a provincial order-in-council required "Orientals" in British Columbia to surrender all their firearms (despite the fact that China was aligned with the Western allies against Japan).[114] Soon afterward, Mr C.E. Louie wrote: "I am one of the hundreds of Canadian-born Chinese, of military age, and glad of the privilege of fighting and dying for Canada. Although my parents are naturalized British subjects for 35 years and myself born in Vancouver, I am not allowed to vote. Second, although I possess registered firearms for hunting, I must surrender them by September 30, 1940. The government's reason, I am an alien. Third, Canada adopts conscription, therefore I am drafted into the Canadian army. The government's reason, I am a British subject."[115]

In fact, Canadians of Chinese origin were not accepted for service when they volunteered and were not drafted until as late in the war as November 1944.[116] The delay hinged partly on the dilemma their service implied for the franchise issue. During the First World War, over 100 Japanese had managed to enlist in the Canadian forces, and in 1931, by a one-vote margin, the provincial legislature had enfranchised eighty Japanese veterans. Alderman Wilson and others saw that 1931 decision as a dangerous precedent, and in September 1940 Vancouver city council carried a motion, presented by Wilson, "to obtain from the Federal authorities the assurance that certain privileges now denied Orientals in Vancouver will not be granted as a result of their serving in the home defence forces."[117]

The tendency of Europeans to conflate "Chinese" and "Japanese" to the single category "Oriental" proved to be a biting affront to people of Chinese origin in Vancouver during the Second World War. In 1941 the CBA supplied Vancouver's 9,000 Chinese with buttons bearing the Chinese flag, so that they would not be confused on the street with people of Japanese origin.[118] Residents of Chinatown also demonstrated their loyalty to the Allied cause with generous contributions to Victory Loan campaigns. In 1941, one city resident of Chinese origin was awarded a silver cup by Mayor Cornett for selling the highest number of loan bonds in Vancouver.[119]

Slowly, the significance of China's war with Japan and its role in the world war against that aggressor began to register in the minds of white Vancouver society and to dissipate the voices of antagonists. Mayor Cornett even joined the executive of the Chinese War Relief Fund in 1943. In an official letter to Foon Sien, about whom we will hear more in chapter 6, he expressed sympathy with the distressed Chinese people and recognized the unity over the cause of "mankind and democracy" that Canada, the British Empire, and China had found in their struggle against Japan.[120] In the same year, council's long-standing unwritten law against leasing market stalls to Chinese in the city market was undone and approval granted to a firm of Chinatown fish dealers for rental space.[121] By 1945, council also lifted its long-standing colour bar on the city's swimming pool in the West End.[122]

Organized labour was among the greatest advocates of political rights "without regard for race," as the phrase often went. In 1938, the president of the Vancouver and New Westminster District Trades and Labour Council, Mr E.A. Jamieson, boasted: "We have Orientals in our council and welcome them there."[123] Union co-operation was also evident in 1943, when some 3,000 Chinese workers in the local shingle and shipyard industries threatened to strike against a 1931 provincial law that denied pension benefits for wives and children of Chinese living in Canada. The unions of automotive workers, ship-building workers, and shingle workers counselled the Chinese against unilateral action, while the International Woodworkers of America presented a brief to the dominion tax authorities on behalf of the aggrieved workers. The demand for equal treatment was met with retroactive payments of benefits, and the threatened strike was aborted.[124] Of course, the unions needed members as much as the Chinese needed labour advocates, and in 1944, the International Woodworkers of America appointed a Chinese representative for British Columbia to build up Chinese sub-locals in the union.[125]

THE TENOR OF PUBLIC OPINION IN British Columbia was clearly changing. By the mid-1940s, open, formal discrimination was no longer a guaranteed vote-getter for politicians. Opponents of Chinese enfranchisement, so clearly in the ascendancy a decade earlier, had been reduced to a fringe group, and in 1945, fifty Chinese war veterans and approximately 400 Chinese then serving were granted the vote.

It took more time – and strenuous lobbying from a range of reform organizations and from Chinese, Japanese, and East Indian groups themselves – but eventually a key mainstay of white domination since the late nineteenth century came also to be rescinded. In 1947, the provincial legislature, under Premier John Hart, passed an amendment to the Elections Act that enfranchised all Canadian-born residents and citizens in British Columbia of Chinese origin. (Two years later, the same right was extended to Japanese.) Following suit, the Dominion Elections Act of 1948 extended the federal vote to all British subjects by birth or naturalization, and, finally, the Union of British Columbia Municipalities and Vancouver city council recommended without dissent in 1949 that the legislature remove the disqualification of "Orientals" from the Municipal Elections Act. Canada's "Chinese" had finally, after more than seventy years, been relieved of the most obvious official marker of outsider status – the denial of a basic right. "Now that Chinese have the franchise," said Foon Sien a few years later, "finally they feel a sense of permanency."[126]

THE QUESTION OF IMMIGRATION PROVED to be the acid test of the new liberal climate. The issue helped to define how far Canada's national political parameters would be stretched. Political rights without regard for race were one thing, but the "continuous infusion of foreign blood and foreign cultures from abroad" was another – and of sufficient concern in 1942 for the dominion government to commission an investigation into Canada's "changing racial structure." Using census data from 1931, that study examined the balance of what were said to be the different "primitive racial stocks" in Canada, based on "geographical association," "cultural makeup," and "biological strain." This might help determine the extent of assimilation or "fusion" of the disparate elements of Canadian society into a "homogeneous type," the report stated.[127]

That such concern about the racial purity of Canada still covertly guided political action in the 1940s was made abundantly clear in the manner of the repeal of the Chinese exclusion legislation. The Chinese Immigration Act of 1923 attracted quite a lot of notice in the post-war years, especially after the Canadian parliament signed the United Nations Charter, which proclaimed freedom, human rights, and equality. Mr A.L. Jolliffe, director of immigration, however, remained a solid defender of the 1923 legislation which he himself had had a large hand in drafting, and by the early 1940s he was prepared to consider only a reciprocal system of temporary renewal immigration permits for approved categories of Chinese.[128] But the authorities in China contested such an operational definition of "reciprocal," as Dr Hugh Keenleyside of Canada's Department of External Affairs had anticipated. "It is necessary to recognise," he told a colleague in 1942, "that the Chinese temper may now be such that they will no longer accept what is essentially an exclusion agreement, even when it is varnished with the lacquer of mutuality and reciprocity."[129]

Notwithstanding all that was changing in the public domain, the dilemma of how to exclude Chinese without telling them as much was still the burning concern of behind-the-scenes immigration administrators in Ottawa and China. Canadian policy-makers simply dismissed a proposal made by a senior Chinese official in early 1947 that his government might be receptive to a quota system enabling the reunification of families in Canada, while restricting the number of new entrants.[130] At a cabinet committee meeting on Chinese immigration in May 1947, federal officials contemplated the spectre of a deluge of immigration to British Columbia, should restrictions on the entry of Chinese wives and children be relaxed.[131] It was noted that in 1941 there was a Chinese population of 34,627 in Canada (in fact less than half a per cent of the country's total population), and of the Chinese, 30,713 were males and 3,914 females.[132] Repeal of the act would allow women to enter and the Chinese population to "multiply," it was argued, a most unacceptable scenario to the officials.

No one would have known of these back-room deliberations from the speech of Prime Minister King in January 1947. Repeal of the 1923 act would, he boasted, "remove all discrimination against Chinese on account of race and ... bring Chinese persons under the general provisions of the Immigration Act and no longer under legislation applying exclusively to persons of Chinese origin."[133] To say the least, a far less breathtaking measure was introduced. In fact, contrary to public expectation, the bill repealing the act of 1923 did not remove, but rather upheld, the principle of discrimination. Under its terms, Chinese were not placed under an order-in-council of March 1931, which covered immigrants and their dependants in general. Instead, they were placed under an order-in-council of September 1930, which denied entry to Canada of any immigrant of "any Asiatic race" except the wife and unmarried children under eighteen years of age of a Canadian citizen.[134]

The House of Commons had been denied the option of a quota agreement with China during the committee stage of the bill, and therefore, despite heated opposition to the measure in the house, no compromise position could be suggested or reached.[135] David Croll of Spadina charged that after twenty-five years of the "Chinese Extermination [sic] Act ... our enemies in two wars may bring their families to Canada, where the Chinese who have been on our side find that their families are inadmissible."[136] John Diefenbaker, Conservative member for Lake Centre, adopted the rhetoric (about which we shall hear much more in later chapters) first articulated by J.M. Gibbon in his 1938 book *The Canadian Mosaic*.[137] Diefenbaker remarked: "This country is great on the basis of the number of races. Canada can never achieve greatness on the basis of intolerance."[138] The BC members (except the one for Cariboo) were conspicuously silent on the issue, and Prime Minister King had shown himself a shrewd political judge – in this instance, of the consequences for BC Liberals of repeal without "effective restriction."

Thus the new legislation, which parliament passed on 14 May, 1947, merely allowed the reunion of wives and children of the few Chinese who were naturalized. (It also eliminated the obligation of Chinese to register.) Effectively the policy achieved "nothing more than removing Chinese from a 'special' discrimination and bringing them under the general rule of discrimination against Orientals in the matter of immigration."[139] As was noted in chapter 4, only 5 per cent of the Chinese population of Canada were naturalized and 19.3 per cent were Canadians by birth in 1941. The discrimination remaining in the new law did not, however, stop the Liberal party from opening an office at 86 East Pender Street in Vancouver or from holding picnics in pursuit of the new "Chinese" vote.[140] King had distinguished himself once again as one of the most effective architects in the making of European domination in Canada.

CONCLUSION

In the wake of Canada's post-war reforms, the white Canadian perception of the Chinese as an exotic people congealed. By the end of the Second World War, Chinatown was Vancouver's cultural enigma: a "glint of the Orient in an Occidental setting," as it was portrayed by a newspaper feature in 1943.[141] The tourist definition first sponsored in the 1936 Jubilee celebrations had taken root and come to supersede (but by no means dissolve) the vice characterization that Colonel Foster and his municipal predecessors had put to such extensive service. Similarly, throughout North America, Dr Fu Manchu, the sinister character made popular in the 1930s by American writer Sax Rohmer, had become the heroic war ally, representative of the hard-working, persevering, law-abiding people of curio stores and dishes.

The transition in images was not tidy or decisive, however, as we have seen, for the neighbourhood, provincial, and national scales. The process of change was slow and ambiguous, with some events in the mid-1930s pointing back to an inflexible past at the same time as others signalled a brighter way forward in Canadian "race relations." But the war had cast doubt on the notion of racial hierarchy. Alistair Stewart, CCF member for Winnipeg North, made this clear in a speech to the house in 1947: "The war taught us there are no superior and inferior races, that the superior races might easily become the inferior races and vice versa, that we are all dependent upon one another for mutual protection, that the old shibboleths are obsolete, that narrow nationalisms must give way to a broader community of nations."[142] There had indeed been a breakthrough in white attitudes that would help lessen inequalities in Canadian society in subsequent years.

It will be clear, however, that the war and other pressures of the 1940s did not challenge the underlying conceptions of the "Chinese race" and "Chinatown" themselves. The rise of liberalism did not prompt white Canadians to question their belief in the essential distinctiveness of the races, each with its own culture. Mosse states: "It was the Nazis who perpetrated the deed, but men and women everywhere believed in the distinction between races, whether white, yellow or black, Aryan or Jew."[143]

The European premise of a separate, if not inferior, Chinese race was enduring, and it set the context for significant streetscape change on Pender Street from the mid-1940s. The romantic assessment of the "Little Orient" gave it a much-needed material boost from tourists by the end of the war. The restaurant industry on Pender Street blossomed, in turn encouraging vertical expansion of grocery stores, butcher shops, and fish markets. Import outlets, bric-à-brac, and curio stores prospered along the principal thoroughfares in response to the increasing traffic of tourists. Merchants did their best to adapt Chinatown's streetscape in conformity with the neighbourhood image that Europeans sought to discover. In particular, they used neon light façades (not used in China's architecture) as part of what Light has called the "purposeful Orientalizing" of North American Chinatowns.[144] The White House Chop Suey restaurant at the foot of Columbia Street began the trend, when it installed "a traditional moor gate in white neon."[145] The same news report gives an account of the growth – and effects – of Chinatown's tourist definition in the 1940s. By the end of the war, we are told, neon had been extended to "whole storefronts with architectural combinations of slick facades and lighting. In some cases it is more than surface, it goes right inside to the alley and up to the second storey. Before the war the White House was patronized exclusively by Chinese. Now they can't find a seat. The Occidental population has moved in en masse." With the sponsorship and consent of certain Chinese themselves, Chinatown had come to suit the imagination and tastes of European consumers.

Beneath the neon façade, Chinatown still embodied for the city's white community the essence of an alien culture and people, just as Chinese physical and cultural features were still the defining characteristics of the area's residents. There remained something primordially distinct about "East" and "West." Moreover, this view still formed the basis for practices that further reproduced the enclave at Pender Street. By the 1940s, the segregated territory stored the history of a sinister connotation and praxis, and bore the landscape imprint of a new exotic association. A guide to the precinct, published by a local newspaper in 1943, captures the deeper continuity in the categorization of place and race underpinning changes in their expression during the late 1930s and the 1940s:

Chinatown! Time was when that foreign quarter between Canton Alley and Jackson Avenue, between Hastings and Georgia Streets, had an aura of wickedness for the Vancouver consciousness. It was a sinister place 'twas said where white girls should not walk alone through its crowded narrow streets. 'Chuck-a-luk' and other gambling games, rumour had it, were played behind mysterious doors without handles ... And when the police raided ... trap-doors into sub-cellars provided emergency exits for white and Chinese players alike to escape by devious underground passages. Or so many Vancouver people believed ... Chinatown! pungent, mysterious, wicked Chinatown where one bought jasmine tea and wicker furniture and rich embroideries, always with a feeling of danger lurking in the dim shadows of the dark shops. How it has changed! Or perhaps, how we, under the impact of World War Two have changed. China is now our ally, and visitors look at Chinatown through new eyes ... In the shopkeepers along East Pender Street they see a counterpart of the Chinese who make up the armies of General Chiang Kai Shek. Chinatown! Chop Suey houses where delicious foods are served with wooden chopsticks ... Chinese theatres with their sing-song voices and their twanging instruments ... Chinatown, indeed, is one of the most interesting places of all for the wartime 'home sightseer' to visit ... [For] even with its Red Cross groups, its first aid classes, its Victory Loan campaigns, its ration book headquarters, its displays of Canadian merchandise, Chinatown still seems 'foreign'.[146]

Therein lay Chinatown's abiding signature on – and vulnerability to – the frames of mind and political agendas of white Vancouver.

CHAPTER SIX

"Slum Clearance,"
1950–1969

—Chinese
identity
—ethnicity

By the end of the Second World War, a racially defined neighbourhood of "Chinese" business and residence was firmly etched as a
social fact in the Vancouver landscape. Incoming relatives from China
and Hong Kong gravitated to the area where their sponsors had made
their lives, where their own language (if not all dialects) was the
medium of exchange, where a familiar diet was catered for, and
where there was easy access to a market for Chinese housing and
employment. With Chinatown having been labelled as "theirs" for so
many decades, many Chinese no doubt felt it to be such, although
probably for different reasons than for those who had so defined it.

Thus there was within Chinatown itself a set of forces promoting
both growth of the community and a measure of self-identification.
As this chapter will demonstrate, however, residents were by no
means left to chart their own course for the balance of the neighbourhood's career. On the contrary, the city of Vancouver and the
federal government set out to rebuild the area during the 1950s and
1960s on the basis of their own neighbourhood classifications and in
flat defiance of residents' views. Indeed, this period in the history of
Chinatown demonstrates transparently the material consequences of
the power relation that had always underpinned European constructs
of identity and place.

In previous chapters, we have seen that in categorizing the "Chinese" and "Chinatown" as "different," white Europeans were at once
defining themselves as a privileged in-group, all the time building
and justifying a form of cultural hegemony over such "racial Others."
We have seen also how the exercise of control was in large part targeted at the distribution of Chinese in Vancouver and at their district
in Pender Street. By the 1950s, the power of definition over Chinatown served the interests of white Europeans in a more explicit manner. In this period, external projections on the area were guided more

by urban planning ideologies than by the racial mythology we have traced to date, and the mythology itself underwent some further change in content, as we shall see in the first part of the chapter. But planners' and politicians' decisions about public projects – in particular, their location – were plainly guided by inherited ideas about a Chinese race and place. This chapter therefore uncovers prior definitions of Chinese identity and Chinatown as they were carried forward into post-war government policy.

One of the intriguing aspects in the history of white European cultural hegemony in Vancouver (and elsewhere) is the way in which it comes to secure the consent of those subordinated to it. Categorizations of identity and place may "act back" across time, as those historically subject to classification begin to project that ascription in the political arena in order to realize interests of their own.[1] That is, the "Chinese" themselves are also subject to the culture of racial representation, as we saw in the last chapter. Whatever else they may subjectively feel about their ethnic identity, they may invoke the fictitious homogeneity out of which the racial classification is built, adopt dominant images, and ideologically represent them as positive themes, in part to offset the history of negative stereotyping and as a means of self-identification and economic gain. The literature on the so-called ethnic revival of the 1970s and 1980s has tended to overlook the significance of this secondary process.[2] In romanticizing the ancestral tie that binds minority individuals to groups, this literature has tended to mystify the affirmation many non-white Europeans have displayed toward their ethnic origins as if it were an autonomous phenomenon.

In the 1960s, one way in which some Chinatown merchants and leaders attempted to defend their area from demolition was to propound their "Chineseness" through the medium of tourist Chinatown, just as they had done for their own reasons in the Jubilee celebrations of 1936. This projection was, in part, a lever to organize resistance against the other, more threatening definition of residential Chinatown as a "slum." A complex relationship between Vancouver's Chinatown and the Canadian state therefore developed in the 1960s as the federal and city governments attempted to impose their own agendas on a community that, in the knick of time, was to find some unexpected new allies.

ENDING STATUTORY "RACE"

Many Canadians were on hand to express their support for a more liberal immigration policy at hearings of the Senate Standing Committee on Immigration and Labour between 1946 and 1953. There was also widespread agreement that all explicitly discriminatory obstacles to the entry of immigrants should be removed. Still, there was never any doubt that selectivity from particular non-traditional immigration sources should continue to be exercised. "Any suggestion of discrimination based upon either race or religion," the committee said in 1948, "should be scrupulously avoided both in the Act and its administration, the limitation of Asiatic immigration being based, of course, on the problems of absorption."[3] All Canadian citizens should be entitled to equal sponsoring privileges, it was argued, but there could be no question of absorbing independent – i.e. unsponsored – immigration from Asian sources. Open immigration would continue to be reserved for white British subjects, and citizens of Ireland, France, and the United States.

The political task was to remove open discrimination that might undermine the belief that, as Lester Pearson outlined in 1950, "it is we and not the Russians who stand for national liberation, economic progress and social justice."[4] The appearance of equality had to be achieved while ensuring there was no "fundamental alteration" to the "present character of the Canadian population," as Prime Minister King had put it in 1947.[5]

For twenty years following repeal of the Chinese Immigration Act in May 1947, successive governments pursued this strategy through regulations that allowed them to circumvent parliament. Orders-in-council allowed the minister of citizenship and immigration to make short-order rules as to the "suitability" of sets of immigrants. In this way, although "race" was exorcised from the statutes, it was by no means erased from the administrative practices of Canadian government. Just as the legally impotent city council in Vancouver had often sought ways of controlling the life chances of Chinese-origin residents through indirect measures, federal officials during the 1950s were adept at avoiding the spirit of post-war international diplomacy.

Although the structure of special legislation for specifically Chinese immigration ended in 1947, the category "Asiatic" or "Asian," into which "Chinese" became subsumed in immigration policy, guaranteed that the history of separate treatment continued. "Asia" had always been defined in opposition to Europe, and to Canada's Liberal government in 1947, Asia meant "almost everything in the Eastern Hemisphere outside Europe."[6] During the first decade after the Chinese Immigration Act was repealed, the only Chinese immigrants who were allowed to enter Canada were certain categories of the kin of those sponsors who were Canadian citizens. Asian immigrants were specifically excepted from provisions that allowed others, even "enemy aliens" from Germany after 1950, to enter as the relatives of both citizens and legal residents. *[handwritten:] #Key.*

THE SPONSORSHIP SYSTEM THEREBY ensured that a major bias continued in favour of the nationalities already dominant in Canada. The
CBA presented some forthright protests against the bias in 1950 and
1951, but the Immigration Act of 1952 continued to restrict the definition of "relatives of Asians" to Canadian citizens' wives and their
children under eighteen years old. The member for Kamloops, E.
Davie Fulton, provided a public rationale for this in April 1953: "We *[handwritten: # sponsor]*
want to take our country as we have it now and we want to develop *[handwritten: issues]*
it, we do not want to change it. These limitations, that we must not
bring in people faster than we can absorb them, in either a physical
or cultural sense, are I think agreed upon by everyone in the House."[7]
Fulton captured the spirit of the views of the House of Commons
on immigration matters throughout the 1950s. The contradiction
between implementing the house's consensus and the new rhetoric
of rights for all without regard for "race" was not considered an
unhappy tension. Of discrimination there should be none, many
members preached, but selectivity of new immigrants was simply
common sense. Jack Pickersgill, Liberal minister for immigration and
citizenship, even used this justification in 1955: "Selectivity is not *[handwritten: # Key.]*
based on race and it is not based upon creed ... It is based upon a *[handwritten: views]*
conception of adaptability to the kind of society we have tried to *[handwritten: (politic]*
build in this country for 300 years."[8] A year later, Pickersgill applied *[handwritten: officials)]*
an analogy redolent of the discourse and politics of a generation
earlier. "As we know," he remarked, "it is easier to transplant into soil *[handwritten: of racism]*
which is similar to that from which you take the plant."[9] The by-
product of a carefully engineered history of immigration recruitment
and regulation – a predominantly "white" Canada – was now for
Pickersgill a natural endowment that justified practices geared to its
maintenance. The point was underlined by Conservative Immigration
Minister Ellen Fairclough in 1960: "A system of selection which is fair
and just, which will bring to Canada those settlers whom we need
and who can become settled in our communities without dislocation
to our way of life or hardship to the immigrants themselves, is a
government prerogative."[10]

Meanwhile, Chinese residents, anxious at the plight of refugees
from China after the revolution of 1949, would have to be satisfied
with minor concessions. A prominent Vancouver resident, Foon Sien,
made repeated trips to Ottawa throughout the 1950s to plead immi-

gration causes, with limited success.[11] The maximum age of entry for unmarried children of citizens was raised to twenty-one years, and from 1957 fiancées of Chinese men who had lived in Canada for two years were allowed to join their fiancés on posting a $1,000 cash bond.[12]

In 1958, John Diefenbaker's Conservative government made what appeared to be a major concession by extending the right to bring relatives into Canada to Asians who were legal residents.[13] This apparently important victory for Foon Sien had already been undermined by an earlier order-in-council that reapplied tight restrictions on the categories of relatives whom Asians could sponsor as migrants. The order-in-council, which followed a court ruling against the government, was a semantic triumph. It removed direct reference to Asians from the relevant immigration restrictions and applied them instead to people from any country other than the United Kingdom, Australia, New Zealand, South Africa, Ireland, France, the United States, all countries of continental Europe, Egypt, Israel, Lebanon, Turkey, Central America, and South America.[14]

ALTHOUGH IN SPIRIT not much had changed, the language of political debate underwent a subtle transformation from the early 1950s on. In 1952, the member for Winnipeg North, Alistair Stewart, even criticized the government for using the word "race" in its immigration legislation and census records, on the grounds that "it is a word which has very little scientific validity."[15] The content of Stewart's argument was ignored, but his charges deepened the insecurity many members were starting to display about the term "race."

Into this setting of uncertainty about vocabulary, the term "ethnic" entered official lexicon. Its usage in the House of Commons was sparse and confused in the 1950s and early 1960s, and no member attempted to clarify the term before using it. Its very ambiguity seemed to be its greatest asset, as the following examples of its usage suggest. One member signalled the shift in language in 1953 when he called Chinese "ethnically difficult of absorption."[16] Another in 1955 interpreted King's statement of 1947 to mean that "immigration shouldn't be the cause of an undue change in the ethnical balance of the two main groups of this country."[17]

In most of its usages in the house, the term "ethnic" or "ethnical" (Wilfrid Laurier's old word) tended to be another term for "race" or "racial" or "stock." One member said in 1955: "Canada must have some process of selection on an ethnical basis but not obvious discrimination towards Canadian citizens of Chinese origin."[18] The same member observed that "several members have picked up the word 'ethnical' and used it instead of 'fundamental character' or racial derivation."[19] Another member, for Winnipeg South, referred to the "basic ethnic divisions in this country" in a speech about the "fundamental racial position" of the two "great basic stocks who originated this country."[20] Others tried to be more precise. "The selectivity we should be practising, is on the basis of cultural factors or ethnic factors if you wish," said Walter Dinsdale (Brandon, Manitoba) in 1955, "and I use the word as applying in a sense somewhat broader than race." For Dinsdale, "the word 'ethnic' means more than race; it refers to a way of life, a system of values."[21]

What emerges from such confusion is that the biological connotation of "difference" was not being jettisoned by Canada's politicians, but rather assimilated into a seemingly more embracing term. Yet the old term "race" had always connoted both a biological and a "way of life" dimension. Chinese slept twelve to a room, for example, to recall one of the earliest charges against them. They were addicted to opium and worshipped strange gods. As Dinsdale wanted to use the term "ethnic," then, it was not altogether different from the old terminology. Biological determinism had become far less rigid and explicit, but the assumption that combined differences of a cultural and biological nature were constant attributes of a category seemed to remain secure in the new liberal climate of attitudes. A softer form of determinism was being incorporated into an ambiguous doctrine of cultural relativism that could be invoked to justify continued selectivity from non-traditional immigration sources at the same time as it could be used to acknowledge favourably the various "contributions" to Canada's "national tapestry," in the words of Prime Minister Louis S. St Laurent in 1953. "It is because our forefathers had the wisdom to recognize that it was not going to be necessary in this Canadian nation to pour all the elements into the same mould that we have a Canadian nation," said St Laurent.[22]

These expressions of "respect" for "differences" grew more fashionable in the Commons as the decade progressed. By 1958, one member was even able to say: "In Fort William, we have several hundred people of Chinese extraction, and they are the most industrious and law abiding citizens ... If we broaden the ethnic origins by immigration from any or all countries it will not harm us. On the contrary, it will be beneficial. Canada's transition to a multiracial society can only make for new strength and stability."[23]

The term "ethnic" also became adjectival short-hand to describe those people who were not of white Anglo or French origin. With amendments to the Immigration Act pending in 1959, Immigration

Minister Fairclough assured the house: "When the proposals are drafted it is my intention to consult with the representatives of the various ethnic groups and with the ethnic press, which is an important line of communication to those of ethnic origin."[24] It appears that only some members of Canadian society – of non-British and non-French origin – would be bestowed with "ethnic status," a point to which we shall return in chapter 7.

NOWHERE WAS CANADA'S SOCIAL FABRIC being more tightly spun in the 1950s and 1960s than in the Canadian visa office in Hong Kong. While a full-scale immigration promotion campaign was being conducted in Europe and the United States, often with the lure of assisted passages, a single office in Hong Kong was established to process what had become an enormous backlog of applicants by the mid-1950s. Whereas the Hungarian upheaval of 1956 held the promise for Canada of considerable labour supplies, the Hong Kong refugee situation triggered only defensive impulses in Ottawa.[25] For instance in 1964, the Liberal minister of citizenship and immigration, René Tremblay, said: "We must look at immigration from Hong Kong in ordinary immigration terms rather than as a special refugee problem."[26]

Furthermore, while processing of prospective immigrants from Europe and the United States involved a superficial medical examination, processing in Hong Kong was an exceedingly protracted affair, even for the immediate family members of Canadian citizens. It was conducted by officials in both Canada and Hong Kong, who delved into the background of applicants, their professed family relationships, the financial status of their sponsors in Canada, their medical condition, and their age. Verification of age was conducted by the dubious method of x-ray examination of a candidate's bone structure – the findings being then forwarded to Ottawa for review. It was not unusual for processing of Hong Kong applicants to take up to three or four years, by which time applicants had often passed the eligible age of entry. And in the event that a sponsorship application failed, sometimes years after being made, there was no requirement that an explanation be given or that appeal provisions be extended.

Some members of the house made the connection between these onerous and discriminatory practices and the problem of Chinese illegal immigration that surfaced in the late 1950s. "The act itself should be changed so that it would not be necessary for these infractions to take place," said William Peters in 1960.[27] Nevertheless, the discovery of an operation in Hong Kong that sold false identities – mostly fictitious family slots – for entry to Canada, New Zealand, Australia, the United States, and South America prompted one of the largest searches in Canadian history. Unsubstantiated allegations by the Royal Canadian Mounted Police (RCMP) that up to 11,000 Chinese entered Canada illegally after the war, and sensational treatment of the issue by the press, provoked and intimidated Chinese communities across Canada from 1959 to 1963. As long as the Conservative government did not clarify the police allegations, the CBA of Vancouver charged, the man-hunt created "the misleading impression that there is a community-wide conspiracy to land immigrants illegally and use them for slave labour ... While we recognize the right of the government to ferret out and to apprehend anyone engaged in an international ring of smugglers," a brief to Prime Minister Diefenbaker stated, "we are alarmed at the wholesale besmirching of an entire group of minority Canadian citizens."[28]

Such accusations did not stop twelve RCMP and two Hong Kong officers from sweeping unannounced through the Vancouver home of Foon Sien in July 1961. They also raided the home of another CBA official, the association itself, at 108 Pender Street, and five fraternal organizations, seizing filing cabinets, membership records, ledgers, correspondence, and other documents.[29] Meanwhile sections of the press revelled in the atmosphere created around the immigration issue. For example, a controversial *Maclean's* article in 1962 spoke of "the laws that rule behind Canada's bamboo curtain" where lurked "a criminal oligarchy with an immigration policy of its own."[30]

HAPPILY OR UNHAPPILY, UNEQUAL SELECTION of the relatives of people who were Canadian citizens was becoming exceedingly difficult to defend and disguise from parliament. By the early 1960s, the House of Commons had grown noticeably more uncomfortable, if not with the injustices themselves, then with their inconsistency with 1960 legislation that professed to protect individual rights and freedoms in Canada without regard for race or creed.[31] Almost by default, then, and in an economic context of growing labour needs, Ellen Fairclough's ministry introduced immigration legislation in 1962 that removed almost all the vestiges of a colour-conscious immigration policy. The new act provided for the entry of unsponsored or independent immigrants of all origins with specific skills. What remained, however, as the opposition was quick to point out, was the provision in the Immigration Act that granted authority to the governor-in-council to limit the admission of persons by reference to ethnic group, nationality, geographic area of origin, and "peculiar customs, habits, and modes of life."

In 1963 and 1964, the Pearson government received repeated exhortations to remove the inconsistency between its rhetoric and practice on immigration matters.[32] Finally, in 1967, twenty years after repeal of the Chinese Immigration Act and restoration of voting rights to Chinese, legislative authority "to discriminate on ethnic, or to put it bluntly, on racial grounds," as one member said, was finally removed. Requirements for independent entry were standardized through a point system, an immigration appeal board was established, and the sponsoring privileges of all citizens of Canada were finally equalized.

In 1967, liberalism triumphed as the ideology of public morality in Canada. In that year, for the first time in its history, the population of Vancouver's Chinatown would not be artificially controlled, nor stigmatized by legislation that formally classified its residents as outsiders. The process of coming to terms with an out-group in a white European society had in a sense been resolved, at least officially, through recognition that as an instrument of control "race" had lost its once unambiguous force.

The removal of statutory race in 1967 did not, of course, eradicate the consequences of its history to that date. While officials and politicians in Ottawa had been slowly limiting the scope for immigration discrimination since the end of the war, other federal and civic employees had been exercising control in ways that grew out of earlier practices and perceptions of Chinatown and its residents. Some of the consequences of former rounds of racial classification had, by the late 1950s, become the context and justification for a new image of Chinatown as a "slum" – a perception that brought with it planning proposals that would affect Chinatown on a scale perhaps unprecedented in its seventy-year history.

POST-WAR URBAN SURGERY

In the immediate post-war period, Canadian cities underwent a period of rapid demographic and economic growth. Competition for downtown land intensified in the early 1950s, and inner cities, increasingly bereft of a middle-class residential tax base, began to fall into decline. Left as they were to poor families, single persons, new immigrants with meagre resources, and people who faced discrimination in their housing choices, Canada's inner cities joined their American counterparts as special candidates for government attention.

The assumption that social disorders and environmental conditions were functionally related, and that problems of the former could be eradicated by improvements to the latter, was not a new idea in the 1950s. During the Depression, the first major attempts at social change by alteration of urban living conditions had been undertaken in Canada; in the United States, environmental improvement policies for the migrant poor had a longer ancestry. But by the 1950s, the problem of a deteriorating inner-city housing stock had become relevant to Canadian policy-makers not simply for its actual or perceived relationship to social ills, but also because of the larger strategic goals of civic bureaucracies. Foremost among these goals was the "rationalization" of urban land uses, to use the vocabulary of the day, in particular the upgrading of areas that were defined as "revenue sinks" and the planning of facilities that would increase the accessibility of central business districts.

The debates of Canada's House of Commons also suggest that in an era of ardent anti-communism, "slums" were thought to represent a challenge to the capitalist distributive system. They were, as one member claimed in 1955, an "indictment of our society in the midst of plenty."[33] Another told the St Laurent government in 1953: "The abolition of slums and the putting of people into proper housing will obliterate any thought of communism."[34] Moreover, without remedial treatment, the "blight" would spread and infect other areas. On that point, members relied on medical analogies (which assimilated some of the imaginative leaps used by eugenists and other commentators dating back to Commissioner Chapleau's "ulcer") to argue that surgical extraction of the tumorous growth and its replacement by brand new tissue would be necessary to arrest disease.[35] In this way, blight could be reversed, "ghettoes" like Chinatown could be dissolved or assimilated, and, in a dawning age of modernization and "progress" in the "free world," the benefits of unprecedented economic growth could be enjoyed by all, or so it was widely believed.

Into this intellectual context came the idea of government-sponsored urban renewal in Canada. It owed much to US precedents designed to expand the supply of low-rental public housing and to wrestle with the problems of deterioration and congestion in urban centres. In Canada, provision for slum clearance had been available to municipalities since 1938, but it was only in 1954 that cost-sharing provisions became attractive to them. In that year, the National Housing Act was amended to allow a federal contribution of 50 per cent to the cost of housing acquisition, slum clearance, and public housing redevelopment projects, the remainder of which was to be split between the province and the municipality.[36]

has to do with "slums", housing, public housing redevelopment projects

A "BLIGHTED AREA"

Although largely residential at the time, the area immediately to the
east of Vancouver's Chinatown had been zoned "light industrial" in
the city's 1931 Zoning Bylaw, allowing for construction of factories
and warehouses up to six storeys high. This zoning classification had
ensured that the mostly Chinese property owners in Strathcona had
been unable to get mortgage money or bank loans for repairs and
renewal of their properties.[37] By the end of the war, much of the
housing stock of this area, including single houses, rooming-houses,
apartments, and cabins, was in various degrees of disrepair.

The objective condition of the area was not as significant, perhaps,
as the perception that those with the power of definition held of the
district. In 1948, Dr Leonard Marsh wrote the report *Rebuilding a
Neighbourhood* in conjunction with civic officials and the federal government's Central Mortgage and Housing Commission (CMHC).
According to Marsh, the area was in a state of "chronic deterioration."
It was not the worst slum area in the city, he noted – "there are worse
pockets of derelict, unhealthy or overcrowded housing blocks" – but
the area had become "a kind of zoning ganglion of mixed uses, badly
in need of rationalization." The main impetus for identifying Strathcona, however, was its "critical town planning importance" the report
stated, the area being "well located in relation to the industrial waterfront and the downtown commercial and business districts." Furthermore, the area was costing the city in public services nearly twice
the tax revenue derived from it, Marsh calculated.[38]

Clearly, the classification of Strathcona as a "slum" was being
guided by agendas other than the objective status of its housing. This
would not be so significant but for the fact that the diagnosis of
"blight" in the 1950s and 1960s carried the prescription of nothing
short of full-scale surgery, without the consent of the patient.

In 1956, the newly established technical planning board of the city
of Vancouver stated: "That part of Pender Street between Carrall
Street and Main Street forms the most important part of Chinatown.
Chinatown is an area which is improving in quality. In fact, it rates
more highly than most of the normal retail areas, in the amount of
money spent on new retail construction and repairs to stores since
the war. This particular part of the whole Chinese quarter is the only
one which can be said to be a tourist attraction. The remainder of
the Chinese quarter to the east of Main Street is at present of significance only to the people who live there."[39]

The area east of Main Street soon acquired another meaning for
the Vancouver Planning Department and the likes of chief civic planner Gerald Sutton Brown. In February 1956, a technical committee

of the building and planning committee was struck to study and select, with the aid of a grant from CMHC, "those areas of predominantly residential use which might require redevelopment in the next 20 years."[40] *Rebuilding a Neighbourhood* was the committee's guide, and attention therefore quickly focused on the area Marsh had described as "unsavoury" and needing to be "completely reconstructed." The area lay east of Main Street, south of Burrard Inlet, west of Clark Drive, and north of False Creek Flats. Within that area, the Strathcona district (see Map 8) had potential for high-density residential use, the committee's 1957 *Vancouver Redevelopment Study* claimed, because, unlike the more "derelict" area to the north of Hastings, it had an existing community that could be brought into more "productive and improved" accommodation.[41] It was estimated that redevelopment in Strathcona would give "two or three times the tax yield of the existing blighted properties" – gains that would conveniently offset the cost of clearing. Meanwhile the proponents of redevelopment were gaining support in parliament. In 1957, the member for Vancouver-Kingsway, referring to Vancouver's "principal blighted area," told the house: "The whole of the area contributes to the toll which we pay in disease, crime, delinquency and vice."[42]

Although area A (the area designated by the 1957 study for comprehensive redevelopment) was not the exclusive preserve of Vancouver's Chinese-origin residents, it did during the 1950s contain a substantial number of them, in particular a large proportion of the Chinese family population. (The other area in the city slated for comprehensive redevelopment housed many "East Indian" people.[43]) After repeal of the Chinese Immigration Act, the district of Chinese settlement became more decisively split between the commercial sector west of Main Street and a residential sector east of Main Street, as reunited families sought homes and some men gave up their communal-style hostel accommodation. It was a period of rapid growth for Vancouver's Chinese community relative to earlier years. During the period 1950–9, the proportion of the total area A population that was said to be "Chinese" increased from one-third to 48 per cent, while the *Vancouver Redevelopment Study* noted that in certain of the blocks closer to commercial Chinatown the proportion of such residents was 70 per cent and growing (see Map 9). Also, as many as 80 per cent of family household owners, 78 per cent of single owners, and 53 per cent of single tenants of the district earmarked for project 2 (roughly equivalent to residential Chinatown) told the survey that they had no desire to move.[44]

In February 1958, city council approved in principle the recommendations of the 1957 report, complete with an operational strategy for rebuilding the district of Chinese settlement, just as such areas

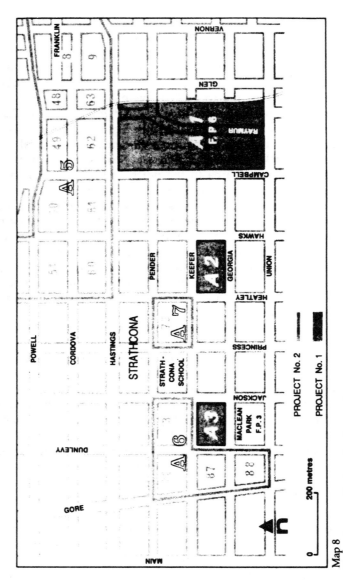

Map 8
Redevelopment Project, Strathcona: Stages 1 and 2
Source: City of Vancouver, Technical Planning Board, *Redevelopment Project No. 2,* 1963

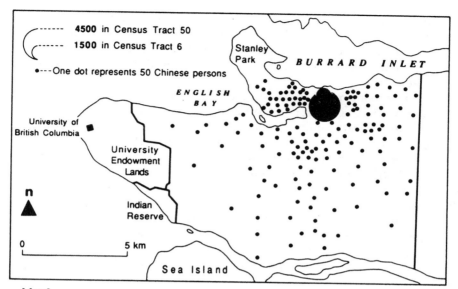

Map 9
Distribution of Chinese in Vancouver, 1961
Source: G. Cho and R. Leigh, "Patterns of Residence of the Chinese in Vancouver,"
in *Peoples of the Living Land*, edited by J. Minghi, B.C. Geographical Series No. 15
(Vancouver: Tantalus 1972), 64

throughout North America were being transformed.[45] As with the
Chinese "ulcer" that was "lodged like a piece of wood," in Chapleau's
words, and treated before the disease had even been detected, Chinatown's diagnosis as a "slum" was to be justified and realized through
the surgery itself. From 1958, applications for building and redevelopment permits in Strathcona began to be rejected, and all property
values were frozen. Residents, discouraged by city staff from improving their homes, waited for the day when they would be told to leave
homes "which we never knew were part of a 'slum'," Shirley Wong
recalled later.[46]

    Chinese homeowners in Strathcona, initially co-operative with the
idea of having improved public services, lost little time organizing
themselves when they discovered that "renewal" meant demolition
of their homes and their relocation to high-density public housing.
Within three days of being acquainted with the plan for Strathcona,
and in the tradition of resistance we have seen displayed by Chinatown's residents, the Chinatown Property Owners Association
(CTPOA) was established. A delegation headed by Foon Sien visited
City Hall to protest the scope of the plan and the fact that the city
had chosen the area adjacent to commercial Chinatown for its first

redevelopment project.[47] It returned with its fears somewhat allayed by the verbal assurance that the 1957 study was merely preliminary. A week later, however, council rezoned ninety acres of area A from light industrial to residential as a first step toward the study's implementation.[48]

The 300–member CTPOA was more wary the following April, therefore, when the still-active "bad member of Council," Alderman Wilson, and Gerald Sutton Brown visited the CBA armed with blueprints of the acquisition and clearance report for project 1. Confiscation of property would leave those who remained in the area "only tenants," association spokesmen protested, while discrimination restricted homeownership possibilities elsewhere in the city. (As Foon Sien had said in 1956: "There are still some areas in Vancouver where we could not buy property if we tried ... so we don't try."[49]) Alderman Wilson again gave his blithe assurance that the plans were "not complete."[50]

STAGE ONE

Within seven months, the report calling for acquisition and clearance in Strathcona was approved by council, and in March 1960 authority was granted to the city's engineers to redevelop the thirty-two-block neighbourhood bounded by Gore Avenue, Raymur Avenue, Hastings Street, and Union Street.[51] The entire district (area A) was earmarked for clearance in stages (see Map 8). The first stage of redevelopment would involve construction of low-rental, high-density public housing between Campbell and Raymur avenues and Hastings and Union streets (the Raymur Park complex – area A-1); clearance of block 83 (area A-2) bounded by Keefer and Georgia streets and Hawks and Heatley avenues, as a replacement park for the MacLean Park site; and clearance of block 86 (area A-3, immediately north of MacLean Park) for public housing, with the possibility of some private development. That block was to be used for the first "housing bank" to accommodate people displaced by project 1 and would be called the MacLean Park complex. By stage 3, it was expected, Strathcona would be entirely rebuilt.

Opposition to the city's acquisitive interests soon swelled in Chinatown, and Foon Sien anticipated that although stage 1 was not as threatening to the district as were the later stages, it would still displace at least a few hundred Chinese. "We are not opposed to the plan as a whole," he said, "we just don't want it to take in all of Chinatown. It would mean the end of Chinatown except for the stores. The program may be a good thing for integration ... but many of our people don't speak English and some are too old to learn."[52]

In the eyes of Mayor Tom Alsbury, however, it was enough to preserve the stores of Chinatown and harness the rest of the area to the
city's needs. On this point he was clear: "I have nothing but com-
mendation for their moral and community life," he said in September
1960, "but our 20-year redevelopment plan must proceed. Other
areas and other citizens will be affected beneficially. Redevelopment
removes the high cost of blight, ill health, delinquency and other
social expenses. Redeveloped areas become revenue instead of deficit
and rehoused citizens get wholesome, healthy homes. In the case of
Chinatown, I hope the City and the Chinese community can work
together to retain its unique character, but in the interests of a
planned city, the redevelopment must go ahead."[53] ✗ Key.

Alsbury's message was extraordinarily blunt and ingenuously provided the reasoning behind an earlier assertion by Alderman Wilson
that redevelopment was "inevitable."[54] But the mayor also identified
a possible source of hesitation in the city's approach, namely, the
commercial value of Chinatown's "unique character." *Beautiful B.C.
Magazine* described it this way in 1961: "With its appealing restaurant neon signs, Chinatown is a treasure of Oriental culture [that]
contributes an exotic flavour to Canada's Oriental gateway."[55] This
version of the area, with its memorable incorporation of neon into
the recipe for tourist appeal, was, it seems, the only Chinatown to
which the city was prepared to concede a place in its planning.
The rest of the district, where its residents lived, had become a
"revenue sink." ✗

Vancouver residents of Chinese origin had never been inclined to
accept passively government encroachments on their life chances, and
the new public-interest logic that singled out their homes for destruction was yet another call to action. Not that all "Chinese," however,
saw the issue the same way. The *Chinatown News*, for instance, voice
of the local-born population and supportive of any means of raising
its constituency's status in the society at large, endorsed the view of
the *Vancouver Redevelopment Study* that relocation should proceed in
such a way as to avoid the formation of "ethnic enclaves." The *News*
urged its readers to "join the ranks of the suburbanites" and "hasten
the assimilation process."[56]

Property owners and merchants were more committed to their
investments and community. In October 1960, in one of the strongest
delegations that Chinatown ever mustered, a contingent of fifty representatives and lawyers from the CTPOA, the CBA, and other Chinese
organizations pleaded a case before city council.[57] A CTPOA brief (also
presented to the Royal Commission on Expropriation Laws and
Procedures the following year) urged retention of private housing in

area A. The brief provides the detailed arguments of those opposing relocation and redevelopment:

> We want to point out the danger to the Chinese Community and the probable disastrous social and economic effects of failing to take every conceivable care to ensure its wellbeing ... Chinese are under a disability as to property ownership and social acceptance generally. Only limited numbers of skilled jobs and white collar positions are available. The disruption of this group could lead to widespread disaster and a very real social problem ... The Chinese population of the City is almost entirely concentrated within Area "A" and there is in Vancouver an estimated 14,000 Chinese people ... Any disruption of Chinatown and a material outflow of Chinese population to another area inevitably means the destruction of the Chinese merchants. Directly affected by the operations now contemplated by the City of Vancouver are 176 businesses ... There are now also 68 fraternal associations ... four Chinese language schools ... six churches ... The expropriation and clearing planned by the City will be a great disruptive force socially ... [Stability] is not provided by rented accommodation, no matter how good ... The private development contemplated would only be available to large investors and [where] private ownership is permitted, there is no guarantee it will be given to [dislocated] Chinese. It is fair to say that all the Chinese whose property will be expropriated are extraordinarily apprehensive as to the price they may receive for their property ... The City, by setting aside this area for redevelopment and marketing it practically as a slum have made properties in the area at the present time almost unsaleable. This has also been reflected in a lowering of assessments which are sometimes used by expert valuers as evidence of the value of property. It is pointed out that this all works to the advantage of the City of Vancouver ... Vancouver's Chinatown has been an asset, it is submitted, and is some place different for Occidentals to go and spend a pleasant evening. Inroads upon the economic life of the Chinese community will have a serious effect upon this and instead of becoming a showplace as in (say) San Francisco, the area will decline.[58]

The appeal to Chinatown's "International Flavour," as the brief worded it, was potentially valuable leverage for Chinese merchants and spokesmen. It afforded them some degree of influence over those with the power to confer visions of Chinatown that, for the inhabitants, held consequences well beyond mere concern for the volume of Occidental tourists.

The strength to be gained from Chinatown's exotic image was slight at this time, however. The merchant élite was able to manipulate the symbols of Chineseness, as we saw in chapter 5, but only to its own advantage, apparently, when they coincided with the interests of those with the power to filter them. The "Chinese Village" of 1936 had brought together the city of Vancouver and Chinese capital, but by the 1960s, the city had little time for the quaint remnants of such ancient civilizations as Chinatown was perceived to embody. Rather, it had unreserved confidence in the logic of progress. A *Province* editorial in August 1961 dismissed the protest from Chinatown: "Slum clearance is going ahead ... and the Chinese community should be cooperating in the process. They should be arranging to house elderly survivors of a past era in the fine new housing that is to be provided. Chinatown can be preserved. But only if the Chinese themselves help to make it a better, more modern and finer Chinatown. Slum clearance is Chinatown's opportunity."[59]

In an optimistic age in the industrial West, with its modern high-rises and urban renewal, the residents merely misunderstood their own best interests. Douglas Jung (whose election to the House of Commons in 1951 signalled the post-war entry of the Chinese in Canada to professional roles) was equally impressed by the logic of progress. "It would be a shame," he said in December 1960, "to hold back something from which the whole city stands to gain."[60]

STAGE TWO

Council was so convinced of the plan's virtue that, having heard the Chinatown brief on 4 October 1960, it decided at the same meeting to hold a further special meeting on the second stage of the Strathcona project.[61] Early in the new year, when expropriation began from stage 1, in areas A-1, A-2, and A-3, the director of planning, George Fountain, summed up the city's position: "I know that if I heard that a big, impersonal City was going to pull my house down I'd be very upset ... But we're sure the Chinese will be very surprised when they find they can have modern Western accommodation at prices they can afford ... I'm sure that once the plan gets going and the first group moves into the new accommodation and appreciates how nice it is, it will be a revelation. It is true their mode of life will change, but it can't be helped. We're not spending public money where it isn't necessary."[62]

The project for stage 2 (see Map 8, above) earmarked for demolition blocks that were in more intensive residential use by Chinese than those identified for stage 1. Area A-6 – blocks 87 and 88, home to approximately 570 people – was to be converted into public housing for the MacLean Park complex, while a private row-house development for senior citizens was planned for blocks 72 and 73. An extension to the Lord Strathcona School on block 75 would displace approximately 200 residents.[63]

The report on stage 2 was circulated by the city to over twenty interested organizations in 1962, but only residents of Chinese origin balked at it. An indignant CTPOA submitted: "The completion of [stage 2] would cut off any future expansion of Chinatown and strangle the Chinese business activities." Not only that, but in denying individual ownership the city was regulating the life of the people residing in area A in a manner that violated "the principle of democracy and individual freedom."[64] The CBA urged that stage 2 be deferred until after assessment of the impact of the first stage. Another seventeen Chinatown organizations opposed the proposal on the grounds that it included five blocks directly adjacent to the area's commercial district. The Christ Church of China objected that Chinatown would be "dismembered" and its own congregation scattered.

City council had appointed a new consultative committee, including Mr Foon Sien, to liaise with the aggrieved parties. After hearing the strong views of the Chinatown organizations, the committee nevertheless recommended, in January 1963, that council approve the "carefully considered and balanced" proposals for stage 2.[65] Foon Sien was not one to be so easily co-opted, however. Before resigning from the committee in protest, he pointed out to council that the intention to disperse the Chinese district had much in common with the forced evacuation of Vancouver's "Little Tokyo" during the Second World War. Even elderly, poor single men preferred furnished housekeeping rooms in private accommodation, he pointed out: many such men had already moved away from the recently completed MacLean Park complex.[66]

THE NEXT DAY, MAYOR WILLIAM RATHIE offered Chinese architects the opportunity to design a private development for area A-3 (Block 86). "Submit your own plans for Chinatown development if you don't like the City's," he said. "The best people to redevelop the area are those most affected."[67] (He neglected to point out the stringent land disposal and density requirements set out by CMHC.) Realtors and CBA members Dean Leung and Faye Leung acted quickly on the offer, and while their Vancouver Chinatown Development Association (VCDA) set about the task of drafting its own redevelopment scheme, council approved stage 2 in principle.[68] By April 1963, the Leungs had completed their plan for presentation to council. Its "Oriental city" of seventy-two individual family units – complete with "moon-gate windows, pagoda roofs and landscapes of bamboo, Chinese maples, Japanese cherries and tea gardens" – conformed well to one of the city's perceptions of the district. "It will provide Vancouver with a marvellous tourist attraction," Mrs Leung promised. "We would also hope to get more land for a big tourist mall complete with *wanted* fountains and temples to display eastern culture."[69] *wanted they wanted*

The Leungs' proposal sparked an interesting controversy in Chinatown itself. The head of a rival project, Gilbert Eng, branded the scheme "outright commercialism." Eng said that his own scheme was based strictly on rehabilitation – "and there aren't any pagodas."[70] The *Chinatown News* also warned against a "Chinese village" as a counterproductive move that would "build a wall around ourselves," while a Chinatown businessman said: "We don't want to be like the Stanley Park Zoo with buses going through our backyards."[71] Despite these objections, the Leungs, with the support of the Greater Vancouver Visitors' and Convention Bureau and the provincial minister of recreation and culture, won council over in July 1963.[72] *oppositions from community itself.*

However, the attempt by the Leungs and their supporters to manipulate Chinatown's landscape in the image of the city's representations met firm resistance at the federal level. The regional officer of CMHC pointed out that the relevant land had been cleared and a redevelopment plan already prepared, at considerable public expense: "The development of Block 86 should be consistent with the broad principles established by this original concept. If, in accordance with the original plan, the City were to request additional public housing on this land to supplement the Maclean Park project, the Corporation would be glad to consider such a request."[73] *→ lied*

This was a stern rebuff for the provincial and civic leaders who had supported the Leungs' proposal. Once again, the attempt by some "Chinese" at commercializing Chinatown proved ineffective so long as it conflicted with the agenda of more powerful architects. The projection of "Chineseness" by those defined in terms of it could "act back" only when, and as far as, hegemonic sectors would have it. Despite Mayor Rathie's concession that "they" knew what was best for themselves, the federal government took as inviolate the logic of progress, and the plan of 1957 had become an inflexible end in itself.

While the city's proposal for a second stage of redevelopment east of Main Street was being reviewed by the provincial and federal governments, the city, in a crude juggling of images, considered a site for the "Oriental Village" more amenable to the federal government's overall plan for the district. The city's Planning Department drafted a proposal that included the area west of Main Street and set out to "show how this area can be improved, its character strengthened and its tourist potential enhanced." Excluded was the shopping area east of Main Street that was patronized by local residents. Redevelopment would reroute heavy traffic from Pender Street to Keefer Street, turn one section into a "park-like Oriental bazaar," and establish a pedestrian mall on Pender, between Carrall and Main. At one entrance to the mall, a sixty-foot "neon-dragon" was to be built, and at the other, an "Oriental gateway." The Planning Department's report also suggested that the "disarray of [other] signs should be ordered to reduce their conflict with the riotous gaiety of the neon signs which should not be restricted."[74]

City council unanimously supported the idea that had first captivated municipal politicians in 1936, and in March 1964 it recommended more research on the report of the planning director.[75] The Town Planning Commission and the civic bureau of the Vancouver Board of Trade agreed that the "improvement plan" would have "economic value to the city, both from the entertainment and tourist point of view."[76] The Vancouver Visitors' Bureau predictably supported the plans, but they also drew endorsement from European and Chinese newspapers. According to the *Province* of 14 November 1964, the proposal would transform Chinatown from "a somewhat drab district into a sparkling area for both tourists and Vancouver residents."[77] And in May of that year, the *Chinatown News* called for major rebuilding in the business district, citing the need for more tourists in the area. "One way to attract them is to keep this area growing. This can only be achieved by a major renovating and rebuilding job. Most of the structures were erected more than half a century ago ... They lack cultural and aesthetic appeal. Architecturally they are neither East nor West – only a caricature of the Orient. With a new generation of architects sprouting up in our community ... these young professionals should be able to produce some blueprints that will truly reflect the architectural splendour of the Orient."[78]

If the *Chinatown News* was eager to cater to the projections of white Vancouver's defining élites, Chinatown's merchants remained fearful about government-initiated projects. A Chinese spokesman at a meeting of the board of trade in early 1964 said that the merchants were especially unreceptive to the "Little China" plan because of "fears that City Council has been trying to drive Chinese out of their residential area."[79] Around the same time, one Chinatown merchant supported the idea of improvement but added "first of all you have to bring people back into the area."[80]

The people still living in the area in 1964 also spoke out. Shirley Wong, of Keefer Street, for example, said that many such as she wished to stay on as homeowners, "not as tiny units in a government

sponsored project. Many of us do not believe we are underprivileged
and in need of a government subsidy."[81] Although the CBA agreed to
form a committee in April to work with the Planning Department,
this plan to "reorient" Chinatown appears to have slid from the civic
agenda as a more imposing plan for the commercial district (discussed below) began to occupy the planning bureaucracy.

more views on the topic.

MERCHANTS' FEARS FOR THEIR nearby clientele, and residents' fears
for their neighbourhood, were realized in December 1964 when the
city began to acquire property under stage 2 of the redevelopment
project. Clearance proceeded apace through 1965 and 1966, taking
with it the resolve of the CTPOA.[82] An estimated 1,600 persons had
been displaced by stage 1, only some of whom were of Chinese
origin, but 1,730 were displaced by stage 2, the majority of whom
were of Chinese origin.[83] Despite considerable turnover in the complexes, including the new Raymur Park complex for 370 tenants,
demand exceeded supply.[84]

The city's response was a proposal in January 1965 for a third and
still more ambitious redevelopment project that would complete the
vision of the 1957 study. By January 1966, homeowners in areas A-7
and A-6 had taken to the desperate strategy of refusing to sell their
homes to the city without the assurance of alternative property in the
same area.[85] Many of their predecessors had been forced to leave the
area (without relocation assistance) because public accommodation
was not available when their properties were acquired. House price
settlements were increasingly interpreted as signs of callousness on
the part of a city trying to cheat owners of their valuable inner-city
land. Displaced families reported anger, frustration, and considerable
disruption to their lives and friendship networks.[86] The property of
the Christ Church of China, which resisted any settlement at all, was
finally expropriated without the offer of another site. "The church
has no architectural value," said Alderman Harry Rankin in 1967,
"and it is holding up 300 units of public housing."[87] *ramifications*

THE CITY'S DECISION TO IMPLEMENT a massive and untried public
venture in Chinatown in defiance of the residents' wishes reflected
the long-standing tendency of European policy-makers to perceive
Chinatown's residents as typifications – essentially as objects for the
projects of others. West of Main Street, the city flirted with the concept of the "Little Corner of the Far East," while east of Main it
imposed its blight classification. Both images, and the practices they

inspired, suggest that the area continued through the 1950s and 1960s to reflect less the career of those who lived there, and more the authority of those with the power to define, and literally to construct, Vancouver's Chinatown.

FIGHTING THE FREEWAY

If city officials in the early 1960s could convince themselves that – despite the opposition of Chinatown's residents – they were providing them with "modern Western accommodation," they could mount no such defence in 1967, when plans were disclosed for an elevated eight-lane freeway through the western wing of commercial Chinatown. "We had been assured that while the City officials knew best about housing for the Chinese people, they would not interfere with the Chinese commercial district," Foon Sien remarked bitterly in December 1967. That same month, Jack Lee, a district lawyer, remarked: "Someone has decided that Chinatown is expendable."[88]

The story of the freeway began in the early 1950s, when, in conjunction with the redevelopment plans for Strathcona, the city's civil servants began to tackle downtown congestion and circulation. Engineers and planners argued that another crossing from Vancouver to the North Shore was necessary to ease access to the downtown area.[89] The committee on Burrard Inlet crossings added that the study of a crossing could not be divorced from transportation planning for the entire Burrard Peninsula. Within six years, a Metropolitan Highway Planning report recommended a new First Narrows crossing to Vancouver that would be integrated with a downtown-oriented network of facilities. Here it echoed planning consensus throughout North America, as policy-makers sought to stimulate investment in central business districts and provide transportation infrastructure that would keep urban cores viable.

Although never formally adopted by council, the report became the working document for Vancouver's transportation plans until 1972. Meanwhile, the appearance on the civic scene of millionaire Mayor William Rathie gave the freeway idea an enthusiastic and influential advocate. In an attempt to implement the idea, Rathie hired a company in 1966 to analyse downtown revitalization and its relationship to transport linkages. Drawing on earlier reports approved by council, the consultants presented an updated version of a system that would increase access to the downtown area via an east–west freeway, a north–south freeway, and a new Georgia viaduct. The mandate of the consultants was simply to take all the pieces in the jigsaw and create explicit routes. Here they replicated almost exactly their terms of reference. That is, as stipulated by the Planning Department, the freeway system would take in a waterfront freeway from a Brockton Point crossing along Abbott Street and a north–south link "in the vicinity of Carrall and Main Streets" which would link up with an east-west freeway. Either of the north–south choices would dissect Chinatown.

Transportation planners and consultants may appear to have simply overlooked Chinatown's existence, but the consultants' study acknowledged the presence of "one of the largest integrated Chinese communities in the Western Hemisphere." It pointed out: "The commercial Chinatown portion of the Old City is one of Vancouver's landmarks and an important tourist attraction. Commercial Chinatown is confined almost entirely in an oblong centred on Pender Street and bounded by Hastings Street, Gore Avenue, Keefer Street and Carrall Street. Residential Chinatown includes this area but extends particularly eastward of this core. The portion of Chinatown of particular interest to tourists is the two blocks of Pender Street between Carrall and Main Streets."[90]

The architectural subconsultant cited in the study was fully aware of the damage a freeway would wreak upon Chinatown: "Whether a freeway facility could be successfully integrated within this old section of downtown Vancouver depends on whether (a) certain of its subtle features are dispensable and (b) the City and senior levels of government are prepared to spend an amount substantially in excess of the cost of the freeway facility itself ... for a timely effectuation of its intent of redevelopment within this area."[91]

In other words, it might be possible for the city to have its "Little China" and its freeway too. The precedent, according to the subconsultant, could be found in "the process of adapting the freeway to Project 200 and vice versa."[92] In fact, Project 200, an eight-block commercial development, had not even been built. The development-oriented city had devised the freeway system with Project 200 in mind, and their invoking it as justification for adapting Chinatown to the freeway plans indicates the degree to which some planners felt Chinatown could be moulded to the city's advantage.

The decision-making behind the choice of Carrall Street for the north–south freeway attests further to this. The possibility of tunnelling the freeway was dismissed on simple cost criteria. Also, it would involve tunnelling the waterfront freeway, which would preclude access to downtown and to Project 200. Locations west of Carrall Street were ruled out because they would "involve relatively more intensive downtown land uses and more valuable property, as well as interference with Project 200."[93] A route east of Columbia to Main

Street would present alignment difficulties, and locations east of Gore Street (in Strathcona) were ruled out. "The City's Planning Director has stated his belief," the consultants' transportation study noted, "that location of any portion of a freeway or its ramps within the Strathcona redevelopment project and its required clearance would involve loss to the City of further financial support to the project by the senior levels of government."[94] The redevelopment scheme, inspired and executed without regard for residents' protests, had now apparently become part of the justification for appropriating the rest of Chinatown. That area, in particular its western border, was the "least disruptive and most feasible" alignment for the north–south connection, the engineering consultants advised.[95]

City council and its Non-Partisan Association (NPA) majority, a major instigator of post-war land use change in Vancouver, found little fault with the choice of its expert advisers and unanimously supported the Carrall Street route on 1 June 1967.[96] In so doing, they unleashed the plans of the civic bureaucracy, which had sought since the early 1950s to superimpose an entire traffic network on the city down routes perceived to be of maximum efficiency – and least resistance.

WHEN FINALLY, IN MID-1967, the merchants of Chinatown were made privy to the city's plans for Carrall Street and the unit block East Pender Street, the "long-divided, fragmented and quarrelsome community," as the *Chinatown News* described Vancouver's Chinese, was galvanized by new heights of fear and indignation.[97] Council had even given approval, just weeks before the freeway decision was disclosed, for the construction by Chinatown interests of a $150,000 centennial pagoda at Pender and Carrall, the site suggested for such a purpose in the 1964 improvement plan.[98] Council obviously hoped that the Chinese would agree that the thirty-foot pillars of an eight-lane freeway were compatible with tourist projects, especially any improvements they cared to pay for themselves.

At that time, however, the city's Chinese community was joined by an unexpected set of allies who possessed the legitimacy often denied Chinese critics. At the forefront of the opposition were members of an influential Vancouver architectural firm, Birmingham and Wood. That firm was the first to acknowledge that the freeway was a threat to the city's "heritage and character," of the kind it argued Chinatown embodied.[99] The architects began a campaign to save the precinct from destruction and first mobilized demand among

Chinatown's leaders, merchants, and property owners for a public hearing before council. "We should be attempting to improve Chinatown, rather than destroy it," said one architect from the firm, while another, Dr Bud Wood, predicted: "If the freeway comes about, it will destroy Vancouver's largest tourist attraction and ancient historic landmarks. The project is 10 to 20 years away but as long as a shadow of it is there, the Chinese community won't attempt to improve Chinatown."[100] In protesting the freeway decision, the firm told council that it could also speak for civic organizations such as the Business Owners' and Managers' Association, the Community Arts Council, the Community Planning Association, the Downtown Business Association, the Townsite Committee, and the Visitors' Bureau. Chinatown had certainly acquired some valuable new advocates.

In mid-June 1967, the CBA was invited to a meeting of council called to enable officials to provide more information on the Chinatown section of the freeway complex. Quickly it became apparent that it was not just the CBA that needed more information, but also a number of aldermen, some of whom queried for the first time why other locations had not even been considered. Mayor Campbell attempted to convince Chinatown's leaders and sceptical councillors that the freeway would be an asset to the area – that it would remove through traffic and bring more local business traffic. The mayor also argued that the underside of the Chinatown freeway need not become a "forest of concrete stilts as in Seattle" but could be turned into an arcade of shops. Neither the Chinatown delegation nor Campbell's colleagues were impressed. Council voted to postpone further action until the opinions of all interested groups had been solicited, and the Chinese group informed council that the centennial pagoda would be shelved until the offer could be treated seriously.[101]

Growing public concern was reflected at a public meeting in July, when no less than seventeen delegations, including a number of non-Chinese groups, attended to declare their opposition. The CBA delegation, sensing a new wave of interest in Chinatown, stepped up the pressure on council with a cleverly worded plea for preservation: "Chinatown is a tradition, a landmark and a major tourist attraction of the City of Vancouver and has been almost since the birth of the City ... Thousands of dollars are spent annually promoting the tourist business in Vancouver and in promoting the city as a Convention City. Chinatown has always been on the agenda of visiting delegates. Vancouver's Chinatown has potentials [sic] of being the largest Chinatown in North America. Unlike the Chinatowns in New York and San Francisco, we have no import restriction. These potentials can be developed with the encouragement from the City Council."[102]

The CBA's selective recollection of Chinatown's past, ignoring its history of harassment "almost since the birth of the City," is an apt example of neighbourhood definition resurfacing, not unreflectively, but as part of a strategic awareness by the Chinese. In an attempt to realize its own interests, the CBA adopted the language and concepts with which the Chinese had long been interpreted, projecting them positively in order to win council's "encouragement." This strategy and the show of force of its many new allies prompted city council to instruct its freeway consultants to study alternative alignments, such as one along Gore Avenue (the eastern border of Chinatown).[103]

Having been assured that they would be invited to the council meeting at which the future of the north–south freeway would be discussed, Chinatown's leaders were outraged to learn later in the year that council had decided to retain the Carrall Street alignment. "It's not only the question of the freeway," charged CTPOA representative Harry Fan, "but the fact that Council acted in bad faith by not allowing a hearing."[104] Chinatown lawyer Jack Lee saw the affront as symptomatic of the entire handling of the freeway decision: "We oppose the freeway plan for our own interests, yet our greatest complaint is the way in which City Council has gone about the whole business ... If the best experts had been free to decide where the freeway should go, and they had settled on Chinatown, we would have had to accept it. But the experts were so sharply restricted that they were virtually forced into recommending Carrall Street and Chinatown."[105]

Foon Sien was incensed and did not mince words at a luncheon hosted by Mayor Campbell in Chinatown on 23 October. He saw it as "the latest abuse in 81 years of discrimination against Vancouver's Chinatown":

When in 1957 the City labelled our residential area blighted, we admitted that some improvement was justified, but more than 500 Chinese protested the scope of the plan. City Hall ignored us of course and went ruthlessly on. Now some 15 blocks of predominantly Chinese homes have been destroyed ... The City boasted it was providing low-income housing. But only some old people who had no choice became tenants in it. Most did not want the stigma of living in subsidized, civic housing and they wanted to be property owners, not just tenants. City officials smiled at our protests and said this would 'make a better Chinatown' ... Now, lo and behold they

announce a freeway to cut 250 feet into the west side of Chinatown ...
Whatever is left in the shadow of the concrete will soon wither away.[106]

The Leungs, meanwhile, claimed that council's decision heralded
the district's slide into dereliction. "They tried to rebuild the Chinatowns of Los Angeles and Toronto after chopping them up in the
name of progress ... but it didn't work," they warned.[107] (Of course
the Leungs had seen no problem with "rebuilding" their own "Oriental Village" from scratch a few years earlier.)

As things evolved, many of the city's residents felt moved to step
in and support the Chinatown protest on a matter of planning principle. Important among them was the provincial member for Vancouver East, Robert ("Bob") Williams, who charged that the freeway
decision was only the most recent expression of the city's tendency
to preclude Chinese from policy-making that directly affected them.
Other such instances, he recalled, were the decisions to turn Pender
Street into a truck route in the 1950s and to clear without consultation
much of the residential area so heavily populated by Chinese.[108] The
student population also became involved. Fifty architecture students
of the University of British Columbia felt moved to march through
Pender Street in October. Others protested outside the hotel where
federal transport minister Paul Hellyer held a press conference the
same month. Another group met with Mayor Campbell to remind
him of the consequences of supporting a link predicated on a whole
freeway network. The Town Planning Commission, the Vancouver
chapter of the Architectural Institute, and Dr Walter Hardwick, a
geography professor, criticized council's subordination to public servants like the city engineer, Mr R. Martin.[109] Martin, for example,
defended the Carrall Street route in November 1967 in terms that
indicated how derogatory stereotypes of Chinatown lived on in the
consciousness of Europeans. "Most ladies wouldn't, nor do they walk
down Carrall at night," he said. "The street isn't any Champs Elysees;
it needs rebuilding."[110]

Other critics invoked Chinatown's value to Vancouver. Larry Kil-
lam, an architect from Birmingham and Wood, warned: "It will be a
tragic blunder if the City demolishes half of Chinatown for a freeway."[111] An architecture professor, one of several academics to speak
out, said: "Chinatown is one of the great things we have in this city."[112]
This had also become the position of the Civic Unity Association,
the Community Arts Council, and the general manager of the Greater
Vancouver Visitors' and Convention Bureau, who asked: "What's a
few million dollars more in costs compared with destroying China-

town – one of our leading tourist attractions?"[113] The support of the board of trade was also important, and, in a brief later in the year – the tenor of which can only be contrasted with one its members submitted to the Special Oriental Immigration Committee in 1921 (see chapter 4) – it declared: "We have every sympathy with the Chinese community and believe that the character of the area should be improved with as little interference as possible."[114] A *Province* news story also remarked: "As a tourist attraction, Chinatown probably ranks second only to Stanley Park, and so contributes greatly to Vancouver's fame abroad. With its restaurants, stores and nightclubs, it adds entertainment spice for resident and visitor alike ... Few Vancouverites are unfamiliar with the colour and romance of Chinatown."[115]

VERY QUICKLY, THIS NEW PERCEPTION of Chinatown was reversing the fortunes of a neighbourhood that had experienced decades of stigmatization. The freeway became politically suicidal for the NPA, as two tumultuous public meetings late in 1967 demonstrated. Early in the new year, council voted to rescind its Carrall Street decision, with only two aldermen refusing to capitulate to what had become a solid change in public attitudes toward Chinatown.[116] Even Alderman Halford Wilson remarked: "I can see their complaints now, it would wipe out Chinatown."[117] Later in the year, Mayor Campbell promised: "We are not out to carve Chinatown in half, in quarters, or bisect or dissect it." An elevated freeway over Carrall Street, he said, "would be like a knife cutting through the area."[118]

The new vision of Chinatown as a civic asset – a refinement of the tourist image – was being forged by an influential liberal reform lobby of architects, academics, lawyers, and community workers, for whom the precinct had become a vehicle to discredit boosterism in urban development and to mount an alternative political and planning agenda. Through these eyes, Chinatown had become an oasis of "difference" in an otherwise uniform downtown. It was a place of "character" and "tradition" in an environment levelled by policies aimed at converting the city to a place of production. It was a symbol of local struggle against land-use change sponsored by ruling élites. The liberal view promised greater justice for the Chinese, to be sure – indeed it was to serve the interests of the Chinese as no other intervention on their behalf ever had. But, as chapter 7 will show, the emerging perception of Chinatown had by no means transcended the culture of racial representation traced in this study. Meanwhile, Vancouver's Chinese community had another battle to fight.

FIGHTING STAGE THREE

For the residents of Strathcona, the decision to rescind the freeway proposal demonstrated that the pro-growth coalitions of free-market politicians, planning-oriented technocrats, and entrepreneurial interests could be challenged, even overcome. Similar development coalitions had also fractured throughout North America under the pressure of a political culture of urban unrest. Encouraged by the reformist turn, including the 1967 federal immigration legislation, the remaining Strathcona residents prepared for the third stage of comprehensive redevelopment with new awareness, incentive, and political clout.

In October 1968, the city submitted to the upper levels of government its plan for stage 3 in Strathcona's redevelopment. The objective was to clear and rebuild the fifteen remaining blocks with a number of "super-block" public-housing and other complexes. The scheme was expected to affect about 3,000 people, most of them "Chinese."[119] In 1967, the proportion of the area that was of Chinese origin was over 70 per cent, while 78 per cent of the families in Strathcona were classified as "Asiatic" in 1966.[120]

Many residents were deeply embittered by the proposal. An indignant Foon Sien, after listening to platitudes about Chinatown beautification at a civic campaign dinner in December 1968, asked his NPA audience: "How can there be a Chinatown without Chinese in it, when you take away our homes by expropriation?"[121] But the Strathcona area council's committee on redevelopment and relocation – an organization of mostly non-resident professionals established in 1965 to liaise with the city on neighbourhood issues – was sufficiently impressed by the proposal to "congratulate City Council and the various departments of the City working on urban renewal, on the excellent proposal to revitalize the Strathcona area."[122]

Obviously the residents needed a voice of their own, and it was the Strathcona Property Owners and Tenants Association (SPOTA) that stepped in to provide it.[123] The organization was established and run predominantly by residents who were committed to salvaging the dwellings of those who remained in Strathcona in 1968. Some politically active Chinese were keen to gain greater control, after decades of unilateral intervention by government, over decisions that affected them, and SPOTA gave them such a forum. At the same time, these local-born "Chinese" hoped to raise their own profile in a community whose power élite had become too insular to contest large-scale public interventions. SPOTA also emerged out of a new mood in Ottawa following the election of Pierre Trudeau's Liberal government in April 1968. The slum clearance–public housing wisdom came under its first real public scrutiny by Trudeau, and it was in December 1968, after the federal minister of transport and his housing task force had visited Vancouver, that Strathcona property owners were first inspired to join forces.[124]

Across Canada, the transport minister, Paul Hellyer, listened to residents relate their experiences of urban renewal. In Strathcona he found further evidence that, for all the advantages clearance programs had for municipalities seeking to alter their assessment ratios, the residents themselves "seemed to know little more than that they were living in an 'urban renewal area' and that this designation should not be interpreted as a compliment to their neighbourhood."[125] In Strathcona, Hellyer described the Chinese as having "a rather exotic, vigorous and cohesive community,"[126] while elsewhere in Canada he observed that other Chinatowns had been special targets of urban renewal plans.

SPOTA cultivated a close relationship with the senior levels of government, especially the favourably disposed Hellyer, as leverage against an unco-operative civic administration. It formulated an alternative redevelopment proposal for Strathcona for which it cleverly lobbied all levels of government. The case for rehabilitation of homes was in the interest of the city, SPOTA argued in one of its many briefs to the governments: "Vancouver City Council and the Vancouver citizens at large have urged that Chinatown be preserved and developed as a business and tourist attraction. These same people must realize that Chinatown cannot continue to exist if there is no residential Chinese community nearby. The present urban renewal scheme for Strathcona is likely to destroy the Chinese residential community and in turn will seriously affect Chinatown as a city asset."[127]

Soon after his return to Ottawa, Hellyer recommended a federal freeze on all renewal projects in Canada, including stage 3 for Strathcona. The federal government had spent approximately $50 million on clearance schemes from 1960 to 1968 and gladly agreed to a moratorium on spending, including in Strathcona.[128]

The city of Vancouver had consistently ignored the link between east and west of Main Street, and it was only when Hellyer's successor, Robert Andras, spelled out the federal government's philosophical shift on Strathcona's redevelopment that the city was forced to take cognizance of the mutuality of commercial and residential Chinatown. "Ottawa is not interested in participating in the City's Strathcona urban renewal scheme," Andras told Planning Department officials in August 1969, "unless the people affected – predominantly Chinese families – and the three levels of government have a full part in the planning."[129] In the same month he told the press: "Since an ethnic group is involved, particular problems arise with the redevelopment, and in consultation with the municipal and provincial authorities, we have agreed to rethink the approach."[130] It was another example of a striking shift in government attitudes toward Chinatown in the late 1960s.

In the following years, the Strathcona Working Committee implemented a rehabilitation project in twenty city blocks east of Gore Avenue – the first cost-sharing arrangement for neighbourhood upgrading in Canada.[131] The experimental project included major public works improvements and housing rehabilitation. A grant-loan system offered owners a federal contribution of 50 per cent, a provincial contribution of 25 per cent, and a city contribution of 25 per cent toward interest-free loans (repayable over five years) for rehabilitation costs to a maximum of $3,000. Sixty-two per cent of the owners of single detached homes in Strathcona participated in the program until its end in 1975, and house prices in Strathcona increased from 55 per cent of the average sale price in Vancouver in 1969 to 80 per cent in 1974. The reversal in the fortunes of Chinatown was signalled by a return of some younger, local-born Chinese to residential Chinatown. Social worker Jonathon Lau said: "Now it seems that they have something they can be proud of. They will stay in the area because it is going to be upgraded."[132]

CONCLUSION

By the late 1960s, there developed a kind of mutually supportive symbiosis between Chinatown and the various levels of the Canadian state that was more congenial to Chinese residents than any previous relationship. Undoubtedly, there had been a change of spirit in the way the Canadian state elected to manage the area, in part because of the resolve of the residents themselves. As we saw in the redevelopment of Strathcona, and in the successful fight against the freeway proposal, the Chinese had been mobilized into action to preserve their neighbourhood in an unprecedented display of shared purpose. They had responded to the full force of a post-war planning imperative that attempted to assimilate their area into an economic master strategy for Vancouver. That the state's plans effectively called for obliteration of the neighbourhood showed the endurance of the European assessment of Chinatown as expendable and served as a rallying point for Chinese, who sought to resist this legacy of their defenceless past and press, once again, the limits of hegemonic control.

Part of their strategy involved appropriating tourist Chinatown as a political symbol. But, as the Leungs' scheme for block 86 and others before it demonstrated, the appeal to "Chineseness" was subject to rules laid out by those more powerful. Moreover, as the CMHC's rejection of the council-approved Leung scheme (and many episodes before it) highlighted, the federal government was the ultimate arbiter of Chinatown's status and definition in Vancouver.

It was only when a new image of Chinatown was forged by a non-Chinese reform lobby in Vancouver sympathetic in outlook to the Trudeau government that appeals to the district's "difference" began to subvert the influential post-war ideology of progress. The "civic asset" label was not altogether new, of course. As throughout Chinatown's history, the area's image as a place of "character" and "tradition" was an outgrowth of historically established discourse, a refinement of the tourist classification first articulated in 1936. But in the increasingly liberal climate of the 1970s, positive perceptions of "Chinese" and "Chinatown" were to find an increasingly solid footing. A *Restoration Report*, commissioned by the city and published in 1969, signalled this new round in the making of a racialized people and place: "The (Pender) Community seems ready to unfold into yet another cycle in its evolution within the multiracial fabric of Vancouver."[133]

CHAPTER SEVEN

Chinatown Re-oriented, 1970–1980

Traces of a positive assessment of "ethnic diversity" in Canada can be found in speeches in the House of Commons from the early 1950s on (see chapter 6), but during the late 1960s and early 1970s enthusiasm for the distinctiveness of Canada's "ethnic groups" began to be loudly proclaimed in the house and elsewhere. This diversity, not only ethnic but regional, held the key to the nation's elusive identity – or so it was often, albeit nervously, suggested. The Royal Commission on Bilingualism and Biculturalism, which held hearings from 1963 to 1968, influenced this sea change in Canada's political rhetoric. As a small part of its mandate, the commission investigated "the cultural contribution of the ethnic groups" with a view to recommending measures to safeguard that contribution, and it found that the ethnic groups – once the fearful embodiment of alien and inferior stock – had become "an inestimable enrichment that Canadians cannot afford to lose."[1] The member for Hamilton-Wentworth captured the new sentiment and displayed a disarming indifference to history when he asked in February 1972: "Has any man in this Chamber ever met a Chinese he did not like? I submit that they enrich our humour, culture and dignity and I hope we have more of them."[2]

This chapter explores the transformation of essentialist thought about the Chinese into a more muted and outwardly sympathetic image and discourse involving "ethnic" difference. We saw the beginnings of this shift in the last chapter, but it was during the 1970s, when a Liberal government held office in Ottawa, that this interpretation of the Chinese became widely endorsed and popularized. Such a language change signalled more than a semiotic shift, however: it facilitated a radically new form of targeting of Vancouver's Chinatown by all three levels of the Canadian state. According to the new vision of Canada as a "multicultural" society, Chinatown was to be celebrated and protected for its uniqueness as one of Vancouver's key "ethnic neighbourhoods." Chinatown had become a local expression of "difference," to be respected and valued for its contribution to the uniquely Canadian ideal of unity through diversity. Without regard for the history of its making, political figures of the 1970s at all levels saw in Chinatown an ethnic element that could not be left to the forces of assimilation and homogenization. It had itself become a powerful symbol of the new Canada, the land where the Chinese were "separate but equal," free ... to be Chinese.

Stuart Leggatt, member for New Westminster, provided a plain statement to that effect in June 1973. "It is interesting to note," he told the House, "that on the west coast we have the second largest Chinatown in North America. They [the Chinese] have made a unique and valuable contribution. Thank God they have not melted themselves into some sort of amorphous North America. They continue to contribute in many interesting ways to the mosaic and originality of this country."[3] The melodious ideal of diversity had become a benchmark for new European constructions of old outsiders, as John Porter implies: "Such diversity is more enjoyed by the beholder – whatever Olympus he might be viewing it from – than any of the actors within their enclaves."[4]

The Canadian state provided the Olympus from which European perceptions of difference were carried into the 1970s. It selected those "cultural contributions" of the Chinese, including Chinatown itself, that it wanted to promote as evidence that the nation was "multicultural." This state control will be seen to be as clear in instances of government courting of Vancouver's Chinatown as in those where, as of old, the state continued to harass Chinatown. In short, the reification of some eternal Chineseness underpinned both the proactive and the reactive reflexes of the Canadian state in the 1970s.

Although seemingly novel and enlightened, the new rhetoric of "ethnic diversity" was based on assumptions carried over from the time when particular (unflattering) qualities were considered inherent to a national type and part of the hereditary process.[5] Multiculturalism was a harmonious metaphor for fashioning a nationalist ideology (as some scholars have argued[6]), but what went unacknowledged was its subtle assimilation of the practice of imputing qualities to national types. Chinese were now to be praised for their industry, fastidiousness, courtesy, and compassion. The *Chinatown News* in January 1970 reported one man's view: "Thousands have come through this court from nearly all countries. They have enriched this nation with their culture and their moral lives and their compassion for the widow, orphan, the infirm and the aged," said Vancouver Citizenship Judge Norman Oreck.

Wong claims that the practice of positive stereotyping is widespread in the United States, including in social science, where the "middleman minority" theory, for example, argues that the "high adaptive capacity" and "commercial acumen" of the Chinese (and Japanese) have made them "model minorities."[7] Note the "masked negativity," to use Wong's words, but also, and more important, the manner in which cultural conceptions about a Chinese race were being re-created by those who controlled the knowledge about, and practice toward, people of Chinese origin in Canada. Liberalism had long erased Darwinist notions of a race hierarchy, but Europeans' faith in the "Chinese" category itself had well outlived the era that gave rise to it.

We have already seen that some groups in Chinatown, in various periods, willingly projected the representations of white Canada to further interests of their own. This is no more apparent than in the 1970s when, in the rush for the spoils of multiculturalism and other public rewards at the neighbourhood level, there was much to recommend a supply of "difference." Indeed the social construction of Chinatown has not been entirely self-serving on the part of Europeans, nor wholly imposed on people of Chinese origin. Europeans' hold on conceptual and instrumental power was unbroken throughout Chinatown's career, to be sure, but so too was the vigilance of "the Chinese" to the assets and liabilities of their racialization. This chapter illustrates the extension of racial concepts in Vancouver society and space into the 1970s and the stamp on the race-definition process left by certain Chinese themselves.

IMMIGRATION POLICY AND CONSOLIDATION OF A "CHINESE" TERRITORY

Throughout the history of Vancouver's Chinatown, the Canadian state exercised a considerable degree of control over the neighbourhood's size and composition. Starting with the head tax in 1885, the federal government helped set conditions for the development of a Chinese enclave in Vancouver's East End. The points system introduced in 1967 did not end publicly expressed concerns for the composition of Canada's population but showed that Ottawa had finally abandoned the direct means to implement these concerns through discriminatory policies. As an immediate result, Canada's Chinese-origin communities swelled in the late 1960s and in the 1970s. In the four years 1967–70, 28,440 immigrants from China, Hong Kong, and Taiwan entered Canada, more than half the number that had arrived in the preceding twenty-two years.[8]

The majority of Chinese-origin immigrants to Canada after 1967 came directly from Hong Kong, where many had acquired English-language education and lived a decade or more in an urban environment not altogether alien to the industrial West.[9] Direct immigration from mainland China had ceased in 1949, but it was resumed in 1974, when Prime Minister Trudeau arranged for the reunification of a small number of families in Canada. There were various other points of origin for the immigration of the 1970s. With the changes in immigration policy, the term "Chinese" in Canada came to signify an ever-increasing range of heritages earned in such diverse points of origin as Britain, Hong Kong, Malaysia, Peru, the Philippines, Singapore, South Africa, Taiwan, the United States, Vietnam, and the West Indies.[10] The diversity prompted an observer of Toronto's Chinatown in 1971 to remark: "Chinese immigrants from Hong Kong, Taiwan, Singapore, Pakistan and even Trinidad have little in common save a culture many of them have left behind by two or three generations."[11]

From 1961 to 1971, the population of Vancouver that was of Chinese origin doubled, from 15,223 to 30,640, reinforcing the marked physical growth of commercial and residential Chinatown that had occurred since the Second World War.[12] In absolute terms, the number of blocks of Strathcona with an occupancy ratio of more than 75 per cent Chinese-origin grew considerably, despite the dispersal effects of the urban renewal program and the out-movement of younger, local-born residents.[13] Strathcona was especially attractive to low-income, non–English-speaking Chinese immigrants because of the employment opportunities in Chinatown's sub-economy. However, by no means all or even the majority of post-war immigrants opted to reside in this area. Although in 1961 it housed over 50 per cent of the people classified as Chinese by the census (see, above, Map 9), the proportion declined rapidly from that time. By 1976, Ng estimates, of a population of 60,000 Chinese in Vancouver, only 10 per cent resided in Chinatown and its immediate vicinity.[14]

These quite dramatic changes are largely explained by the decline in the conditions promoting spatial concentration during the 1970s. The sex ratio of the Chinese-origin population of Canada came at last to approximate the national average; as many as 77 per cent were in command of the English language in 1971;[15] there was a generally high level of educational and professional achievement among the unsponsored new immigrants; and informal pressure against Chinese-origin residence in neighbourhoods outside Strathcona became a thing of the past (at least until the late 1980s, when feeling ran high once more against the "Hong Kong immigrant who buys his house with cash"[16]).

The residential base of Strathcona was nevertheless strengthened *helped* in the 1970s by the efforts of SPOTA and other organizations, such as *act* the Shon Yee Association. They also had the support of both the city *after.* and provincial governments, which were by this time keen to boost housing in the area for the local Chinese residents, particularly the elderly. This shift in government priorities was revealed in 1973, when the city rescinded its decision to build a firehall on the block bounded by Pender, Keefer, Jackson, and Gore streets – acquired previously by the city under urban renewal. Council donated the site instead for construction of non-profit family and senior citizen's housing.[17] Growing civic awareness of the links between Chinatown's residential and commercial districts was also apparent in a report on the status of the Chinatown Planning Program in April 1976. The director of planning emphasized, among other goals, the need to correct the housing loss for Chinatown.[18] In turn, SPOTA successfully negotiated with the city and provincial governments to co-ordinate the objective, and by 1980 there was some evidence of a middle-class return to the area.[19]

The rush of immigration after 1967 deepened the crisis of space in commercial Chinatown. Already in December 1967, physical constraints on expansion there had prompted lawyer Harry Fan to write to council:

In the short street blocks on Pender Street East, there are 115 business establishments. There are: 13 Chinese supermarkets, 11 grocery stores, 7 butchers, 4 chicken houses, 2 fish shops, 12 restaurants, 11 tea shops, 9 gift shops, 4 banks, 3 law offices, 6 real estate offices, 4 barber shops and 27 businesses such as taxis, hotels, travel agencies, and newspaper offices, and in the upstairs of these 115 shops, there are 75 associations, including the Chinese Benevolent Association, the Veteran's club, the farmers' co-op, the unions, and 3 musical societies. Not anywhere in any city in Canada do we have so many business establishments in such a concentrated area of three street blocks, and thus they are unable to serve Vancouver because of the lack of space ... The Chinese merchants have spent $750,000 in the past five years to improve the appearance, and re-model their facilities, but there is no space to expand.[20]

With such constraints on growth, Chinatown became a profitable field of investment from the late 1960s, not unlike the turn of the century, when property purchase in the area was first being negotiated. New immigration regulations encouraged small and large entrepreneurs from Hong Kong to look to Canada and the United States as a means of escaping unstable investment conditions. In 1968, for example, 8,000 Hong Kong residents entered Canada, half of them in the skilled or professional category, bearing an average of $29,000 on entry, compared with the $4,000 to $7,000 brought by immigrants from England, West Germany, and France.[21] Questions about the future of Hong Kong after the expiration of Britain's lease from China in 1997 also encouraged entrepreneurs to divert capital to North America. In Vancouver, the result was inflated land and building values in Chinatown and exorbitant rents by the early 1970s. By 1976, Chinatown had become so competitive an environment that tenants were being asked for rents as high as those of downtown shopping malls.[22]

Land use in Vancouver's Chinatown (and also in its North American and Australian counterparts) underwent rapid change during the 1970s. No longer simply a commercial district serving a nearby residential community and non-Chinese tourists, Chinatown was becoming a prosperous investment, service, and marketing centre. Chinese and non-Chinese visitors from throughout the Lower Mainland provided a large clientele for the district's growing number of specialized restaurants, while the variety of imported foodstuffs and specialty items that Chinatown stores began to offer in the 1970s also attracted many suburbanites to the busy district for weekend shopping.

Vancouver's Chinatown owed much to changes in government immigration practices for its physical revitalization in the 1970s. The Canadian state also instigated redefinition of this place in the 1970s, as the remainder of this chapter attempts to show. Since the freeway victory, Chinatown had become a valuable asset in the eyes of Vancouver society, and this image prompted special government programs to preserve and promote the district's character. Chinatown was to be revitalized around the premise of difference in a new guise—one that cannot be understood without first looking at the wider context of state ideology regarding Canada's "Others."

THE MOSAIC IDEOLOGY

In the late 1950s and early 1960s, the grievance of one of Canada's "charter groups" which had shared, but unequally, in the fruits of white European cultural domination surfaced in a dissent that seemed to challenge the nation's unity. Prime Minister Pearson appreciated that some means of acknowledging the heightened consciousness of French Canada would have to be found, and it was at his initiative that a Royal Commission on Bilingualism and Biculturalism was launched in 1963. As to the commission's major focus – on the balance of power between Anglo-origin and French-origin Canadians – it is sufficient for this study to note that the commission's final recommendations outlined sweeping measures for linguistic and cultural partnership and equality that helped intercept (if only for a while) the political reassertion of Quebec.

Announcement of the commission in 1963 raised a flurry of protest among some articulate men of Ukrainian and Jewish origin who were well connected to Ontario's Liberal élite.[23] Senator Paul Yuzyk of Alberta spearheaded their agitation for the inclusion of Canadians of all origins in the commission's inquiry. Pearson needed little persuading, however, believing as he said in 1963 that "the only way in which we can maintain unity in Canada is by recognizing and glorying in our diversity."[24] Three years later he said: "Our unity must recognize the duality of our origin and the multiracial character of our social and cultural development."[25] Thus the group's demand was happily met by a government searching for ways of incorporating a growing electorate of non-anglophone/non-francophone citizens within the framework of white Canada. Agreement to broaden the commission was consistent with the increasingly popular nationalist ideology whose controlling metaphor was the "mosaic," as distinct from the "melting pot" to the south.

The mosaic metaphor had its origins in the notion that "Canada" consisted of two societies, both committed to building a European civilization in Canada. This plural structure always set Canada apart in the minds of its nationals from the American neighbour. After the Second World War, politicians frequently invoked in debate in the House of Commons a vision of Canada as a "grand design consisting of many different elements, each of which retains its own character and quality while simultaneously contributing to the realization of the design as a whole."[26] And, by the 1960s, when biological essentialism was subsumed into the discourse of cultural relativism, the architects of the mosaic metaphor were making room in it for non-whites. Long-standing asymmetries of power and privilege between whites and non-whites were thereby obfuscated in a colourful image of harmony and equality.

The notion of each population as "separate but equal" was belied by the assumptions of the commission. Unlike the two dominant white societies, which were conceptualized for the purposes of the commission as competing structural wholes – politically, economically, and culturally – the residual "third force" became known as "the ethnic groups" whose "cultural distinctiveness should find a climate of respect and encouragement to survive ... within these two societies."[27] It was as if there were "such a thing as a Canadian society which exist[ed] more or less independent of ethnic groups and toward whose development ethnic groups [were] encouraged to make their various contributions."[28]

With the objective of studying such "contributions to the life of the country," the commission held a hearing in Vancouver's Chinatown in June 1965. Three Canadians of Chinese origin were asked to attend, one of whom was the editor of the *Chinatown News*. In the early 1960s editorials in that paper had appealed to its readers to abandon the "ghetto" and integrate as quickly as possible into the larger society (see chapter 6). By 1964, however, the first reflection on "the tragedy of the younger generation's loss of culture" appeared in the paper,[29] and a year later, the three spokesmen before the commission were requesting recognition of the Chinese language as well as the two official languages. By 1966, the editors were making a strong appeal for recognition of linguistic and cultural heritage: "No less a person than Prime Minister Pearson has reminded us," the *News* said, "that the greatness and the glory of this country comes from the fact that we are being moulded from 30, 40 or 50 racial fabrics."[30]

These shifts in editorial opinion at the *Chinatown News* appear to have followed changes in the racial discourse of the wider society. It can even be argued, as one scholar has done, that in the late 1960s and early 1970s claims of the kind the three spokesmen articulated to the commissioners were as much an outcome as a cause of the mosaic ideology.[31] In June 1968, on the eve of his election victory, Pierre Trudeau led the way in expressing the new version of the old racial frame of reference. "People of European descent have a great deal of value to learn from those of Oriental origins," he told a throng of people on Pender Street. "We don't want the people of Canada to assimilate. We don't want to eliminate cultural differences – we want everyone to get along in one united Canada."[32]

In October 1971, the Trudeau government announced a policy of "multiculturalism within a bilingual framework" that institutionalized the mosaic concept. For Kallen, the policy was the most recent "version of the myth of the mosaic," only with "more clarity and national legitimation."[33] Multiculturalism was indeed a self-conscious policy; in Trudeau's words, it was an attempt to "support and encourage the various cultures and ethnic groups that give structure and vitality to our society. They will be encouraged to share their cultural expression and values with other Canadians and so contribute to a richer life for us all."[34] Furthermore, by encouraging minorities to be minorities and Chinese to express themselves as Chinese, the policy "will help break down discriminatory attitudes and cultural jealousies," he claimed. Trudeau had an inventive rationale for this curious assertion: "National unity if it is to mean anything in the deeply personal sense must be founded on confidence in one's own individual identity; out of this can grow a respect for that of others and a willingness to share ideas, attitudes and assumptions. A vigorous policy of Multiculturalism will help create this initial confidence."

Yet the history of British- and French-origin people in Canada had demonstrated precisely the opposite tendency; confidence in the integrity of the in-group had been more a source of ethnocentrism than "sharing," as a 1977 survey, commissioned by the federal government, was itself to show.[35] Trudeau was insistent, however. "We are free to be ourselves," he proclaimed, "but this cannot be left to chance. It must be fostered and pursued actively."[36] Chinese, it seemed, would now be free to be that which had, for many decades, been seen as the embodiment of a foreign stock; further, they would be encouraged, through a program of grants and advertising in the "ethnic" press, to promote themselves as "Chinese."

By 1972, a policy of multiculturalism to foster the will to exist of Canada's ethnic groups was fully operational. Six programs were developed to implement the policy under the Citizenship Branch of the Department of the Secretary of State. They included a grants program for "multicultural encounters," a program of "ethnic histories," development of a "Canadian ethnic studies program," and one promoting among all Canadians "an awareness of the cultural heritage of all of Canada's ethnic groups." The National Museum of Man would receive funds for the purchase of artifacts representing Canada's ethnic diversity, while the National Film Board would expand its production of films about the contributions and problems of the various ethnic groups. Advertising in the "ethnic press" of the kind undertaken in the *Chinatown News* from 1973 would promote "ethnic awareness." One such advertisement of the multiculturalism directorate in February 1979 proclaimed "All Canadians Are Not Alike. Vive la Différence!"[37]

Although there were many acerbic exchanges in the house during the 1970s over operational details of the policy – in particular, its scant budget and its manipulation for election purposes – its objectives and spirit received unambiguous support in political circles. On the announcement of the policy in the house, the leader of the opposition, Robert Stanfield, expressed his expectation that "this declaration by the government of the principle of preserving and enhancing the many cultural traditions which exist within our country will be most welcome."[38] The following year, when Trudeau appointed a minister to implement the policy, the prime minister said: "There is no uniformity, no flatness to Canadians. Canada is richer five million times through the presence here of that many people whose cultural heritage is other than British or French. We dare not attempt to imagine how bland Canada would be ... were these people not part of our society."[39]

Other speeches, long on polemic, praised the new official definition of Canadian society. In February 1977, for example, the year in which a "Cultural Enrichment Program" was initiated, the member for Hamilton West remarked: "No Canadian race, no melting pot, no fashioning all into one mould but rather, we are pursuing the attainment of an identity which is based on intelligence, tolerance and decent neighbourly attitudes. We are in the midst of the great Canadian experiment."[40] The new multiculturalism minister, Norman Cafik, spoke of the experiment in October that year as

an example to other nations as to how best to live together in a bilingual, multicultural and multiracial society ... Our granting funds ... enables cultural groups to work and to interface together, to share their backgrounds and traditions with all the community in which they live. In that way that which is theirs will become that which is ours, and all of us will benefit as a result ... Our national unity problem shall disappear when Francophones, Anglophones, our native peoples and our ethno-cultural groups fully realize that we are all better off ... if we are living in a spirit of understanding, tolerance and good will ... The impact of the directorate of multiculturalism is broader than grants of money; it is as broad as the government itself.[41]

A strong advocate of the policy, Cafik informed the house of expanded programs during 1978 "to encourage cultural pluralism among the ethno-cultural groups" and "to ensure that multiculturalism and its objectives are taken into account by the government at all levels."[42]

THROUGH THE 1970S, THEN, a variety of means were used to demonstrate public commitment to the new "multicultural fact of Canada." Important among them were special programs and dispensations for what policy-makers (and some social scientists) have uncritically called "ethnic neighbourhoods" – uncritically, because the adjective "ethnic" is often used without consistency, to apply in Vancouver, for example, to Chinatown but not Shaughnessy, the long-time home of British-origin residents (until recently, when people of Chinese and other origin have moved in). It is to these government-inspired projects, which represent a different form of neighbourhood targeting of Vancouver's Chinatown to that which we have seen for earlier periods, that this chapter now turns.

CIVIC AND PROVINCIAL INITIATIVES

By the 1970s, the earlier interest shown by the city of Vancouver in revitalizing Chinatown was escalated into a full-scale effort to beautify and preserve the district. "The Chinese community is the only truly ethnic group within the study area," a city-commissioned *Restoration Report* observed of the Old Granville Townsite heritage area in 1969, adding that Chinatown was an area "the general urban population finds both agreeable and enriching."[43] Chinatown's new status seemed to incorporate the earlier tourist image into a deeper sense of the neighbourhood's historical integrity and idiosyncrasy – its "character and personality," as the *Province* put it in 1969. The crude "Oriental" motif courted in 1936 and in 1964 was being assimilated into a more nuanced sense of Chinatown's "ethnic" quality.

Like earlier projections, this new concept belonged to white Canada's culture of racial representation. Chinatown's defining characteristic in the minds of Europeans was still that which set it distinctly apart. But such an interpretation was not unilaterally imposed on an uncritical Chinese community. Eventually this latest European image of Chinatown secured the participation of some Chinese, as they came to recognize their own interests in implementation of idealized notions of their district. Some of their receptivity was no doubt economically based, geared to the tourist trade; for some people, government courting of Chinatown probably sparked pride in Chinese identity against the long history of negative stereotyping. Whatever the motivation, the acceptance of European forms of racialization has been testimony to their very hegemony and part of their contemporary reproduction.

In order to encourage "the imaginative re-use of existing, but declining neighbourhoods," the *Restoration Report* recommended preservation of the "historic areas" of Gastown, Chinatown, and Hastings Street. They formed "an indelible series of images for Vancouver," the report noted, and "can contribute to the quality and richness of city life."[44] For Chinatown, the task was to maintain, not betray through decoration, "the charm of an honestly evolved area." The report's recommendations included: an interim six-month hold on any demolition permit; appropriate zoning by-laws; protective and historic legislation; a formula of tax relief to encourage restoration; and a low-rental, long-term lease of the city-owned land at the Pender-Keefer diversion for a Chinese community centre. The report also advised the city to consider allowing Chinatown to expand southward.

The city's director of planning, Bill Graham, advised council in June 1970 of "possible techniques for protecting Vancouver's historic area."[45] The most promising strategy, he submitted, was for the city to rezone Chinatown (and Gastown) so as to preserve its land-use character. But while rezoning "could ensure the development and maintenance of desirable uses, [it] would not prevent unwanted demolitions and alterations from occurring." That control could be secured, he pointed out, only by declaring Chinatown and Gastown historic precincts through the provincial Historic Monuments Act. But the higher assessments that accompanied increased tourism and real estate values also encouraged uses incompatible with the historic designation, he warned. The challenge was to change Chinatown without "endangering the area's essential character."

In early December 1970, the initiative to preserve Vancouver's Chinatown through protective legislation received unanimous support in the provincial parliament. The provincial secretary and the minister for municipal affairs declared their willingness to designate the historic site and gave assurances of provincial financial assistance. Following cabinet's approval, an order-in-council on 2 February 1971 designated Chinatown a historic site under the Archaeological and Historic Sites Protection Act.[46] According to this new legislation, the province became vested with control over all major changes, demolitions, and renovations to buildings in the district. Also, a Historic Area Advisory Board was established to consider administrative matters bearing on the area's preservation. The extent of government control was not lost on the *Chinatown News*, which noted the following year that "our preservation and restoration regulations require the Planning Department approval for all facelifting work done to buildings in Chinatown before a single penny can be spent."[47]

The provincial order to preserve Chinatown, while a victory for planners, was not considered such a triumph among those expected to bear a considerable part of the cost. The merchants' reluctance was apparent in the ultimatum of the director of planning to Chinatown's owners and merchants on 1 November 1972: "In 1964 the City Planning Department presented a beautification proposal to the Chinese community but there was not sufficient interest for the proposal to proceed ... If Chinatown is to benefit from the City assistance contained in the Five Year Plan it is important that discussions with the community are started as soon as possible so that the necessary community support for whatever proposal is finally developed, can be assured. If the community support is not evident it is possible that the funds presently set aside for Chinatown may be used elsewhere where the interest is greater."[48]

Planning Director Graham promptly organized a meeting in Chinatown to present the city's proposals to the merchants, but they remained distinctly unimpressed. When Mike Egan of the Planning Department suggested that the merchants bear two-thirds of the cost of beautification, the audience burst into laughter, according to the *Chinatown News*. "We might be pardoned for our ill-timed sense of humour," wrote the *News* on 18 November 1972. "Fact is the cost is so unrealistic that there is little chance the community would buy either of these proposals."

The Chinatown Property Owners and Merchants Association (CTPOMA) – an organization of entrepreneurs interested in the tourist trade of Chinatown – was established early in 1973 to negotiate with the city over planning matters. It bluntly put the concerns of its constituency to local officials. For the merchants, parking space, not beautification, was the pressing issue. But the city did not share the merchants' priority, and, as part of a strategy to ensure that the city's concept was implemented, the deputy director of planning, Harry Pickstone, wrote to Egan on 27 March 1973: "I believe that the approach should be that we would consider recommending to Council the purchase of property for parking, but only tying it to some kind of undertaking by the Chinatown Property Owners and Merchants Association to carry out a beautification project."[49] CTPOMA's suggestion to use the $100,000 available for beautification to build continuous free-standing canopies along the three-block length of Pender Street met with an equally cool response.[50] In the words of the new Chinatown planner, Mike Kemble, the design had "little regard to the variety of actual building facade conditions that exist on Pender Street and which give the street its charm and visual interest."[51] The canopy idea was quashed, parking space was made conditional, and the area's façade was secured, unencumbered, for the city's visual enhancement program. For whom was there a Chinatown? the merchants might well have asked.

Kemble's three alternative schemes for district beautification revolved around street improvements to eliminate "the gap in activity" and "meld together" the two areas east and west of Main Street.[52]

In 1964, the city had been concerned only with the tourist precinct
to the west of Main. By the 1970s, however, Chinatown had become
an "ethnic neighbourhood," as the planners described it – "a people
and an atmosphere" – where "individual charm was the keynote" and
"some of the City's most attractive buildings are to be found."[53] Kemble's proposals recognized this unity by fusing east and west of Main
on Pender with various combinations of street improvement, tree
planting, sidewalk paving, parking facilities, and street furniture.

At a presentation in Chinatown in November 1973, the CTPOMA
registered some approval for the second scheme costing $400,000,
including a $100,000 contribution from the city toward land acquisi-
tion for a parking facility.[54] (The third, least expensive scheme, contained no provision for parking.) Kemble advised Harry Fan,
chairman of the merchants' association, that scheme 2's parking contribution was conditional on initiation of joint street improvement by
June 1974. "If a project for Chinatown has not been initiated by this
time," Kemble warned, "consideration will be given to re-allocating
beautification funds presently committed for the Chinatown area to
other projects and priorities."[55] But by June no such commitment was
forthcoming from the merchants; they remained "basically interested
in parking improvements and only secondly in street improvements."[56] The city did not shelve the project as it had threatened,
however, and Kemble and others set about scaling down their aspirations for the district's beautification.

UNDETERRED BY ITS FAILURE TO GET the merchants on side, the city
pursued its vision of Chinatown still more actively on other fronts.
In 1974, the city charter was amended to give the city power to
designate heritage buildings or areas, and in preparation for bestow-
ing this special status on Chinatown a set of proposed sign guidelines was devised. The preamble to the report on sign guidelines
stated:

These guidelines are intended to ensure the preservation and encouragement
of some of the environmental aspects which contribute to its [Chinatown's]
present attractiveness and distinctiveness ... Much of the character of Chinatown, in fact, is directly attributable to the multitude of complex, decorative
signs. Signing policies in this area should, therefore, be more tolerant of the
number, size and placement of all signs except in the case of those structures
deemed of the highest historic and aesthetic significance. All new signing in
this area should, however, incorporate Chinese motifs, symbols and forms

rather than the stereotyped sign types which dominate other commercial areas ... The use of neon tubing for illumination purposes should be emphasized ... Signs must reflect the traditional motifs and ethnic character of Chinatown.[57]

In April 1974, an environmental psychology professor at the University of British Columbia praised the sign guidelines and "the incentives for neon [which] suggest a cute return to the good old Thirties when Chinatown prospered sufficiently to afford neon and argon."[58] The *Chinatown News* did not share the professor's rather dubiously based enthusiasm for the new guidelines. "Does it mean that owners of structures with 'highest historic and aesthetic significance' will not be able to select the signs of their own choice?" the editors asked. "And who is to rule which building has the highest significance? While sign guidelines do not rate top priority for Chinatown, they should not be overlooked by the CTPOMA," the *News* warned.[59]

The sign guidelines were a significant element in the city's plan to make the district more legible as a "Chinese" enclave. Equally important was the city's initiative to devise its own legislation to "make it easier to maintain the character of the area," as Harry Pickstone told the Technical Planning Board on 21 June 1974. "The Zoning Bylaw," he said, "is intended to give the City authority to control building changes and building additions in the context of the Historic Area."[60] The new zoning schedule was "designed to recognize the area's unique ethnic quality and to ensure the protection, restoration and maintenance of Chinatown's historical, architectural and cultural character," to quote from the preamble to the zoning schedule. It also recognized new physical perimeters of Chinatown (see Map 10), which expanded on the former provincial boundaries, including as they did the southeast section of Strathcona to Union Street. In the words of Nancy Oliver of the Heritage Advisory Board: "The whole designation was judged on a general feeling of 'character' which pervaded the area."[61]

If the basis for Chinatown's designation seemed "general" to Oliver, it was sufficiently specific for Vancouver's aldermen, who at a special public meeting of council on 9 July 1974 unanimously agreed to amend the Zoning and Development Bylaw to establish the new district known as HA-1 Chinatown Historic Area District.[62] A Chinatown Historic Area Planning Committee was also established the following year to advise the city's Planning Department in its efforts to "preserve and protect the heritage and character of the Chinatown area."[63]

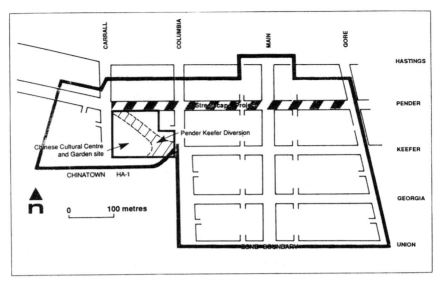

Map 10
HA-1 Historic Area Zone and Chinatown Streetscape Project
Source: Based on City of Vancouver Planning Department, *Vancouver' Heritage:
Twenty-two Buildings and Two Historic Areas,* 1974, p. 44

In these ways, Chinatown was once again being identified for special status by white Vancouver society. The local government continued its long tradition of interpreting the area in terms of an essential "Chineseness" and, moreover, of inscribing its beliefs in the physical landscape. Just as council had formally designated Chinatown an entity for the medical health officer's rounds in the 1890s, so in the 1970s the municipality perceived and officially targeted the area for its distinctiveness. Through rezoning, the city even drew the physical contours of the district and further objectified the remarkably enduring idea of the "East" in the "West" – a construction that consistently involved the use of place and geographical boundaries to confirm cultural and political ones.

Given the deeper continuity of the European racial frame of reference, it is perhaps not surprising to find remnants of prior characterizations of Chinatown carried forward into ensuing ones. According to one Main Street merchant and CTPOMA member, council's way of seeing "Chinatown" in the 1970s was not far removed from the side-show image of earlier days. In September 1974, the month in which the new zoning by-law was enacted, the merchant wrote to the Planning Department:

The City Hall powers that be are trying to force new or rebuilding type construction to conform to copies of tourist photos of temples in Asia. In other words construction cannot proceed unless it would be a museumized version with artificial red posts and verticle [sic] window stripes. Most of the commercial buildings in downtown Hong Kong, Kowloon, Teipeh and Singapore are not built in the old temple style, but rather in their own forms and fronts that lend themselves to the ready view of the products or merchandise that is offered to the visitors and passers by ... We were supplied with a new sign guidelines brochure which contained two photos of old Chinatown scenes showing garbage cans and horse drawn wagons. Are we to presume that they are trying to force us in Chinatown to revert to grubby buildings and horse wagons?[64]

Clearly the vision of Chinatown being promoted in the 1970s was not this merchant's own. Local entrepreneurs were, however, able to frame interests of their own in the European discourse about difference, and – as earlier – they did not always or necessarily contest government initiatives. In this instance, CTPOMA's chair, Thomas Mah, described the merchants' willingness to accommodate the city's rezoning intentions: "The defined boundary of Chinatown will give us some elbow space for expansion of business activities."[65]

THE CHINATOWN HISTORIC Area Planning Committee (CHAPC), formed in July 1975, was called on to rally, where other organizations had failed, local support for the much-delayed beautification project. The committee, in consultation with the director of planning, was vested with considerable discretionary power over matters of landscape form in the new district. For example, the new zoning schedule's rules governing issue of development permits specified height limitations on buildings, but alterations to exteriors required the approval of the director and the committee. Where painting was to be done, the schedule laid down that "colours traditional of the Chinatown area should be considered." In a dispute over a permit, applicants could appeal to council, whose decision was final.

Given the committee's powers, its composition was important and was duly contested. The city initially insisted on a non-Chinese majority, but by July of the following year, when CHAPC was formally approved by council, it comprised eight Chinatown figures and one each from the Architectural Institute, the Community Arts Council, and the University of British Columbia.[66]

Unlike Gastown (the other historic area), where only a small number of property owners had to be convinced of the wisdom of change, approximately seventy-five owners on Pender Street had to be mobilized to support revitalization.[67] This was no small task for CHAPC, given that the community had been on the receiving end of so many externally inspired plans. In late November 1976, when the new improvement guidelines of the Planning Department's "Chinatown Work Program" were unveiled at a meeting of CHAPC, the editor of the *Chinatown News*, an ardent supporter of tourist promotion, lamented: "City planners Don Hickley and Mike Kemble possess such boundless patience even Job would envy. For the umpteenth time they have come up with an imaginative set of plans designed to upgrade the physical appearance of Chinatown. Unfortunately, whenever financial commitment is involved, prospects of having Chinatown property owners accepting the proposals are exceedingly dim."[68]

Kemble's project provided options "to add the desired atmosphere to the ethnic character of the area." However, the reaction of the thirty-six people who turned out for the meeting (of whom only five were property owners) was "far from enthusiastic," according to the *News*. A more modest set of proposals was devised early in the new year, in consultation with CHAPC, and the worried CHAPC chair, Harry Con, warned Chinatown's businesses: "The options contain many realistic proposals. If merchants and property owners still manifest indifference and disinterest, I doubt whether City planners would come up with any more plans to improve this area for a long, long time."[69] The revised project again offered three options: basic improvements, at a cost of $300,000 (merchants would pay one-third); limited improvements, for $400,000 (merchants would pay 30 per cent); and moderate improvements (again, one-third).[70] In turn, CHAPC did its part by undertaking a conscientious campaign among the Pender Street merchants.

CHAPC's efforts, as with those of the relentless Kemble and others of the Planning Department, were finally rewarded in the spring of 1977, when the merchants saw their way to offering $300,000 toward the streetscape project, largely in the interests of an upgraded business district and tourism.[71] City planners accepted quickly and formulated "moderate improvements" for the unit, 100-, and 200- blocks of Pender Street, with a special sidewalk and cross-walk treatment, new stone curbing, a mid-block crossing in the 100- block, the planting of some trees native to China, sidewalk furniture, brass bilingual street name signs from Hong Kong, and special "lantern-like" street lighting at street corners. Council also acted quickly and approved the plan in principle in October 1977.[72] The estimated cost of the streetscape project was $700,000, of which the city would contribute $200,000 and the owners one-third in taxes over fifteen years.

Provincial support for the streetscape project was not the routine matter that city planners hoped it would be, despite the earlier guarantees of cabinet. The political climate in the provincial capital had changed during the years of delay. In March 1978, the Ministry of Recreation and Conservation declined an application from the city for provincial participation under provisions of the Heritage Conservation Act, on the grounds that the proposal involved "civic beautification and not heritage conservation."[73] However, on the advice of the director of planning, the city resubmitted its application for at least 20 per cent of the cost in July of that year. "This is particularly appropriate," he said, "as this improvement project affects perhaps the most important Provincially designated heritage area in the City."[74] CHAPC also introduced its own strategy by insisting that Chinatown be "de-designated" and developed as owners alone would have it, if the province refused to commit money to its historic site.[75]

By late 1978, with a provincial election pending, the Social Credit government began to see its own opportunity in the project. It was especially attracted by Chinatown's tourist potential, and, like generations of predecessors, provincial politicians could see the legitimacy to be had from manipulations of Chinese "difference." Also it was eager to support the district in a way that distanced it from the Chinatown project (to be discussed in the next section) which had been inspired by the previous New Democratic Party (NDP) government. The result was a substantial offer of $200,000 toward the $700,000 streetscape project. The deputy premier, Grace McCarthy – a friend of some of Chinatown's entrepreneurs – presented the offer to Mayor Volrich and the CHAPC chair, Gibb Yipp, at a Chinatown reception on 30 November 1978.[76]

The Chinatown landscape of the 1970s was quite self-consciously styled. Planning Department professionals were especially heavily involved, in consultation with both CHAPC and the utility-oriented Engineering Department. Often, the latter overruled the Planning Department's proposals for decorative details on simple cost criteria. At other times, the city engineer would offer a compromise, as when he agreed to paint the street lighting poles tile red in keeping with "the ethnic character of the area and the traditional Chinese use of red" – but not the traffic signs and street furniture as well.[77] Such bureaucratic battles continued throughout the project. The Planning Department enjoyed one triumph over the engineers in February 1979, when council agreed to retain the old incandescent lamps – as, in the words of the director of planning, "a concession to Chinatown's unique quality."[78]

A YEAR LATER, IN FEBRUARY 1980, the Chinatown Streetscape Project was opened by Grace McCarthy and Mayor Volrich amid the festivities of the Chinese New Year.[79] It was a symbolic occasion that signalled the magnitude of change in the reception of Chinese settlers in Canada. To be sure, the residents and entrepreneurs of Chinatown were much better placed than their predecessors earlier in the century. But while attitudinal change was significant, both for the "Chinese" and "whites," the novelty of the event should not be misconstrued. Chinatown had tight links with the past, and an enduring ideology of difference was perpetuating old idioms of classification and separation. Beautification required and rewarded Chinese participation, but the state's presence in the precinct in the 1970s was not inspired to meet those interests. Rather, Chinatown had become a symbol for the new "multicultural Canada." For European Canada and its urban planners (and for their counterparts in Australia[80]), Chinatown's essential "Chineseness" had become its very asset, and that premise continued to shape policies that remade both the vision and the reality of an enclave and a people apart through the 1970s.

THE CHINESE CULTURAL CENTRE AND GARDEN

One of the main responsibilities of Canada's Multiculturalism Directorate after 1972 was to "encourage and assist ... the full realization of the multicultural nature of Canadian society through programs which promote the preservation and sharing of cultural heritages."[81] Federal involvement in Vancouver's Chinatown during the 1970s demonstrated that the responsibility was not held lightly. Although the directorate's participation in the district was limited, substantial capital works projects undertaken there were clearly predicated on Ottawa's new definition of Canadian society. Other levels of government also took up the challenge to facilitate the expression of "difference" in Canada. In the case of Vancouver's Chinese Cultural Centre (CCC) and Garden complex, all three levels of government worked together.

As early as 1968, Mayor Tom Campbell urged the Chinese community to take the initiative in enlisting city support for a community centre in Chinatown.[82] In an election speech the following August, NDP member Emery Barnes also promised provincial support for a Chinese cultural centre of the kind recommended by the *Restoration*

Report in the same year.[83] Equally encouraging was the new NDP premier, Dave Barrett, at a Wong Association reception in Chinatown in October 1972. At the same reception, other dignitaries to endorse the idea included Attorney-General Alex Macdonald and federal Urban Affairs Minister (and SPOTA ally) Ron Basford. The regional liaison officer of the Department of Secretary of State went further in a letter read to the reception: "Such assurance [from three levels of government] does not come often and I urge your association and other Chinese organizations to give some serious thought to such an offer ... I am writing to see if the Wong Benevolent Association would act as chairman of the ad hoc committee on a Chinese Cultural Centre if such a meeting were to be called in the near future."[84]

So enthusiastic were the officials, said architect Joe Wai, that "in the euphoria of the Cantonese banquet, the three levels of government publicly pledged to pay what someone later calculated to be 160 per cent of the projected cost of the centre."[85]

Soon afterward, 150 people representing forty-three organizations in Chinatown, and Brian Marshall of the Citizenship Department of Secretary of State, duly attended an exploratory meeting in the Wong Benevolent Association's quarters at 123-A Pender Street. The meeting resolved to form a Chinese Cultural Centre Building Committee and elected a twenty-one-member board to negotiate with government officials. It was noted that the project would require a cohesive community effort – a significant challenge, as the *Chinatown News* remarked: "The gulf has remained as wide as ever. What is needed is something to bring us together – a catalyst for community action. That something may be the Chinese Cultural Centre. It is fairly obvious that if we want something done for our community, we'd do well to compose our differences. The time has come for a massive coalition to get the centre built. We have the functional resources in the community. And the three levels of government have already pledged their support. But we need to coalesce and move toward a unified goal ... Chinatown merchants and property owners should be eager to participate too ... It is in their interest and profitability to bring the Centre plan to fruition."[86]

Despite government endorsement, only persistent lobbying by a core of interested "Chinese" got the project implemented. The process boosted the political power of certain figures within Chinatown, who saw in the proposals some economic and status benefit for the district and for Vancouver's Chinese-origin people. Details of the project's history highlight the practical complexities of co-ordination among three levels of government and expose the enduring beliefs about "Chinese difference" that were informing government practice and community response in Chinatown during the 1970s.

The attention of the CCC's building committee and of some interested members of the Historic Area Advisory Board focused first on locating a site for the proposed project. At a lunch in Chinatown in early June 1973, chair George Wong informed Mayor Art Phillips and some councillors that the site at the corner of Pender and Carrall streets was the most appropriate (see Map 10, above). As long as the Engineering Department's controversial scheme "G" for the Quebec-Columbia connector was destined to link up with the site, however, the city was not prepared to commit itself.[87] Not surprising, therefore, the site committee was among the most outspoken of six delegations to protest the Quebec-Columbia connector at a public meeting at City Hall on 12 June 1973. "The six-lane connector," they claimed, "effectively reduces the chosen site for the cultural centre complex to a tiny triangular plot."[88] Other organizations such as SPOTA expressed astonishment that the professedly reform-oriented council appeared to have learned so little.[89] Even the city's own director of planning warned that the connector could seriously limit expansion of Chinatown toward the west and southwest. In a decision that signalled the last gasp of the freeway era, council rescinded the connector scheme and set up a planning process to deal with "the north-east side of False Creek and the link with the Chinese community."[90]

Council had effectively freed the site at Pender and Carrall; the challenge remained to link the actual project to that free site. To this end, discussions began between planners, engineers, B.C. Hydro (as owner of land to the south of Keefer Street), the site committee, and many other interested parties. They set out to find ways to close or reroute the Pender-Keefer traffic diversion, remove the CPR tracks and railyard to the south of Keefer, and consolidate the triangular site at Carrall and Pender into one developable entity (see Map 10). It was no small engineering task, and deliberations and negotiations in both Vancouver and Victoria dragged on from 1973 through 1978.[91] In an important breakthrough in 1975, council approved a downtown plan that incorporated a new bypass road system south of Chinatown. Such a route would put greater pedestrian emphasis on Chinatown and permit closing of the Pender-Keefer diversion, which in turn would allow consolidation into one site of the adjacent city-owned land (with an estimated market value in 1975 of more than $3 million).[92]

Meanwhile the CCC's building committee, with the support of several other groups interested in the scheme, set out to persuade council to grant the land at Pender and Carrall to the project. An important ally was the director of planning, who saw in the proposal the chance to boost his department's Chinatown beautification project. In 1974, and again in the same terms in 1976, he reported to council: "There is a need for new development on the western edge of Chinatown to act as a 'pull' for increasing pedestrian retail shopping activity in the blocks west of Main Street. The Cultural Centre location would be very beneficial to the existing Chinatown commercial area by strengthening the weak areas that presently exist. Pender Street, from Carrall to Gore, must be preserved and strengthened as an intense and lively pedestrian shopping area, for both the local Chinese community, visitors and tourists."[93]

The Community Arts Council endorsed these arguments in July 1976, saying that the proposed centre would "serve as a catalyst for an exciting rebirth of Chinatown as one of our city's major attractions."[94] The appeal to a more "liveable city" was also used by CHAPC: "The CCC project and related garden/park development will provide an impetus and the first step towards changing the entire area back to an exciting focus for Chinatown and Vancouver."[95]

The various lobbies for the CCC had their long-awaited victory on 26 July 1976. On that day council unanimously agreed to negotiate a land-lease arrangement with the 3,000-member CCC organization for the 3.5-acre site at Carrall and Pender.[96] Soon afterward, Mayor Volrich made political capital out of the decision and, ultimately, of beliefs about the Chinese, in an election speech in Chinatown. He said: "We want to encourage you to preserve and continue the great traditions and customs of the Chinese people."[97]

ALL WAS NOT YET SECURE FOR THE project, however. The manipulation of "Chineseness" by the state was precipitating an internal struggle among competing élites for the right to speak as the "real" Chinese on behalf of Chinatown.[98] The election of a Social Credit provincial government in 1975 proved a catalyst in this process. Encouraged by the legitimacy the new government gave to conservative interests in Chinatown, a Chinese-Canadian Activity Centre Society was established in February 1977 to recapture power from the CCC organization.[99]

The new society, some members of which had links to the cabinet, was set up to build its own cultural centre in Chinatown. Its main support came from the CBA, which had gradually been losing its power base as younger, Canadian-born citizens had taken on neighbourhood causes and the provision of welfare services to immigrants. The CCC organization, progressive and oriented to local-born rather than Taiwanese concerns, gave form to these developments and thus filled a political void in Chinatown. By the late 1970s, it commanded considerable support from Chinese-origin people throughout Vancouver – sufficient to mobilize a movement against the seemingly archaic, élitist, and insular CBA.

The cultural centre counter-proposal exacerbated this rift and provoked CCC activists to set up a Committee to Democratize the Chinese Benevolent Association.[100] The progressives were further inflamed in August 1977, when the provincial government hosted a luncheon in Chinatown for delegates to the CBA's national convention (a gathering to which the federal Multiculturalism Directorate had also granted $5,000). A protest demonstration outside condemned the CBA as undemocratic and unrepresentative and urged senior levels of government to withdraw their support.

The Committee to Democratize the CBA next adopted more dramatic tactics. Early in 1978, it took the association to the BC Supreme Court, arguing that the CBA had repudiated its own constitution by holding closed elections for eight executive positions. In the spring of that year, the court ordered open elections.[101] The litigation had the desired effect of discrediting the Chinese-Canadian Activity Centre Society. In April 1979, when the conservative lobby applied for a lease of the city land then under two-year lease to the CCC organization, Mayor Volrich "indicated that he was satisfied with the Cultural Centre group, [which] having in excess of 6,000 members, was fairly representative of the community ... and had sufficient funds, amounting to $900,000 to proceed with Phase 1."[102] Soon afterward, in the spring of 1979, the city formally signed over the site to the CCC organization.

IN MAY 1977 OTTAWA COMMITTED $1.5 million of Urban Demonstration capital to a fund for development of an East End False Creek garden and park. The garden was expected to conform to the Chinatown landscape and would, in the words of the agreement made on 12 September 1978 between the Ministry of State for Urban Affairs and the city of Vancouver, "aid in the re-establishment of a viable Chinatown and arrest the eastward drift and dispersal of this unique community." In addition, it would "provide a public amenity ... which, besides providing a recreational area for local residents, is seen to become a major tourist attraction."[103]

The image of Chinatown as an "ethnic neighbourhood" whose distinctiveness was to be courted and protected had certainly come to enjoy the support of the most senior level of Canadian government. It was also an image that CHAPC and certain members of the CCC organization were keen, and knew how, to deliver. Dr Marwyn

Samuels, a geographer and CHAPC member, helped to mount the proposal for "an authentic Chinese garden, conforming to traditional concepts and incorporating traditional elements of Chinese garden design."[104] In Ottawa, the response was favourable, while Mayor Volrich saw fit to praise the proposal in words reminiscent of Mayor McGeer in 1936: "We wish our Vancouver 'Chung Shan' Garden to be of world-class calibre and a great asset to our city and to the Chinese community," he said in a letter to the consul general for the People's Republic in May 1980.[105]

The classical garden idea seems to have appealed to all the romantic notions of the "Flowery Kingdom" that had captivated council during the Jubilee celebrations and, long before then, the earliest Western visitors to China. One local magazine boasted: "The garden will be a mecca for Far Eastern scholars and a tourist showpiece unique in the Western hemisphere."[106] The $6-million garden was to be called the Dr Sun-Yat Sen Gardens, in honour of the founder of the republic of China, whose status in his nation's history was acknowledged by a rare consensus in Chinatown. It was also to be strictly "traditional," using "authentic" materials and elements and technical advice from China itself, much like the project undertaken by the Metropolitan Museum of Art in New York City (and, more recently, by the Darling Harbour Authority in Sydney). No pagodas, no chinoiserie, no willow patterns, no dragons – this was to be the classical East, recreated anew in (and for) the West. *East in the West.*

AN INDEPENDENT JURY SELECTED the winning architectural submission for the CCC itself, said to be inspired by Beijing's Imperial Palace. But the concept then had to run the gauntlet of both client and bureaucracy. The client, the CCC organization, was concerned less with aesthetics and character than with function, space, and cost. The ultimate product therefore turned out to be something of a compromise – as Chinatown planner Mike Kemble conceded – among the cost criteria of the clients, the intentions of the architects, and the demands of the city and CHAPC.[107]

The input of the city's planners and CHAPC is evidence, as is the garden, of the version of Chinatown that the levels of government were trying to achieve in Vancouver through manipulation of landscape imagery. Kemble was anxious that the design of the exterior of the centre be integrated with the larger Chinatown streetscape. For this reason he was concerned at the lack of "Chinese" architectural features in the application. He was troubled in particular by the lack of a recessed entrance balcony to the upper wall facing Pender Street;

the type of roofing surface, which should be "a glazed or natural finish type of tile commonly used in China"; the balcony handrail design facing Pender, for which he recommended "the use of traditional, decorative design features to relate [them] to the older character of the adjacent area"; and the "apparent lack of bright accent colours on the exterior of the building," which would "give the building a more distinctive 'Chinese' character, and ... relate it more sympathetically to adjacent historic buildings on Pender Street." Kemble also suggested that stepped gable walls be incorporated into the entry area, because of "their possible association with the form of traditional ancestral halls common to South China," and that a ccc logo, backlit with neon tubing, might be more in keeping with the sign guidelines for the Chinatown Historic Area.[108] All these recommendations for a stronger "Chinese" motif were incorporated into the final design for stage 1 of the ccc.[109]

When Social Credit had come to power in 1975, the ccc project had been downgraded by cabinet. But just as the Chinatown beautification project suddenly captured the attention of the government on the verge of the 1979 election, so the ccc appeared more worthwhile by that time. "My government has a strong commitment to promote Multiculturalism in British Columbia," said Premier William Bennett at a Chinatown function in May 1979. While presenting a cheque for $400,000 toward construction of stage 1 of the ccc, he went on: "I want to underline the policy of our government to help fund these centres as one of the best opportunities to preserve the cultures that will strengthen our country."[110]

On 14 September 1980, representatives of all three levels of government and numerous other dignitaries were on hand at the opening of the $900,000 first stage of the ccc. Through the nexus of this enclave called "Chinatown" – the very embodiment, it was believed, of "Chineseness" – the mosaic ideology was being discovered and further objectified. "The project reflects the great culture of the Chinese people," Mayor Volrich declared amid what the *Chinatown News* called "a colourful extravaganza of lanterns, lions, unicorn dances, songs and firecrackers."[111] But if the project reflected that "great culture," it also surely distinguished Chinatown's beholders, who, through all the rhetoric, ambience, and government largesse, were ceaselessly inventing the "Chineseness" of Chinatown.

BONHAM'S BARBECUED MEATS

Earlier chapters of this book have traced how the presence of people from China in Vancouver was interpreted in the perceptions and practices of the Canadian government. In the 1970s, the government's sanction of popular beliefs about a Chinese culture sui generis was apparent no less in instances where it courted particular symbols of "difference" for public expression than in those where it continued its established tradition of suppression. The "cultural contribution" of Vancouver's Chinese has assuredly been a regulated one.

It was the celebrated barbecued meats issue that most clearly demonstrated that the Canadian government, even in the tolerant 1970s, was not above flexing its regulatory muscle when expressions of the "peculiar" Chinese were considered less as contributions than as threats to white Canadians. It also demonstrated the speed with which dormant ideas of Chinatown as a public nuisance could be resurrected at the whim of those more powerful. On hand to contest the recycling of vice associations, however, was a Chinatown lobby which again tested the limits of European hegemony in Vancouver.

In October 1972, Prime Minister Trudeau visited Chinatown to a welcome of firecrackers that sent him running for quick cover. Within weeks, the use of firecrackers was restricted through an amendment to the Explosives Act.[112] Also in October, city health authorities – in the spirit of selective regulation that had so coloured their work over the decades – sponsored new health regulations aimed specifically at meat merchants in Chinatown. The new rules required barbecued meats, which hung in the windows of the district's stores and restaurants, to be stored at temperatures below 4.4 degrees or above 60 degrees celsius. Professing concern for the presence of salmonella, the city suddenly insisted that Chinatown's meats be stored in specially built glass ovens. The merchants, maintaining that this would destroy the flavour and texture demanded by customers, closed off their barbecued meats section and circulated a petition.[113]

Faced with 2,000 signatories to the petition, the medical health officer, Dr Gerald Bonham, adamantly declared that the city would not back away from the new regulation. "Our problem has not been that we've been picking on Chinatown merchants," he said, "rather it has been tolerating them for so long and allowing too much for language problems and customs."[114] The merchants, with the assistance of a member of the provincial legislature, Emery Barnes, demonstrated to the city's Health Department the high turnover of the product in dispute, and for the time being the issue was shelved.

Dedicated officer Bonham certainly did not forget the issue, however. In July 1973, he stated to the press that the city would close down fourteen merchants who were not complying with the regulations, rather than spend money watching over them.[115] The merchants' lawyer, Douglas Jung, pointed out that Chinese had been happily cooking and selling barbecued products for over 2,000 years. Moreover, his clients had installed equipment and retained the services of a doctor from Biomedical Laboratories Ltd, "even though it has not yet been proven that any one of the Chinatown merchants has been guilty of causing food poisoning resulting from improper cooking or handling." Food poisoning could result from improper storage by the consumer, Jung argued.[116] Charges against the merchants were dropped, and although the Health Department introduced further food-handling regulations in August 1973, nothing more was heard of the controversy for two years.

Then the medical health officer struck again. In September 1975, five Chinatown stores selling barbecued meats were served with closure notices by Bonham's inspectors for alleged violations of regulations.[117] Six other stores promptly shut down in protest, and the merchants raised a petition with no less than 8,000 signatures. On this occasion, however, Bonham was joined, if a little belatedly, by federal health inspectors bearing thermometers and threats of fines. They sporadically descended on Chinatown's ducks in the spring of 1977, to check the merchants' conformity to regulations of the newly amended Food and Drug Act.[118]

With a $6–million-a-year industry at stake, the newly founded Committee to Save Chinese Barbecued Products resorted to co-opting the one element of society that could be relied on to take an anti-bureaucratic stance. On 22 February 1978, media representatives were treated to a demonstration of Chinese barbecuing techniques. Afterward, reporters were invited to taste the products, and there were no refusals or complaints.[119] A microbiologist, Sid Andersen, argued at a news conference that there could not be any pathogenic bacteria in the meats, since none could possibly survive the firing process used to barbecue them. With the health by-laws defied by the media without incident or illness, it was clear that the merchants had won a public-relations victory. No action was taken against merchants found in violation of the regulations, and Dr A. Morrison, head of the Health Protection Branch in Ottawa, also publicly acknowledged that "the department has no documented cases of food poisoning due to barbecued meat."[120]

By this time, the Committee to Save Chinese Barbecued Products had mobilized sufficient support across Canada to adopt more dramatic strategies against federal and civic scrutiny. In April 1978, the committee organized a fifty-five-member delegation, including a chef, which went to Parliament Hill in Ottawa. To the beat of a lion dance, a parade of "succulent delicacies" was circulated under the noses of scores of legislators at the parliamentary restaurant. Members were invited to try for themselves the products that Bonham was so keen to administer out of existence. Trudeau, earlier so shy of the trappings of Chinese culture, declared his approval of the taste, and most members "attacked the roasts with relish" and returned for second and third helpings.[121] Two months later, the federal government shifted the emphasis of its regulations from temperature to microbiological standards – which the merchants were confident they could meet. Bonham still persisted, however, with his inspections of Chinatown. "If the Federal Government change their regulations they are just setting up rules for their branch to follow – it doesn't affect my responsibilities," he said.[122] It was a defiant but final stand. The microbiologist Andersen denounced Bonham's harassment, and within months the medical health officer had left Vancouver for a new posting, and presumably more sanitized conditions, in Victoria.

THE ENDURING CONCEPT OF RACE IN CANADA

A number of social scientists have documented the effort expended at all levels of the state to remove "race" as a determinant of life chances after the passage of the Canadian Bill of Rights in 1960.[123] Less widely acknowledged has been the persistence of the racial frame of reference in white Canadian thought and practice into the 1970s. Yet the mosaic ideology, well intentioned as it was, represented at root a reaffirmation of the we/they distinctions that had informed Canadian culture throughout the twentieth century. "Multiculturalism" was a form of incorporation of minority groups that promised them tolerance, while reproducing their targeting in both a semiotic and a political sense. It retained the premise of "difference" while altering its connotations. The point would not be so significant but for the following factor: as long as the classification "Chinese" was given new forms of currency within the European community, cultural relativism could give way to classical forms of wielding outsider status.[124] The following examples demonstrate, at the community and national political levels, just how easily this could happen.

IN AUGUST 1974, THE LITTLE MOUNTAIN Ratepayers' Society took to task a Montreal Trust real estate agent who had been advertising neighbourhood homes for sale in "Oriental" papers. In the society's opinion, his action was inviting the formation of ghettoes, where "it will soon be impossible to sell homes to Canadians."[125] A letter from the society's president to the *Sun* newspaper called openly for residential quotas based on race, backed by municipal and provincial legislation. The *Chinatown News* hit back swiftly, criticizing the re-emergence of such attitudes. The ratepayers' letter, said the *News*, "trots out all the ugly cliches in vogue at the time of the Oriental Exclusion Act." The charge that Chinese tended to form ghettoes was growing familiar by the early 1970s, the *News* said, noting the irony in Chinatown itself, where "only commercial interests, aided and abetted by well meaning planners, have encouraged the retention of the ghetto."

IN THE MID-1970S, DURING A DOWNTURN in the Canadian economy, a more serious revival of the baggage attached to the category "Chinese" appeared in debates of the House of Commons. A number of members decided to voice their concern for the "changing composition" of Canada's population and the "absorptive capacity" of the country, in the face of growing flows of immigration from Asia. In 1975, the Canadian government published a green paper for immigration and population, which declared: "It would be astonishing if there was no concern about the capacity of our society to adjust to a pace of population change that entails after all as regards international immigration, novel and distinctive features."[126] Stripped of semantics, the words revealed the flip side of the "novelty" and "distinctiveness" we have seen officials so keen to court at the local level.

Some members were more blunt, like the member for Capilano, Ron Huntington, in December 1974: "These people [from China and the Indian subcontinent] are coming in so rapidly that they are not fitting into the fabric of Canadian society ... They are locating in ghettoes, dozens to a house. Does this give them respect for the Canadian system and our government? ... If there is one thing we need in our immigration policy it is planned assimilation of other races, people who are foreign to our ideologies and way of life."[127] Huntington was quickly called to order – though for being "prejudiced," a "racist," not for trading in fictions. He apologized, and other members learned to be more discreet.

The green paper outlined proposed restrictions on immigration to Canada for people of lower socioeconomic status and certain categories of sponsored dependants and nominated relatives. One of many protest groups across Canada, the Immigration Policy Action Committee (IMPAC, representing forty-one organizations in Vancouver's Chinatown) saw the proposed bill as a disguised attempt to restrict "third world" immigrants in favour of long-established, traditional sets of immigrants.[128]

Some public officials, including Mayor Phillips of Vancouver, disputed the claim. After an address at the University of Winnipeg on

5 March 1975, Phillips was charged by IMPAC with providing "bigots with a cloak of responsibility." He replied in a letter to the *Chinatown News* that showed the confusion wrought in official thinking by the assimilation of cultural to biological essentialism: "What I suggest is that we cut down on the pace of immigration and that we realize that a community can only assimilate immigrants from a drastically different culture at a particular rate ... I want Vancouver to be a liveable, exciting and diverse community. I have pushed for activities such as Folkfest and the Multicultural Centre because I believe our ethnic communities have a great deal to offer to the city. It is in all our interest to keep Vancouver a good place to live. To achieve that goal, we have to keep our growth under control."[129] As long as the likes of Phillips did not have to confront the deeper connection between his two seemingly opposed positions – immigration restriction and ethnic promotion – such politically veiled arguments for discrimination would continue to be tolerated.

The race idea was also plainly manifest during debate in the House of Commons over the proposed new Immigration Bill. "Today there is increasing concern that we are losing, to some extent, the way of life that made our country great," said William Scott of Victoria-Haliburton (Ontario) on 11 March 1977. "Perhaps one of the reasons for this change in outlook has been the influence of immigrants whose lifestyle is often foreign to that which has been traditionally Canadian." Similarly, Mr S. Schumacher of Palliser (Alberta) asked: "Do Honourable Members really think we can accept the introduction of large numbers of culturally different people without changing our way of life?" For Mr F. Philbrook of Halton (Ontario), the new bill was an effective balance between "helping the world with its problems and trying to maintain our way of life," while G. Ritchie of Dauphin (Manitoba) wondered "whether Canadians would support an immigration policy which could make a fundamental change in the nature of the Canadian population." No support at all was expressed in the house for Andrew Brewin's motion in July 1977 that the objectives of multiculturalism be incorporated into the spirit of the Immigration Bill – not even from the minister of state for multiculturalism, Joseph Guay. One BC member captured the sentiments of many politicians in March 1977 when he said: "Multiculturalism is all right in its place."[130]

IN THE SUMMER OF 1979, the National Film Board (NFB) of Canada launched a documentary that revealed how derogatory stereotypes about "the Chinese" still structured white Canadian perception and praxis. As part of the federal government's promotion of multiculturalism, the NFB produced numerous films about "the contribution of the ethno-cultural groups" to Canadian history and society. The Chinatown film, *Bamboo, Lions and Dragons*, took four years to produce and cost the government of Canada $100,000 for what the *Chinatown News* described as a "take-off" of Chinatown. According to the *News*, the film conveyed an image of early immigrants as "strange and sinister" and suggested that "it was natural for whites to fear and loathe the settlers ... because there were so many of them." The film also implied that "exposure to white society has finally transformed Chinese into not-so-perfect but perfectly acceptable copies of white folks." It portrayed a "typical third generation Chinese-Canadian" as owning a forty-foot yacht and implied that all immigrants from Hong Kong were professionals or merchants. Finally, it warned that "you can't be too careful of the Chinese" because "Yellow China" has turned "Red."[131]

At its première in the CBA's headquarters on 27 July 1979, the film was bitterly condemned as "misleading, inaccurate, exploitative, offensive, degrading, an embarrassment, an insult to the Chinese community and a way to perpetuate the worst stereotypes." A committee was formed to protest the film and agitate against its distribution. Dr Edgar Wickberg, of the History Department at the University of British Columbia, said the film had "serious historical inaccuracies," while other critics attacked it as "totally lacking in educational value and completely unacceptable for circulation and presentation to school children and to the general public." An embarrassed NFB quickly agreed to halt the film's circulation.[132]

ANOTHER, MORE DRAMATIC INTERVENTION by the media provoked one of the largest protests of Chinese-origin people ever rallied in Canada. On 30 September 1979, CTV's W5 public affairs program televised a segment entitled "Campus Giveaway," alleging that 100,000 foreign students, especially Chinese, were pre-empting the places of "Canadians" in the country's universities. These "foreigners," like the early "sojourners," were said to be coming to Canada to reap the benefits of its educational facilities, after which, the story went, they returned to their countries of origin with their taxpayer-subsidized degrees in hand. "As long as qualified Canadian students can't get into schools," said the program host, "the foreign student program has gone too far."[133] The school of pharmacy at the University of Toronto, for instance, had denied entry to an aspiring pharmacist from St Catharines. While the heroine related her plight, cameras roamed a classroom, focusing on "Chinese" faces while Chinese music played in the background.

Omitted from the segment was the evidence from the associate dean of pharmacy that the student did not have sufficient merit to be admitted into the school. The president of the Association of Universities and Colleges of Canada also corrected the grossly inflated original figure of 100,000 "foreigners."[134] More serious, the investigative program overlooked the fact that the pharmacy faculty at the university admitted only Ontario residents; visa or foreign students were barred. Of the five faces singled out by the camera, one student was born in Canada and all the others were Canadian citizens.

Slowly the message of the program registered among Chinese-origin residents throughout Canada, and the Chinese, united by a common mission that revealed the weight of their history of outsider status, politicized as a group.[135] In all major cities, ad hoc committees were formed by professionals and activists in Chinese communities. By February 1980, complaints had been filed to provincial and federal human rights bodies and a petition supporting the grievance had been signed by 20,000 people, including more than 7,000 from Vancouver. CTV's apology, which dwelt on the use of inaccurate statistics, further inflamed the agitation. Only some months later, after further lobbying and a national meeting of the ad hoc committees, was the real issue – that of assuming that "Chinese" were foreigners – finally brought home to the network. The day after the national meeting of ad hoc committees in Toronto, the network's president issued a public apology that acknowledged the affront the program had unwittingly levelled at the institution of Canadian citizenship and to permanent residents of the country.

CONCLUSION

The W5 incident, perhaps more than any other, brought to a head the tension between the avowed policy of multiculturalism, with its respect for Chinese contributions to Canadian society, and the abiding reality, where race continued to be a principle around which white Canadians organized themselves. In the wake of the NFB and W5 events, what could Chinese come to expect from the governing voice of Canada? Not, it seems, a new language for dealing (or not dealing) with the Chinese; nor, it would seem, recognition of the "masked negativity of positive stereotypes." It is evident from the debate in the House of Commons on 16 June 1980 that in the symbolic universe of white Canada Chinese were as pre-eminently "Chinese" then as they had been a century before. Qualified approbation may have taken the place of indignation, but the concept of a Chinese race – assimilated into the hegemonic culture and embedded locally at Chinatown – remained constant and avaliable for further service.

On 16 June, Ian Waddell, member for Vancouver-Kingsway, moved: "That this House recognizes the contribution made to the Canadian mosaic ... by the people of Chinese background."[136] Referring to the people slighted by the Chinatown documentary and the students singled out by W5, he said, reminiscent of Judge Oreck's statement about the industrious Chinese: "We will hear from these people. I think that the House of Commons should celebrate the energy and talent of these young Canadians." In support of the motion, Steve Paproski of Edmonton North remarked that the students' achievements "have put the people of Chinese background into the category of one of the most rapidly developing groups of Canadian citizens."[137] Finally, Gordon Taylor of Bow River (Alberta) could not let the opportunity go by without paying tribute to Canadians of Chinese origin: "The attributes of the Chinese people are qualities for which we should all be grateful. I go so far as to say we can all learn from them. They are hard workers; they do not expect handouts from government. They want to contribute to their country and they want a good life for themselves. I congratulate them for that."[138] Waddell's motion was unanimously carried.

positive comments about the chinese

CHAPTER EIGHT

The End of a Fiction?

Few concepts that have governed human life chances in Western societies so decisively have been as fraught with ambiguity and ignorance on the part of the lay public, the media, and governing bodies as that of race. Until recently, this confusion has been compounded by the social science of race relations, where terms like "race," "ethnic," "ethnic pluralism," "race relations," "cultural diversity," and "multiculturalism" have often been used in ways that mask uncritical assumptions about "difference" and "otherness." This book has attempted a more rigorous approach to the race question which critically examines the cognitive leap made in many Western societies from physical and cultural differences to something more fundamental which has been called "race." Its objective has been to present a way of conceptualizing the twin concepts of a Chinese race and place different from that which has featured in the social science of such racialized minorities and their enclaves.

Within the liberal tradition of research on the "Chinese" in British settler societies, race has more often been taken for granted as a discrete fact than made an object of explanation itself. As was noted in chapter 1, idealist approaches tend to invoke a universal white "prejudice" in their explanations of colour-based stratification, chronicling the sins of discrimination and stereotyping to which people of Chinese origin have been subjected. By extension, the enclaves of such settlers have been conceptualized as "ghettoes" or victimized colonies of the East. Orthodox structural Marxist approaches, in contrast, have emphasized the economic sources of conflict between groups distinguished by colour, arguing that race, like other ideologies, is derivative of more decisive economic pressures under capitalism. More recently, a field of sociobiology has emerged that draws from evolutionary principles and raises again the lingering spectre of primordial explanations in the field of race relations.[1] In contrast to those perspectives, I have traced the construction of knowledge about the Chinese, demonstrating how it informed government practices and conditioned the territorial arrangements through which racial concepts were inscribed and reproduced. Consistent with recent constructivist research in social science, I have examined the contextualized process through which "race" was constituted as fact.

The tradition of symbolic interactionism in sociology has always been sensitive to the fact that people process reality in ways that reveal as much about the beholder as some a priori order of things. "The nature or essence of an object does not reside mysteriously in the object itself, but is dependent upon how it is defined by the namer," Strauss said back in 1959.[2] One well-known piece of sociology that developed this epistemological perspective examined the "definition of the situation" in Chicago's inner city, where social categories of in-group and out-group were negotiated in the competition for territory.[3] At the time, such work contributed in no small measure to restoring subjective meanings to functionalist approaches to social order.

The tradition of symbolic interactionism has as a whole, however, been impoverished by its eclipse of history and its silence on issues of power.[4] With regard to the race question, it will be clear that these are serious omissions indeed. The existence of socially based insider and outsider processes does not alone explain why "race" was, and for so long continued to be, selected as an idiom of exclusion and inclusion in Vancouver society. Nor does it account for the distribution of power between the reference groups so defined or the configuration of social relations in that setting. As I argued in chapter 1, such groups do not come in ready-made packages, nor is the pattern of their relations somehow fixed in advance, and thus they must be examined with reference to the historical contexts which led to and sustained their formation.

The hegemony concept helps illuminate precisely the negotiated nature of the cultural and political process known as racialization. Far from being part of the natural world, race has been a historically specific way of seeing and practice, linked in circular relation to the global extension of European domination. The Canadian experience of people of Chinese origin owes some of its character even to times as far removed as the classical era, when the collective notion of "Europe" first came to signify an "us" as distinct from a "different" (and usually inferior) "them." The expansion of Christianity from the tenth to the thirteenth centuries and colonialism from the sixteenth century further influenced Europeans' interpretation of those people over whom colonial powers attempted to exert control. By the nineteenth century, Europe's cultural strength brought the elaboration of theories about race that fastened on classical and medieval stereotypes and prepared British Columbians for the likes of the "heathen Chinee" and his vice-ridden "Chinatown." Thereafter, for 100 years, the screen through which Vancouver's Chinese community was filtered to Europeans was subtly revised and recycled, not radically transcended.

It is in the context of that long rise to hegemony of a European historical bloc that the category Chinese needs to be situated, because out of the quest for power the classification acquired its meaning of non-white, non-Christian – in short, of "them" as opposed to "us." Such a connotation cannot alone explain the category's endurance, however. In late-nineteenth-century New World settings like British Columbia – where this book's story began – I tried to show how the power relations implicit in beliefs about "difference" were extended and cemented. With the imprimatur of the Canadian state, the premise of a Chinese race acquired a legitimacy that popular agitation could not alone have afforded it. The state sponsored and enforced beliefs about race, often for political purposes, and always to affirm the identity and privilege of a white Canadian in-group. Moreover, with the linkage to territory, the premise took on a spatial referent. The enclave on Vancouver's Pender Street provided a continuous context for the reproduction of racial beliefs giving them the appearance of being in some kind of "natural" correspondence with the physical presence of settlers from China.

The study of racial consciousness might seem to be invoking an outmoded idealism in a new guise that emphasizes the power of conceptual and linguistic systems. This book has attempted to show through substantive historical analysis, however, that bodies of theory that focus on ideological formulations like race can be compatible with those that emphasize their political, economic, and spatial articulation. It has not attempted the ambitious task of relating all these dimensions to the history of a "Chinese race" in Vancouver, and, in particular, the complex relationship that exists in capitalist societies between racial consciousness and economic forces needs to be further unpacked. But the record of European hegemony suggests the value of linking "in process in time" the two (often polarized) ideological and material regions.[5] One scholar in race relations argued a similar, but largely neglected epistemological case nearly twenty years ago: "The historical task is ... to relate satisfactorily the psychological, 'material' and other aspects of society to each other in such a way as to present reality as integrated social process."[6]

The evidence in this study also suggests the merits of attempting to synthesize – rather than treat as incompatible levels of analysis – the "micro-cognitive order of sense making" and the macro-structure "of social institutions and socio-cultural change on an aggregate level."[7] In the example of nineteenth-century European beliefs about a Chinese race, it has been possible to show that they acquired strength and resilience as they became reciprocally embedded in institutional and spatial structures. The micro-cognitive order of racial representation, as mediated through Chinatown, informed a macro-structure of European hegemony in a thoroughly dialectical dynamic, the complexity of which can be grasped only by integrating levels of analysis and situating the process in time and space.

The concept of hegemony often evokes images of a massive, anonymous entity driven by its own internal logic and momentum. Williams, for one, has warned of the "totalizing tendencies" of the hegemony concept.[8] The focus of this study on the agency of politicians and bureaucrats in the process of race definition has in part been by way of avoiding such abstraction. It will be clear from the substantive chapters of this book that the members of the Canadian state were active in constituting, legitimizing, and, with the rise of liberalism, modifying white society's racial frame of reference. The idea of a Chinese race was put to great service by successive administrations which all the time sought to build the fabric of, and gain their legitimacy from, a white European in-group. In chapters 2 and 3, we saw that the late-nineteenth-century provincial and municipal régimes adopted a position of bold opposition to the territory of "Chinatown" which it considered alien. And almost one hundred years later, under the aegis of the policy of multiculturalism, Chinatown was still being refurbished in ways that conformed to policy-makers' images of the East. The influence of changing conceptions of the "Chinese" on successive generations of policy-makers has indeed been extensive, as has been the reciprocal effect of such governing élites on the conceptions themselves. Their influence was by no means boundless, however, and the courts and Canada's constitutional structure set limits that also defy totalizing claims about European hegemony.

The internal complexity of European racial thought likewise cautions us against adopting neat models of domination. We have seen co-existing and even contradictory dimensions to white Vancouver's vision of the "Chinese" and "Chinatown," to the extent that at Vancouver's Jubilee celebrations in 1936 "John Chinaman" could be praised for his connection to the opulent East, at the same time as being harassed for his reputed amoral intentions toward white women in Chinatown's cafés. From that time on, both negatively and positively evaluated characteristics were ascribed deterministically to people of Chinese origin to either suppress or capitalize on expressions of their "difference." And to this day, benign conceptions of the resplendent East and the industrious Chinese persist alongside "Hongcouver's" more classical fears about its wealthy new "Yacht-people."[9]

These multiple voices in the European perspective suggest that perceptions of a Chinese race and place cannot be reduced to a unitary white viewpoint.[10] Reverse essentializing of the European is, after all, no corrective to Orientalizing the Chinese. Nonetheless, the categories "Chinese" and "Chinatown" did enjoy an official authority and coherence that sustained them for a century. The categories also gained credibility as they became the focus of claims to inclusion of some of Vancouver's Chinese. Such was the case in the many instances of Chinese protests against violations of their life chances, as chapters 3 through 6 laid out, and in moments when people of Chinese origin combined to promote the "Chineseness" of "Chinatown," as we saw in chapters 5 through 7. The examples highlight the sense in which Chinatown's ideological construction has not been a simple process of cultural imposition on an unreflective audience. In 1936, Chinatown's merchants appropriated to lucrative effect the conceptual symbols of Chineseness, and during the stages of redevelopment in Strathcona community organizations attempted to harness tourist Chinatown to the cause of neighbourhood preservation. And again, in the 1970s, the merchant and community élite came to endorse the image of Chinatown that the city of Vancouver sought to inscribe on its streetscape.

Many merchants and community figures seemed strategically aware of the benefits of framing their neighbourhood plans in the language of the representations that filtered them and their enclave to white Vancouver. Moreover, there were Chinese (such as Gilbert Eng, who objected to the Leungs' "Oriental Village" in 1963) who seemed alert still more to the ultimate struggle, which lay in transcending the conceptual categories that for so long had marginalized Chinatown. Chinese were not falsely conscious of the mechanisms sustaining their outsider status, therefore, and while on occasion they colluded in their own oppression they were always on hand to test the limits of, and extract their own advantage from, dominant ideological renderings of their identity and territory.

Regional and neighbourhood studies in geography have too rarely taken measure of the role of powerful agents in defining places. Yet those with the power of definition can, in a sense, create places by arbitrarily regionalizing the external world and attaching to them symbolic significance. Concepts of the "Dark Continent," the "Third World," the "Pacific Rim," and the "inner city" are cases in point.[11] Of course, not all places are as heavily laden with cultural baggage as "Chinatown." But Chinatown points up once again the more general principle that a negotiated social process lies behind the apparently neutral-looking taxonomies of census districts and world regions.[12] More important, perhaps, the manipulation of racial ideology by institutions is additional testimony to the fact that a set of power relations may underpin and keep alive our spatial categories.

Not that Chinatown has exclusively been an artifact of European imagining. Its importance in the history of the racialization of Vancouver's "Chinese" is that it has been at once symbolic and concrete; it has been a set of meanings, at the same time as informing and objectifying racialist ideas and practices. Moreover, we have seen that Europeans directed a great deal of their effort at defining themselves and safeguarding their privilege through the medium of Chinatown. This, too, attests to the significance of such enclaves in the making of systems of racial classification.

Recently, there has been something of a retreat on the part of social scientists from broad explanatory paradigms and grand theorizing. With the critique has come a call for case studies that weave "the most local of local detail and the most global of global structures in such a way as to bring both into view simultaneously."[13] Geertz's prescription is perhaps too exacting an appeal to be scrupulously practised. But it is an ideal we can strive to approximate. Thus it will be clear from these concluding comments that, while this book has traced the history of the race-definition process in one setting, the Vancouver case study points beyond itself to more "global" themes concerning power and racial discourse, the social construction of identity and place, the relation between ideology and institutional practice, and the transformation of conceptual structures into material forms. Similarly, while the narrative could not have been constructed without reference to the images and actions of the likes of Commissioner Joseph Chapleau, Health Inspector Robert Marrion, Prime Minister William Lyon Mackenzie King, Alderman Halford Wilson, Mayor Tom Alsbury, and Chinatown planner Mike Kemble, such figures have wider significance – their contribution to making racial concepts which have themselves been indelibly linked to European hegemony in a British settler society. Methodologically speaking, then, the "descriptive" and the "analytical" have been mutually interdependent axes of the "problematic of structuring," to use the terms of Abrams's program for a historical sociology.[14]

Demystification of the interacting orders and moments in Vancouver's race-definition process has been a primary aim of this book. More specifically, this study has attempted to expose the premises and interests immanent in government practices toward Chinatown in such a way as to challenge the sense of necessity and eternity implicit in conventional descriptions of this "ethnic community." Of course, the argument presented in these pages does not exhaust the ways of conceptualizing the Chinatowns of Western settings. For one thing, an interpretation that entertains only some of the views of Chinatown's residents can hardly be said to be complete. But after many decades of research into the "cultural stuff" that distinguishes the Chinese from their "host" societies, it seems timely to show the sense in which Europeans' constitution of "Chinatown" has its own exotic quality.

A study that does the same for people of Chinese origin in Vancouver might be equally illuminating – showing more carefully the ways in which different classes and sectors of that community interpreted and managed the classification of their identity and territory and how they perceived the society at large (if such a shared vision existed).[15] A limitation of cultural relativist research on Canada's minority communities has been that immigrants from China and elsewhere have often been conceptualized in the one-dimensional terms of their ethnic status, so emphasizing their cultural bonding and obscuring the complexity of their lived experiences. One must be wary of the reverse error of denying people's attachment to ancestral traditions, but to impute and reify them is also dubious, and there is perhaps a more valid basis for examining substantive differences among the world's communities once we have accepted their fundamental commonality.[16] The problem, after all, is not group differences themselves, but rather the exclusionary habits of mind and practice that such differences have attracted.

ALL OF THE WORLD'S SOCIETIES IMPOSE what Said has called "corrections upon raw reality, changing it from free-floating objects into units of knowledge."[17] That the external world is known only selectively by people is by now commonplace to cultural geographers and many other social scientists. The issue is not so much that we transform or "convert" the external world. Significant of course are the categories we use to do so, the particular field of meaning our categories accrue, the functions they perform for us, and the social relations they support.[18] Labyrinthine textual explorations have grown in popularity in recent social science writings, and they require precisely this kind of deeper confrontation to avoid lapsing into academic exercises inside the hermeneutic circle.

In the case of racial categories, it will be apparent to all readers that they do something of a disservice to reality, reducing the range of human variation – mental, moral, physical, social, institutional – down and backward to a set of primordial types. We end up unable to see people as they are (if we ever did), because of the seductive convenience of types that rob people of their particularity. These categories have been used to justify the erection of spatial and cognitive boundaries that enslave representer and victim alike. Yet, as we have seen in this study, our representations are deeply engraved in our culture, language, institutions, and environments. We live by our abstractions – indeed, as Olsson has pointed out, we are bound by them, for to remove them "is to tear the world asunder."[19]

Such a message is overly pessimistic, however. In a statement that applies to one of the most pernicious abstractions of all – that of race – Olsson states: "When we cease to believe in a word, it no longer has power. And when words lose their power, so do the institutions that are built upon them."[20] The pressures that have made the Other into our designated image are never complete and always reversible. European hegemony is not a formation without boundaries, limits, or cracks, as the struggles and strategies of people of Chinese origin in Vancouver so clearly demonstrate. Nor are our racial categories inherently enslaving, but they rather are open to challenge and scrutiny, by whites and non-whites alike.

Neutralizing the colour line does not require initiatives to turn the Other into the Same. It does, however, suggest the need for today's policy-makers to rethink potentially divisive assumptions about "difference" implicit in cultural relativist rhetoric like "multiculturalism," while at the same time continuing to silence classical forms of racism. The policy challenges obstructing the transition to a non-racial Canada are considerable, but, just as this book has tried to reconstruct the understanding of a macro-level structure from the bottom up, so policy-makers might take some direction from shifts that are possible at the street and personal levels. Racial categories can be transcended by visions that promise more creative human relations than those conducted behind capriciously conceived borders. Such borders conceal a fiction that cultural pressure can as readily dispel as defend.

Notes

CHAPTER ONE

1 An exception is the work on Europeans in New World settings by historical geographer R. Cole Harris. See for example his article, "The Simplification of Europe Overseas." See also J. Duncan and N. Duncan, "A Cultural Analysis."
2 See for example G. Barth, *Bitter Strength*; Palmer, *Patterns of Prejudice*; Price, *The Great White Walls*; Roy, "British Columbia's Fear."
3 The most comprehensive study of the internal dynamics of Canadian Chinese communities is Wickberg et al. *From China to Canada*. See also Thompson, "The State." On Vancouver, see Willmott, "Chinese Clan Associations," and Straaton, "The Political System." On the social organization of American communities, see for example Nee and Nee, *Longtime Californ'*; Weiss, *Valley City*.
4 See for example D. Lai, "Socio-economic Structures"; Cho and Leigh, "Patterns of Residence"; Salter, *San Francisco's Chinatown*.
5 D. Lai, "Socio-economic Structures," 101.
6 Dear, "The Post-Modern Challenge," 270.
7 The following discussion has been guided by a reading of Stepan, *The Idea of Race*; Miles, *Racism*, chap. 1; and Montagu, ed., *The Concept of Race*.
8 See for example Farish, *Biology*, 361.
9 Appiah, "The Uncompleted Argument," 22.
10 Lewontin, Rose, and Kamin, *Not in Our Genes*, 124. Another scientist states that the blood types of two caste communities in Bombay are at least as different as American whites and blacks, yet "there would be a good deal of hesitation in referring to the two Indian caste communities as belonging to different races"; Dunn, "Race and Biology," 291.
11 Marger, *Race and Ethnic Relations*, 12.

12 Fried, "A Four-Letter Word."
13 Lewontin et al., *Not in Our Genes*, 127.
14 See for example Park, "The Concept of Social Distance."
15 For a collection of essays in the ecological tradition, see Peach, ed., *Urban Social Segregation*. See also some essays in Jackson and Smith, eds., *Social Interaction*; Peach, Robinson, and Smith, eds., *Ethnic Segregation*; Burnley, "Ethnic Factors"; Massey and Eggers, "The Ecology of Inequality."
16 See for example Palm, "Ethnic Segmentation"; Berry, *The Open Housing Question*.
17 See for example Clark, "Residential Mobility"; Rose, "Spatial Development."
18 See for example R. Johnston, *Residential Segregation*.
19 See Jackson, ed., *Race and Racism*; S. Smith, *The Politics of "Race"*.
20 See note 14.
21 Marshall, "Racial Classifications," 151.
22 Farley, "Segregated City."
23 Solomon, *Ancestors*, cited in Marshall, "Racial Classifications," 157.
24 Hughes and Kallen, *The Anatomy of Racism*, 85.
25 See Cowlishaw's article ("Colour") for a critique of the reification of the category "Aboriginal" by anthropologists.
26 Worsley, *The Three Worlds*, 242.
27 Fried, "A Four-Letter Word," 358.
28 Brotz, "Multiculturalism," 42.
29 F. Barth, ed., *Ethnic Groups*, 14.
30 See for example Jackson, "A Transactional Approach"; Peach, "Force"; Wallman, ed. *Ethnicity at Work*, chap. 1; Yancey, Ericksen, and Juliani, "Emergent Ethnicity."
31 For a critique of the reification of culture in American ethnic studies, see Steinberg, *The Ethnic Myth*. A critique of the conceptualization of ancestral culture used in some of the recent Generation series of Canadian monographs commissioned by the Department of the Secretary of State is provided by Perrin, "Clio as an Ethnic." See also J. Duncan, "The Superorganic," and Chan, "Neither French nor British." In Singapore, "Chinese" culture is, in the words of Clammer, "an amalgam of many bits of tradition, many of them utterly transformed by their transplantation to Southeast Asia, some more Malayan than Chinese, and very few any longer practised in China"; "Institutionalization," 133. As it turns out, in Singapore, where there is a high degree of spontaneous ethnic consciousness among the Chinese-origin majority, "Chinese" is a strongly felt self-concept to the point where that majority has insisted on its own "four-race-model" of classification for that society.
32 Loh Kok-Wah, "The Chinese in Australia," 70.

33 Banton, *Racial and Ethnic Competition*, 104; see also Hughes and Kallen, *The Anatomy of Racism*, chap. 6; and Jenkins, "Social Anthropological Models," 177–8.

34 Cohen, "Ethnicity," 383.

35 Padillo, *Up from Puerto Rico*, cited in Jackson, "Ethnic Groups," 18.

36 Miles, *Racism*.

37 See for example de Lepervanche and Bottomley, eds. *Cultural Construction*; Fenton, "Race Relations"; Fields, "Ideology and Race"; Gates, "Writing 'Race'"; Gilroy, "You Can't Fool the Youths"; Husband, ed., *"Race" in Britain*; Jackson, ed., *Race and Racism*; Jennett and Stewart, eds., *Three Worlds of Inequality*; Lawrence, "Just Plain Commonsense"; S. Smith, *The Politics of "Race"*.

38 See for example Green and Carter, "'Races'"; Carter, Harris, and Joshi, "The 1951–55 Conservative Government"; and Satzewich, "Racisms."

39 Banton, *The Idea of Race*, 19.

40 Allport, *The Nature of Prejudice*.

41 P. Ward, *White Canada Forever*, 169. See also Palmer, *Patterns*, and Roy, "British Columbia's Fear."

42 Said, *Orientalism*.

43 Schutz, "The Social World," 208. In geography this point is taken up by Ley in his "Social Geography."

44 See Marcus and Fischer, *Anthropology*, and the writings of Foucault – for example, *Discipline and Punish*. See also Sibley on the "ideological aspect of the outsider problem"; Sibley, *Outsiders*.

45 See for example Castells, *The Urban Question*, and Clark and Dear, *State Apparatus*.

46 Breton, "Production and Allocation," 127.

47 Greenberg, *Race and State*. For an orthodox structural Marxist interpretation of racial ideology, see Magubane, *Political Economy*. On the autonomy of "levels" within the problematic of a "structured totality," see Gabriel and Ben-Tovim, "Marxism," 118–54.

48 Warburton, "Race and Class," 84.

49 For internal critiques of economic determinism, see for example Wolfe, "Class Concepts". See also the original insights of Stuart Hall and his colleagues, including Paul Gilroy, in Centre for Contemporary Cultural Studies (Birmingham), *The Empire Strikes Back*. More generally, a non-Marxist critique of economic reductionism in geographic explanation is provided by J. Duncan and Ley, "Structural Marxism." David Harvey, "Between Space and Time" continues the debate, linking the "world of ideas" to "social reproduction of the capitalist sort," 424.

50 Boswell, "A Split Labor Market Analysis," 352–3.

51 See for example Boxer, *Race Relations*, and Ross, ed., *Racism and Colonialism*.

52 See for example Bastide, "Colour"; Hay, *Europe*; Jordan, *White over Black*; and March, *The Idea of China*.

53 See Said, *Orientalism*.

54 Prager, "American Racial Ideology," 103.

55 Gramsci, *Selections from the Prison Notebooks*.

56 See Williams, *Marxism and Literature*, 108–14.

57 In 1881, 51.9 per cent of the population of British Columbia was "Indian." "British" comprised 29.6 per cent, "Asiatic" 8.8 per cent, and there were minorities of others. *Census of Canada 1880–1*, Vol. 1, 299.

58 Western, *Outcast Capetown*, 8.

59 Lears, "The Concept of Cultural Hegemony," 570.

60 See for example Connell, *Gender and Power*.

61 See MacLaughlin and Agnew, "Hegemony."

62 Satzewich, "Racisms," 325.

63 On the process by which identity ascriptions come to be appropriated by indigenous populations in post-colonial societies in the Pacific, see Keesing, "Racial and Ethnic Categories."

64 A number of useful texts have been compiled. See for example Agnew, *Place and Politics*; Agnew and Duncan, eds., *The Power of Place*; Anderson and Gale, eds., *Ways of Seeing the World*; Dear and Wolch, eds., *The Power of Geography*; Gregory and Urry, eds., *Social Relations*; Murgatroyd et al., *Localities*; and Thrift and Williams, eds., *Class and Space*.

65 See for example J. Duncan and N. Duncan, "(Re)reading the Landscape"; Lewandowski, "The Built Environment"; and Ley, "Styles."

66 Stuart Hall has written widely on ideology, insisting on both its practical and its reflective dimensions. See for example Hall, "Race."

67 D. Lai, *Chinatowns*.

68 Lyman, "Chinese Social Organization," cited in Young, "Street of T'ongs," 30. See also Lyman, "Contrasts." Specifically on Canadian communities, see Baureiss and Driedger, "Winnipeg Chinatown"; Hoe, *Structural Changes*; Johnson, "Chinese Family"; and Sedgwick and Willmott, "External Influences." See also note 3, above.

69 The point suggests the problem of reducing European constructs to the constant of a single viewpoint – that is, of implicitly treating Europeans as a "type." While members of the European community did not always share the same evaluation of people of Chinese origin, the ideas of a Chinese race and place overrode regional, gender, and class-based variations in the perceptions and persisted whatever evaluation (negative or positive) was placed on the "Chinese."

70 Said, *Orientalism*, 55.

71 Mills, *The Sociological Imagination*.

72 Abrams, *Historical Sociology*; Giddens, *Central Problems*.

73 See for example Marcus and Fischer, *Anthropology*.

74 Dear, "The Post-modern Challenge," 270. See also Soja, "Post-moderni-zation," and the body of "localities research" in human geography – for example, Savage, "Locality Research."

75 The phrase "movement in formation" is taken from Gramsci, *Selections*, 353.

76 Durkheim, "Individual and Collective Representations"; see also Rabi-now, "Representations."

CHAPTER TWO

1 Wickberg et al., *From China to Canada*, 14.

2 D. Lai, "Chinese Immigrants." By the 1870s, the push factors in China were as powerful as the inducements in the New World. South China experienced a difficult period of reconstruction following the Taiping Rebellion, and many people were forced by their impoverished circum-stances to leave. Chan, *Gold Mountain*, 52.

3 Wynne, "Reaction," 145.

4 Ibid., 146. In absolute terms, the colony in 1867 had a population of 5,635 "Whites," 2,195 "Chinese," and over 35,000 "Indians."

5 In cannery work, Chinese were paid $25 to $35 per month, and "whites" $40. Road building earned Chinese $15 to $20 per month, and "whites" $40. Canada, *Sessional Papers*, 1885, No. 54a, "Royal Commission on Chinese Immigration" (hereafter cited as Canada, *Report*, 1885), 26 and 11.

6 Ibid., 14, 70, 49.

7 Ibid., 69.

8 Ibid., 128.

9 Canada, *Sessional Papers*, 1902, No. 54, "Royal Commission on Chinese and Japanese Immigration" (hereafter Canada, *Report*, 1902), 144.

10 Canada, *Report*, 1885, 41.

11 Ibid., 156.

12 Cited in P. Ward, *White Canada Forever*, 25.

13 Ibid., 169. Elsewhere he writes that the "pattern of racial awareness was ... ultimately founded ... on the white community's continuing psycho-logical tendency to cling to the ideal of the homogeneous society," 54.

14 See Tuan's figure of traditional Chinese world views with circles of increasing barbarism away from the Chinese court in his book, *Topophilia*, 38. Berger and Luckmann discuss the general applicability of "symbolic universes" described here for Europeans; see their *Social Construction of Reality*.

15 March, *The Idea of China*, 23–4. See also the chapter "East Is East" in Dawson, *The Chinese Chameleon*. Dawson notes (p. 91) that in the fifth century BC the term "Asia" was not an unemotive geographical term but

a reference to "despotic authority and barbaric splendour." Said (*Orientalism*, 56) also claims that the demarcation between East and West was "bold" by the time of the *Iliad*. See the discussion of the idea of the "heathen Chinee" below in chapter 3.

16 Cited in March, *The Idea of China*, 30.

17 Snowden, *Before Colour Prejudice*.

18 Montagu, *The Idea of Race*, 13.

19 See Bastide, "Colour."

20 Montagu, *The Idea of Race*, 33.

21 Jordan, *White over Black*, 94. Jordan notes (p. 95) the change in the terminology that English colonists applied to themselves during the seventeenth century. "From the initially common term Christian, at mid-century, there was a marked drift toward English and free. After about 1680 taking the colonies as a whole, a new term appeared – white." Thereafter colonists turned to the difference in complexion, and by the end of the seventeenth century "dark complexion had become an independent rationale for enslavement" (p. 96).

22 The references to these eighteenth-century texts are taken from M. Harris, "Race," 265; Gates, "Writing 'Race,'" 10; and Montagu, *The Idea of Race*, 37.

23 The deficient shape and size of the skulls of "the Mongol, Indian and Negro, and all the dark-skinned races," Nott contended in 1849, were "especially well marked in those parts of the brain which have been assigned to the moral and intellectual faculties"; cited in Miller, *The Unwelcome Immigrant*, 156.

24 Stepan, *The Idea of Race*, 4.

25 For a more extended discussion, see ibid., chap. 2.

26 Cited in Miller, *The Unwelcome Immigrant*, 145.

27 In particular, see Jones, *Social Darwinism*.

28 Stepan, *The Idea of Race*, 55.

29 Jones, *Social Darwinism*, 142.

30 Canada, *Report*, 1885, 98.

31 M. Harris, "Race," 266.

32 See Livingstone, "Science and Society," 188.

33 Bannister, *Social Darwinism*, 190–6.

34 Stepan, *The Idea of Race*, 18.

35 Canada, *Report*, 1885, 61.

36 Ibid., 166. By the turn of the century, these conceptions of the Chinese were picked up by BC fiction writers. See for example Hiebert, "The Oriental."

37 Canada, *Report*, 1885, 99, 19–44, 136, 60–6, 155–60, 94, 92.

38 Ibid., 72.

39 Voegelin, "Growth," 283–317.

40 Canada, *Report*, 1885, 94, 72, 95, 103. See also the testimony of the general manager for the Wellington Collieries, 111.

41 Porter, *The Vertical Mosaic*, 61, 63; P. Ward, *White Canada Forever*, Table 1.

42 British Columbia, *Statutes*, 1872, 35 Vict., chap. 37, s. 13. The act was reserved by the lieutenant-governor. It was not until 1875 that the jurisdictional competence of the provincial legislature to deny Chinese the franchise was affirmed and Chinese were removed from the voters' lists. British Columbia, *Statutes*, 1875, 35 Vict., ch. 26, s. 22.

43 British Columbia, *Statutes*, 1883, 51 Vict., chap. 15.

44 British Columbia, *Journals of the Legislative Assembly of British Columbia* (hereafter *JLABC*) 1, 1872, 15, 16.

45 Unfortunately, no record of the debates of the legislature is available. Wynne has retrieved from newspapers the debates surrounding these resolutions; see his "Reaction," 155, 161.

46 P. Ward, *White Canada Forever*, 32.

47 *JLABC*, 1876, 5, 46.

48 *JLABC*, 1878, 7, 82.

49 British Columbia, *Statutes*, 1878, 42 Vict., chap. 35.

50 P. Ward, *White Canada Forever*, 33.

51 *Tai Sing v. Maguire*, [1878] BCR 101 (BCSC), 101.

52 La Forest, *Disallowance*.

53 Wynne, "Reaction," 345.

54 *JLABC*, 1879, 8, 24–5 and 55.

55 Canada, *Report*, 1885, 12. For a critique of the common view that Chinese were "sojourners" rather than "settlers," see Chan, "Orientalism."

56 See Robin, *The Rush for the Spoils*, chap. 2.

57 *JLABC*, 1883, 12, 17.

58 Ibid., 83.

59 *JLABC*, 1882, 11, 10.

60 Berton, *The Last Spike* , chap. 2.

61 British Columbia, *Sessional Papers*, 1885, "Correspondence in connection with the mission of Hon. W. Smithe to Ottawa relating to Chinese immigration and other questions," 2. British Columbia, *Statutes*, 1884, 47 Vict., chap. 3.

62 British Columbia, *Statutes*, 1884, 47 Vict., chap. 4.

63 Ibid., chap. 16.

64 See Bonacich, "Theory." On the BC context see Creese, "Immigration Policies."

65 *JLABC*, 1885, 14, 46. See also British Columbia, *Sessional Papers*, 1886, "Destitute Condition of Chinese Recently Discharged from the CPR Works, 1885."

66 British Columbia, *Statutes*, 1885, 48 Vict., chap. 13.
67 *JLABC*, 1891, 20, 145. Without access to the debates, it is not possible to establish why that motion was carried, nor the numerous others involving what became called "the usual Chinese clause."
68 British Columbia, *Statutes*, 1897, 60 Vict., chap. 1.
69 *JLABC*, 1900, 28, 99.
70 Ibid., 1894, 23, 117; 1897, 28, 57.
71 Ibid., 1900, 24, 58–9.
72 Canada, *Report*, 1885, 11.
73 Ibid., 97.
74 Canada, House of Commons, *Debates* (hereafter *DHC*) 18 March 1878, 1209.
75 *DHC*, 16 April 1879, 1262.
76 Ibid., 12 May 1882, 1477.
77 Ibid., 30 April 1883, 905.
78 Warburton, "Race and Class," 82. Basran also argues that Canadian immigration practices can be explained by "the general role of the Canadian state," which has been "to help capitalists in the accumulation process and to assist them to increase their profits"; "Canadian Immigration Policy," 11.
79 *DHC*, 18 March 1878, 1208; 16 April 1879, 1253.
80 Canada, *Report*, 1885, 69.
81 Ibid., 94.
82 *DHC*, 2 July 1885, 3002–11.
83 Canada, *Statutes*, 1885, 48–49 Vict., chap. 71. In the same session, Macdonald introduced an amendment to the Franchise Act that prevented any "person of Mongolian or Chinese race" from the dominion franchise; ibid., chap. 40, s. 2. Macdonald was one of the most ardent supporters of the amendment. He said "The Chinaman ... has no British instincts or British feelings or aspirations, and therefore ought not to have the vote"; *DHC*, 4 May 1885, 1589.
84 *DHC*, 4 May 1887, 277.
85 Ibid., 31 May 1887, 643.
86 Canada, *Report*,1885, 98.
87 *DHC*, 4 September 1891, 5059.
88 The telegram was sent to the *Vancouver World*. See *DHC*, 25 June 1900, 8175.
89 "For my part," said Prime Minister Laurier in 1903, "I make a distinction between Japan and China. Japan is one of the rising nations of the present day. It has shown itself to be very progressive ... among the civilized nations of the world." *DHC*, 27 March 1903, 599.
90 Ibid., 7 July 1899, 6836.
91 Ibid., 7 July 1899, 6846.

92 Canada, *Report*, 1902, 273. Chinese immigration and Japanese immigration were investigated separately in the report.

93 Ibid., 274.

94 Ibid., 277.

95 Cited in *Report*, 1902, 13.

96 The amendment passed its third reading on 5 May 1903; *DHC*, 5 May 1903, 2399. The amendment was passed despite the protest of the president of the Canadian Pacific Railway, Mr T. Shaughnessy, who claimed that "legislation by Canada would deprive us of the revenue from the carriage of Chinamen back and forth between this country and their own and would so seriously affect the revenue of our Pacific steamships that we could not afford to keep them running"; Canada, *Report*, 1902, 201.

97 *DHC*, 27 March 1903, 597–8.

98 Ibid., 599.

99 Parkin, *Marxism*, 95.

100 Li, "A Historical Approach," 324.

101 Morton, *In the Sea*, 144.

102 The two newspaper references are taken from Roy, "Preservation," 45.

103 *Vancouver News*, 2 June 1886.

104 Morley, *Vancouver*, 73.

105 *Vancouver News*, 27 July 1886.

106 City of Vancouver Archives (hereafter CVA), Vancouver City (hereafter Van. City), *Council Minutes*, Vol. 1, 8 November 1886, 164.

107 *Vancouver News*, 30 December 1886.

108 Ibid., 9 November 1886.

109 See *Vancouver News*, 8, 9, 14, January 1887, on local response to McDougall.

110 Ibid., 9, 11 January 1887.

111 Morton, *In the Sea*, 148.

112 *British Columbia Federationist*, 9 December 1911.

113 Morton, *In the Sea*, 148.

114 Robson to Vancouver City Council, cited in *Vancouver News*, 15 March 1887.

115 British Columbia, *Statutes*, 1887, 50 Vict., chap. 33.

116 On the squatters, see CVA, Van. City, Council Minutes, Vol. 3, 3 June 1889, 33; ibid., Vol. 3, 30 June 1890; ibid., Clerk's Incoming Correspondence (hereafter In Corresp.), Vol. 3, 27 June 1890, 2103.

117 Canada, *Report*, 1885, 143.

118 Canada, *Report*, 1902, 296, 235.

119 For accounts of the 1907 riot, see Sugimoto, "The Vancouver Riot," and P. Ward, *White Canada Forever*, chap. 4.

120 On the renewal of anti-Chinese feeling in Vancouver during the late 1890s, see *World* 6, 7, 9, 15 July and 12 August 1896 and 6 January and 6 February 1897.

121 *Province*, 26 May 1902.

CHAPTER THREE

1 Canada, *Report*, 1902, 278.

2 Ibid., 13.

3 CVA, Van. City, In Corresp., Vol. 17, 26 November 1900, 13,292.

4 Canada, *Report*, 1902, 13; see also Adilman, "A Preliminary Sketch."

5 The figures for 1901 cited in this section are taken from Canada, *Report*, 1902, 213, and the newspaper report of Cumyow's testimony in *Province*, 11 May 1901.

6 See Yee, "Business Devices."

7 Ibid., 47.

8 *Province*, 27 May 1908.

9 Yee, "Chinese Business," chap. 3.

10 Ibid., 43.

11 See Lal, "The Chinese Benevolent Association." The CBA was active in the intervening years. Lee Kee, a wealthy merchant, represented it before council in 1902, for example, to request permission to erect altars and furnaces for funeral services; *Province*, 25 August 1902.

12 Yee, "Chinese Business," 51.

13 *Province*, 5 February 1910.

14 Yee, "Chinese Business," 83.

15 *Province*, 27 May 1908.

16 Yee, "Chinese Business," 42. A number of the companies that invested in real estate bought property outside Chinatown. By April 1915, the Lee Yuen Co., for example, owned $279,500 in land assets, only five blocks of which were in the Pender Street area. The other purchases were in North Vancouver, West 15th Avenue, the East End, and elsewhere. Lee Family Papers, Special Collections Division, University of British Columbia Library, Box 4. Sam Kee owned five hotel sites and other buildings in central Vancouver as well as numerous other holdings across the city. Yee, "Chinese Business," 47-8.

17 *Province*, 30 September 1902. One Hastings Street businesssman claimed: "I am convinced that a row of Chinese stores, the same as line Dupont Street on the south side of the same block, would make it decidedly bad for the other business people in that vicinity."

18 Yee, "Chinese Business," 83. The growth of the "Chinese" district was accompanied by an out-movement of non-Chinese residents in the vicinity. One pioneer from Keefer Street said in 1906: "Finally the Chinaman from Chinatown approached so much about us, that we moved to Mount Pleasant ... Gradually too, the high class residential district east of Westminster Avenue slowly deteriorated." CVA, J. Matthews, Early Vancouver:

Narratives of a Pioneer in Vancouver, BC, unpublished manuscript, Vol. 7, 413.

19 *Province*, 5 February 1910.

20 Canada, *Report*, 1902, 236, 65.

21 *Province*, 9 November 1907. The majority went to nearby Central School.

22 L. Ma, "A Chinese Statesman."

23 Cited in Lee, "A History of the Overseas Chinese in Canada," 1967, translated by Ma Sen, 1973, 18, in Chinese-Canadian Project, Box 9, Special Collections Division, University of British Columbia Library (hereafter Chinese-Canadian Project).

24 D. Lai, *Chinatowns*, 35.

25 Canada, *Report*, 1885, 130.

26 Ibid., 126.

27 *World*, 9 July 1896.

28 Canada, *Report*, 1885, 130.

29 *DHC*, 2 July 1885, 3006.

30 Canada, *Report*, 1885, 109.

31 *DHC*, 2 July 1885, 3010.

32 *Vancouver News*, 7 December 1886.

33 Ibid., 13 January 1887.

34 *Henderson's British Columbia Directory* (Victoria: L.G. Henderson, 1889), 426.

35 CVA, Van. City, In Corresp., Vol. 17, 26 November 1900, 13,301–2. In 1893, Health Inspector Brenton advised council that the same fate he had sealed on the Chinese-owned piggeries at False Creek – "wiped out to become a thing of the past" – should be administered to the dispersed Chinese laundries; CVA, Van. City, In Corresp., Vol. 6, 4 July 1893, 5,275.

36 *Regina v. Corporation of Victoria* [1888] BCR 331 at 331.

37 CVA, Office of the City Clerk, Bylaw 176, May 1893.

38 CVA, Van. City, In Corresp., Vol. 15, 6 August 1900, 11,766. In response, council carried a motion to "instruct the proper authorities to stop the erection of the Chinese washhouse"; ibid., Council Minutes, Vol. 9, 6 August 1900, 736. For similar protests against outlying laundries, see In Corresp., Vol. 8, 27 April 1895, 6,860; Vol. 9, 10 October 1895, 8,107; Vol. 15, 18 January 1900, 11,738.

39 Yee, "Chinese Business," 34.

40 See CVA, Van. City, Council Minutes, Vol. 9, 17 December 1900, 936.

41 See ibid., Vol. 10, 9 April 1901, 133.

42 *Province*, 12 May 1904.

43 *News*, 30 August 1890.

44 *World*, 23 March 1893; 23 February 1892.

45 CVA, Van. City, In Corresp., Vol. 17, 26 November 1900, 13,292. See health committee minutes for references to inspections of Chinatown.

For an account of similar practices by late-nineteenth-century officials in Melbourne's Chinatown, see McConville, "Chinatown."

46 CVA, Van. City, In Corresp., Vol. 17, 26 November 1900, 13,291.

47 Ibid., 13,298.

48 Ibid.

49 *World*, 1 November 1899.

50 CVA, Van. City, In Corresp., Vol. 17, 26 November 1900, 13,299. The following year, the health committee resolved that the medical health officer "instruct the residents on Dupont Street that they must be vaccinated within seven days otherwise they will be prosecuted"; CVA, Van. City, Council Minutes, Vol. 9, 26 February 1900, 498.

51 *Province*, 18 June 1902.

52 Ibid., 30 September 1902.

53 *World*, 6 April 1899.

54 Canada, *Report*, 1902, 14,16.

55 *World*, 6 July 1896.

56 CVA, Van. City, In Corresp., Vol. 17, 26 November 1900, 13,301.

57 Canada, *Report*, 1902, 297.

58 CVA, Van. City, In Corresp., Vol. 17, 26 November 1900, 13,295.

59 CVA, Van. City, Council Minutes, Vol. 7, 20 January 1896, 4.

60 Ibid., Vol. 8, 5 December 1898, 568.

61 Ibid., In Corresp., Vol. 14, 14 June 1899, 10,433.

62 Ibid., Council Minutes, Vol. 13, 22 May 1905, 395; ibid., 30 January 1905, 146.

63 *Province*, 9 February 1906.

64 CVA, Van. City, In Corresp., Vol. 11, 20 August 1897, 9,119– 35.

65 Ibid., In Corresp., 28 August 1890, 2,018; Council Minutes, Vol. 4, 15 September 1890; ibid., Vol. 4, 22 February 1891, 215.

66 Ibid., In Corresp., Vol. 15, 4 December 1899, 11,705.

67 Canada, *Report*, 1902, 14; CVA, Van. City, Council Minutes, Vol. 10, 9 April 1901, 49.

68 *Province*, 16 September 1907. The term "Cellestialland" is taken from ibid., 28 May 1908.

69 Foucault has said that "the problem is not one of drawing the line between that in a discourse which falls under the category of scienticity or truth, and that which comes under some other category, but with seeing historically how effects of truth are produced within discourses which are themselves neither true or false"; cited in Rabinow, ed., *The Foucault Reader*, 60.

70 *Province*, 27 January 1910; *Times*, 29 January 1910.

71 *World*, 3 March 1911.

72 S.S. Osterhout, "A Religious and Missionary Survey of the Chinese," United Church of Canada Archives, typescript, 1919, in Chinese-Cana-

dian Project, Box 15. The council's resolution was reported in the *Province*, 26 September 1911.

73 *World*, 12 February 1912.

74 Osterhout, "Survey." See also Wickberg et al., *From China to Canada*, 121.

75 *Sun*, 31 March 1914.

76 See for example Sunahara, *The Politics of Racism*.

77 CVA, Van. City, Council Minutes, Vol. 20, 8 April 1914, 122.

78 *Province*, 27 January, 19 February 1910.

79 *Sun*, 8 April 1914; CVA, Van. City, In Corresp., Vol. 53, Solicitor's file, 7 April 1914, Clerk to Council.

80 *Sun*, 10 April 1914. Employment agent Hop Wo and Co., of Carrall Street, reported that sixty "China-boys" were dismissed from Vancouver homes following the incident. The *Colonist* stated that "the disposition of the body and the callousness of the murder indicates a phase of character which is exceedingly rare among people of our own race"; 8 April 1914. Such a description seems to have stemmed from the popular conception of the Chinese as inhumane, an idea perhaps related to the view of China as a hugely populous country where human life was deemed to be cheap.

81 *Sun*, 24 May 1915.

82 See for example 25 February and 4 March 1915.

83 *Sun*, 31 March 1914.

84 On this campaign, see ibid., 20, 27 April, 5 October, 30 November 1915.

85 *Province*, 19 February 1917.

86 Ibid., 7 October 1907.

87 See Gates, "Writing 'Race'," and other essays in the same issue of *Critical Inquiry*, 12, 1 (1985).

88 For evidence that it was more the white European view that was "the same everywhere" and less Chapleau's "Chinaman," see accounts from other places, for example: Paupst, "A Note." On images of American Chinatowns, see for example Light, "From Vice District to Tourist Attraction"; Salter, "Urban Imagery"; and Steiner, *Fusang*, chap. 15. Melbourne's Chinatown was portrayed by the press and politicians in an almost identical fashion to Vancouver's; see McConville, "Chinatown." Some of the themes, especially those concerning white women in slavery, were common in interpretations of other racially defined out-groups, such as "blacks" in the United States. See for example Ley, *The Black Inner City*, chap. 1.

89 See for example Hill, "Anti-Oriental Agitation"; Roy, "British Columbia's Fear"; and Saxton, *The Indispensable Enemy*.

90 See Geertz, *The Interpretation of Cultures*, chap. 8.

91 March, *The Idea of China*, 27.

92 See Dawson, *The Chinese Chameleon*, chaps. 2, 3.

93 Cited in Miller, *The Unwelcome Immigrant*, 42.

94 See for example Dawson, *The Chinese Chameleon*; Hay, *Europe*; and Said, *Orientalism*.

95 Miller, *The Unwelcome Immigrant*, chap. 2.

96 Ibid., chap. 3.

97 *World*, 10 February 1912.

98 Nilsen, "The 'Social Evil'," chaps. 2, 3.

99 *World*, 20 February 1892.

100 Nilsen, "The 'Social Evil'," 27.

101 Letters to the editor cited in ibid., 37, 31.

102 For an example of the treatment the press gave the Chinese New Year's celebrations, see *Province*, 29 January 1900. That year, the mayor of Vancouver was invited to attend the celebrations, and the report also noted that "white citizens always gather to see the fireworks display."

103 See Pettman, "Whose Country Is It Anyway?," for a critical discussion of the way in which the white Australian category "Aboriginal" collapses the different experiences of men and women of Aboriginal origin. Gender differences in the responses of those doing the classifiying have also been examined. See for example Knapman's discussion of the variation in the views of British men and women in colonial Fiji; Knapman, *White Women*. Research is increasingly available that examines the links between race, gender, and class formation. See for example Jennett and Randal, eds., *Three Worlds*.

104 Cited in *Province*, 3 February 1908.

105 Ibid., 3 July 1908.

106 Ibid., 10 February 1912.

107 King discovered that almost as much opium was sold to white people as to Chinese; Canada, *Sessional Paper*, 1908, No. 36b, "Report by W.L. Mackenzie King on the Need for the Suppression of the Opium Traffic in Canada," 7. McConville states a similar finding for Melbourne in his article, "Chinatown," 65.

108 *Province*, 17 June 1907.

109 Giffen, "Rates of Crime," 434.

110 Canada, *Report*, 1902, 236.

111 *Province*, 26 January 1915.

112 *Sun*, 19 June 1915; see also 24 May 1915.

113 *Province*, 16 July 1913.

114 Cited in Young, "The Vancouver Police Force," 65.

115 *World*, 12 February 1914.

116 *Chinese Times*, 22 December 1917.

117 *Province*, 5 February 1906.

118 *Chinese Times*, 16 January 1939.

CHAPTER FOUR

1 Samuels, "A Biography of Landscape," 71–2.
2 See for example Philo, "Enough to Drive One Mad," and Sibley, *Outsiders*.
3 Stepan, *The Idea of Race*, 111, 112.
4 Livingstone, "Science and Society," 200.
5 Haller, *Eugenics*, chap. 10.
6 Stepan, *The Idea of Race*, 130.
7 *DHC*, 8 May 1922, 1523.
8 Stoddard, *The Rising Tide*, 301, 229. For a similar statement of concern for the decline of "Nordic" influence in the United States, see Grant, *Passing*. One of the best discussions of the American "tribal twenties" is provided by Higham, *Strangers*.
9 On scapegoating, see Allport, *The Nature of Prejudice*, 349–53. See also Simpson and Yinger, *Racial and Cultural Minorities*, 53–61.
10 On links between "race" and "nation," see for example Miles, "Recent Marxist Theories."
11 Wickberg et al., *From China to Canada*, 119.
12 *JLABC*, 1919, 49, 272.
13 *Colonist*, 9 August 1913.
14 Ibid., 7 February 1920.
15 See ibid., 24 February 1920; 17 February, 1 March 1921; Premier's Correspondence, 1919–27, File 60, in Chinese-Canadian Project, Box 8.
16 British Columbia, *Report*.
17 *Colonist*, 1 March 1922.
18 L. Johnston, "The Case of the Oriental," 316.
19 Cited in Board of Trade files, Vol. 1, 21 July 1921, CVA, Add. MS 300.
20 *Colonist*, 2 November 1921.
21 Ibid., 21 November 1922.
22 Ibid., 15 November 1922.
23 Ibid., 6 July 1922. See also *Colonist*, 13 September 1923.
24 See ibid., 2 March 1926, and *Chinese Times*, 26 July, 2 December 1926. In that year, the Asiatic Exclusion League went on record as favouring a minimum wage for all forms of labour in the province.
25 *Colonist*, 3 June 1922.
26 Ibid., 14 November 1922.
27 *JLABC*, 1920, 49 , 246; *Colonist*, 2 April, 9 September 1921; 12, 13 December 1922; 22 February 1923.
28 In particular, see P. Ward, *White Canada Forever*, chap. 7; Roy, "The Oriental 'Menace'" and "Protecting Their Pocketbooks."
29 Roy, "British Columbia's Fear," 162.
30 *Colonist*, 11 November 1922.
31 *JLABC*, 1922, 52, 60.

32 Ibid., 137–8.
33 A copy of the circular is printed in C. Ma, *Chinese Pioneers*, 34–5. See also *Province*, 26 July 1913.
34 *Province*, 7 April 1914.
35 CVA, Van. City, Council Minutes, Vol. 20, 23 March 1914, 107.
36 *Sun*, 16 March 1916; *Province*, 16 March 1916. See also *Chinese Times*, 28 March, 14 April, 22 June 1916.
37 Lin Shih-Yuan to board of licence commissioners, 13 April 1915, Consul-General for China Letterbook, 1914–15, copy in Special Collections Division, University of British Columbia Library.
38 *World*, 24 June 1916.
39 *Province*, 16 September 1908.
40 Ibid., 16 October 1913.
41 *Colonist*, 10 February 1915.
42 Cited in *Chinese Times*, 26 May 1915.
43 Ibid., 13 August 1918. A month later, the dominion government began its wartime campaign against organizations considered subversive and dissolved a number of labour groups and connected associations in Vancouver's Chinatown; *Chinese Times*, 12 October, 4, 15 November 1918; *Colonist*, 12 March 1919. Chinese shingle workers were particularly well organized, and, in March 1919, 1,000 went on strike to protest a reduction in their salaries and to negotiate a shorter working day; see *Chinese Times*, 7 March, 9 April, 27 May, 14 June, 27 October 1919.
44 Koliang Yih to Finance Committee, 13 December 1918, CVA, Van. City, In Corresp., Vol. 69.
45 Cited in *Chinese Times*, 18 January 1919.
46 Yang Shu Wen to Mayor, 24 April 1919, CVA, Van. City, In Corresp., Vol. 74, C File.
47 See references to the homeworker lobby in *Chinese Times*, 3, 20 December 1919. The reference to the 1920 petition is taken from a caption in the photographic exhibition "Saltwater City: The Chinese in Vancouver, 1886–1986," Chinese Cultural Centre, Vancouver, October 1986.
48 *Chinese Times*, 30 January 1920. The number of pedlars for 1923 is cited in the speech of BC member Mr A. Neill, *DHC*, 16 April 1923, 1,900.
49 *Province*, 9 March 1914.
50 Koliang Yih to Mayor, 23 January 1919, cited in CVA, Van. City, In Corresp., Vol. 74, C File.
51 Ibid.
52 *Province*, 8 February 1919.
53 Ibid., 20 February 1919.
54 CVA, Van. City, Outgoing Corresp., Vol. 29, 1910, 501.

55 Wickberg et al., *From China to Canada*, 95; figure included 210 families.
56 CVA, Van. City, Council Minutes, Vol. 22, 8 March 1919, 413.
57 *Province,* 8 February 1919.
58 *World*, 25 October 1921.
59 Koliang Yih to Council, 28 February 1919, CVA, Van. City, In Corresp., Vol. 74, C File.
60 CVA, Van. City, Council Minutes, Vol. 22, 8 March 1919, 414.
61 Williams to Clerk, 1 May 1923, CVA, Van. City, In Corresp., Vol. 95, Solicitor's File.
62 A US Supreme Court decision of 1917 put an end to legalized residential discrimination in American cities. In that year, the court declared a Louisville residential segregation law unconstitutional on the grounds that it denied an owner the legal right to dispose of his own real estate in the manner of his choosing. Fredrickson, *White Supremacy*, 254.
63 See the discussion of Point Grey in chapter 5; on the University Endowment Lands, see *Sun*, 12 June 1954. The Capilano Highlands and British Properties barred people of African and Asian descent from living there except as servants, by the same clause that excluded people from keeping swine, sheep, poultry, and other animals; *Sun*, 5 March 1951; *News Herald*, 5 July 1941.

The operation of an "iron curtain" in Shaughnessy, Kerrisdale, the British Properties, and Capilano Highlands was exposed in 1956, when a Jewish person took his exclusion from property ownership in one of the areas to the Supreme Court of Canada. See Kloppenborg, ed., *Vancouver's First Century*, 139.

A covenant in the estate of Joseph Martin in the Hastings Townsite read as follows: "No Asiatic, Negro or Indian should have the right or be allowed to own, become tenant of, or occupy the said land ... and that all of said land, whether sold at public auction or private sale, should be subject to said condition"; Corporation Counsel to Wilson re restrictive covenants, 19 July 1939, Halford Wilson Papers, Provincial Archives of British Columbia (hereafter PABC), Catalogue No. E/D W69, Vol. 1/19.

It is known that Orientals were excluded by a clause in the title of a property in the vicinity of Kamloops and Nanaimo streets from the late 1920s (personal communication with new owner, 1986). Unfortunately, it is impossible to assess how systematic this process was across the city. A gentlemen's agreement existed in a section of the Mount Pleasant Subdivision that excluded Orientals; Petition to CPR re sale of property in the Little Mountain Area to a Chinese, 28 January 1940, Halford Wilson Papers, Vol. 2/27 (Wilson lived at 650 West 30th Avenue).

Whether other such agreements were entered into with the CPR, a large landholder in the city, is unknown.

64 Koliang Yih to Mayor, 24 January 1919, CVA, Van. City, In Corresp., Vol. 74, C File.

65 *Chinese Times*, 26 February 1921. In 1918, when two Chinese tried to enter law school in Vancouver, the law students' association prohibited their registration. *Chinese Times*, 19 January 1918, 30 October 1920; *Sun*, 3 March 1951.

66 *Chinese Times*, 8 January 1921; *Colonist*, 8 October 1922; *Chinese Times*, 20 October 1922. In Vancouver, in 1921, 434 of the city's 18,035 elementary school children were of Chinese origin. Most of the agitation for school segregation in the early 1920s took place in Victoria. See P. Ward, *White Canada Forever*, 127–8.

67 *Province*, 5 June 1922.

68 Jolliffe to Scott, 7 February 1922, National Archives of Canada (hereafter NAC), Immigration Branch, RG 76, Vol. 121, File 23,635, Part 5, copy in Box 28, Chinese-Canadian Project.

69 Related to House of Commons by Mr W. McQuarrie, *DHC*, 8 May 1922, 1,514.

70 *Sun*, 5 October 1921. Odd copies of the publication are kept in the Special Collections Division, University of British Columbia Library.

71 Anon., *British Columbia Monthly*, Vol. 17, February 1921, 8.

72 *Chinese Times*, 28 March 1919; CVA, Van. City, Council Minutes, 19 May 1919, 488.

73 CVA, Van. City, Council Minutes, 7 April 1919, 435; *Chinese Times*, 24 January 1920.

74 *Chinese Times*, 4, 8 March, 5 April 1921.

75 CVA, Van. City, Council Minutes, Vol. 23, 24 April 1922, 467; *Chinese Times*, 12 July 1922; *World*, 6 February 1922.

76 *Chinese Times*, 28 March 1921.

77 Ibid., 13 February 1922.

78 Ibid., 27, 31 March, 5, 9 April 1920.

79 *Sun*, 14 April 1921.

80 *World*, 16 January 1922.

81 *Chinese Times*, 15 April 1922.

82 *Sun*, 24 March 1920.

83 See also *The Black Candle*, written by Judge Emily Murphy. It was first published in 1922 after being serialized in *Maclean's* magazine. The book highlighted Chinese involvement in the trafficking of narcotics and is known to have had an impact on legislative changes regarding the drug trade. For a discussion of the book's influence, see Palmer, *Patterns of Prejudice*, 84–5.

84 *DHC*, 26 April 1921, 2,598.

85 Ibid., 8 May 1922, 1,529.

86 Ibid., 1,536.

87 Canada, *Statutes*, 12–13 George V, 1922, chap. 35.

88 Scott to McArthur, December 3, 1913, NAC, Immigration Branch, RG 76, Vol. 121, File 23,635, Part 3, copy in Box 28, Chinese-Canadian Project.

89 Canada, *Sessional Papers*, 1910, No.10, Department of Trade and Commerce, Statement showing transactions under the Chinese Immigration Act to 31 March 1909, 12.

90 Cited in Andracki, *Immigration*, 151–2.

91 Canada, *Statutes*, Edward VII, 1908, chap. 14. See also *DHC*, 22 June 1908, 11,020.

92 Canada, *Sessional Papers*, 1913, No. 207, "Report of [Madam] Justice Murphy, Royal Commission Appointed to Investigate Alleged Chinese Frauds and Opium Smuggling on the Pacific Coast, 1910–11."

93 Scott to Cory, 24 April 1913, 70, Canada, *Sessional Papers*, 1914, No. 25, Department of Interior.

94 See, *DHC*, 2 March 1914, 1,220.

95 Canada, *Sessional Papers*, 1917, No. 25, Department of Interior, "Report on Chinese Immigration," 70.

96 In 1909, for example, the railway entrepreneur Charles Hays asked Prime Minister Laurier for a more liberal immigration policy for Chinese labour. However, the race question was a critical political issue for Laurier. In the 1908 dominion election, his Liberals had lost five of their seven BC seats. Laurier's stand reveals these concerns: "The condition of things in British Columbia is now such that riots are to be feared if Oriental labour were to be brought in. You remember that in our last conversation upon this subject I told you that if the matter could be arranged so that you have an absolute consensus of [Premier] McBride, that dangers would probably be averted, but with the local government in active sympathy with the agitators, the peace of the province would be really in danger and that consideration is paramount to me." Cited in Avery, "Canadian Immigration Policy," 53–4. In 1917, Scott wrote to the Trades and Labour Council of Ontario: "The Government has been strongly urged to rescind the orders-in-council by large employers of labour, so as to permit a large number of Chinese arrivals. So far, their requests have been refused." NAC, RG 76, Vol. 121, File 23,636, Part 3, 21 August 1917, copy in Box 28, Chinese-Canadian Project.

97 The commissioner for Canada in London, England, suggested that when the war is over "we can greatly increase our propagandist efforts ... to the advantage of Canada"; Canada, *Sessional Papers*, 1919, No. 18, Department of Immigration and Colonization, "Report of the Commissioner of Immigration for Canada, London, England," 21. See also *Col-*

onist, 29 November 1922; *DHC*, 19 March 1923, 1,287. In an effort to settle the tracts of land in western Canada, Ottawa offered incentives to white homesteads; *Province*, 27 April 1921.

98 In a speech to the Local Council of Women in Vancouver in 1917, an election year, Stevens described Oriental immigration as "an unmitigated curse, and foul from the bottom up"; *Province*, 14 April 1917. In a campaign speech to the Vancouver branch of the Retail Merchants' Association in 1921, he stated: "History holds many examples where large bodies of Occidentals have been swallowed up by Orientals"; ibid., 31 October 1921. See also ibid., 24 February, 15 November 1922.

99 *DHC*, 2 March 1914, 1,242.

100 Ibid., 2 March 1914, 1,220–1.

101 Ibid., 8 June 1917, 2,149.

102 Scott to Cory, 17 February 1919, NAC, RG 76, File 23,635, Part 4, copy in Box 28, Chinese-Canadian Project.

103 Canada, *Statutes*, 11–12 George V, 1921, chap. 21. See also *DHC*, 11 May 1921, 3,207–8, 3,827–9.

104 Jolliffe to Scott, 7 February 1922, NAC, RG 76, File 23,635, Part 5, copy in Box 28, Chinese-Canadian Project.

105 D. Lai, *Chinatowns*, 61.

106 Andracki, *Immigration of Orientals*, 131. For more on the attitudinal climate of the time, see Nelson, "Shall We Bar the Yellow Race?"

107 *DHC*, 8 May 1922, 1,509.

108 Ibid., 1,516.

109 Ibid., 1,518, 1,522, 1,524, 1,529.

110 Ibid., 1,554.

111 Ibid., 1,521, 1,527.

112 Ibid., 1,559.

113 Ibid., 1,577.

114 Wickberg et al., *From China to Canada*, 141.

115 Ibid., 142–5.

116 Canada, *Statutes*, 13–14 George V, 1,923, chap. 38.

117 On the anxiety that registration caused Chinese, especially those who had entered Canada to build the railway and were not issued entry certificates, see *Chinese Times*, 28 March, 14, 23 June 1924, 13 January 1925.

118 *DHC*, 30 April 1923, 2,315.

119 Ibid., 4 May 1923, 2,485.

120 Ibid., 8 May 1922, 1,536.

121 *Province*, 28 February 1938.

122 Wickberg et al., *From China to Canada*, 149.

123 Cited in *Chinese Times*, 11 October 1924.

124 The murder led to a prolonged discussion in the provincial legislature about a bill that would exclude white women from working in homes where Chinese were employed. See *Province*, 13, 28 November, 5 December 1924. Eventually, having made considerable political capital out of the issue, Manson suggested that the bill would be ultra vires and dropped the matter. In the mean time, the press relished in Manson's supervision of a morbid post mortem on Smith's body undertaken to search for incriminating evidence against the "China-boy." See ibid., 19 November 1925.

125 Ibid., 25 February 1927. Manson continued: "It is well established that the Eurasian is a very unsatisfactory product in that in nearly every case he absorbs the weaknesses of both races without acquiring the virtues of either race."

126 *Chinese Times*, 31 October 1927.

127 Ibid., 12 March 1927.

128 Cited in W. H. Malkin Papers, CVA, Add. MS 237. *Colonist*, 12 October 1928. A Vancouver lawyer inflamed the issue of Chinese diffusion with a campaign in the press about the "extending tentacles" of Pender Street East. See for example *Province*, 17 July 1927. Malkin carried out his election promise with an investigation of Oriental trading in the city. His government also gave consideration to a Provincial Trades License Bill that would extend enabling power to an independent board to deny licences in the "public interest." Council's determination to restrict the licensing of Orientals, however, did not extend to relinquishing its own power over city-wide licensing, and council voted against using the power. Counsel McCrossan to Malkin, 16 November 1928, CVA, Van. City, In Corresp., Vol. 126, L File.

129 *Province*, 4 May 1931; *Sun*, 10 March 1931.

130 Andracki, *Immigration of Orientals*, 213–4.

131 CVA, Van. City, In Corresp., Vol. 154, 1932, Petitions File.

132 Cited in Hillaby, "Report on Chinese Relief," ibid., Vol. 193, 1935, Medical Health Officer File.

133 Ibid., 3.

134 CVA, Van. City, In Corresp., Vol. 198, 1935, Unemployed Organizations File.

135 Bone to Smith, 29 June 1936, ibid., Vol. 207, 1,936, Relief Officer File, April-June.

136 In 1934, a few hundred elderly and destitute Chinese from British Columbia were returned to China by the provincial government. See *Province*, 28 December 1934, 3 May 1935.

137 Provincial Worker's Council on Unemployment to City Clerk, 22 February 1935, CVA, Van. City, In Corresp., Vol. 198, 1935, Unemployed Organizations File.

CHAPTER FIVE

1 CVA, Van. City, In Corresp., Vol. 198, 1935, Unemployed Organizations File. The Provincial Workers' Council on Unemployment charged that "the insufficient and low-grade food breaks down the resistance of the Chinese ... Since the soup kitchen has been started many Chinese workers who have been forced to eat there have died."

2 The term "category legislation" is borrowed from Reeves, *British Racial Discourse*, 7.

3 Rex, "Racism," 198. Rex would of course accept that race is problematic.

4 Husband, *"Race" in Britain*, 11–23.

5 C. Ma, *Chinese Pioneers*, 56.

6 These figures were used by Mun Hope of Victoria in a letter to the editor in 1935 to correct the use of "inflated, misleading statistics flung around as vote-catching ammunition" by those opposed to Oriental enfranchisement; *Colonist*, 8 October 1935.

7 *Province*, 22 January 1938.

8 Ibid., 15 October 1941.

9 See figures in Halford Wilson Papers, PABC, Vol. 1/19. Re: Trade and Licensing, 1939.

10 Yip, *Vancouver's Chinatown*, 9.

11 Canada, Dominion Bureau of Statistics, Census of Canada, 1931: "Orientals, 10 years of Age and Over, Gainfully Employed by Race, Occupation and Sex, in the Province of British Columbia," Ottawa, 1934, copy in CVA, Pamphlet 1931–12.

12 British Columbia, "Report," 17. The drop in employment in the lumber industry was also caused partly by the Depression, when the value of timber production plummeted. See Robin, *The Rush for Spoils*, 235. A news report in 1927 stated that minimum wage legislation had been introduced in December 1926 "with a view to the elimination of Orientals from the lumber industry"; *Colonist*, 1 February 1927.

13 See Kwong, *Chinatown*.

14 Robin, *The Rush for Spoils*, chap. 9.

15 Ireland, "Canadian Trade Unionism," 19.

16 *Chinese Times*, 10, 14 June 1919.

17 Loat to Mayor, minutes of meeting held 27 November 1929, 5, CVA, Van. City, In Corresp., Vol. 126, L File, 1929.

18 *Province*, 29 August, 1931; *Colonist*, 27, 29 August 1931.

19 *Sun*, 12 October 1935.

20 Angus, "Asiatics in Canada," "The Legal Status," and "Underprivileged Canadians."

21 The Chicago school of sociologists, for example, began to argue that the attitudes and conduct of the host society were obstacles to the assimi-

lation of blacks and certain immigrants. See the collection of Robert Park's essays, *Race and Culture*. In a chapter on racial prejudice first published in 1928, Park wrote (pp. 237–8): "The fact seems to be that what we ordinarily regard as instinctive and biologically determined in our behaviour and attitudes toward people and races other than our own is merely, in the first instance at least, the spontaneous response to what is strange and unfamiliar."

22 Angus, "Contribution." 23–33. Angus lobbied his cause to many Vancouver groups, including the board of trade; *Province*, 13 November 1934; *Sun*, 10 February 1937. He advocated enfranchisement among workers as a policy of "self interest," arguing that discrimination was counterproductive because it promoted occupational segregation; *Sun*, 20 November 1934.

23 *DHC*, 22 June 1934, 4,207; *Sun*, 14 December 1934. For a discussion of Woodsworth's political vision, see MacInnis, *J.S. Woodsworth*.

24 *Colonist*, 27 November 1934. See also Winch's letters to the editor, *Sun*, 8 October 1935, 23 July 1936; *Colonist*, 13 October 1935, 21 August 1936, 2 July 1937.

25 *DHC*, 20 February 1936, 373.

26 *Province*, 1 December 1929.

27 *Colonist*, 2 March 1932.

28 See for example *Province*, 13 November 1934; *Colonist*, 12 October 1935.

29 *Province*, 1 September 1934.

30 Ibid., 14 May 1936. See letters to *Sun*, 19, 25 July 1936, 7 September 1937.

31 *Sun*, 14 December 1914.

32 *Province*, 11 October 1929. See Dawson, *The Chinese Chameleon*, chap. 2, on the romantic view of China held by early European travellers; chapter 6 discusses the aesthetic appeal of Chinese civilization.

33 CVA, Van. City, Council Minutes, Vol. 37, 11 May 1936, 265; *Chinese Times*, 26 February 1936.

34 Yip, *Vancouver's Chinatown*, 6.

35 See Light, "From Vice District to Tourist Attraction"; also Salter, "Urban Imagery," 17, which reproduces a resolution of the Chinese Chamber of Commerce issued through the *Los Angeles Times* (25 January 1924) to help dispel derogatory images of Chinatown and promote tourism.

36 *Sun*, 11, 20 July 1936.

37 Ibid., 13 July 1936.

38 *Province*, 18 July 1936.

39 *Sun*, 20 July 1936.

40 Ibid., 2 August 1936.

41 CVA, Van. City, Special Committee Files, No. 1, Vancouver Golden Jubilee Committee, Report of the Managing Board, 1936.

42 *Sun*, 18 July 1936.

43 Ibid., 13 July 1936. At the time, the city of Vancouver was more generally beginning to recognize its tourist potential, and in the late 1930s council extended its market, exhibition, and industries committee to include tourist development.

44 Ibid., 16 April 1938. An undated news report in the Foon Sien papers states that the CBA provided McDevitt with the first "passport" to conduct tours of Chinatown; Foon Sien (Wong Mun-po) Personal Papers and Newspaper Clippings, Special Collections Division, University of British Columbia Library, Box 3. Concerning the Grayline sightseeing arrangements, see Superintendent B.C. Motor Transportation Limited to Mr Y. Leong, 31 March 1938, Halford Wilson Papers, PABC.

45 Gilmour, "What, No Opium Dens?" 30.

46 *Province*, 6 July 1940.

47 CVA, Van. City, In Corresp., Vol. 126, L File, Minutes of meeting of White Canada Association held 16 December 1929. See also *Province*, 27 November 1929; *Sun*, 20 February 1930; *Province*, 11 January 1931; *Colonist*, 25 February 1931; *Province*, 29 July 1939.

48 *Colonist*, 29 November 1929.

49 For the protests, see Yang Shu Wen to Mayor, 24 April 1919, CVA, Van. City, In Corresp., Vol. 74, C File; PABC, Premier's Correspondence, 1919–27, File 75, in Box 8, Chinese-Canadian Project. See British Columbia, *Statutes*, 1923, 14 George V, chap. 76.

50 Jordan, *White over Black*, chap. 4; Fredrickson, *White Supremacy*, 99–108.

51 *Province*, 23 December 1931.

52 CVA, Van. City, Council Minutes, Vol. 36, 9 October 1935, 576; 28 October 1935, 614, 640.

53 Foster to W. King, Dep. Minister of Trade and Industry, Edmonton, 18 July 1938, CVA, Van. City, Mayor's Correspondence, Vol. 37.

54 Ibid.

55 Foster to Mayor Miller, 3 September 1937, CVA, Van. City, Mayor's Correspondence, Vol. 26. On the Restaurant Bylaw amendment, see Council Minutes, Vol. 37, 26 January 1937.

56 Ibid.

57 Foster to Mayor Miller, 5 February 1937, ibid.

58 Foster to Mayor Miller, 3 September 1937, ibid.

59 *Chinese Times*, 8 February 1937.

60 CVA, Van. City, Mayor's Correspondence, Vol. 26, Minutes of meeting held 9 April 1937 re white waitresses employed in Chinese restaurants.

61 Murphy to Mayor Miller, 6 May 1937, ibid.

62 Foster to Mayor Miller, 6 March 1937, ibid. In the letter, Foster requested the co-operation of the Licence Department, asking that it "make an example" through cancelling the licence of one of the cafés that was acting in defiance of the "agreement." Miller replied, assuring Foster that

he had contacted the licence inspector, "asking him to take the necessary action." Mayor Miller to Foster, 9 March 1937, ibid.

63 Orr to Foster, 7 September 1937, ibid.
64 *Sun*, 14 September 1937.
65 Ibid., 16 September 1937.
66 Ibid., 16, 17, 18, 22 September 1937.
67 *Sun*, 16 August 1938.
68 Ibid., 18 September 1937.
69 Ibid., 17 September 1937.
70 Ibid.
71 CVA, Van. City, Council Minutes, Vol. 38, 27 September 1937, 422.
72 Murphy to Orr, 29 September 1937, CVA, Mayor's Correspondence, Vol. 26.
73 *Province*, 12 October 1937.
74 Ibid.
75 CVA, Van. City, Council Minutes , Vol. 39, 12 September 1938, 303.
76 CVA, Van. City, Council Minutes, Vol. 39, 15 March 1939.
77 *Sun*, 17 August 1938.
78 Brook, "Chinese-Canadians in the Depression," 2, in Box 8, Chinese-Canadian Project.
79 *Province*, 10 September 1936; *Sun*, 20 July 1937, 8 February 1938.
80 *Chinese Times*, 9 February 1936.
81 Ibid., 10 July 1937.
82 CVA, Special Committee Files, Restaurant conditions, 1939.
83 CVA, Van. City, Council Minutes, 16 May 1935, 250.
84 Ibid., Vol. 37, 29 June 1936, 412.
85 Ibid., Vol. 38, 28 February 1938, 725.
86 Ibid., Vol. 39, 30 May 1938, 86.
87 R. Barton to Wilson, 29 August 1940, Halford Wilson Papers, PABC.
88 R. Barton to Wilson, 1 October 1940, ibid.
89 *Province*, 7 September 1938.
90 CVA, Van. City, Council Minutes, Vol. 39, 19 September 1938, 340.
91 *Province*, 18 October 1938.
92 *Sun*, 23 November 1938.
93 CVA, Van. City, Council Minutes, Vol. 39, 1 May 1939, 156.
94 Ibid., Vol. 42, 16 December 1940, 95, Report of Special Committees.
95 *Province*, 27 April 1939.
96 CVA, Van. City, Council Minutes, Vol. 44, 13 October 1942, 465.
97 *Province*, 2 March 1937.
98 Ibid., 3 November 1936. See also *Colonist*, 3 November 1936.
99 *Province*, 24 October 1936.
100 Ibid., 13 March 1937.
101 Ibid., 4 February 1941.

102 *Chinese Times*, 10 August 1938.
103 CVA, Van. City, Council Minutes, Vol. 41, 27 May 1940, 369; see correspondence from these organizations in Special Committee Files, No. 12, 1940, Legislation.
104 *Province*, 4 February 1941.
105 MacGill, "The Oriental Delinquent," 433.
106 *Sun*, 4 February 1941. CVA, Special Committee Files, 1941, "Oriental Penetration into Better Class Residential Districts."
107 *Province*, 4 February 1941.
108 Ibid., 5 February 1941.
109 *Sun*, 4 February 1941.
110 Personal communication from Ann Broadfoot, Vancouver Real Estate Board.
111 *News Herald*, 4 February 1941.
112 *Province*, 7 November 1940.
113 Ibid., 2 July 1943, 18 October 1944, 16 March 1945.
114 Ibid., 27, 29 August 1940. Attorney-General Wismer said: "The object of the order-in-council is to disarm our enemies no matter what their nationality, and also to preserve law and order. Under the latter head, it has been thought desirable to refuse registration of guns to Japanese and Chinese."
115 Ibid., 2 October 1940.
116 See Roy, "The Soldiers." In November 1944, 132 males of Chinese origin were called up in Vancouver; *Province*, 1 November 1944.
117 CVA, Van. City, Council Minutes, Vol. 41, 24 September 1940, 713.
118 *Province*, 12 December 1941.
119 *Chinese Times*, 25 June 1941.
120 CVA, Mayor's Correspondence, Vol. 56, 1943, Chinese relief. Later, Cornett was presented with a miniature Chinese dragon by the consul-general for China as a symbol of friendship between Canada and China; *Sun*, 8 September 1945.
121 *Province*, 23 November 1943.
122 *Sun*, 8 November, 1945. CCF parks board commissioner Mr A. Webster challenged the city to "reconcile an act of racial discrimination on the part of a public body in Vancouver with the principles of Canadian democracy in defence of which we are engaged in the present war"; *Sun*, 10 April 1943.
123 Ibid., 16 February 1938.
124 On this issue, see *Chinese Times*, 6, 7, 8, 15 July 1943; *Sun*, 6, 8 July 1943; *Province*, 2 August 1943.
125 Ireland, "Canadian Trade Unionism," 26.
126 *Sun*, 25 May 1955.
127 Hurd, *Racial Origins*, 568–71.

128 See draft articles for inclusion in a treaty between Canada and China concerning commerce and navigation, NAC, RG 76, Immigration Branch, Vol. 122, File 23,636, Part 6, copy in Box 28, Chinese-Canadian Project. On events leading to repeal of the Chinese Immigration Act, see McEnvoy, "Symbol."

129 Memorandum for Mr Robertson, 17 November 1942, NAC, RG 76, Vol. 122, File 23,636, Part 6, copy in Box 28, Chinese-Canadian Project.

130 Ibid., Part 6, Minutes of meeting held re Chinese immigration, 6 December 1943; ibid., Part 7, Keenleyside memorandum for file re Chinese immigration.

131 Ibid., Part 7, Minutes of a meeting held in the office of the Deputy Minister of Mines and Resources, 2 May 1947.

132 Ibid., document titled "Possible Numbers as a Result of the Repeal of the Chinese Immigration Act, and Prospects for Actual Arrivals."

133 Cited in speech of David Croll, member for Spadina, DHC, 11 February 1947, 324–5.

134 See DHC, 5 May 1947, 2,779–95.

135 Andracki, Immigration of Orientals, 208.

136 DHC, 11 February 1947, 321.

137 Gibbon, The Canadian Mosaic. Gibbon's was a study of the "history and folkways" of Canada's "European racial groupings." Each chapter discusses a different "race" and includes a sketch of the face and the dress of "the Welsh-Canadian type," "the Norwegian-Canadian type," the "Ukrainian-Canadian type," and so on.

138 DHC, 11 February 1947, 321. See also the speeches of Mr M.J. Coldwell, Mr D. Ross, and Mr B. McKay.

139 Andracki, Immigration of Orientals, 211.

140 Chinese Times, 3 August 1948, 9 August 1949.

141 Sun, 1 May 1943.

142 DHC, 4 February 1947, 114.

143 Cited in Stepan, The Idea of Race, 140.

144 Light, "From Vice District to Tourist Attraction," 391.

145 Sun, 10 January 1947.

146 Ibid., 1 May 1943.

CHAPTER SIX

1 Two Canadian sociologists state: "It was not until very recently, with the emergence of Pan-Indian or Canadian Indian consciousness, that the various peoples categorized as Indians by outsiders began to believe themselves to be of common ancestry and to categorize themselves as ethnically alike on the basis of that belief"; Hughes and Kallen, The Anatomy of Racism, 87. Prager argues a similar case for the United States,

where the "manipulation of cultural symbols of blackness" by blacks is widespread; Prager, "American Racial Ideology," 109. See also Berger, *Invitation to Sociology*, 157.

2 In the Canadian literature, a number of collections have focused on the cultural aspects of ethnic communities, to the neglect of economic, political, and historical processes that also shape forms of ethnic identification. See for example Migus, ed., *Sounds Canadian*. Some of the monographs in the Generations series commissioned by the Department of Secretary of State have tended to characterize ethnic communities as standard-bearers of an ancestral culture. See for example Abdu-Laban, *An Olive Branch*, which explains the economic success of Arabs in Canada in terms of the "Levantine ethic." For the American context, see for example Greeley, *Ethnicity*. One collection that has attempted to demystify ethnic affiliation is Dahlie and Fernando, eds., *Ethnicity*. See also note 28 to chapter 1.

3 Cited in Hawkins, *Canada and Immigration*, 84.

4 *DHC*, 22 February 1950, 138. Cold War psychology permeated the House of Commons through the early 1950s. See also 23 June 1950, 4,048; 6 February 1951, 123; and 3 February 1953, 1,567.

5 See King in *DHC*, 6 May 1947, 2,644–7. The speech is typical of King – cautious and indicative of "a dislike of the world beyond the North Atlantic Triangle"; Hawkins, *Canada and Immigration*, 91.

6 Hawkins continues: "Its [Asia's] north-west frontier ran along the southern border of the Soviet Union and the Black Sea and round the eastern and southern coasts of the Mediterranean. All Turkey and lands to the south, including Egypt, were in Asia. Only the Armenians managed to slip out of the Asian net." By 1956, "Asia" had been adjusted to exclude Turkey, Egypt, and Israel. Hawkins, *Canada and Immigration*, 94.

7 *DHC*, 24 April 1953, 4,337–8.

8 Ibid., 6 May 1955, 3,545.

9 Ibid., 8 August 1956, 7,219.

10 Ibid., 9 June 1960, 4,712.

11 For a summary of the requests Foon Sien took to Ottawa between 1950 and 1955, see Francis, "Wong Foon Sien." By 1961, he had made twelve trips to Ottawa on immigration matters. See *Chinatown News*, 9 no. 5, 3 November 1961.

12 *DHC*, 28 June 1951, 4,853, and 5 April 1957, 3,134–5.

13 Referred to in ibid., 30 January 1958, 4,061.

14 Following a court case that went against the government in 1956, the wording of the regulations was changed to exclude direct reference to "Asians." Instead, a geographic principle was used that allowed Pickersgill to boast: "People are no longer penalized because of their race"; *DHC*,

9 June 1960, 4,713. The new principle can be seen from the wording of the 1956 order-in-council. According to that regulation, a person who was a citizen of a country other than the United Kingdom, Australia, New Zealand, South Africa, Ireland, France, the United States, all countries of continental Europe, Egypt, Israel, Lebanon, Turkey, and countries in Central and South America could enter Canada if he/she were related to a Canadian citizen – as the husband, wife, or unmarried child under twenty-one years old; as the father, where he was over sixty-five; or as the mother, where she was over sixty. Canada, *Gazette* Part II, Vol. 90. SOR/ 56–180, copy in Box 8, Chinese-Canadian Project.

15 *DHC*, 2 June 1952, 3,079.

16 Ibid., 24 April 1953, 465.

17 Ibid., 15 February 1955, 1,188.

18 Ibid., 26 June 1954, 6,811.

19 Ibid., 17 February 1955, 1,290.

20 Ibid., 1,271.

21 Ibid., 1,290.

22 Ibid., 3 February 1953, 1,567.

23 Ibid., 2 August 1958, 4,027; see also 5 March 1959, 1,645.

24 Ibid., 22 April 1959, 2,937.

25 Between 1956 and 1958, 35,000 Hungarian refugees entered Canada; Hawkins, *Canada and Immigration*, 114.

26 *DHC*, 14 August 1964, 6,829.

27 Ibid., 16 June 1960, 5,001.

28 Cited in *Globe and Mail*, 23 June 1960, copy in Box 13, Chinese-Canadian Project.

29 *Sun*, 15 July 1961; *Chinatown News*, 8 no. 22, 3 August 1961.

30 Phillips, "The Criminal Society," 11.

31 In 1960, an Act for the Recognition and Protection of Human Rights and Fundamental Freedoms was passed by the House of Commons that enshrined the "right of individuals to protection of the law without discrimination by reason of race, national origin, religion or sex." See discussion in Kallen, *Ethnicity*, chap. 2.

32 See for example *DHC*, 14 December 1963, 5,885; 23 June 1964, 4,607–9. See also Chinese Canadian Citizen's Association, "A Brief Concerning Immigration Laws," Presented to Hon. J. Nicholson, March 1965, copy in Box 32, Chinese-Canadian Project.

33 *DHC*, 11 January 1955, 84.

34 Ibid., 24 April 1953, 4,390.

35 Statement of Minister of Resources and Development, *DHC*, 21 January 1954, 1,318.

36 Hardwick, *Vancouver*, 86.

37 L. Marsh, *Rebuilding*, 3, 7, 9.
38 See Ward's discussion of pseudo-scientific medical analogies like Commissioner Chapleau's "ulcer" that have been used at various periods, including in recent debates, to make sense of the experiences of inner-city, migrant communities in the United States. D. Ward, *Poverty*.
39 City of Vancouver, *Downtown Vancouver*, 26.
40 City of Vancouver, *Vancouver Redevelopment Study*, 2.
41 Ibid., 111.
42 *DHC*, 18 December 1957, 2,538.
43 L. Marsh, *Rebuilding*, viii and 65; Hardwick, *Vancouver*, 115. The "racial" bias of urban renewal projects in Canada is also highlighted by Clairmont and Magill, *Africville*. In American cities, the term "slum" had "distinctly racist overtones" during the period of urban renewal. See Mollenkopf, "Post-war Politics," 256.
44 *Province*, 6 April 1959. City of Vancouver, *Vancouver Redevelopment Study*, 49.
45 CVA, Van. City, Council Minutes, Vol. 68, 4 February 1958, 113. The fate of Canadian Chinatowns is discussed in Sien Lok Society of Calgary, *Proceedings*. The encroachments on Montreal's Chinatown are discussed by Louder, "Montreal's Downtown," 32–9. The Sien Lok *Proceedings* reported (p. 37) that US Chinatowns had decreased from twenty-eight in 1940 to fewer than sixteen in 1969; some had stagnated through lack of immigration, while others were destroyed by renewal projects. On the effects of core expansion on San Francisco's Chinatown, see Hartmann, *Yerba Buena*; on Boston's, see *Chinatown News*, 12 no. 8, 18 December 1964; Seattle's is now the site of a domed stadium.
46 *Sun*, 2 December 1967. S. Chan, "Overview."
47 H. Lai, "Integration," 83–4. On Chinese resistance to the Strathcona plan, see Kim and N. Lai, "Chinese Community Resistance."
48 City of Vancouver, Technical Planning Board, *Redevelopment*, 9.
49 Foon Sien (Wong Mun-po), Personal Papers and Newspaper Clippings, Special Collections Division, University of British Columbia Library, Box 3, CBC interview with Foon Sien, 1956. In 1951, a couple of Chinese origin was declined entry to a city-owned suite in the West End; *New Citizen*, 24 April 1951. In 1958, a Chinese family was denied an apartment in the West End; *Sun*, 12 December 1958. In 1962, the Vancouver Real Estate Board still honoured article 32 of its code of ethics which read: "A member should never be instrumental in introducing into a neighbourhood, a character, or occupancy or any individual whose presence will clearly be detrimental to property values in that neighbourhood"; *Sun*, 24 February 1962. By 1967, Foon Sien claimed that resistance to Chinese home purchases had passed in all but "one or two areas"; *Province*, 27 May 1967.

50 *Province*, 6 April 1959.
51 CVA, Van. City, Council Minutes, Vol. 73, 10 March 1960, 144.
52 *Province*, 15 September 1960.
53 Ibid., 26 September 1960.
54 *Sun*, 6 April 1959.
55 *Beautiful B.C. Magazine*, 3 no. 2 (1961), 27–33. See also *Sun*, 30 May 1962, for a similar feature on Chinatown's "exotic flavour."
56 *Chinatown News*, 7 no. 7, 3 December 1959.
57 Ibid., 8 no. 4, 18 October 1960.
58 Brief of the CTPOA submitted to the Hon. J. Clyne, Royal Commission on Expropriation Laws and Procedures, 17 July 1961, copy in Box 11, Chinese-Canadian Project.
59 *Province*, 7 August 1961.
60 *Chinatown News*, 8 no. 8, 18 December 1960.
61 CVA, Van. City, Council Minutes, Vol. 74, 4 October 1960, 675.
62 *Chinatown News*, 8 no. 11, 18 February 1961.
63 Numbers to be displaced are reported in *Sun*, 19 January 1963. Stage 2 also included area 5, north of Hastings Street, outside Strathcona.
64 The responses of the Chinese organizations and the counter-responses of Fountain are included in the appendices to City of Vancouver, Technical Planning Board, *Redevelopment Project No. 2*.
65 *Sun*, 19 January 1963.
66 Ibid., 23 January 1963; S. Chan, "Overview," 2; *Chinatown News*, 10 no. 10, 23 February 1963.
67 *Sun*, 31 January 1963.
68 *Province*, 8 February 1963.
69 *Sun*, 27 April 1963.
70 Ibid., 29 April 1963.
71 Cited in *Chinatown News*, 11 no. 21, 18 July 1964; *Province*, 19 June 1964.
72 Minute of Council 23 July 1963, cited in report from Director of Planning, 1964, City of Vancouver, Technical Planning Board, *Redevelopment Project No. 1, Area A-3*, Appendix C.
73 Regional officer to W. Graham, 17 January 1964, in ibid., Appendix H.
74 City of Vancouver, Planning Department, *Chinatown, Vancouver*.
75 CVA, Van. City, Council Minutes, Vol. 83, 24 March 1964, 651–2.
76 *Sun*, 2 May 1964, quotation taken from a board of trade report reprinted in part in *Chinatown News*, 11 no. 18, 3 June 1964.
77 *Province*, 14 November 1964.
78 *Chinatown News*, 11 no. 17, 18 May 1964.
79 *Province*, 24 February 1964.
80 *Sun*, 25 March 1964.
81 Ibid., 27 January 1964.

82 H. Lai, "Integration," 97.

83 Ibid., 98. Figures for stage 1 are taken from S. Wong, "Urban Redevelopment," 258.

84 In the MacLean Park complex, provision existed for only 300 persons, and in 1963 requests were made by many Chinese to the *Chinatown News* for assistance in securing a space; ibid., 10 no. 15, 18 April 1963.

85 *Sun,* 20 January 1966.

86 See Nann, *Urban Renewal.*

87 *Sun,* 15 November 1967.

88 Both quotes are taken from *Province,* 2 December 1967.

89 Details of the background to the Chinatown freeway are taken from Pendakur, *Cities.*

90 Parsons, Brinkerhoff, Quade and Douglas Inc., *Vancouver Transportation Study,* 42.

91 Ibid., 43.

92 Ibid., 49.

93 Ibid., 46.

94 Ibid., 47.

95 Ibid.

96 Pendakur, *Cities,* 60.

97 *Chinatown News,* 15 no. 5, 3 November 1967.

98 Ibid., 14 no. 18, 3 June 1967; *Sun,* 17 May 1967.

99 *Sun,* 10 June 1967.

100 Ibid.

101 Ibid., 13 June 1967.

102 Parsons et al., *Vancouver Transportation Study,* 52.

103 CBA, Brief re proposed freeway through Chinatown, July 1967, copy in CVA, Public Document 788.

104 *Sun,* 18 October 1967.

105 *Province,* 2 December 1967.

106 Ibid.

107 Ibid.

108 *Chinatown News,* 15 no. 5, 3 November 1967.

109 See detailed discussion of these protests in Pendakur, *Cities,* chap. 4.

110 *Sun,* 18 November 1967.

111 Ibid., 18 October 1967.

112 Ibid., 19 October 1967.

113 Ibid., 18 October 1967.

114 Board of trade brief presented at public meeting, December 1967; reprinted in part in *Chinatown News,* 15 no. 8, 18 December 1967.

115 *Province,* 2 December 1967.

116 Pendakur, *Cities,* 73.

117 *Province,* 12 December 1967.

118 *Sun*, 22 November 1968.

119 Ibid., 25 November 1967.

120 Bell and Moore, *Urban Renewal Scheme 3 – Strathcona*, 2.

121 *Sun*, 5 December 1968.

122 Brief to City Council from Strathcona Area Council re Urban Renewal plans for Strathcona area, 22 October 1968, in S. Chan, "Overview," Appendix B.

123 See CVA, Add. MS 734, SPOTA Files.

124 S. Chan, "Overview," 8.

125 Canada, *Report of the Task Force*, 13.

126 Bell, *The Strathcona Rehabilitation Project*, 127. See DHC, 20 January 1968, 4,480, for expenditures. For discussion in the House of Commons on the task force and freeze on spending, see DHC, 25 March, 30 May, 2 June, 11 June, 25 June 1969.

128 Brief to City Council from SPOTA, 27 January 1969, in S. Chan, "Overview," Appendix B; see also *Sun*, 20 January 1969.

129 *Province*, 8 August 1969.

130 *Sun*, 14 August 1969.

131 Details of the Strathcona rehabilitation project are taken from S. Wong, "Urban Redevelopment," 261–8.

132 *Sun*, 3 October 1970.

133 City of Vancouver, Planning Department, *Restoration Report*, 40.

CHAPTER SEVEN

1 Canada, *Report of the Royal Commission on Bilingualism and Biculturalism*, Vol. 4, 3. The phrase "Chinatown re-oriented" is borrowed from the *Sydney Morning Herald*, 16 May 1989.

2 DHC, 21 February 1972, 88.

3 Ibid., 22 June 1973, 5,037.

4 Porter, *The Measure of Canadian Society*, 131.

5 See also ibid., 103–37. A sustained critique of the reification of ancestral culture in American social science is provided by Steinberg, *The Ethnic Myth*.

6 Djao, "Asian Canadians," 91. On this theme as it relates to the experience of European communities in the New World, see R.C. Harris, "Simplification," and Wynn, "Ethnic Migrations." On the subculture that has grown out of the history of subordinate status in Canada for Chinese-origin people, see A. Chan, "Neither French nor British."

7 E. Wong, "Asian American Middleman."

8 Hawkins, *Canada and Immigration*, 55–6.

9 Wickberg, et al., *From China to Canada*, 245. Djao writes ("Asian Canadians," 92) that "the overall cultural background of the Hong Kong immi-

grant is not 'traditional' Chinese. The cultural system of Hong Kong is a mixture of British colonial and Chinese influences."

10 After 1967, statistics were kept not on "ethnic origin" but rather for "country of former residence" and "country of citizenship." It is therefore difficult to assess the number of people of Chinese origin entering Canada.

11 Cited in *Chinatown News*, 19 no. 4, 18 October 1971.

12 Ng, "The Vancouver Chinese Immigrant Community," 75.

13 Cho and Leigh, "Patterns of Residence."

14 Ng, "The Vancouver Chinese Immigrant Community," 76.

15 Wickberg et al., *From China to Canada*, 246, 250.

16 Quotation from a Canadian of Chinese origin when describing the stereotypes about the Chinese in Canada, cited in *Weekend Australian*, 13–14 January 1990.

17 On the firehall issue, see CVA, Add. MS 734, SPOTA files, Vol. 15, file 1; *Chinatown News*, 19 no. 10, 3 February 1972; 20 no. 7, 3 December 1972; 20 no. 8, 18 December 1972; 20 no. 9, 18 January 1973. SPOTA, the Chinatown Lions, the Christ Church of China, and the Shon Yee Association lobbied for the site, and after many delays council approved SPOTA's application. See *Chinatown News*, 20 no. 17, 18 May 1973; 21 no. 14, 3 April 1974; 27 no. 9, 18 January 1980.

18 City Manager's Report to Standing Committee on Planning and Development, 14 April 1976, City of Vancouver, Planning Department, Chinatown Beautification file (hereafter Chinatown Beautification file), B03.C01.

19 For SPOTA, revitalization of residential Chinatown did not end with the rehabilitation project. The non-profit infill housing program was begun in 1973, and the first co-operative project for family living at 730 Union Street was completed in 1975 with financing under the federal government's non-profit housing program. *Chinatown News*, 21 no. 17, 18 May 1974; 22 no. 8, 18 December 1974. Stage 2 involved eight Strathcona locations and was financed under the provincial government's non-profit housing scheme. Ibid., 23 no. 12, 3 March 1976; 23 no. 14, 1976; 23 no. 23, 18 August 1976.

20 H. Fan to Council of City of Vancouver, 4 December 1967, reprinted in City of Vancouver, Technical Planning Board, *Strathcona Sub-Area Report*, Appendix A, 1–2.

21 *Chinatown News*, 16 no. 12, 3 March 1969.

22 Ibid., 24 no. 4, 18 October 1976.

23 Personal communication from Mr B. Marshall, Regional Office of the Secretary of State for Multiculturalism.

24 *DHC*, 12 November 1963, 4,647.

25 Ibid., 20 January 1966, 72.

26 A. Smith, "Metaphor and Nationality," 249.
27 Canada, *Report of the Royal Commission on Bilingualism and Biculturalism,* Vol. 4, 10.
28 Peter, "Myth," 56.
29 *Chinatown News,* 11 no. 13, 18 March 1964.
30 Ibid., 13 no. 14, 3 April 1966.
31 Moodley, "Canadian Multiculturalism."
32 Cited in *Chinatown News,* 15 no. 19, 18 June 1968.
33 Kallen, "Semantics," 23.
34 *DHC,* 8 October 1971, 8,545.
35 In 1977, a study of attitudes commissioned by the federal government revealed the dubious nature of the assumption that respect for others increases directly with respect for one's own heritage. The study demonstrated that the "multicultural assumption" was "clearly not supported." An ethnocentric pattern of attitudes emerged, with "the most positive ingroup attitudes being associated with negative outgroup attitudes." The study also found that those people perceived to be racially distinct were the most negatively evaluated. See Berry, Kalin, and Taylor, *Multiculturalism.*
36 *DHC,* 8 October 1971, 8,546.
37 *Chinatown News,* 26 no. 11, 18 February 1979.
38 *DHC,* 8 October 1971, 8,546.
39 Ibid., 18 February 1972, 38.
40 Ibid., 17 February 1977, 3,145. In the same speech, the member submitted: "Our country has been enriched by the beautiful and noble culture of the first Canadians; by the gaiety and passion of the French Canadians; by the measured dignity of the Anglo-Saxons; by the stern efficiency of the Teutonic races; by the vivid tones of the Celts; by the moving processional of 1,000 years by the Baltic people; by the diligence of the Italian community; by the beauty of the age-old mystique of Asia and Africa; and the grandeur and pathos of the Jewish pilgrims."
41 Ibid., 25 October 1977, 240–1.
42 Ibid., 21 March 1978, 3,979.
43 City of Vancouver, Planning Department, *Restoration Report,* 5. The report was commissioned after council approved a beautification program for the "Old City" in August 1968.
44 Ibid., 16.
45 Director of Planning Report to the Board of Administration, 12 June 1970, CVA, City of Vancouver, Social Planning 77-D-2, file 17.
46 Board of Administration to Council, 4 March 1971, ibid., file 18.
47 *Chinatown News,* 20 no. 6, 18 November 1972.
48 Graham to Owners and Merchants of Chinatown, 1 November 1972, Chinatown Beautification file, B03.Coo.
49 Pickstone to Egan, 27 March 1973, ibid.

50 Minutes of meeting held in Pickstone's office, 11 April 1973, ibid.

51 Memorandum from Mike Kemble to B03.C00 regarding conversation with Harry Fan, 20 June 1973, ibid.

52 Minutes of meeting held 22 November 1973, ibid.

53 The reference to Chinatown as "depicting a people and an atmosphere" is taken from City of Vancouver, Planning Department, *Chinatown Planning Newsletter*, CVA, Public Document 663, ibid.

54 Minutes of meeting re Chinatown Improvement Project held 22 November 1973, Chinatown Beautification file, B03.C00.

55 Kemble to Fan, 4 December 1973, ibid.

56 Cited in Notes of meeting re Chinatown Improvement Project held 21 February 1974, ibid., B03.C01.

57 City of Vancouver, City Planning Department, *Chinatown Sign Guidelines*, 1974, 2, copy in CVA, Public Document 163.

58 Seaton to Ellis, 8 April 1974, Chinatown Beautification file, B03.C01. Seaton's statement regarding Chinatown in the Depression would seem no more sound than the assumption that neon is a traditional feature of Chinese architecture.

59 *Chinatown News*, 21 no. 16, 3 May 1974.

60 Cited in Minutes of the Technical Planning Board, 21 June 1974, Chinatown Beautification file, B03.C01.

61 Minutes of the Technical Planning Board, 28 June 1974, Kemble to file, 24 May 1974, ibid., B03.C01.

62 Minutes of special public meeting of Council, 9 July 1974, ibid.

63 Cited in Manager's report to Standing Committee on Planning and Development re Chinatown Planning Program, 14 April 1976, Chinatown Beautification file, B03.C01.

64 Goldberg to City Planning Department, 25 September 1974, Chinatown Beautification file, B03.C01. Goldberg's judgment about the resilience of the crass tourist image would seem to be borne out by magazine portrayals of Chinatown in the 1970s. See for example, Moon, "Chinatown," and Wood, "The Year of the Horse."

65 *Cited in Chinatown News*, 21 no. 21, 18 July 1974.

66 Ibid., 22 no. 5, 3 November 1974. City of Vancouver, Planning Department, *Chinatown Planning Newsletter*, 1976, 2.

67 Personal communication from Mike Kemble.

68 *Chinatown News*, 24 no. 7, 3 December 1976.

69 Ibid., 24 no. 9, 18 January 1977.

70 City of Vancouver Planning Department, *Chinatown Streetscape Improvement Project*, 1977, in Chinatown Beautification file, B03.C02.

71 Chinese Cultural Centre Reports, July–August 1978, 2.

72 Cited in Manager's report to Vancouver City Council, 23 May 1978, Chinatown Beautification file, B03.C03.

73 Bawlf to Volrich, 28 March 1978, ibid.
74 Cited in Manager's report to Council, 23 May 1978, ibid.
75 Kemble to Fleming, 21 June 1978, Appendix A of Manager's report to Council, 7 July 1978, ibid.
76 McCarthy to Volrich, 18 October 1978, ibid. The federal minister of state for urban affairs, André Ouellet, declined Volrich's request for matching funds from Ottawa on the grounds that the appropriate federal source – the Community Services Contribution Fund – was distributed according to provincial discretion. Volrich to Ouellet, 22 December 1978, ibid.
77 Kemble to Curtis, 2 October 1979, Rudberg to Kemble, 28 November 1979, Chinatown Beautification file, B03.C04. See various exchanges in this file on other decorative features.
78 Planning and Engineering Department reports to City Manager for Standing Committee of Council on Planning and Development, 12 February 1979, ibid. See also the communication of Kemble with the city director of planning, Melbourne, Australia, regarding the street lighting (and other) features chosen by that city to "orientalize" its Chinatown. The planning departments of both Sydney and Melbourne have undertaken similar streetscape projects in their Chinatowns in the 1970s. See Melbourne City Council, *Chinatown Action Plan.*
79 *Chinatown News,* 27 no. 11, 18 February 1980.
80 See Anderson, "Chinatown Re-oriented."
81 Canada, Minister of State for Multiculturalism, *Multicultural Update,* 14.
82 *Chinatown News,* 16 no. 8, 18 December 1968.
83 *Province,* 16 August 1969.
84 *Chinatown News,* 20 no. 3, 3 October 1972.
85 Rossiter, "Exodus Reversed," 58.
86 *Chinatown News,* 20 no. 12, 3 March 1973.
87 For relevant city documents on the connector and the protest that surrounded it, see CVA, Add. MS 734, SPOTA files, Vol. 15, file 6.
88 *Chinatown News,* 20 no. 18, 3 June 1973.
89 Chinese Cultural Centre Building Committee Report, "An Incredible Story," 3–4, CVA, Add. MS 734, SPOTA files, Vol. 15, file 6.
90 Extract from minutes re Columbia–Quebec Connector and Pender–Keefer Diversion of the Vancouver city council meeting, 12 June 1973, Chinatown Beautification file, B03.C00. The *Chinatown News* noted that "communication between City Hall and the Chinese-Canadian community has improved a snippet since the TEAM-dominated Council took office this year"; 20 no. 18, 3 June 1973.
91 See the numerous reports and communications concerning these matters, City of Vancouver, Planning Department, Chinatown Beautification files, B03.C00, B03.C01, B03.C02, and Chinese Cultural Centre file, B03.C25, B03.C26.

92 See discussion of the implications of road arrangements for Chinatown in Manager's report re Chinese Cultural Centre to Standing Committee on Planning and Development, 22 June 1976, City of Vancouver, Planning Department, Chinese Cultural Centre file (hereafter ccc file), B03.C25.

93 Director of Planning to Standing Committee on Civic Development, April 22, 1974, ibid., cited in Manager's report re Chinese Cultural Centre to Standing Committee on Civic Development, 22 June 1976, ibid.

94 Lepage to Mayor and Council, 5 July 1976, ibid.

95 Mah to Mayor and Council, 22 July 1976, ibid.

96 Extract of Council meeting, 26 July 1976, ibid.

97 *Chinatown News*, 24 no. 5, 3 November 1976.

98 On the manipulation of "Chineseness" by the old China-born élite to claim the right to represent New York's Chinatown community to the larger society, to Taiwan, and to itself, see B. Wong, "Elites." In their interactions with the Taiwanese government, members of the élite assume the identity of the "overseas Chinese" (for special concessions); to the local Chinese community, they are the "real Chinese" (as opposed to Hong Kong– or local-born); and to the larger society, they adopt the identity of "Chinese-Americans" (for political and economic gains).

99 *Chinatown News*, 24 no. 10, 3 February 1977; 24 no. 12, 3 March 1977. For details of the political rift in Chinatown in the early 1970s, see Koch, "Taiwan."

100 *Chinatown News*, 24 no. 23, 18 August 1977; 25 no. 2, 18 September 1977.

101 Ibid., 25 no. 9, 18 January 1978; 25 no. 11, 18 February 1978; 25 no. 12, 3 March 1978.

102 Cited in extract from minutes of the Vancouver City Council meeting re land lease agreement, 10 April 1979, ccc file, B03.C26.

103 Copy of agreement made 12 September 1978, ibid.; see also Ouellet to Volrich, 20 April 1978, ibid.

104 The chapc meeting of 14 June 1978 decided to respond to the federal invitation with the offer of a classical Chinese garden. See Kemble to Chee, 27 June 1978, ibid.

105 Volrich to Yi Zhu, 6 May 1980, ibid., B03.C27. For further details on the garden project, see other documents in the file.

106 Rule, "A Classical Chinese Garden," 36. See also City of Vancouver, Planning Department, *Dr Sun Yat-Sen*, copy in cva, Public Document 679, 1980; Eng, "Inside Chinatown."

107 Personal communication from Mike Kemble.

108 Kemble to Chee, 17 April 1979, ccc file B03.C25.

109 Personal communication from Mike Kemble.

110 Cited in *Chinatown News*, 26 no. 17, 18 May 1979. Earlier his government had sponsored a Multicultural Conference in Vancouver, 3–4 April 1979,

on the theme "Toward a Provincial Multicultural Policy." The proceedings were later published.

111 *Chinatown News*, 28 no. 2, 18 September 1980.

112 Ibid., 20 no. 3, 3 October 1972; see also 20 no. 5, 3 November 1972.

113 Ibid., 20 no. 4, 18 October 1972.

114 Cited in ibid., 20 no. 5, 3 November 1972.

115 Ibid., 20 no. 21, 18 July 1973.

116 Ibid.

117 Ibid., 23 no. 1, 3 September 1975.

118 See CVA, Add. MS. 734, SPOTA files, Vol. 14, file 4. For an example of a letter of warning, see Lukey to the Wing Hing Co., 13 June 1977. The owners were threatened with a fine of $500. On the federal inspections, see *Province*, 26 January 1978; *Chinatown News* , 25 no. 10, 3 February 1978.

119 For further details of the media event, see *Chinatown News*, 25 no. 11, 18 February 1978; *Province*, 23 February 1978; *Sun*, 23 February 1978.

120 Cited in *Chinatown News*, 25 no. 11, 18 February 1978.

121 Ibid., 25 no. 15, 18 April 1978.

122 Ibid., 25 no. 20, 3 June 1978.

123 See for example Kallen, *Ethnicity*.

124 This point is borrowed from Prager, "American Racial Ideology."

125 *Chinatown News*, 21 no. 22, 3 August 1974.

126 Cited in ibid., 22 no. 12, 3 March 1975.

127 *DHC*, 9 December 1974, 2,085.

128 See the arguments of IMPAC in *Chinatown News*, 22 no. 12, 3 March 1975; 22 no. 14, 3 April 1975; 22 no. 18, 3 June 1975; and 23 no. 2, 3 September 1975.

129 Ibid., 22 no. 15, 18 April 1975.

130 *DHC*, 11 March 1977, 3,904; 21 March 1977, 4,186; 14 March 1977, 4,018; ibid., 3,944; 16 March 1977, 4,047; 11 March 1977, 3,904.

131 *Chinatown News*, 26 no. 22, 3 August 1979.

132 Ibid., 27 no. 3, 3 October 1979.

133 Cited in ibid., 27 no. 5, 3 November 1979.

134 For a detailed discussion of the incident, see A. Chan, *Gold Mountain*, 161–86.

135 For a discussion of the protest, see Kwan, "The W5 Movement."

136 *DHC*, 16 June 1980, 2,145–50.

137 Ibid., 16 June 1980, 2,148.

138 Ibid., 2,149.

CHAPTER EIGHT

1 Sociobiologists argue that attachment to our respective ethnic groups is a natural extension of kinship and ultimately an expression of a drive

to optimize the production of common genes. See van den Berghe, *The Ethnic Phenomena*. Van den Berghe claims (p. 32) that his selectionist theory "accounts better for the appearance and disappearance of racism in various times and places than competing theories that attribute racism either to ideological factors or to the capitalist mode of production." For a critique, see for example Barker, *The New Racism*, and Sahlins, *The Use and Abuse of Biology*, chap. 1.

2 Strauss, *Mirrors and Masks*, 20, cited in Western, *Outcast Capetown*, 8.
3 Suttles, *Social Order*.
4 See Zaret, "From Weber to Parsons," and Giddens, *New Rules*.
5 The phrase "in process, in time" is taken from Abrams, *Historical Sociology*, xviii.
6 Genovese, *In Red and Black*, 46.
7 Knorr-Cetina and Cicourel, eds., *Advances*, Introduction.
8 Williams, *Marxism and Literature*, 112.
9 *Daily Telegraph*, 23 April 1989.
10 See the author's writings on gender and class positionings within the white Canadian category in her chapter "Engendering Race Research: Unsettling the Self/Other Dichotomy" in *(Re)placings: Destabilizing Geographies for Gender and Sexuality*, edited by N. Duncan (London: Routledge, forthcoming).
11 See for example Naipul, "Illusion," and Brantlinger, "Victorians."
12 See also Lowman, "Conceptual Issues," and Ley, *Social Geography*, 293–4.
13 Geertz, *Local Knowledge*, 69.
14 Abrams, *Historical Sociology*, 332–3.
15 A recent history of Vancouver's Chinese is Yee, *Saltwater City*.
16 Marcus and Fischer, *Anthropology*, 138.
17 Said, *Orientalism*, 67.
18 On the way anthropologists have supplied and steered our knowledge of foreign cultures, see for example Fabian, *Time*.
19 Olsson, "Social Science," 297.
20 Ibid., 304.

Bibliography

ARCHIVAL SOURCES

GOVERNMENT DOCUMENTS

British Columbia. *Journals of the Legislative Assembly of British Columbia (JLABC)*, various dates, 1872–1950.
– *Reports.* 1878, 1885, 1888.
– *Sessional Papers,* 1880, 1885, 1886, 1894.
– *Statutes,* 1872, 1875, 1878, 1883, 1884, 1885, 1886, 1897, 1900, 1919.
Canada. *Debates of the House of Commons (DHC)*, various dates, 1879–1980.
– *Sessional Papers,* 1885 (No. 54a); 1902 (No. 54); 1908 (No. 36b); 1908 (74f); 1910 (No. 10); 1913 (No. 207); 1914 (No. 25); 1917 (No. 25); 1919 (No. 18).
– *Statutes,* 1885, 1908, 1921, 1922, 1923.
The Canadian Parliamentary Companion and Annual Register, 1862–1897. Ottawa: Gazette Printing Ltd. Continues *Canadian Parliamentary Guide, 1898–1900.* Montreal: Gazette Printing.
Census of Canada, 1881, Vol. 1.
City of Vancouver. Chinatown Beautification files, 1972–80.
– Chinese Cultural Centre files (CCC files), 1975–80.
– Department of Permits and Licences, Licence Registry, 1910–12.
City of Vancouver. Office of the City Clerk, Council Minutes, various dates, 1886–1964.
– Health Committee Minutes, 1899–1906.
– Incoming Correspondence, various dates, 1886–1939.
– Mayor's Correspondence, 1937, 1938, 1943.
– Special Committee files, 1936, 1939, 1940, 1941.
– Social Planning files, 1970–1.

OTHER DOCUMENTS

Board of Trade files, Additional Manuscript 300, City of Vancouver Archives, 1921.

Chinese-Canadian Project. Special Collections Division, University of British Columbia Library, Boxes 1–32.

Consul-General for China Letterbook, 1914–15. Special Collections Division, University of British Columbia Library.

W.A. Cumyow Papers. Special Collections Division, University of British Columbia Library.

Henderson's Directory. British Columbia. L.G. Henderson, 1889, 1910, 1920.

Lee Family Papers. Special Collections Division, University of British Columbia Library.

W.H. Malkin files. Additional Manuscript 237, City of Vancouver Archives.

SPOTA files. Additional Manuscript 734, City of Vancouver Archives.

Halford Wilson Papers. Provincial Archives of British Columbia, Catalogue No. E/D W69.

Williams' Illustrated Official British Columbia Directory. Victoria: R. Williams, 1892.

Foon Sien (Wong Mun-po) Personal Papers and Newspaper Clippings, 1930s–1950s. Special Collections Division, University of British Columbia Library.

NEWSPAPERS

British Columbia Federationist, 1911.

Chinatown News, 1958–80.

Chinese Cultural Centre Reports, 1978.

Chinese Times, English translations in Chinese-Canadian Project, various dates, 1914–37.

Colonist, 1908–28.

News Herald, 1941.

Province (some years titled *Vancouver Province*), 1901–78.

Sun (some years titled *Vancouver Sun*), 1914–79.

Sydney Morning Herald, 1989.

Vancouver News (some years also *Daily News-Advertiser*), 1886–9.

Weekend Australian, 1990.

World (some years also *Vancouver World* or *Daily World*), 1889–1922.

BOOKS, ARTICLES, AND THESES

Abdu-Laban, B. *An Olive Branch on the Family Tree.* Toronto: McClelland and Stewart, 1980.

Abrams, P. *Historical Sociology.* Bath: Pitman Press 1982.

Adilman, T. "A Preliminary Sketch of Chinese Women and Work in British Columbia 1858–1950." In *Not Just Pin Money*, edited by B. Latham, R. Latham, and R. Pazdro, Victoria: Camosun College 1984: 53–78.

Agnew, J. *Place and Politics: The Geographical Mediation of Society*. Boston: Allen and Unwin 1987.

Agnew, J., and Duncan, J. eds. *The Power of Place: Bringing Together Geographical and Sociological Imaginations*. Boston: Unwin Hyman 1989.

Agnew, J., Mercer, J., and Sopher, D. eds. "Introduction." In *The City in Cultural Context*. Boston: Allen and Unwin 1984: 1–30.

Allport, G. *The Nature of Prejudice*. Reading, Mass.: Addison-Wesley 1954.

Almirol, E. "Confucius to Charlie Chan: Stereotyping Chinese-Americans." *East-West Perspectives*, 2 (1981): 35–40.

Anderson, K. "Chinatown Re-oriented: A Critical Analysis of Recent Redevelopment Schemes in a Melbourne and Sydney Enclave." *Australian Geographical Studies*, 28, no. 2 (1990): 137–54.

– "Community Formation in Official Context: Residential Segregation and the 'Chinese' in Early Vancouver." *Canadian Geographer*, 32 no. 4 (1988): 354–7.

– "Cultural Hegemony and the Race Definition Process in Chinatown, Vancouver: 1880–1980." *Environment and Planning D: Society and Space*, 6 (1988): 127–49.

– "East Is West: State, Place and the Institutionalization of Myth in Vancouver's Chinatown." PHD dissertation, Department of Geography, University of British Columbia, 1986.

– "The Idea of Chinatown: The Power of Place and Institutional Practice in the Making of a Racial Category." *Annals, Association of American Geographers*, 77 no. 4 (1987): 580–98.

Anderson, K., and Gale, F., eds. *Inventing Places: Studies in Cultural Geography*. Melbourne: Longmans 1992.

Andracki, S. *Immigration of Orientals into Canada with Special Reference to Chinese*. New York: Arno Press 1978.

Angus, H. "Asiatics in Canada." *Pacific Affairs*, 19 (1946): 402–8.

– "A Contribution to International Ill-Will." *The Dalhousie Review*, 13 (1933): 23–33.

– "The Legal Status in British Columbia of Residents of Oriental Race and Their Descendants." In *The Legal Status of Aliens in Pacific Countries*, edited by N. Mackenzie, London: Institute of Pacific Relations 1937: 77–88.

– "Underprivileged Canadians." *Queen's Quarterly*, 38 (1931): 445–60.

Anon. *British Columbia Monthly* Vol. 17, February 1921.

Appiah, A. "The Uncompleted Argument: Du Bois and the Illusion of Race." *Critical Inquiry*, 12 no. 1, (1985): 21–37.

Avery, D. "Canadian Immigration Policy and the 'Foreign' Navvy, 1896–1914." In *The Consolidation of Capitalism, 1896–1929,* edited by M. Cross and G. Kealey, Toronto: McClelland and Stewart 1983: 47–73.

Bannister, R. *Social Darwinism: Science and Myth in Anglo-American Social Thought.* Philadelphia: Temple University Press 1979.

Banton, M. *The Idea of Race.* London: Tavistock 1977.

– *Racial and Ethnic Competition.*Cambridge: Cambridge University Press 1983.

Barker, M. *The New Racism.* London: Junction Books 1981.

Barth, F., ed. *Ethnic Groups and Ethnic Boundaries: The Social Organization of Cultural Difference,* Boston: Little, Brown 1969.

Barth, G. *Bitter Strength: A History of the Chinese in the United States, 1850–1870.* Cambridge, Mass.: Harvard University Press 1964.

Basran, G. "Canadian Immigration Policy and Theories of Racism." In *Racial Minorities in Multicultural Canada,* edited by P. Li and B. Singh Bolaria, Toronto: Garamond Press 1983: 3–14.

Bastide, R. "Colour, Racism and Christianity." *Daedalus,* 96 (1967): 312–27.

Baureiss, G., and Driedger, L. "Winnipeg's Chinatown: Demographic, Ecological and Organizational Change, 1900–80." *Urban History Review,* 10 no. 3 (1982): 11–24.

Beautiful B.C. Magazine, 3 no. 2 (Fall 1961): 27–33.

Bell, L., and Moore, R. *The Strathcona Rehabilitation Project: Documentation and Analysis.* Vancouver: Social Policy and Research: United Way of Vancouver 1975.

– "Urban Renewal Scheme 3 – Strathcona." Research Department, United Community Services, July 1966, 2.

Berger, P. *Invitation to Sociology: A Humanistic Perspective.* New York: Anchor Books 1963.

Berger, P., and Luckmann, T. *The Social Construction of Reality.* Harmondsworth: Penguin 1966.

Berry, B. *The Open Housing Question.* Cambridge, Mass.: Ballinger 1979.

Berry, J., Kalin, R., and Taylor, D. *Multiculturalism and Ethnic Attitudes in Canada.* Ottawa: Supply and Services Canada 1977.

Berton, P. *The Last Spike.* Toronto: McClelland and Stewart 1971.

Bonacich, E. "A Theory of Ethnic Antagonisms: The Split Labor Market." *American Sociological Review,* 37 (1972): 547–59.

Boswell, T. "A Split Labor Market Analysis of Discrimination against Chinese Immigrants, 1850–82." *American Sociological Review,* 51 (1986): 352–71.

Boxer, C. *Race Relations in the Portuguese Colonial Empire, 1415–1825.* Oxford: Clarendon Press 1963.

Brantlinger, P. "Victorians and Africans: the Genealogy of the Myth of the Dark Continent." *Critical Inquiry,* 12 no. 1 (1985): 166–203.

Breton, R. "The Production and Allocation of Symbolic Resources: An Analysis of Linguistic and Ethno-Cultural Fields in Canada." *Canadian Review of Sociology and Anthropology*, 21 (1984): 123–44.

British Columbia. *Report on Oriental Activities within the Province*. Victoria: Charles Banfield 1927.

Brook, T. "Chinese-Canadians in the Depression: A Summary of Readings in the *Chinese Times* from the 1930s." Unpublished paper, n.d.

Brotz, H. "Multiculturalism in Canada: A Muddle." *Canadian Public Policy*, 6 no. 1 (1980): 41–6.

Burnley, I. "Ethnic Factors in Social Segregation and Residential Stratification in Australia's Large Cities." *Australian and New Zealand Journal of Sociology*, 11 (1975): 12–23.

Canada. Dominion Bureau of Statistics. *Seventh Census of Canada*, 1931. Orientals, 10 years of age and over, Gainfully Employed by Race, Occupation and Sex, in the Province of British Columbia. Ottawa 1934.

– Minister of State for Multiculturalism. *Multicultural Update*. Department of Secretary of State 1978.

– *Report of the Royal Commission on Bilingualism and Biculturalism*. Ottawa: Queen's Printer 1969.

– *Report of the Task Force on Housing and Urban Development*. Ottawa: Queen's Printer 1969.

Carter, B., Harris, C., and Joshi, S. "The 1951–55 Conservative Government and the Racialization of Black Immigration." *Immigrants and Minorities*, 6 no. 3 (1987): 335–47.

Castells, M. *The Urban Question: A Marxist Approach*. London: Edward Arnold 1977.

Centre for Contemporary Cultural Studies (Birmingham). *The Empire Strikes Back*. London: Hutchinson 1982.

Chan, A. "'Orientalism' and Image Making: The Sojourner in Canadian History." *Journal of Ethnic Studies*, 9 (1981): 37–46.

– *Gold Mountain*. Vancouver: New Star Books 1983.

– "Neither French nor British: The Rise of the Asianadian Culture." *Canadian Ethnic Studies*, 10 no. 2, (1978): 114–17.

Chan, S. "An Overview of the Strathcona Experience with Urban Renewal by a Participant." Unpublished paper for Action Research, Department of Secretary of State, 1971.

Chinatown Property Owners Association, Vancouver. Brief to the Royal Commission on Expropriation Laws and Procedures, 1961.

Chinese Benevolent Association, Vancouver. Brief re: Proposed Freeway through Vancouver Chinatown to Mayor and Council, 1967.

Cho, G., and Leigh, R. " Patterns of Residence of the Chinese in Vancouver." In *Peoples of the Living Land*, edited by J. Minghi, BC Geographical Series no. 15, Vancouver: Tantalus (1972): 67–84.

City of Vancouver. *Downtown Vancouver, 1955–76*, Prepared for City Council by the Technical Planning Board, 1956.

– *Vancouver Redevelopment Study*. Planning Department of the Housing Research Committee, 1957.

City of Vancouver. Planning Department. *Chinatown, Vancouver: Design Proposal for Improvement*. 1964.

– *Chinatown Planning Newsletter*. 1976.

– *Chinatown Sign Guidelines*. 1974.

– *Chinatown Streetscape Improvement Project*. 1977.

– *Dr Sun Yat-Sen: A Classical Chinese Garden*. 1980.

– *Restoration Report: A Case for Renewed Life in the Old City*. 1969.

– *Vancouver's Heritage: Twenty-Two Buildings and Two Historic Areas*. 1974.

City of Vancouver. Technical Planning Board. *Redevelopment: Acquisition and Clearance*. 1959.

– *Redevelopment Project No. 1, Area A-3*. 1964.

– *Redevelopment Project No. 2*. 1963.

– *Strathcona Sub-Area Report, Urban Renewal, Scheme 3*. 1968.

Clairmont, D., and Magill, D. *Africville: The Life and Death of a Canadian Black Community*. Toronto: McClelland and Stewart 1974.

Clammer, J. "The Institutionalization of Ethnicity: The Culture of Ethnicity in Singapore." *Ethnic and Racial Studies*, 5 no. 2 (1982): 127–39.

Clark, G., and Dear, M. *State Apparatus*. London: Allen and Unwin 1984.

Clark, W. "Residential Mobility and Neighbourhood Change: Some Implications for Racial Residential Segregation." *Urban Geography*, 1 (1980): 95–117.

Cohen, R. "Ethnicity: Problem and Focus in Anthropology." *Annual Review of Anthropology*, 7 (1978): 379–403.

Connell, R. *Gender and Power*. Sydney: Allen and Unwin 1987.

Cowlishaw, G. "Colour, Culture and the Aboriginalists." *Man*, 22 no. 2 (1987): 221–37.

Creese, G. "Immigration Policies and the Creation of an Ethnically Segmented Working Class in British Columbia, 1880–1923." *Alternate Routes*, 7 (1984): 1–34.

Crissman, L. "The Segmentary Structure of Urban Overseas Chinese Communities." *Man*, 2 (1967): 185–204.

Cybriwsky, R. "The Community Response to Downtown Redevelopment: The Case of Philadelphia's Chinatown." Paper presented at the Association of American Geographers Conference 1986.

Dahlie, J., and Fernando, T., eds. *Ethnicity, Power and Politics in Canada*. Toronto: Methuen 1981.

Dawson, R. *The Chinese Chameleon: An Analysis of European Conceptions of Chinese Civilization*. London: Oxford University Press 1967.

de Lepervanche, M., and Bottomley, G., eds. *The Cultural Construction of Race*. Sydney: Sydney Association for Studies in Society and Culture 1988.

Dear, M. "The Post-modern Challenge: Reconstructing Human Geography." *Transactions, Institute of British Geographers*. New Series 13 (1988): 262–74.

Dear, M., and Wolch, J., eds. *The Power of Geography: How Territory Shapes Social Life*. Boston: Unwin Hyman 1989.

Djao, A. Wei. "Asian Canadians and the Welfare State." *Canadian Ethnic Studies*, 2 (1982): 91–8.

Duncan, J. "The Superorganic in American Cultural Geography." *Annals, Association of American Geographers*, 70 (1980): 181–98.

Duncan, J., and Duncan, N. "A Cultural Analysis of Urban Residential Landscapes in North America: the Case of the Anglophile Elite." In *The City in Cultural Context*, edited by J. Agnew et al., Boston: Allen and Unwin 1984: 255–76.

– "(Re)reading the Landscape." *Society and Space*, 6 (1988): 117–26.

Duncan, J., and Ley, D. "Structural Marxism and Human Geography: A Critical Assessment." *Annals, Association of American Geographers*, 72 (1982): 30–59.

Dunn, L. "Race and Biology." In *Race and Science*, UNESCO, New York: Columbia University Press 1969: 263–98.

Durkheim, E. "Individual and Collective Representations." In *Sociology and Philosophy*. Translated by D. Pocock. London: Cohen and West 1953: 1–34.

Eng, R. "Inside Chinatown." *Vancouver Magazine*, 13 no. 11 (1980): 114–21.

Fabian, J. *Time and the Other: How Anthropology Makes Its Object*. New York: Columbia University Press 1983.

Farish, D. *Biology: The Human Perspective*. New York: Harper and Row 1978.

Farley, J. "Segregated City, Segregated Suburbs: To What Extent Are They Products of Black-White Socioeconomic Differentials?" *Urban Geography*, 7 no. 2 (1986): 164–71.

Fenton, S. "'Race Relations' in the Sociological Enterprise." *New Community*, 8 (1980): 162–8.

Fields, B. "Ideology and Race in American History." In *Region, Race and Reconstruction*, edited by J. Kousser and J. McPherson, Oxford: Oxford University Press 1982: 143–77.

Foucault, M. *Discipline and Punish: The Birth of the Prison*, New York: Pantheon Books 1977.

Francis, R. "Wong Foon Sien Wants Better Deal for Chinese Immigrants." *Canadian Business*, 28 (1955): 78–86.

Fredrickson, G. *White Supremacy*. New York: Oxford University Press 1981.

Fried, M. "A Four-Letter Word That Hurts." *Saturday Review*, 2 October 1965: 358–62.

Gabriel, J., and Ben-Tovim, G. "Marxism and the Concept of Racism." *Economy and Society*, 7 no. 2, (1978): 118–54.

Gates, H. "Writing 'Race' and the Difference It Makes." *Critical Inquiry*, 12 no. 1 (1985): 1–20.

Geertz, C. *The Interpretation of Cultures*. New York: Basic Books 1973.

– *Local Knowledge*. New York: Basic Books 1983.

Genovese, E. *In Red and Black: Marxian Explorations in Southern and Afro-American History*. New York: Pantheon 1971.

Gibbon, J. *The Canadian Mosaic: The Making of a Northern Nation*. Toronto: McClelland and Stewart 1938.

Giddens, A. *Central Problems in Social Theory: Action, Structure and Contradiction in Social Analysis*. Berkeley: University of California Press 1979.

– *New Rules of Sociological Method*. London: Hutchinson 1976.

Giffen, P. "Rates of Crime and Delinquency." In *Critical Issues in Canadian Society*, edited by C. Boydell et al., Toronto: Holt, Rinehart and Winston 1971: 430–45.

Gilmour, C. "What, No Opium Dens?" *Maclean's*, 15 January 1949: 16 and 27–30.

Gilroy, P. "You Can't Fool the Youths ... Race and Class Formation in the 1980s." *Race and Class*, 2/3 (1981–2): 207–22.

Glynn-Ward, H. (Mrs H. Howard). *The Writing on the Wall*. Vancouver: Sun Publishing 1921.

Gramsci, A. *Selections from the Prison Notebooks*, edited by Q. Hoare and G. Smith. London: Lawrence and Wishart 1971.

Grant, M. *The Passing of the Great Race*. New York: Charles Scribner's Sons 1916.

Greeley, A. *Ethnicity in the United States*. New York: John Wiley 1974.

Green, M., and Carter, R. "'Races' and 'Race-Makers': The Politics of Racialization." *Sage Race Relations Abstracts*, 13, no. 2 (1988): 4–30.

Greenberg, S. *Race and State in Capitalist Development: Comparative Perspectives*. New Haven and London: Yale University Press 1980.

Gregory, D., and Urry, J., eds. *Social Relations and Spatial Structure*. London: Macmillan 1985.

Hall, S. "Race, Articulation and Societies Structured in Dominance." In UNESCO, *Sociological Theories: Race and Colonialism*, Poole, UK: Sydenhams 1980: 305–46.

Haller, M. *Eugenics: Hereditarian Attitudes in American Thought*. New Brunswick, NJ: Rutgers University Press 1963.

Hardwick, W. *Vancouver*. Don Mills, Ont.: Collier-Macmillan 1974.

Harris, M. "Race." In *International Encyclopedia of the Social Sciences*, New York: Macmillan, 13 and 14 (1972): 263–8.

Harris, R.C. "The Simplification of Europe Overseas." *Annals, Association of American Geographers*, 67 no. 4 (1977): 469–83.

Hartmann, C. *Yerba Buena*. San Francisco: Glide 1974.

Harvey, D. "Between Space and Time: Reflections on the Geographical Imagination." *Annals, Association of American Geographers*, 80 no. 3 (1990): 418–34.

Hawkins, F. *Canada and Immigration: Public Policy and Public Concern*. Montreal: McGill-Queen's University Press 1972.

Hay, D. *Europe: The Emergence of an Idea*. New York: Harper and Row 1966.

Hiebert, A. "The Oriental as He Appears in Some of the Novels of British Columbia." *British Columbia Library Quarterly*, 34 no. 4 (1971): 20–31.

Higham, J. *Strangers in the Land: Patterns of American Nativism, 1860–1925*. New Jersey: Rutgers University Press 1955.

Hill, H. "Anti-Oriental Agitation and the Rise of Working Class Racism." *Society*, 10 no. 2 (1973): 43–54.

Hillaby, H. Report on Chinese Relief, as administered to Chinese on Provincial Relief at 143 Pender Street East, under auspices of Anglican Board of Oriental Missions. 1935.

Hoe, B. *Structural Changes of Two Chinese Communities in Alberta, Canada*. Canadian Centre of Folk Culture Studies, No. 19. Ottawa: National Museum of Man 1976.

Hofstader, R. *Social Darwinism in American Thought*. Boston: Beacon Press 1955.

Hope, C. "British Columbia's Racial Problem: Part One." *Maclean's*, 1 February 1930: 3–4 and 62–4.

– "British Columbia's Racial Problem: Part Two." *Maclean's*, 15 February 1930: 8, 45–6, 48.

Hope, C., and Earle, W. "The Oriental Threat." *Maclean's*, May 1933: 12 and 54–5.

Hughes, D., and Kallen, E. *The Anatomy of Racism: Canadian Dimensions*. Montreal: Harvest House 1974.

Hurd, W. *Racial Origins and Nativity of the Canadian People*. Census of Canada, Vol. XIII, 1931, Monographs. Ottawa: Edmond Cloutier 1942.

Husband, C., ed. *"Race" in Britain: Continuity and Change*. London: Hutchinson 1987.

Ireland, R. "Canadian Trade Unionism and Oriental Immigration: A Study of Ideological Change." *Indian Journal of Economics*, 46 (1965): 1–31.

Jackson, P. "Ethnic Groups and Boundaries: 'Ordered Segmentation' in Urban Neighbourhoods." Research Paper No. 26, Oxford University, 1980.

– "A Transactional Approach to Puerto Rican Culture." *Review/ Revista/ Interamericana*, 11 (1981): 53–68.

Jackson, P., ed. *Race and Racism: Essays in Social Geography*. London: Allen and Unwin 1987.

Jackson, P., and Smith, S., eds. *Social Interaction and Ethnic Segregation.* London: Academic Press 1981.

Jenkins, R. "Social Anthropological Models of Inter-ethnic Relations." In *Theories of Race and Ethnic Relations,* edited by J. Rex and D. Mason, Cambridge: Cambridge University Press 1986: 170–86.

Jennett, C., and Randal, S., eds. *Three Worlds of Inequality: Race, Class and Gender.* South Melbourne: Macmillan 1987.

Johnson, G. "Chinese Family and Community in Canada: Tradition and Change." In *Two Nations, Many Cultures,* edited by J. Elliot, Scarborough, Ont.: Prentice Hall 1978: 353–71.

Johnston, L. "The Case of the Oriental in British Columbia." *Canadian Magazine,* 57 (1921): 315–18.

Johnston, R. *Residential Segregation, the State and Constitutional Conflict in American Urban Areas.* London: Academic Press 1984.

Jones, G. *Social Darwinism and English Thought: The Interaction between Biological and Social Theory.* Sussex: Harvester Press 1980.

Jordan, W. *White over Black: American Attitudes toward the Negro, 1550–1812.* Baltimore: Penguin 1968.

Kallen, E. *Ethnicity and Human Rights in Canada.* Toronto: Gage Publishing 1982.

– "The Semantics of Multiculturalism." In *Consciousness and Inquiry: Ethnology and Canadian Realities,* edited by F. Manning, Ottawa: National Museum of Man 1983: 22–46.

Keesing, R. "Racial and Ethnic Categories in Colonial and Post-Colonial States: Sociological and Linguistic Perspectives on Ideology." In M. O'Callaghan, ed., *Studies on the Adequacy of Theories, Paradigms and Assumptions in the Social and Human Sciences,* Paris: UNESCO (forthcoming).

Kim, H., and Lai, N. "Chinese Community Resistance to Urban Renewal: The Case of Strathcona in Vancouver, Canada." *Journal of Ethnic Studies,* 10 no. 2 (1982): 67–81.

Kloppenborg, A., ed. *Vancouver's First Century: A City Album, 1860–1960.* Vancouver: J.J. Douglas 1977.

Knapman, C. *White Women in Fiji, 1835–1930: The Ruin Of Empire?* Sydney: Allen and Unwin 1986.

Knorr-Cetina, K., and Cicourel, A., eds. *Advances in Social Theory and Methodology: Toward an Integration of Micro- and Macro-Sociologies.* Boston: Routledge and Kegan Paul 1981.

Koch, T. "Taiwan versus Peking on Pender Street." *Vancouver Magazine,* 11 no. 1 (1978): 22–4.

Kwan, C. "The W5 Movement." *Asianadian,* 2 (1980): 11–13.

Kwong, P. *Chinatown, New York: Labor and Politics, 1930–1950.* New York: Monthly Review Press 1979.

La Forest, G. *Disallowance and Reservation of the Provincial Legislation.*
Ottawa: Department of Justice 1955.

Lai, D. *Chinatowns: Towns within Cities In Canada.* Vancouver: University of
British Columbia Press 1988.

– "Chinese Immigrants into British Columbia and Their Distribution, 1858–
1970." *Pacific Viewpoint,* 14 no. 1 (1973): 102–8.

– "Socio-economic Structures and the Viability of Chinatown." In *Residential and Neighbourhood Studies in Victoria,* edited by C. Forward, Western
Geographical Series, No. 5, Victoria: University of Victoria 1973:
101–29.

Lai, H. "Integration of Physical Planning and Social Planning: A Case
Study of the Strathcona Urban Renewal Area." MA thesis, University of
British Columbia, 1970.

Lal, B. "The Chinese Benevolent Association of Vancouver, 1889–1960."
Unpublished manuscript, Special Collections Division, University of British Columbia Library, 1975.

Lawrence, E. "Just Plain Commonsense: The 'Roots' of Racism." In *The
Empire Strikes Back: Race and Racism in 70s Britain,* edited by Centre for
Contemporary Cultural Studies, London: Hutchinson 1982: 47–94.

Lears, T.J. "The Concept of Cultural Hegemony: Problems and Possibilities."
American Historical Review, 90 no. 3 (1985): 567–93.

Lee, C. "The Road to Enfranchisement: Chinese and Japanese in British
Columbia." *B.C. Studies,* 30 (1976): 44–76.

Lee, D. *A History of the Overseas Chinese in Canada.* Taibei, 1967.

Lewandowski, S. "The Built Environment and Cultural Symbolism in Post-
Colonial Madras." In *The City in Cultural Context,* edited by J. Agnew et
al., Boston: Allen and Unwin 1984: 237–54.

Lewontin, R., Rose, S., and Kamin, L. *Not in Our Genes: Biology, Ideology
and Human Nature.* New York: Pantheon Books 1984.

Ley, D. *The Black Inner City as Frontier Outpost.* Association of American
Geographers, Monograph No. 7, Washington, D.C., 1974.

– "Social Geography and the Taken-for-Granted World." *Transactions, Institute of British Geographers,* new series 2 (1977): 498–512.

– *A Social Geography of the City.* New York: Harper and Row 1983.

– "Styles of the Times: Liberal and Neo-Conservative Landscapes in
Inner Vancouver." *Journal of Historical Geography,* 13 no. 1 (1987):
40–56.

Li, P. "A Historical Approach to Ethnic Stratification: The Case of the Chinese in Canada." *Canadian Review of Sociology and Anthropology,* 16 no. 3
(1979): 320–32.

Light, I. "From Vice District to Tourist Attraction: The Moral Career of
American Chinatowns, 1880–1940." *Pacific Historical Review,* 43 (1974):
367–94.

Livingstone, D. "Science and Society: Nathaniel S. Shaler and Racial Ideology." *Transactions, Institute of British Geographers*, New Series 9 (1984): 181–210.

Loh Kok-Wah, F. "The Chinese in Australia: An Overview." In *The Chinese In Australia*, edited by P. Hanks and A. Perry. Working Paper 12 on Migrant and Intercultural Studies, Monash University, 1988: 67–72.

Louder, F. "Montreal's Downtown Moves East." *City Magazine*, 1 (1975): 32–9.

Lowman, J. "Conceptual Issues in the Geography of Crime: Toward a Geography of Social Control." *Annals, Association of American Geographers*, 76 no. 1 (1986): 81–94.

Lyman, S. "Chinese Social Organization in Nineteenth Century America." PHD thesis, University of California, 1961.

– "Contrasts in the Community Organization of Chinese and Japanese in North America." *Canadian Review of Anthropology and Sociology*, 5 no. 2, 51–67.

Ma, C. *Chinese Pioneers*. Vancouver: Versatile Press 1979.

Ma, L. "A Chinese Statesman in Canada, 1903: Translated from the Travels of Liang Ch'i-ch'ao." *B.C. Studies*, 59 (1983): 28–43.

McConville, C. "Chinatown." In *The Outcasts of Melbourne: Essays in Social History*, edited by G. Davison, D. Dunstan, and C. McConville, Sydney: Allen and Unwin 1985: 69–90.

McEnvoy, F. "A Symbol of Racial Discrimination: The Chinese Immigration Act and Canada's Relations with Chinese, 1924–47." *Canadian Ethnic Studies*, 14 (1982): 24–42.

MacGill, H. "The Oriental Delinquent in the Vancouver Juvenile Court." *Sociology and Social Research* (1938–9): 428–38.

MacInnis, G. *J.S. Woodsworth: A Man to Remember*. Toronto: Macmillan 1953.

MacKenzie, R. *Oriental Exclusion*. Chicago: University of Chicago Press 1928.

MacLaughlin, J., and Agnew, J. "Hegemony and the Regional Question: The Political Geography of Regional Industrial Policy in Northern Ireland, 1945–1972." *Annals, Association of American Geographers*, 76 no. 2 (1986): 247–61.

Magubane, B. *The Political Economy of Race and Class in South Africa*. New York: Monthly Review Press 1979.

March, A. *The Idea of China: Myth and Theory in Geographic Thought*. New York: Praeger 1974.

Marcus, G., and Fischer, M. *Anthropology as Cultural Critique: An Experimental Moment in the Human Sciences*. Chicago: Chicago University Press 1986.

Marger, M. *Race and Ethnic Relations*. Belmont: Wordsworth Publishing 1985.

Marsh, D. "Vancouver's Old and New Chinatown." *Profile*, 2 no. 2, August 1965: 7.

Marsh, L. *Rebuilding a Neighbourhood*. Research Publications No. 1, University of British Columbia, 1950.

Marshall, G. "Racial Classifications: Popular and Scientific." In *Science and the Concept of Race*, edited by M. Mead et al., New York: Columbia University Press 1968: 149–63.

Massey, D., and Eggers, M. "The Ecology of Inequality: Minorities and the Concentration of Poverty." *American Journal of Sociology*, 95 no. 5 (1990): 1,153–88.

Matthews, J. Early Vancouver: Narratives of Pioneers in Vancouver, B.C. Unpublished manuscript, n.d.

Meinig, D., ed. "Editor's Introduction." In *The Interpretation of Ordinary Landscapes*, New York: Oxford University Press 1979: 1–7.

Melbourne City Council, City Strategic Planning Division. *Chinatown Action Plan*. 1985.

Migus, P., ed. *Sounds Canadian: Languages and Cultures in Multi-Ethnic Society*. Toronto: Peter Martin 1975.

Miles, R. *Racism and Migrant Labour*. London: Routledge and Kegan Paul 1982.

– "Recent Marxist Theories of Nationalism and the Issue of Racism." *British Journal of Sociology*, 38 (1987): 24–43.

Miller, S. *The Unwelcome Immigrant: The American Image of the Chinese, 1785–1882*. Berkeley: University of California Press 1969.

Mills, C.W. *The Sociological Imagination*. New York: Oxford University Press 1959.

Mollenkopf, J. "The Post-War Politics of Urban Development." *Politics and Society*, 5 no. 3 (1975): 247–95.

Montagu, A. *The Idea of Race*. Lincoln: University of Nebraska Press 1965.

Montagu, A., ed. *The Concept of Race*. New York: Free Press 1964.

Moodley, K. "Canadian Multiculturalism as Ideology." *Ethnic and Racial Studies*, 6 no. 3 (1983): 320–1.

Moon, M. "Chinatown: Where the West Meets the East on the Coast." *B.C. Motorist*, 12 (1973): 14–19.

Morley, A. *Vancouver: From Milltown to Metropolis*. Vancouver: Mitchell Press 1961.

Morton, J. *In the Sea of Sterile Mountain: The Chinese in British Columbia*. Vancouver: J.J. Douglas 1977.

Mouffe, C. "Hegemony and Ideology in Gramsci." In *Gramsci and Marxist Theory*, edited by C. Mouffe, London: Routledge and Kegan Paul 1981: 168–204

Murphy, E. *The Black Candle*. Reprinted Toronto: Coles 1973.

Murgatroyd, L., et al. (Lancaster Regionalism Group). *Localities, Class and Gender*. London: Pion 1985.

Naipul, S. "The Illusion of the Third World." *Harpers*, September 1985: 15–18.

Nann, R. *Urban Renewal and Relocation of Chinese Community Families.* Ottawa: Department of Secretary of State 1970.

Nee, V., and Nee, B. *Longtime Californ'.* Boston: Houghton Mifflin 1974.

Nelson, J. "Shall We Bar the Yellow Race?" *Maclean's*, 15 March 1922: 13–14 and 60.

Ng, R. "The Vancouver Chinese Immigrant Community and Social Services." *Rikka*, 4, no. 3 (1977): 72–85.

Nilsen, D. "The 'Social Evil': Prostitution in Vancouver, 1900–20." BA honours essay, University of British Columbia, 1976.

Olsson, G. "Social Science and Human Action or on Hitting Your Head against the Ceiling of Language." In *Philosophy in Geography*, edited by S. Gale and G. Olsson, Dordecht: Reidel 1979: 287–308.

Padillo, E. *Up from Puerto Rico.* New York: Columbia University Press 1958.

Palm, R. "Ethnic Segmentation of Real Estate Agent Practice in the Urban Housing Market."*Annals, Association of American Geographers*, 75 (1985): 58–68.

Palmer, H. *Patterns of Prejudice: A History of Nativism in Alberta.* Toronto: McClelland and Stewart 1982.

Park, R. "The Concept of Social Distance." *Journal of Applied Sociology*, 8 (1924): 339–44.

– *Race and Culture.* New York: Free Press 1950.

Parkin, F. *Marxism and Class Theory: A Bourgeois Critique.* New York: Columbia University Press 1979.

Parsons, Brinkerhoff, Quade and Douglas Inc. *Vancouver Transportation Study.* Vancouver 1968.

Paupst, K. "A Note on Anti-Chinese Sentiment in Toronto before the First World War." *Canadian Ethnic Studies*, 9 no. 1 (1977): 54–9.

Peach, C. "The Force of West Indian Island Identity in Britain." In *Geography and Ethnic Pluralism*, edited by C. Clarke et al., London: George Allen and Unwin 1984: 214–30.

Peach, C., ed. *Urban Social Segregation.* London: Longman 1975.

Peach, C., Robinson, V., and Smith, S., eds. *Ethnic Segregation in Cities.* London: Croom Helm 1981.

Pendakur, S. *Cities, Citizens and Freeways.* Vancouver: V.S. Pendakur 1972.

Perrin, R. "Clio as an Ethnic: The Third Force in Canadian Historiography." *Canadian Historical Review*, 64 no. 4 (1983): 441–67.

Peter, K. "The Myth of Multiculturalism and Other Political Fables." In *Ethnicity, Power and Politics in Canada*, edited by J. Dahlie and T. Fernando. Toronto: Methuen 1981: 56–67.

Pettman, J. "Whose Country Is It Anyway? Cultural Politics, Racism and the Construction of Being Australian." *Journal of Intercultural Studies*, 9 no. 1 (1988): 1–24.

Phillips, A. "The Criminal Society That Dominates the Chinese in Canada." *Maclean's*, 75 no. 7 (1962): 11 and 40–8.

Philo, C. "'Enough to Drive One Mad': The Organization of Space in 19th-Century Lunatic Asylums." In *The Power Of Geography: How Territory Shapes Social Life*, edited by J. Wolch and M. Dear, Boston: Unwin Hyman 1989: 258–90.

Porter, J. *The Measure of Canadian Society*. Toronto: Gage 1979.

– *The Vertical Mosaic: An Analysis of Social Class and Power in Canada*. Toronto: University of Toronto Press 1965.

Prager, J. "American Racial Ideology as Collective Representation." *Ethnic and Racial Studies*, 5 no. 1 (1982): 99–119.

Price, C. *The Great White Walls Are Built: Restrictive Immigration to North America and Australia, 1836–1888*. Canberra: Australian University Press 1974.

Rabinow, P. "Representations are Social Facts: Modernity and Post-Modernity in Anthropology." In *Writing Culture: the Poetics and Politics of Ethnography*, edited by J. Clifford and G. Marcus, Berkeley: University of California Press 1986: 234–61.

Rabinow, P., ed. *The Foucault Reader*. New York: Pantheon Books 1984.

Reeves, F. *British Racial Discourse: A Study of British Political Discourse about Race and Race Related Matters*. Cambridge: Cambridge University Press 1983.

Rex, J. "Racism and the Structure of Colonial Societies." In *Racism and Colonialism: Essays on Ideology and Social Structure*, edited by R. Ross, The Hague: Martinus Nijhoff 1982: 199–218.

Robin, M. *The Rush for Spoils: The Company Province 1871–1933*. Toronto: McClelland and Stewart 1972.

Rose, H. "The Spatial Development of Black Residential Sub-Systems." *Economic Geography*, 48 (1972): 43–65.

Ross, R., ed. *Racism and Colonialism: Essays on Ideology and Social Structure*. The Hague: Martinus Nijhoff 1982.

Rossiter, S. "Exodus Reversed." *Equinox*, 2 no. 8 (March–April 1983): 48, 63.

Roy, P. "British Columbia's Fear of Asians, 1900–50." *Social History*, 13 no. 25 (1980): 161–72.

– "The Oriental 'Menace' in British Columbia." In *Historical Essays on British Columbia*, edited by J. Friesen and H. Ralston, Toronto: Gage 1980: 243–55.

– "The Preservation of Peace in Vancouver: The Aftermath of the Anti-Chinese Riots of 1887." *B.C. Studies*, 31 (1976): 44–59.

– "Protecting Their Pocketbooks and Preserving Their Race: White Merchants and Oriental Competition." In *Cities in the West: Papers of the Western Canada Urban History Conference, 1974*, edited by A. McCormack and I. MacPherson, Ottawa: National Museum of Man 1975: 116–38.

- "The Soldiers Canada Didn't Want: Her Chinese and Japanese Citizens."
  Canadian Historical Review, 49 (1978): 341–58.
- *Vancouver: An Illustrated History*. Ontario: James Lorimer 1980.
- "White Canada Forever: Two Generations of Studies." *Canadian Ethnic
  Studies*, 11 (1979): 97–109.
Rule, C. "A Classical Chinese Garden." *Western Living*, September 1981: 36–
  40.
Sahlins, M. *The Use and Abuse of Biology*. Ann Arbor: University of Michi-
  gan Press 1976.
Said, E. *Orientalism*. New York: Random House 1978.
Salter, C. *San Francisco's Chinatown: How Chinese a Town?* San Francisco:
  R. & E. Research Associates 1978.
- "Urban Imagery and the Chinese of Los Angeles." *Urban Review*, 1 (1984):
  15–20, 28.
Samuels, M. "The Biography of Landscape." In *The Interpretation of Ordinary
  Landscapes*, edited by D. Meinig, New York: Oxford University Press
  1979: 51–88.
Satzewich, V. "Racisms: The Reactions to Chinese Migrants in Canada at
  the Turn of the Century." *International Sociology*, 4 no. 3 (1989): 311–27.
Savage, M. "'Locality Research': The Sussex Programme on Economic
  Structuring, Social Change and the Locality." *Quarterly Journal of Social
  Affairs*, 3 no. 1 (1987): 27–51.
Saxton, A. *The Indispensable Enemy: Labor and the Anti-Chinese Movement in
  California*. Berkeley: University of California Press 1971.
Schutz, A. "The Social World and the Theory of Social Action." *Social
  Research*, 27 (1960): 205–21.
Schwantes, C. *Radical Heritage*. Vancouver: Douglas and McIntyre 1979.
Sedgwick, C., and Willmott, W. "External Influences and Emerging Iden-
  tity: The Evolution of Community Structure among Chinese Canadians."
  Canadian Forum (1974): 8–12.
Shaw, C. "The Oriental Wants to Vote." *Maclean's*, April 1937: 24, 44, and
  46.
Sibley, D. *Outsiders in Urban Societies*. Oxford: Basil Blackwell 1981.
Sien Lok Society of Calgary, Alberta. *Proceedings of National Conference on
  Urban Renewal as it Affects Chinatown*. Calgary: Sien Lok Society 1969.
Simpson, G., and Yinger, J. *Racial and Cultural Minorities: An Analysis of
  Prejudice and Discrimination*. New York: Harper and Brothers 1953.
Skinner, G. *Leadership and Power in the Chinese Community of Thailand*. Ith-
  aca: Cornell University Press 1957.
Smith, A. "Metaphor and Nationality in North America." *Canadian Histori-
  cal Review*, 61 (1970): 247–75.
Smith, S. *The Politics of "Race" and Residence*. Cambridge: Polity Press 1989.
Snowden, F. *Before Colour Prejudice: The Ancient View of Blacks*. Cambridge,
  Mass.: Harvard University Press 1983.

Soja, E. "The Post-modernization of Geography." *Annals, Association of American Geographers*, 77 (1987): 289–94.

Solomon, B. *Ancestors and Immigrants*. Cambridge, Mass.: Harvard University Press 1956.

Steinberg, S. *The Ethnic Myth: Race, Ethnicity and Class in America*. New York: Atheneum 1981.

Steiner, S. *Fusang: The Chinese Who Built America*. New York: Harper and Row 1979.

Stepan, N. *The Idea of Race in Science: Great Britain, 1800–1960*. London: Macmillan 1982.

Stoddard, L. *The Rising Tide of Color*. New York: Charles Scribner's Sons 1920.

Straaton, K. "The Political System of the Vancouver Chinese Community: Associations and Leadership in the Early 1960s." MA thesis, University of British Columbia, 1974.

Strauss, A. *Mirrors and Masks: The Search for Identity*. Glencoe, Ill.: Free Press 1959.

Sugimoto, H. "The Vancouver Riot and Its International Significance." In *East across the Pacific*, edited by H. Conroy and T. Miyakawa, Santa Barbara: Clio Press 1972: 92–126.

Sunahara, A. *The Politics of Racism: The Uprooting of Japanese Canadians during the Second World War*. Toronto: James Lorimer 1981.

Suttles, G. *The Social Order of the Slum*. Chicago: University of Chicago Press 1968.

Thompson, R. "The State and the Ethnic Community: The Changing Social Organization of Toronto's Chinatown." PHD thesis, University of Michigan, 1979.

Thrift, N., and Williams, P., eds. *Class and Space: The Making of Urban Society*. London: Routledge and Kegan Paul 1987.

Tuan, Y.-F. *Topophilia*. Englewood Cliffs, NJ: Prentice Hall 1974.

van den Berghe, P. *The Ethnic Phenomena*. Amsterdam: Elsevier 1981.

– *Race and Racism: A Comparative Perspective*. New York: John Wiley 1967.

Voegelin, E. "The Growth of the Race Idea." *Review of Politics*, 2 no. 3 (1940): 283–317.

Wallman, S., ed. *Ethnicity at Work*. London: Macmillan 1979.

Warburton, R. "Race and Class in British Columbia: A Comment." *B.C. Studies*, 49 (1981): 79–85.

Ward, D. *Poverty, Ethnicity and the American City, 1840–1925*. Cambridge: Cambridge University Press 1989.

Ward, P. *White Canada Forever: Popular Attitudes and Public Policy toward Orientals in British Columbia*. Montreal: McGill-Queen's University Press 1978.

Weiss, M. *Valley City: A Chinese Community in America*. Cambridge: Schenkman 1974.

Western, J. *Outcast Capetown*. Minneapolis: University of Minnesota Press 1981.

Wickberg, E., Con, H., Johnson, G., and Willmott, W.E. *From China to Canada: A History of the Chinese Communities in Canada*. Toronto: McClelland and Stewart 1982.

Williams, R. *Marxism and Literature*. Oxford: Oxford University Press 1977.

Willmott, W. "Chinese Clan Associations in Vancouver." *Man*, 64 (1964): 33–7.

Wolfe, H. "Class Concepts, Class Struggle and Racism." In *Theories of Race and Ethnic Relations*, edited by J. Rex and D. Mason, Cambridge: Cambridge University Press 1986: 110–30.

Wong, B. "Elites and Ethnic Boundary Maintenance: A Study of the Role of Elites in Chinatown, New York City." *Urban Anthropology*, 6 no. 1 (1977): 1–22.

Wong, E. "Asian American Middleman Minority Theory: The Framework of an American Myth." *Journal of Ethnic Studies*, 13 no. 1 (1985): 31–88.

Wong, S. "Urban Redevelopment and Rehabilitation in the Strathcona Area: A Case Study of an East Vancouver Community." In *Vancouver: Western Metropolis*, edited by L. Evenden, Victoria: University of Victoria 1978: 255–69.

Wood, D. "The Year of the Horse." *Western Living*, 8 no. 2 (1978): 17–20.

Worsley, P. *The Three Worlds: Culture and World Development*. Chicago: University of Chicago Press 1984.

Wynn, G. "Ethnic Migrations and Atlantic Canada: Geographical Perspectives." *Canadian Ethnic Studies*, 18 no. 1 (1986): 1–15.

Wynne, R. "Reaction to the Chinese in the Pacific Northwest and British Columbia, 1850–1910." PHD thesis, University of Washington, 1964.

Yancey, W., Ericksen, E., and Juliani, R. "Emergent Ethnicity: A Review and Reformulation." *American Sociological Review*, 41 (1976): 391–403.

Yee, P. "Business Devices from Two Worlds: The Chinese in Early Vancouver." *B.C. Studies*, 62 (1984): 44–67.

– "Chinese Business in Vancouver, 1886–1914." MA thesis, University of British Columbia, 1983.

– *Saltwater City*. Vancouver: Douglas and McIntyre 1988.

Yip, Q. *Vancouver's Chinatown: Vancouver Golden Jubilee, 1886–1936*. Vancouver: Pacific Printers 1936.

Young, D. "Street of T'ongs." MA thesis, University of British Columbia, 1976.

Young, D. "The Vancouver Police Force, 1886–1914." BA honours essay, University of British Columbia, 1976.

Zaret, D. "From Weber to Parsons and Schutz: The Eclipse of History in Modern Social Theory." *American Journal of Sociology*, 85 (1980): 1,180–1,201.

Relevant Geographical Scholarship on Vancouver's Chinese since First Publication of Vancouver's Chinatown

For sympathetic auto-critiques of the book, one from a feminist perspective, another using a political economy frame, see:

Anderson, K. "Engineering Race Research: Unsettling the Self-Other Dichotomy. In *Bodyspace: Destabilising Geographies of Gender and Sexuality* edited by N. Duncan. London and New York: Routledge, 1996, 197–211.

– "Sites of Difference: Beyond a Cultural Politics of Race Polarity. In Fincher, R. and Jacobs, J.M. eds. *Cities of Difference*, edited by R. Fincher and J.M. Jacobs. New York: Guilford, 1996: 201–25.

Ley, D. "Between Europe and Asia: The Case of the Missing Sequoias." *Ecumene: Journal of Environment, Culture, Meaning* 2 (1995): 185–210.

Mitchell, K. "Conflicting Geographies of Cemocracy and the Public Sphere in Vancouver, B.C." *Transactions, Institute of British Geographers* 22 (1997): 162–79.

– "Reworking Democracy: Contemporary Immigration and Community Politics in Vancouver's Chinatown." *Political Geography* 17 no. 6 (1998): 729–50.

Olds, K. "Globalisation and Urban Change: Tales from Vancouver via Hong Kong." *Urban Geography* 19 no. 4 (1998): 360–85.

Rose, J. "Immigration, Neighbourhood Change and Racism: Immigrant Reception in Richmond, Bc." Vancouver Centre of Excellence, Research on Immigration and Integration in the Metropolis (RIIM) Working Paper Series, 99-09, 1999.

Index

Peru, 214

Peters, William, 184

Philbrook, F., 241

Philippines, 214

Phillips, Arthur, 240, 241

Pickersgill, Jack, 181

Pickstone, Harry, 223, 225

Planta, Clive, 167

Point Grey, 159, 168, 169, 269n63

police, 25; *see also* Chinatown (Vancouver): harassment; raids; Royal Canadian Mounted Police; Vancouver: and Chinatown's vice image

politics of race: *see* race: politics of

poll tax: *see* head tax

polygenist beliefs, 41, 42

population genetics, 10, 11

Port Moody, 66

positive ascription and stereotyping, 27, 95–6, 145, 164, 210, 211, 212–13, 243, 244, 249, 287n40

positivism, 13

Powell Street, 90

power of definition, 10, 24, 25, 31, 92, 178, 188, 194, 200, 210, 213, 249

power relations, 6, 7, 19, 20–8, 32, 54, 74, 88, 104, 140, 178, 217, 246, 247, 250, 251

"prejudice," 19, 38, 43, 49, 54, 60, 63, 72, 85, 94, 126, 137, 152, 164, 240, 245, 275n21

Prior, Edward, 60

Produce Marketing Act (1927), 168

prostitution: *see* Chinatown (Vancouver): vice image: prostitution

Provincial Elections Act, British Columbia, 53, 152, 173

Provincial Workers' Council on Unemployment, 144, 274n1

public housing, 187, 189, 191, 192, 195, 199, 207

"Puerto Rican," 17

Puget Sound, 35

Quebec, 217

Quebec-Columbia connector, 232

Quebec Street, 165

Queensland (Australia), 5

Quene Yip, 147, 156

"race," 4, 6, 10, 11, 12, 14, 15, 18, 19, 27, 94, 109, 245, 246

race: as a biological notion, 10–13, 243n10; as a social construct, 13–15, 20, 44; beliefs in existence, 10, 11, 13, 27, 61, 62, 104, 145, 152, 170, 176, 231, 233, 247, 248; constructivist approach to, 4, 23, 246; "contamination," 27, 44, 107, 113–14, 137, 138, 139; ecological research on, 13–14, 244n15; geographical, 11; hierarchy, 22, 36, 40, 43, 56, 62, 71, 84, 88, 104, 110, 145, 152, 170, 176, 213; history of idea, 5, 22, 38–44, 247; "hybridization," 44, 273n125; idea of, 18, 24, 45, 46, 61, 63, 71, 86, 94, 107, 112, 135, 137, 138, 153, 170, 241, 243; idealist views of: *see* "prejudice"; race relations; liberal tradition; white racism thesis; inferiority: *see* race: hierarchy; language of, 5, 19, 42, 46, 85, 92, 108, 110, 135, 137, 158, 170, 175, 182–4, 211, 213,

218, 227, 243; Marxist views of, 21–2, 38, 63, 72, 94, 245, 255n47, 260n78, 292n1; politics of, 26, 46–7, 55, 57, 60, 62, 63, 82, 114–15, 135, 137, 138, 140, 153, 166, 167, 169, 172, 180, 219, 229, 233, 271n96, 273n124; reification of, 14, 44, 212, 254n25; riots, 67–8, 69, 70, 82, 88, 261n119; science of, 10–11, 41–4, 61, 71, 96, 107–9, 170; and the state, 20–8; statutory, 179–80; territorial arrangements of, 5, 20, 23, 28–32, 63–71, 72, 74, 92, 104, 106, 112, 247, 250

race-definition process, 6, 17–20, 23, 26, 28, 29, 31, 248, 250, 251

"race hygiene," 107–9; *see also* race: contamination, "hybridization"

race relations, 4, 14, 19, 21, 94, 144–5, 152, 176, 245, 247; liberal tradition, 19, 86–7, 145, 245, 257n13; *see also* "prejudice"; white racism thesis

racial classifications, 4, 7, 8, 11, 14, 16, 18, 20, 27, 58, 73, 94, 132, 213, 239, 247, 250, 252; *see also* Chinese racial category

racial consciousness, 19, 21, 22, 23, 109, 118, 226, 247, 248

racial discourse: *see* race: language of

racial frame of reference, 6, 19, 55, 164, 218, 239, 248

racial ideology, 19, 20–3, 25, 26, 27, 28, 73, 74, 178, 230, 250